IARS

Funded by the Criminal Justice Programme of the European Union

Project Partners - Restorative Justice in Europe: Safeguarding Victims & Empowering Professionals

Restorative Justice Nederland

Restorative Justice Nederland (RJN) is a center of expertise and innovation in the field of restorative justice. Our aim is to encourage a participatory society of active citizens who are involved as much as possible in the handling of their own conflicts and the restoration of the consequences for victims, offenders and the community. As a grassroots charity we bring together policy makers, scientists, practitioners from different societal sectors and other stakeholders in order to stimulate where possible the application of restorative justice and restorative practices.

EPLO European Public Law Organization

The European Public Law Organisation (EPLO) is an international inter-governmental organization headquartered in Athens, Greece, whose specific mandate is the creation and dissemination of knowledge in the area of public law and the promotion of European values through public law throughout the world. The Organization's Board of Directors comprises its 13 Member States, the European Commission, the Council of Europe and 63 Universities and institutions from 33 countries. Professor Vasso Artinopoulou is Head of the Crime and Criminal Justice Unit, since 2011.

HfÖ Hochschule für Öffentliche Verwaltung Bremen

The **Institute for Police and Security Research (IPoS)** at the University of Applied Sciences and Administration has been researching for many years in the field of Restorative Justice. It has also been a partner in the project Mediation and Restorative Justice in Prison Settings (MEREPS) and is supervising the national-wide Victim-offender-mediation statistics in Germany. IPoS is an interdisciplinary oriented institute which has conducted and still conducts numerous studies in the research areas legal psychology, law, criminalistics and criminology.

INSTITUTE OF CONFLICT RESOLUTION

The **Institute of Conflict Resolution** is an association of lawyers, researchers and university professors. It follows a number of objectives, including: exploration of creative conflict resolution methods, based on the culture of dialogue; practice of mediation, negotiation and other peaceful methods for dispute resolution, focusing on restorative justice; preventing violence, youth offending and other antisocial behaviour; protection of rights of crime victims; strengthening civil society and European integration.

The Restorative Justice in Europe Programme is co-financed by the European Commission (EC Grant Agreement JUST/2011-2012/JPEN/AG/2951)

IARS Publications – Restorative Justice Series

A Victim-led Criminal Justice System: Addressing the Paradox

T. Gavrielides (Ed.) (2014)

London: IARS Publications. ISBN: 978-1-907641-27-5. Price: £9, 99

The European Union has recently entered into a process of legislative and policy reforms with the aim of strengthening the rights of victims in criminal proceedings. By November 2015, all EU member states will need to have demonstrated that they have modified their domestic laws to give effect to the Directive 2012/29/EU "Establishing minimum standards on the rights, support and protection of victims of crime" (Victims' Directive). For the first time, restorative justice is explicitly regulated at the EU legal level, as the Victims' Directive aims to establish a baseline for its safe implementation across member states.

This ground-breaking and timely edited collection aims to contribute to this international debate. The book aims to challenge current thinking while highlighting good practices that respect and safeguard victims in the criminal justice and restorative justice processes. The book uses a combination of theoretical and empirical analysis while utilising original research data collected by the EU funded "Restorative Justice in Europe" (RJE) project. The book is partly funded by the European Commission (EC Grant Agreement JUST/2011-2012/JPEN/AG/2951) through the Restorative Justice in Europe project.

E-book: Restorative Justice and Domestic Violence: A Critical Review

G. Loseby A. Ntziadima and T. Gavrielides (2014)

London: IARS Publications. ISBN: 978-1-907641-28-2. Price: £4, 99

This e-book reports on the current developments, practices and policies on the use of restorative justice in cases of domestic violence in the UK and it aims to stimulate an open and honest discussion about using restorative justice in such cases. The research also reflects on limitations, inefficiencies and complexities of the current criminal justice system in the UK.

The "Restorative Justice and Domestic Violence: A critical Review" forms the first stage of the research that was conducted in the framework of the 2 year EU funded project "Restorative Justice in cases of domestic violence: Best practice examples between increasing mutual understanding and awareness of specific protection needs", a programme that aims to generate and pilot new knowledge on practices of restorative justice and domestic violence and to identify criteria for offering restorative approaches to such cases, in accordance with the Victims' Directive.

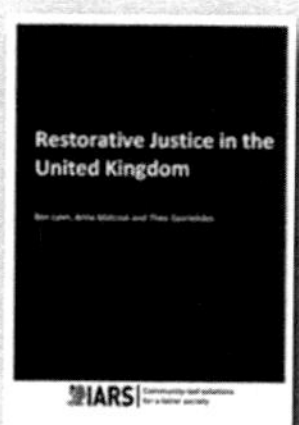

E-book: Restorative Justice in the United Kingdom

B. Lyon, A. Matczak and T. Gavrielides (2012)

London: IARS Publications. ISBN: 978-1-907641-14-5. Price: £4, 99

The e-book explores and discusses the current provisions, legislation and practice of restorative justice in the United Kingdom.

Comparisons between England, Northern Ireland and Scotland are drawn, and contrasts between youth and adult practice are highlighted.

The struggles with the traditional criminal justice system and restorative practices' place in it are also considered.

IARS Publications – Restorative Justice Series

Waves of Healing: Using Restorative Justice with Street Group Violence

T. Gavrielides (2012)

London: IARS Publications. ISBN: 978-1907641-10-7. Price: £9, 99

Despite the impressive literature on restorative justice, the potential of its paradigm with street group violence remain largely unexplored.

The financial, political and social implications that recent riots are having on governments across the world spark a new debate on the appropriateness of restorative approaches in relieving the overstretched and costly criminal justice system.

The book uses the case study method to investigate examples in India, Greece, Canada and England, where restorative justice is considered within the context of street group violence. Key issues are identified and recommendations are posited, as new policies, practices and research are being proposed in this grey area of restorative justice.

Rights and Restoration Within Youth Justice

T. Gavrielides (Ed.) (2012)

Witby: de Sitter Publications. ISBN: 978-1-897160-62-6. Price: £37.00

Rights & Restoration within Youth Justice unites the principles and practices of human rights and restorative justice. Leading international experts challenge current thinking on evidence-based youth justice policy.

Through international case studies, a framework emerges for connecting human rights and restorative justice approaches to criminal justice policy and practice.

This book is written by leading scholars in the field of restorative justice, human rights, youth justice and policy and criminal justice. The project was carried out under the auspices of IARS and the book was published by de Sitter Publications.

Restorative Justice and the Secure Estate: Alternatives for Young People in Custody

T. Gavrielides (2011)

London: IARS Publications. ISBN: 978-1-907641-08-4. Price: £9, 99

This book focuses on the use of restorative justice with young people in custody in the UK, and aims to achieve three objectives. Firstly, to provide and up-to-date descriptive account of restorative practices within the secure estate.

This account looks at issues of classification, definition and understanding. Secondly, to prevent a critical overview of existing restorative practices with the objective of establishing the extent to which they influence the regimes and programmes of the secure estate.

Based on qualitative data from young people, practitioners, policy makers, victims, offenders and academics, the book posits evidence-based recommendations for policy and strategy analysts, researchers and practitioners at a critical point in time for the restorative justice movement.

Table of Contents

Editor's Note & Acknowledgements

Theo Gavrielides

It is a great privilege to edit this book at a critical point in the development of new criminal justice policies internationally. These reforms will arguably see the victim moved from the margins to the centre of state attention. This is particularly true for Europe.

We tend to forget that the criminal justice system is a modern construct. In fact, much of what we understand today as 'crime' was seen by early communities as a conflict between individuals, while the terms 'offender' and 'victim' were coined as a result of our modern, legal positivistic framework. Despite my legal background, the term 'victim' makes me feel uncomfortable as it fails to acknowledge that in the harsh and complex reality of crime, the lines between labels are often blurred. However, for the purposes of this book and a constructive debate that will hopefully help us move the forgotten stakeholders out of the shadows, I accept the term.

According to historians, the victim was gradually pushed to the margins as the interests and power of the state overtook those of the individual. This created a paradox that has endured for centuries. Moving victims out of the shadows cannot be an easy task, as the same power structures that put them there remain strong even in our modern societies.

It took humanity two World Wars and many civil conflicts to come to the table to agree to minimum standards of behaviour for states. These were intended to control this state-led attitude including that impacting on criminal justice. We called them 'human rights' and recorded them in international documents such as the Universal Declaration of Human Rights (UDHR) and the European Convention on Human Rights. I have always argued that the criminal process and the administration of criminal justice by state agents is the field of battle in which human rights are tested. Therefore, over many years, questions were being raised by communities, the victims' movement and other civil society organisations about states' behaviour and compliance with the human rights of victims in the criminal process.

In Europe, its Union had no other choice but to respond to this questioning. In the hope of achieving consistency in victims' rights protection across the EU, in 2001, the Commission passed a Framework Decision, but this did not go far and deep enough. As a result, we now have a Victims' Directive which must be translated into domestic laws and policies by November 2015. It is hoped that this will provide a baseline for minimum guarantees for victims.

Since passing the Directive, the EC invested resources in order to prepare member States for its implementation. After a competitive process, IARS' project Restorative Justice in Europe: Safeguarding Victims and Empowering Professionals (RJE) was successful in receiving an EU grant and I had the honour of coordinating its scientific and practical ambitions and outputs. Over twenty-four months, IARS worked closely with its four European partners Restorative Justice Nederland (Netherlands), the Institute of Conflict Resolution (Bulgaria), European Public Law Organization (Greece), and University of Applied Sciences (Germany). We were also supported by 12 Associate Partners who are experts in the area of victims and restorative justice: the University of Cyprus (Cyprus), Restorative Thinking (UK), the Register of Restorative Practitioners (UK), Restorative Justice International (USA), the Forgiveness Project (UK), HM Prison Altcourse (UK), the European Forum for Restorative Justice (Belgium), the

Centre for Restorative Justice at Simon Fraser University (Canada), Prof. Gerry Johnstone (UK), Foresee (Hungary), Ulster University (Northern Ireland) and Victim Support (UK).

We were adamant that our results were produced not just in English, but in all participating country languages i.e. Greek, German, Dutch and Bulgarian. The victims and restorative justice literature is still very thin when it comes to non-English sources and thus we hoped to make material accessible by going the extra mile by making them accessible to local people.

After a thorough review of the extant literature and existing best practice, we produced over 20 reports sharing this information for free across Europe. Following this, we carried out fieldwork with over 272 victims and offenders and 280 professionals working with victims either by providing victim support, restorative justice or criminal justice services.

This gave us the evidence base to construct training material, manuals, best practice guidance and protocols. In total, 27 face-to-face pilots were carried out in the five participating countries reaching 1,131 individuals and 383 organisations. We also used this material to produce an online course for victims, which was downloaded 200 times. A separate e-course was also created for professionals. At the time of writing, this was downloaded 50 times and like the face-to-face course it received CPD accreditation (Continuing Professional Development). At the same time, we organised conferences and seminars and made various presentations at national and international conferences while meeting with our national and local decision makers.

The structure of this book was carefully considered bearing two objectives in mind. First, I wanted to explore and propose a new narrative for victim policy. To achieve this, I combined evidence from international guest papers (Part I) and the findings of the RJE project (Part II and III). Most of the guest articles are written by victims who had the courage to share their personal experiences. My experience and the evidence that we have gathered suggest that contrary to what many criminal justice professionals believe, victims do want to talk and be included in the formation of practices and policies that impact on them. I have always said that a true democracy is one that not only offers its citizens the opportunity to participate, but also supports them in doing so. As we become more honest about our intentions and available resources for criminal justice reforms, we must become more accountable whenever we choose not to include victims directly in policy making. Therefore, an obligation is created for national and European governments to respond to this call. Second, I wanted to offer a comparative and critical perspective of current evidence and emerging themes that will facilitate the implementation of this new narrative for victim policy including the Victims' Directive.

I hope that the knowledge that we produced through the programme and this book, as well as the tools that we made available will be used by professionals, decision makers and policy makers in their efforts for a better criminal justice system. Having set up IARS, a user-led international institute that aims to change policy and practice from the bottom up, it will not be suprising to read that my biggest hope is that individuals/ users are empowered through our work and the training that we produced to seek their rights under the new law. The victims and offenders whom we spoke feel that the existing gatekeepers, entrenched practices and mind-sets are the true barriers in the implementation of our proposed narrative for victim policy including the Victims' Directive. The practitioners and other experts who took part in our research also confirm this conclusion. While we foster an attitudinal change and a cultural shift within our criminal justice systems, we must allow the human rights values of Freedom, Respect, Equality and Dignity to guide us through our policy, institutional and legislative reforms.

I am proud to safely claim that the RJE project and this book went way beyond what we had originally promised to the European Commission and it is to the credit of my team, our partners and guest authors. This would not have been possible without the participation of the victims and other users of the criminal justice system as well as the professionals who kindly gave their time. I am also grateful to the Independent Advisory Group that we set up in order to provide advice and scrutinise our direction.

I am particularly grateful to Ben Lyon (IARS' trainer), Grace Loseby (IARS' Justice Project Coordinator) and Andriana Ntziadima (IARS' Communications Manager). Special thanks go to IARS' Finance Manager, Hatixhe Demushi who very patiently kept track of our spent. Many thanks also go to the country project leads Professor Artinopoulou (Greece), Professor Hartmann (Germany), Dr. van Hoek (the Netherlands) and Professor Chankova (Bulgaria), and their respective research teams. Thanks also go to the UK Ministry of Justice which provided us with support letters that made our fieldwork easier and gave us access to various decision makers including relevant ministers and decision making bodies such as the National Restorative Justice Implementation Board, prisons and NOMS.

- Dr. Theo Gavrielides (Founder and Director of Independent Academic Research Studies, Co-Director of the Restorative Justice for All Institute, Visiting Professor at Buckinghamshire New University and Adjunct Professor at Simon Fraser University, School of Criminology), Unit 14, Dock Offices, Surrey Quays Road, Canada Water, London SE16 2XU, UK, T.Gavrielides@iars.org.uk +44(0)20 70644380.

October 2014, London.

Professor Theo Gavrielides

Foreword

Olivier Tell

The European Commission has made the protection and support of victims of crime a priority and is taking steps to ensure that their needs are met. Therefore, it is a great pleasure to write this Foreword for Theo Gavrielides' new book "A victim-led Criminal Justice System: Addressing the paradox".

As the title of the book suggests, we have been living a paradox in our modern criminal justice systems. Although justice and criminal justice are primarily meant to restore the power imbalance and hurt that are caused by crime, victims continue to be disempowered. At the European Union (EU) level, therefore, we have taken recent legislative action to rectify this paradox by creating a baseline of minimum safeguards and guarantees for victims across Europe.

The package of measures presented by the European Commission in May 2011 – and in particular the Directive 2012/029/EU of the European Parliament and of the Council establishing minimum standards on the rights, support and protection of victims of crime (the "Victims' Directive") – will ensure that victims are treated appropriately and without discrimination. Our aim is to ensure that victims get access to justice though a range of rights that will allow them to actively participate in criminal proceedings, to access support and assistance services, to be protected from secondary and repeat victimisation, to be informed throughout the course of proceedings and to seek compensation and restoration. Meeting the needs of victims plays an important role in assuring victims' rights and achieving a high quality of justice in the European Union. It is crucial to acknowledge victims, to take their suffering seriously and to help them get on with their lives.

Once the transposition date of the Victims' Directive on 16 November 2015 has passed, EU Member States must implement at least the Directive's minimum standards. In our attempt to prepare Member States appropriately for the implementation of the Directive, we made funding available through a competitive and open process. One of the projects that we co-financed was the "Restorative Justice in Europe: Safeguarding Victims & Empowering Professionals" (RJE). This was run by the UK based international NGO Independent Academic Research Studies (IARS) in partnership with four other partners in Germany, the Netherlands, Greece and Bulgaria.

The appropriate treatment of victims is a demonstration of our societies' solidarity with each individual and recognition that such treatment is essential to the moral integrity of society. It is therefore crucial not only to combat and prevent crime, but also to properly support and protect individuals who do fall victim to crime. One of the primary concerns of the RJE project and this book is restorative justice. While we are still learning about the strengths and limitations of restorative justice, this book helps us to reflect on its implications for victims and their rights. One of the aims of the Victims' Directive is to ensure that restorative justice practices are delivered safely and in the interest of the victim. It is important that as we move forward with the implementation of the Directive that the concerns and wishes of victims and professionals are heard.

Therefore, I commend the RJE project and the authors of this book for including victims' voices in the construction of their scientific and practical results. I was particularly pleased to see chapters written by victims as well as material that aim to empower victims directly in pursuing their rights.

I want to congratulate the Editor, the authors and everyone who was involved in writing this book, which brings together the key finding from the project that we have co-financed. While it summarises the extant literature, it also provides new evidence on effective practice and key recommendations for the improvement of our criminal justice and restorative justice processes.

- Olivier Tell is Head of Procedural Criminal Law, Directorate-General Justice, European Commission.

October 2014, Brussels.

PART I:
A NEW NARRATIVE FOR VICTIM POLICY

Why Victims' Voices Matter in Criminal Justice Policy and Reform

*Gabrielle Browne**

Abstract

This chapter provides an examination of how criminal justice policy has altered as a result of victims' influence. The chapter also provides a critical analysis from a victim perspective of whether these changes go far enough. Victims are critical to the instigation of the criminal justice process and how their treatment affects outcomes for society. The State undertakes the responsibility for bringing offenders to justice and attempting to reform offenders behaviour. The adversarial system does not provide an equal position for the victim. Recent changes to legislation, such as EU Victims' Directive have been influenced by victims, go some way to treat victims as valued participants. The effectiveness of such legislation lies in its application and implementation by criminal justice professionals. The concept of criminal justice is explored as a process to disable harm as an overarching focus, yet still encompassing the standard range of court disposals and punitive measures but to actively seek to engage with victims so that their pain is recognised and their harm repaired as far as possible.

Victims' Needs and Realities: A Personal Account

In that moment when the man asking me the time, spun on his heels and violently yet deftly swung his right arm around my neck, I did not know whether I would survive. In my naivety, I thought if apprehended and sentenced he would not be able to do this to anyone else.

In addition to the subsequent sexual violation of my body, significant further harm was caused to me by the criminal justice process. A process, which any right thinking member of society, would assume it to be there, to protect my interest and that of any of my offender's potential future victims.

Victims are often a forgotten voice. We are broken by the devastating consequences caused by the actions of an offender. Naively, we look to the criminal justice system to protect us from further harm and yet it is all too often the criminal justice process itself that causes us the most harm. "The systems failings have caused me on some days, more stress, anguish and depression than the original crime."(Waxman, July 2014). Marginalised, used and abused, we are a desperate, broken group of human beings, whose rights are not upheld. We should not have to manage the criminal justice process, yet if we don't, it fails us.

The extreme stress caused by victimisation can *"shatter the very basic assumptions victims have about themselves and the world around them"* (Peterson, 2003; as cited in DeValve 2005). Victims need rehabilitation. The consequences of crime can range from broken family life, lost friends, loss of employment, stress and panic attacks.

* Ms. Gabrielle Browne (a victim of crime and an Advisor on the RJE project), contact: gbrownecontact@gmail.com

Victims not only have to struggle with primary injuries in the aftermath of the crime, but they must also battle with the "secondary" injuries. Secondary injuries are injuries that occur when there is a lack of proper support. These injuries can be caused by friends, family and most often by the professionals victims encounter as a result of the crime. Law enforcement officers, prosecutors, judges, social service workers, the media, coroners, clergy, and even mental health professionals can cause secondary injuries. Those individuals may lack the ability or training to provide the necessary comfort and assistance to the victim. Often, those individuals blame the victim for the crime. Failing to recognize the importance of the crime or to show sympathy can be damaging to the victim's self-worth and recovery process (Bard, and Sangrey, 1986).

We would like as far as possible, for policy and practice within criminal justice agencies to stitch us together again – perhaps always leaving a scar however good the repair, but sufficient for us to become worthy contributors and participants in society, rather than in the other metaphorical sense, to stitch us up.

"There is a growing consensus that our criminal justice system does not serve victims well" (Guardian, 2014). There is no criminal justice process without victims. Victims are as diverse as any population group, we respond in different ways. However, all victims deserve to be treated with consideration and respect. Our world as we knew it has been blown apart by the trauma of the crime and yet we are often marginalised by those authorities whose role it is to bring the offender to justice. "The breaking of the law, which is designed to protect the rights and freedoms of every individual, causes immeasurable harm to the victim of the crime. Even in comparatively less severe crimes, victims can still be seriously violated mentally, physically, emotionally or spiritually. Continuing losses resulting from the crime, such as marriage failure, job loss and social dysfunction, can also continue to disable the victim from continuing his or her life as before. Thus the question of who is going to cover the cost of the losses and help the victim recover from the harm is an important expectation of the justice-making process" (Derksen, 2009).

In terms of recovery, in my own case, the criminal justice process caused greater emotional damage than the offender ripping out my soul as he tried to rape me. We, as victims are human beings traumatised by what has befallen us. Give us the bad news, we can handle it, treat us like we matter. This will then help us to free ourselves from our self-imposed confinement, afraid to go out for fear of who we might be with, yet equally suffering from fear of being alone.

Victims' Voices in Criminal Justice Policy and Reform

Should a victim's voice matter in criminal justice policy and reform? Yes, if we accept the premise that victims are the instigators of the criminal justice process. How society treats its victims is a reflection of how they are valued (or not). The treatment of the victim should be delivered in a manner that upholds the five broad categories of the needs of victims as laid out in the EU Victims' Directive:

- respectful treatment and recognition as victims, both within the justice system and more widely by society;
- protection both from intimidation, retaliation and further harm by the accused or suspected and from harm during criminal investigations and court proceedings, such as by avoiding repeated interviewing of the victim;

- support, including immediate assistance following a crime, longer-term physical and psychological assistance and practical assistance during proceedings to help victims understand, participate and to reduce their distress;
- access to justice to ensure that victims are aware of their rights and understand them both linguistically and legally, are able to provide additional information and to participate in proceedings; and
- compensation and restoration, whether through financial damages paid by the State or by the offender or through mediation or other form of restorative justice that allow victims to face the accused, with a view to reaching a voluntary agreement between them on how to repair the harm to the victim.

This significant victim legislation is to be adopted into national law by member states no later than 16 November 2015. In particular, we as a society need to do significantly more to help a victim re-integrate into society. "Crime is a wrong against society as well as a violation of the individual rights of a victim" (Official Journal of the European Union, 2012)

Victims are either actively or passively discriminated against by family, friends, community, employers, work colleagues. Perhaps this is a lack of education, people not knowing how to communicate or not wanting to say anything to cause distress, but the lack of communication and shutting off from the victim causes even further distress. However, a law is only as good as its enforcement. I would therefore urge all victims and criminal justice professionals to understand the EU Victims Directive in its entirety and to apply pressure to ensure the victim rights defined, are upheld if society's treatment does not equate to these rights.

Within the context of public discussion on crime and justice we should attempt to seek common ground between those who seek retribution and those who seek reformation. If you ask the majority of victims of crime what is important they will say, as I did, "for this not to happen to anyone else".

Perhaps first we should seek a common definition of the Criminal Justice System. "The justice system must punish the guilty, protect our liberties and rehabilitate offenders" (Government website, 2014). For the purposes of the Victims' Code, a 'victim' is:

- a person who has suffered harm, including physical, mental or emotional harm or economic loss which was directly caused by criminal conduct;
- a close relative of a person whose death was directly caused by criminal conduct (CPS website, 2014).

No two circumstances of offences, even if committed by the same offender are the same. The reaction by the victim(s) is as likely to be diametrically opposed as it is likely to be the same, yet the following would relate to most victims nonetheless:

- The wish for this to never happen to anyone else
- The wish for what has happened to be acknowledged
- The wish to be updated proactively
- The Criminal Justice System should help the recovery process rather than hinder it by causing further harm

Have victims merely become the anecdote, or the "buzz word" within criminal justice? "To better tailor services to individual victims, adding for the first time restorative justice and the victim personal statement" as defined on the Government website under "Helping and supporting victims of crime."

> *"I want to create a fairer criminal justice system where victims have a louder voice and those who break the law are more likely to go to prison for longer. I also want to ask everyone working with victims to help deliver the promises in the new Code and make sure their needs are put first."* (Grayling, accessed July 2014).

Our voice on how the offence has made us feel, is limited to our words when submitting a Victim Personal Statement (VPS). This is enshrined in Article 10 of the Victims' Directive, Right to be Heard. One researcher states "Conceivably, this puts victims with lower writing abilities at a disadvantage compared to those who are better able to express themselves through the written word – possibly giving rise to a trend of harsher sentences being passed on offenders who commit crimes against more intelligent victims" (Harper, 2013).

On this point, the raw emotion, is as real whatever the intelligence of the victim; it has less to do with intelligence but more to do with how much a victim cares about justice and the victim finding a supreme inner strength to deal with the frustrations suffered. His view is the victims' pivotal role in criminal proceedings in the vast majority of crimes as being: "Crimes are first reported to the police by victims, who help investigators to collect evidence that lead to charges being brought against suspects. They then testify against defendants in court by providing first-hand accounts of alleged offences. These are examples of positive victim involvement in justice – involvement that directly facilitates, as stated earlier, the detection, and conviction of offenders. However, this is where victim involvement in criminal proceedings should stop" (Harper, 2013).

My continued involvement with criminal justice reform, despite my case conclusion, will continue until the majority of criminal justice cases actively work towards supporting and aiding a victim's recovery rather than causing significant further harm. I had many discussions on the positive use of a victim personal statement with the Ministry of Justice (MoJ) when discussing the Victims' Code. It is important and useful as it can inform the sentencing judge the impact the crime has had on the victim. This may not be heard through standard questioning/cross examination of witnesses and indeed is the only "voice" of the victim heard in those cases where the defendant pleads guilty. The Judge may refer to the victim personal statement as a part of the sentencing remarks. The sentencing remarks are the lasting statement that will carry through to any bail hearings or Parole Board review and where applicable to Immigration Tribunals, so irrespective of a further VPS, the original VPS can still have a significant impact on sentencing.

However, the Ministry of Justice leaflet "Making a Victim Personal Statement" states: "Your VPS can be seen by everyone involved in the case, including the defendant and their lawyer(s), police, prosecution, and the judge or magistrate if the case goes to court. However, your VPS will only be considered by the court if the defendant either pleads guilty or is found guilty by the court. The court and/or the defence could cross-examine you about the contents of the VPS in order to clarify or challenge certain points. This may be reported on in the media." Indeed, it mentions no less than three times that it could be "reported on in the media". Is this a deliberate attempt to put off victims from using their only chance to have their say? My case was widely reported, my VPS was not. Most cases do not make the media but the net effect might be victims are reluctant to put their emotion on paper for fear of their rawest emotions being dissected in court and publicised.

To add further insult to victims, a Judge in a Parole Board hearing in August 2014 was reported as saying "I feel so sorry for these families. They make these statements thinking they are going to make a difference, but they make no difference at all. Someone should tell them" (BBC News, August 2014), In my own experience I refute this and have received confirmation that the Parole Board acknowledged victim impact information which led them to extending my offender's licence period and keeping him in custody until end of sentence. However, this is the perfect example to show the mind-set of many criminal justice professionals - they do not want victims involved in the process. Without victims there is no process. Whilst it would be wrong to sentence an offender on the basis of the eloquence of the victim, it is equally wrong to ignore the impact of an offence on the victim. This information is directly relevant to informing the complicity of the offender and may also have some benefit in making the offender face up to the offence and with the assistance of Restorative Justice find a new way of living.

The criminal justice system and its professionals do not unanimously appreciate the impact a crime can have on a victim, nor do they see that we, as victims, are part of their remit. This is a very sad realisation and in contravention to the Victims Directive "Crime is a wrong against society as well as a violation of the individual rights of a victim" (Official Journal of the European Union, 2012). I would urge all victims to challenge their poor treatment in the European Court and let's hold the justice system to account. The extreme stress caused by victimisation can *"shatter the very basic assumptions victims have about themselves and the world around them"* (Peterson, 2003).

The Victims Directive, Article 18 Right to Protection includes protection for the victim against the risk of secondary and repeat victimisation and emotional of psychological harm. According to the United States National Criminal Justice Services recommendation on Victim Impact Statements (Web access, July 2014) :"Victims' overwhelming desire to have an active role in the prosecution and disposition of a criminal case does not stem from a need to retaliate, but rather to promote fair and sensitive treatment of victims, to have their role in the justice process acknowledged, and to alert the justice process to the emotional, physical and financial impact of crime on its victims and our nation as a whole."

The Government have just announced the following measures which when implemented will underpin in national law the rights of the victim (Victim's Law). The additional measures of an information line and online "one stop shop" for case tracking and signposting to local services may lead to a reduction in re-victimisation and the double abuse so often caused by the criminal justice process. The Government's plans include:

1. Establishing a new nationwide Victims' Information Service by March 2015, and developing this into a comprehensive service that allows victims to access the information and support they need.
2. Strengthening the protection for vulnerable victims by making the experience of going to court a better one.
3. Increasing transparency and accountability, to ensure criminal justice agencies are held to account for the services they provide to victims.
4. Introducing a Victims' Law to guarantee key entitlements for victims.

The Role of the Media

Malcolm Dean (Dean, 2011) refers to "Penal Populism returns" "Alas 5 months after the Green Paper, the heart of the plan was abandoned. It was triggered by a Radio 5 live phone-in, by a woman caller,

Gabrielle Browne who had suffered a sexual assault"; (Green Paper, Breaking the Cycle: Effective Punishment, Rehabilitation and Sentencing of Offenders).

Was I, as a single victim likely to have had a voice with Ministers without the assistance of the media? No. This was made clear to me much earlier when I wrote to the Justice Secretary, Jack Straw in 2007 following his statement he wanted to enter into a public debate on the greater use of community sentences. My letter was all but ignored.

I raised many of the issues I subsequently raised with Ken Clarke, Justice Secretary, in 2011 which led to the following responses: "Thank you also for your suggestions about how things could be improved for victims" (letter, Justice Secretary, June 2011) "I am aware that you are already in contact with my officials and I have asked them to keep you updated on the progress of the work...... If you have any further observations or queries on this, my officials will give them careful consideration" (letter, Immigration Minister February 2012)."I am grateful for the time you have taken to assist us in improving our processes for dealing with victims of crime" (letter Home Secretary, May 2012).

It is all very well to comment on the influence of media stories, but this is one person's perspective based on "facts" gleaned from a journalist's view point. The media's involvement was central to the pressure I was able to place and therefore a key component, leading to my case conclusion when my offender was deported. I received more respect for my feelings, and more assistance from media outlets than I did any criminal justice agency or Victim Support.

There are unscrupulous journalists definitely, but still some I trust and respect to this day and to whom I will always be grateful. My subsequent input has helped to shape significant changes within the Victims Code, the Probation Victim Contact Scheme, the Victim Personal Statement and Parliamentary Health Service Ombudsman reform. The media opened the door to constructive discussions with Ministers and their officials. Irrespective of the validity of my arguments, I would not have had influence if the media had not taken an active interest. Beyond opening the door, I was able to validate my arguments. I was true to my values and desire to improve how victims of crime are treated. I would not succumb to the pressure from the some elements of the media to take the scalp of a Minister. This would not have furthered change for victims and therefore would have hindered my objective.

Similarly, the media was instrumental in raising publicity that ultimately led to the introduction of Sarah's Law. Lead by the News of the World newspaper in the summer of 2000 after the murder of Sarah Payne by a paedophile, it was to take another decade to be rolled out nationally following successful trials. (Hughes, M. 2010) otherwise known as the Child Sex Offender Disclosure Scheme.

It is an indictment as to the state of systems to protect victims' interests, if the only way for these to be converted to better practices is to rely on the media.

The offence of stalking has come about as the direct result of successful victim campaigning showing the power of the victim in bringing about change. Stalking and harassment prosecutions between April 2013 and March 2014 rose to 10,535, up 20% on the previous year (BBC, 2014) The Protection of Freedoms Act 2012 created two new offences of stalking by inserting new sections 2A and 4A into the Protection from Harassment Act 1997.

The changes to the law followed a campaign by a number of organisations, including Protection Against Stalking. The campaign led to an unusual "Independent Parliamentary Inquiry" by the Justice Unions' Parliamentary Group. Their report, published in February 2012, found that victims of stalking had a profound lack of confidence in the criminal justice system, and recommended that the 1997 Act be amended as part of a package of reforms. The Domestic Violence, Crime and Victims Act 2004 Act makes provision for the Victims' Commissioner. Yet the Commissioner, although able to air general views of victims to Ministers, does not have the right of intervention in cases brought to her attention.In her annual report, Baroness Newlove concludes "A victim's voice which does not lead to action is no voice at all" (Newlove, 2014). This could also be said of the lack of power for the Commissioner, herself, to effect immediate change to a victim's experience.

Restorative Justice: A Victim's Perspective

The definition for Restorative Justice in the Directive under Article 2 Definitions "means any process whereby the victim and the offender are enabled, if they freely consent, to participate actively in the resolution of matters arising from the criminal offence through the help of an impartial third party.

I agree with the need for a court to act objectively and it is reasonable that a victim whose soul has been blown apart by the actions of the offender cannot be objective, hence the adversarial system. Yet, does this really invalidate the victim's voice? It is surely directly relevant for the court and the offender to understand the trauma caused and perversely is this not the very success of Restorative Justice that is referred to as working "particularly will in cases...with the restorative approach leading to higher rates of victim satisfaction and offender accountability than any other sentencing type" (Harper, 2013)

The significance of Restorative Justice lies very much with the introduction of the EU Victims' Directive to **establish minimum standards on the rights support and protection of victims of crime**. Article 12 of the EU Victims Directive requires Member States to carry out restorative justice services only in the interest of the victim subject to any safety considerations and are based on a victim's free and informed consent which may be withdrawn at any time.

A restorative intervention, if led under the principles of Article 12 of the EU Victims Directive, can empower a victim to ask those questions of the offender often left unanswered by the adversarial system. It requires both the offender's and the victim's co-operation. The offender to accept full responsibility for the harm done; for the victim to be a willing participant, not pressured, but free to decide if it is the right course of action for that victim. The timing of such an intervention, may or may not fit in with the allowances made in the Crime and Courts Act 2013 to allow sentencing to be deferred for an intervention to take place. The implied pressure on the victim may be a cause for concern and may also be too early after a crime for the victim to be ready for an intervention at this early stage.

The other contradiction is the Payment by Results for Restorative Services. Again, this implies a pressure for an RJ intervention to be written up as successful in order for the provider to receive full payment. Sometimes the process of exploring the option of Restorative Justice, will lead a victim to decide that its continued pursuit is not right. If it leads to positive decision making for the victim then its instigation was right and compliant with Article 12 EU Victims Directive.

However, the caveat to the focus on Restorative Justice is that not every offender accepts the facts of the case, some are psychopaths and are not suitable. Recovery from trauma for a particular crime by a victim, does not have a standard time line. The approach to the aftermath of a crime is unique to the individual victim. Restorative Justice is not the right path for every victim, we should not pursue it as though it will work in most cases. That being said, I do not believe there should be any restriction on its consideration, whether for low level juvenile offending or domestic violence but each case dealt with if appropriate with the necessary risk assessments (Loseby, Ntziadima and Gavrielides, 2014). Because of the accumulated physical, emotional and spiritual harm caused by violent crime, victims feel that there needs to be some recognition of these losses, preferably through compensation, perhaps indirectly through healing or rehabilitation programs, or at the very least through a sincere apology (Derksen, 2009).

Earlier this year, I discussed a case with the victim whose request for a Restorative Justice intervention with the offender turned down by the Victim Liaison Officer (VLO). I checked the policy in the Victim Guidance Manual in PI 11/2013. The VLO had not applied the latest guidance in dealing with this request. I raised the broad issue of front line delivery of the policy with the relevant victims' team. I was heartened by the response "it may prove beneficial to make clearer the advice VLOs can give on Restorative Justice and to this end we will seek to amend the relevant section during the next revision (email from Policy Advisor, April 2014).

In my experience dealing directly with policy officials there has been much cooperation with improving practices. As the above example demonstrates, the policy can exist but it does not always translate at the point of service delivery.

The lifecycle I have experienced as a victim of a serious sexual assault has brought me to a different standpoint than I held at the outset.

My focus is very much on, not only reducing the impact and long lasting effects of crime on the victims and their wider peer group but also to seek measures that will help to deter reoffending, as it is this more than anything else, that will improve outcomes for society as a whole. We need to deviate away from having a viewpoint too offender, or too victim focussed. Why are Restorative Justice interventions successful not only on recidivism rates but also victim satisfaction? I would suggest it is about compromise and genuinely listening to another's viewpoint.

Most victims, although emotionally traumatised by the damage meted out by the offender, are still reasonable thinking human beings, often offended by the fear criminal justice professionals often show towards them. It is possible they are more likely to be open to a restorative intervention than might be expected. A victim is as equally capable as any other human being to deal and cope with information that may be different from what they would like to hear. Victims need honest open dialogue delivered with some empathy. It is often the how, that determines the response rather than the what.

However, as the evidence suggests, Restorative Justice is not an easy fix for all of society's ills. It is an approach that will work very effectively at times. These times should be pursued because although investment of time is high, the reward is a more integrated society, with a greater likelihood of the offender and the victim, contributing more positively. We should not avoid the challenge but should adopt a realistic assessment of when it will work.

I have undergone training as a volunteer Restorative Justice Facilitator. This is the training of novice facilitators, to deliver an in-prison project, funded by the Ministry of Justice. Whether it will be delivered in the ethos of the Victims' Directive remains to be seen. This is where the delivery at the front end of services can differ so much from the policy. This is also an issue with Restorative Justice practitioners with many years of experience primarily focussing on the needs and motivations of the offender, who now have to rethink their starting strategy to ensure delivery is compliant with the EU Victims Directive.

I have dealt with a unique set of circumstances because I dared to challenge practitioners, Government Ministers and their officials when the case was not handled as it should have been. Either I as a victim had been singled out deliberately for poor treatment or the more likely explanation that my experience is widespread. Even, despite my efforts, poor treatment of victims is still endemic. In an ideal criminal justice system, a victim reports a crime, the offender is apprehended and society benefits because the offender is either not free to reoffend or is rehabilitated to the extent that the offender chooses not to ever again.

I will continue to demand greater respect and fairness to victims until the time arrives when the criminal justice process aids recovery rather than prolonging the pain and suffering and in so doing causes further harm and re-victimisation. If victims allow the status quo to be deemed acceptable there will be no progress, we have had much progress recently but only due to relentless campaigning by victims and organisations across Europe that represent them, which has led us to the EU Victims Directive.

At no stage however frustrated with the way I was treated, did I ever want a nominal suspect to be put forward. I only wanted the perpetrator, the person who took away my inner soul, to be put before the court. This initial injustice and the subsequent research I did to prove how unjust the criminal justice system is to victims, has led me to the path of campaigning and working with Government Ministers and their officials to improve policy and practices so that at some point in the future there will be a time, when the criminal justice process positively contributes to the recovery of a victim rather than at present hindering the recovery of the victim.

There is a discrepancy where policy without question, has a much stronger, "in the interests of victims" slant but where those responsible for the delivery of front line services have yet to absorb and apply the policy. "Victims play a critical part in criminal justice – victims and witnesses giving evidence – and having the courage to do so is critical to the functioning of the criminal justice system" (Government response to Getting it Right for Victims and Witnesses).

The victim feels let down by everyone. Those close family and friends are given no guidance as to the trauma and increased sensitivity of the victim. The criminal justice agencies focus on the accused. The adversarial system works this way. However by focussing on the accused the victim is often marginalised. The victim's voice is imperative for justice. The court process is important to deliver unbiased reasoned balance to sentencing, but has only recently started to listen to the voice of the victim, in the form of a Victim Personal Statement (VPS). This has been available for many years, but all too often most victims have not been informed that they can complete one. Now, although the policy is in place to ensure a victim is asked as to whether a VPS is completed, the guidance on the policy does not read as being victim friendly. I hope that by challenging and reforming no other victim will ever have to suffer as I did.

Concluding Thoughts

If the level of abuse and damage caused to victims by the criminal justice system was in fact caused by a perpetrator, that perpetrator would be brought before the courts. That is how serious the state of our criminal justice system currently is.

The long lasting effects of being treated badly by the State as a victim is not conducive with any State's first duty "to protect its citizens". A victim led agenda is not mutually exclusive to punishing and rehabilitating offenders. Victims are the people to whom the State owes the greatest responsibility as there is no criminal justice system without their input. Their vital input and co-operation demands that they are treated as valued human beings with a role to play as the criminal justice process unfolds. The challenge is to ensure professionals safeguard victims and deliver a service to them whereby the criminal justice process aids rather than hinders recovery.

The adversarial system does not allow for an equal position for the victim (state vs offender). The expression of grief, anger, and feelings of revenge interfere with the impartial objective and rational character of the procedure. The system is designed around the priorities for the offender. The victim can also be a broken member of society and as defined in the EU Victims' Directive "Crime is a wrong against society as well as a violation of the individual rights of victims". So why does the criminal justice system deal with one strand but not the other? "Research also indicates two key post-victimization factors that can increase the likelihood of victims to develop mental health problems:

- A lack of or poor social support systems.
- The degree of exposure to the justice system" (Wasserman and Ellis, 2007)

This is a problem that criminal justice systems are failing to address despite the implied responsibility within the Victims' Directive. I hope that practitioners will ensure that future the front-end delivery of policy takes into account the needs of victims.

In the UK, does the Victims' Code go far enough to meet the victims' rights as defined in the EU Victims Directive? The Victims' Law should allow victims to challenge in court the provision of services in line with their rights. Does the practitioner position on Restorative Justice meet the criteria as defined in the Victims Directive? If victims are to get a fair deal, more of us need to the challenge the authorities using our rights as clearly defined in the Directive and the Victims Law. Although practitioners working within criminal justice have a responsibility to treat us in accordance with our rights, unless we are aware, informed and challenge when necessary to uphold our rights, the impact of the EU Victims Directive and Victims Law legislation is not likely to fulfil its potential.

If a member state fails to pass the required national legislation, or if the national legislation does not adequately comply with the requirements of the directive, the European Commission may initiate legal action against the member state in the European Court of Justice. This may also happen when a member state has transposed a directive in theory but has failed to abide by its provisions in practice.

On a personal note, in my own experience dealing with practitioners, it was not the lack of policy to keep me informed that failed, but the lack of implementation of that policy. I have had an influence on UK policy because I have challenged existing processes. The more of us who challenge, the greater impact we will have on future policy.

Variation in the provision of victims' services has come about through the introduction of Police and Crime Commissioners (PCCs) who are now responsible for the local commissioning. This leads inevitably to local variation in service provision and therefore some victims not receiving the support needed.

The Minister for Policing and Criminal Justice has stated with reference to Police and Crime Commissioners "'How victims are treated is essential to maintaining public trust in policing and the criminal justice system The needs of victims vary locally and PCCs, much more than central government, will be best placed to decide what their communities want" (Herbert, 2012). The converse view is Police & Crime Commissioners have added further bureaucracy, cost and mistrust into the system (for example the South Yorkshire Commissioner who has refused to stand down despite being the Council member responsible for children's social care during the Rotherham child abuse scandal) (BBC, Sept 2014). This is a role in which he is responsible for all the victims of crime and is bringing the office of Police and Crime Commissioner into disrepute. In my opinion, it is as "criminal" to ignore offending as it is to commit offending. Victims need confidence in those that are tasked with delivering services to them.

The UK Justice Secretary has recently announced the introduction of the Victims' Law to replace the Victims' Code and in a press release has stated:

"A new law will guarantee key entitlements for victims, previously set out in the Victims Code.... Transparency and accountability will also improve, with criminal justice agencies held to account and required to publish information on how they have improved services" (Grayling, 2014).

This important and significant announcement has come about following significant pressure from Victims and the implied pressure from the European Directive to be embedded into National law no later than 16 November 2015. Where provision does not meet the minimum standards in the Directive, or the Victim's Law after its introduction, we, as victims and as society, need to challenge to uphold our rights and make the rhetoric the reality.

References

Bard, M. & Sangrey, D., (1986). *The Crime Victim's Book*. Secaucus, NJ: Citadel Press

BBC News online (5th August, 2014) *Family hears judge say victim statements make 'no difference'* http://www.bbc.co.uk/news/uk-28644799

BBC News online (11th September 2014) *Rotherham abuse: 'No confidence' in PCC Shaun Wright* from: http://www.bbc.co.uk/news/uk-england-south-yorkshire-29157337

BBC News online (11th September 2014) *Stalking prosecutions at record high after new law* http://www.bbc.co.uk/news/uk-england-28334035

CPS accessed July 2014, http://www.cps.gov.uk/legal/v_to_z/code_of_practice_for_the_victims_of_crime_(victim_s_code)_-_legal_guidance/#a04

Dean M. (2011), *Democracy under attack: How the media distort policy and politics Bristol*: Policy Press

Derksen, W. Director, Victims' Voice, Mennonite Central Committee, Winnipeg, Manitoba, Canada - Posted 2009-10-23 15 *The 15 Elements of the Crime Victim Detour* http://www.iirp.edu/iirpWebsites/web/uploads/article_pdfs/77270_Beth09_Wilma_Derksen.pdf

Directive 2012/29/EU of the European Parliament and of the Council of 25 October 2012 establishing minimum standards on the rights, support and protection of victims of crime, and replacing Council Framework Decision 2001/220/JHA 14.11.2012 Official Journal of the European Union L315/57 (9) http://db.eurocrim.org/db/en/doc/1828.pdf

Government response to *Getting it Right for Victims and Witnesses*, p80. https://consult.justice.gov.uk/digital-communications/victims-witnesses/results/a-gov-response-getting-right-victims-witnesses.pdf

Government website (15 May 2013) *Helping and supporting victims of crime*, https://www.gov.uk/government/topics/law-and-the-justice-system

Herbert, N. (2nd July 2012) *Police and Crime Commissioners to determine local victims' services* https://www.gov.uk/government/news/police-and-crime-commissioners-to-determine-local-victims-services

Grayling, C. (10 December 2013) https://www.gov.uk/government/news/victims-put-first-in-the-criminal-justice-system

Grayling, C. (September 2014) Press release

Harper, Craig A. *Can We Balance Victim and Offender Interests in the Criminal Justice System?* August, 2013 http://craigaharper.wordpress.com/2013/08/03/victims-and-offenders-cjs

Hughes, M. The Independent Online: (2010) *'Sarah's law to be rolled out nationally'*. http://www.independent.co.uk/news/uk/crime/sarahs-law-to-be-rolled-out-nationally-1914989.html

Impact Statements, (accessed 28th July 2014) *National Recommendation 1* https://www.ncjrs.gov/ovc_archives/reports/impact/impact.htm

Loseby, G. Ntziadima, A. and Gavrielides, T. (2014) *Restorative Justice and Domestic Violence: A Critical Review*, London: IARS

Newlove, Baroness, (8th July, 2014) *Commissioner for Victims and Witnesses: Report for the Secretary of State for Justice 2013-14* http://www.justice.gov.uk/downloads/about/victims-commissioner/victims-commissioner-annual-report-2013-14.pdf

Peterson, 2003 cit in DeValve, E., *A Qualitative Exploration of the Effects of Crime Victimisation for Victims of Personal Crime, Applied Psychology in Criminal Justice*, 2005, 1(2)).

Starmer, K. Guardian 6th April 2014; *A voice for victims of crime* http://www.theguardian.com/commentisfree/2014/apr/06/victims-law-criminal-justice-labour-plan

Wasserman, E. Ellis, C. A; PARTICIPANT'S TEXT; 2007 National Victim Assistance Academy, Track 1, Foundation-Level Training; *Chapter 6: Impact of Crime on Victims VI* -http://www.ccvs.state.vt.us/sites/default/files/resources/VVAA%20Ch%206%20Impact%20of%20Crime.pdf

Waxman, C., accessed 17th July, 2014 www.voice4victims

The Fluidity of Victimhood

*Elaine Shpungin**

Abstract

The victim-centered movement has resulted in legislation outlining minimal rights and supports for individuals experiencing harm as a result of criminal actions (e.g., the EU Victims' Directive). However, victimhood is a fluid concept that is (a) socially constructed; (b) imperfectly captured by our legal systems; (c) obfuscated by contextual factors and systemic inequities (e.g., domestic violence, implicit bias); and (d) often shared by multiple parties in a conflict. Thus, this chapter argues for *multi-partiality*, a justice response that goes beyond a bifurcated idea of victimhood and offenderhood to encompass multiple parties who may be victimized by an act of harm. Case studies from a Restorative Circles practice (a community-based restorative justice response) illustrate specific ways in which on-the-ground justice responses can go beyond the letter of victim-centered law to the heart of its spirit.

Introduction

> *There is a higher court than courts of justice and that is the court of conscience. It supercedes all other courts.* - Mahatma Gandhi

> *We must take sides. Neutrality helps the oppressor, never the victim. Silence encourages the tormentor, never the tormented.* - Elie Wiesel

In the dawning of an age in which victim rights and victim-centred justice responses are gaining momentum, inspiring nation-wide debate, and giving birth to new legislation and action, we must, more than ever, consider taking sides. Indeed, if we are to truly improve the "justness" of our justice responses, we must seek neither neutrality nor partiality as our guiding motto, but take the side of every individual who comes within our custody, our care, our Circle, and our conflict community. This is because mounting research shows that victimization is socially constructed, imperfectly captured by our legal systems, obfuscated by contextual variables, and often shared by multiple parties in a conflict. Thus, uniting the reality of victim needs and the need for a more shared reality about victimization, this chapter calls for an increase in multi-partiality, an approach that allows us to speak up for not only "official" victims but all those who experience victimization when acts of harm occur.

* Elaine Shpungin (Director, Psychological Services Center at University of Illinois, USA, Urbana Champaign), contact shpungin@illinois.edu

Beyond the Act of Harm: Limits and Opportunities of Victim-Centred Legislation

Victim-centred legislation around the world (e.g., *1994 Australian Victims of Crime Act; 1996 Service Charter for Victims of Crime in South Africa; 2012 E.U. Victims' Directive; 2013 U.K.* and *Wales Code of Practice for Victims of Crime; U.S. Victims' Rights State Amendments;* proposed *2014 Canadian Victims' Bill of Rights*) tries to expand the rights and protections of individuals harmed by acts of crime. Minimally, these laws often address common victim needs such as privacy, information, and respect; in some cases, as with the EU Victims' Directive, they also attend to other needs, including cultural and linguistic needs (e.g., interpreters, literacy), gender specific needs (e.g., violence against women), and age-related needs (e.g., of children).

In terms of opportunities, the vast majority, if not all, victim-centred legislation limits the definition of victim to an individual who has suffered harm as a result of a criminal act. The EU Victims' Directive, for example, defines a victim as "... a person who has suffered harm... which was directly caused by a criminal offense" and, somewhat less commonly, also "family members of a person whose death was directly caused by a criminal offense." The offender is defined as the "... person who has been convicted of a crime... [or] a suspected or accused person..."

While defining victims and offenders in this specific way, most legislation also notes that the provisions therein are "minimum rules" which, as the EU Victims' Directive explicitly states, may be extended "... to provide a higher level of protection." Thus, this chapter highlights both ways in which constricted definitions of "victim" may limit our victim-centred responses, and ways in which they provide us with an opportunity to go beyond the letter of the law to more fully capture its spirit. That is, the issues and arguments raised in this chapter do not aim to diminish or contradict victim-centred provisions and recommendations, but to extend them to all involved parties – including, perhaps controversially, to the party currently thought of as the offender or perpetrator.

Victimhood as a Social Construction

The first danger of defining victimhood using a particular act of harm is that victimhood is socially and politically constructed. Just as scholars have written about the social and political construction of the "deserving" and "underserving" poor (e.g., Will, 1993), and of the phenomenon of "victim blaming" social policies which stem from the belief that individuals and groups who are disenfranchised are responsible for their problems and lower economic status (e.g., Ryan, 1976), scholars have also discussed the social and political construction of victimhood. These differing, and sometimes contradictory, constructions by media, law enforcement, and scholars serve as a reminder that victimhood is a dynamic and changing social creation.

For instance, Christie (1986) talks about a socially ideal victim being a person who holds certain characteristics that combine vulnerability (e.g., seemingly weak, physically harmed by a powerful offender) and respectability (e.g., did not provoke the offender, was doing something socially appropriate while harmed). Consistent with Christie's conceptualization, Strobl (2004) and Vrij and Fisher (1997) found that persons who appear shy, sad, weak, and vulnerable are indeed more likely to be given victim status by law enforcement officials.

Others have written about different sets of characteristics that embody the construction of the ideal victim in different contexts. For instance, Walklate (2007), shows that historical and political influences propel certain types of victims centre-stage while keeping others behind the curtain:

> *Appreciating the ways in which the state operates sometimes in the interest of its citizens, but always in the interests of self-maintenance, is central to understanding the underlying (generative) mechanisms that contribute towards the kinds of victimizations which we "see" as compared to those which we do not "see"...* (p.49)

This bifurcation is also seen in conceptualizations of "deserving" and "undeserving" victims, meaning both individuals who deserve to be victimized (e.g., Knox, 2001, regarding political violence in Northern Ireland) and individuals who deserve to be considered victims. For instance, Smolej (2010) examined the construction of the ideal victim by analysing violence vignettes from Finnish crime-appeal television programmes (which involve the public in solving criminal cases). Contrary to Christie's conception of the ideal victim as vulnerable and innocent-seeming, Smolej found that victims who were included in the TV vignettes were middle class, middle-aged, well-off, and part of nuclear families, and that individuals with more marginal roles (e.g., homeless, young) were excluded from the status of victimhood.

Others (e.g., Fattah, 2003; Kinsella, 2012) have also noted that people who are marginalised are often simultaneously more likely to be victimized and rejected as victims. For instance, Kinsella (2012) discusses the social and legal (i.e., in terms of police response) construction of the feared homeless perpetrator, when, in reality, those who are homeless are more likely to be victims, rather than perpetrators, of crime. Kinsella notes that all attempts at naming or noting victimhood stem from judgments that reflect moralistic, philosophical, cultural and political biases:

> *Since the emergence of academic interest in the victims of crime, a preoccupation with the status of the victim has, either explicitly or implicitly, been a feature of victimology in all its forms. More specifically, academics exploring victimisation have prioritised establishing who is to blame for victimisation, and who is worthy, or deserving, of support, respect, and dignity – who is in the 'right'. From the positivist approaches of Von Hentig, who attempted to identify proneness in victims via the development of victim typologies (Mawby and Walklate, 1994), and Mendelsohn, who categorised crime victims "from the 'completely innocent' to the 'most guilty victim'" (ibid , p.12); through feminist critiques of victimology, which highlighted women as the forgotten victims of crime and sought to absolve them from 'blame' (Wolhuter et al., 2009); and radical victimology, which shifted blame by shining a light on the crimes of the powerful (Quinney, 1972); to critical victimology, and its concern with who has the power to attribute victim/perpetrator status – the notion of who is at fault, who is in the 'wrong', is key. Within each of these victimological frameworks, the demarcation between who the victims are and who is to blame for their victimhood is clearly established according to the standpoint and political motivation of those academics developing the theory. Be it the traditional approach of the positivists focusing on the crimes of the street, or the radical approach of those drawing attention to more abstract understandings of criminal 'harm', there are always symbolic conceptions of 'good' and 'evil' at play* (Weisstub, 1986: p.126)

Similarly, Winkel (1991) and others have shown that culturally normative behaviours expressed by individuals from non-mainstream groups (e.g., immigrants) can lead police to label some individuals as victims and reject that status for others. Not only does the social and legal construction of victimhood affect obvious outcomes for individuals (e.g., whether they receive help), but it may also affect relationships between individuals involved in conflict. For instance, Sahlin (2004), through examination of in depth interviews with individuals involved in obtaining contact prohibition orders (i.e., orders of protection), found that the need to bifurcate their own roles as pure victims and the roles of the other as pure "villain" (in criminal proceedings) encouraged the reconstruction of themselves, the other, and their relationship along victim-offender lines.

Attempting to capture how this occurs, scholars have created models that describe the construction and "triaging" of victimhood. Miers (1990), for instance, discusses how determinations of victimhood are an interaction between the societal recognition of an individual's victimhood and the individual's self-identification as a victim. As a result of this combination, a person may be considered, in this model, as (a) an *actual victim*, recognized by both society and self; (b) a *rejected* victim, recognized only by oneself; (c) a *designated* victim, recognized only by society; or (d) a non-victim, recognized as a victim by neither. Strobl (2004) proposes a different model, which examines whether the "offender" was motivated to create harm and whether the harm was targeted at the individual(s) who felt harmed. This model also results in four possible victimization classifications: (a) *personal victimization* (directly harmed as a result of being personally targeted by harmer); (b) *vicarious victimization* (directly harmed by accident, such as a pedestrian caught in a crossfire); (c) *mediated victimization* (harm experienced by those who are impacted by someone else's victimization, such as family members, loved ones, and classmates); and (d) *collective victimization* (harm experienced via the indirect impact of being part of a targeted group). Strobl also discusses the complications of communication, culture, and social biases in the law enforcement response to people calling for help (e.g., a large, strong-looking man may have a harder time being seen as a victim in some cultures, compared to a smaller woman), and how these factors come together to create a "social ascription" of victim status.

What is relevant for our increased clarity of how to approach the question of victim fluidity is not the pros and cons of a particular model or definition of victimhood, but the clear understanding that victimhood is, indeed, constructed by society, media, law enforcement officials, scholars, attorneys, and our unconscious biases. These social constructions and biases result in unequal designations of some individuals – and/or individuals from some groups – as victims, while systematically rendering others as offenders on a more regular basis, as discussed below.

Offenders as Victims of Maltreatment

The social construction of victimhood underlies other ways in which victimhood and offenderhood can be fluid, or even interchangeable, concepts. For instance, systemic and contextual factors between individuals involved in an act of harm can shape victimhood beyond the actual criminal or harmful act, as with the phenomenon of the "Burning Bed."

The Burning Bed, the 1980s book (McNulty, 1980) and film (Avnet & Greenwald, 1984) about Francine Hughes, a real-life mother and wife who killed her ex-husband, James "Mickey" Hughes after 13 years of brutal and well-documented[1] physical abuse, rape, terrorizing, and control, popularized the phenomenon of "fighting back" by victims of continuous maltreatment. After pouring gasoline on James while he slept, and setting him and the house on fire (while the children waited in the car in their coats), Francine turned herself in to the police, later to be acquitted of the murder in a Lansing, Michigan courtroom.

While examples of legislative recommendations for "victims who fight back" have seen an increase since Francine's case (e.g., Mackenzie & Colvin, 2009; Wimberley, 2007), and similar dramatic acquittals of victims of maltreatment occasionally make it into the media (e.g., Susan Falls in Australia; Nicole Ryan in Canada; Barbara Sheehan, Donna Fryman and Lisa Donion of the U.S.), the "battered wife defence" is still frequently denied (e.g., the case of Lavern Longsworth in Belize) and considered by scholars to be under-considered in criminal cases (e.g., Kinport, 2004). In addition, international scholars and advocates note that the legal response to survivors of domestic violence who offend continues to focus on the severity of the act (i.e., a knife stab is a knife stab is a knife stab) without giving sufficient attention to the context in which the act occurred, such as a pattern of abuse. For instance, writing on the criminal justice response to domestic violence in Australia, Douglas (2005) notes:

> *...On the one hand the criminal justice system has continuously refused to recognise harms perpetrated against women in the private sphere as crimes... On the other hand, where harms perpetrated in the intimate sphere are prosecuted as criminal acts, the approach of criminal law often results in these criminal offences being treated like other crimes, that is, as 'one off' incidents that are abstracted from their context...* (p.441)

Wright (1996), in *Justice for Victims and Offenders*, also states:

> *It has become commonplace to observe that court proceedings are based on win/lose, guilty/not guilty principles. Only at the margins are background details such as provocation or contributory negligence allowed to introduce shades of grey into the black-and-white decision. Thus, both defendants and victims are liable to be cut short if they try to mention background information which they regard as relevant* (p.23).

Similarly, Miller (2005) and Swan, Gambone, Caldwell, Sullivan & Snow (2008), reviewing the literature on women's violence against their partners, show that contextual factors are critical when examining violence and aggression in intimate relationships. For instance, they find that, while the frequency of violent and aggressive incidents seems "equal" for men and women, women's aggression against men occurs most frequently in the context of self-defence and abuse by their partners (while men's violence is more likely to be a way to exercise control) and men are significantly more likely to perpetuate sexual abuse, coercive control, serious and violent "intimate terrorism" and stalking. Women are also more likely than men to suffer injury in the context of domestic violence and to be further victimized by a gender neutral and acontextual social service and legal response to intimate partner violence.

Thus, Douglas (2005) and others (e.g., Mills, 2006) have argued that rather than being either "neutral" (applying an unbiased one-size fits all approach) or purely "victim centred" as defined by the harmful act (i.e., centring victim supports on the person who happens to be the target of that particular violent act) justice responses to domestic violence should focus on the contextual factors and social interpersonal patterns between involved parties.

Research on survivors of domestic violence can also inform our understanding of the complexity of victimhood and offenderhood in cases of less obvious or seemingly less egregious maltreatment and harassment in families, schools, and organizations.

A case from our Restorative Circles practice, involving an adolescent girl and her family, provides a useful illustration.

"You Fat Cow": Offenderhood and Victimhood in a Family Shooting[2]

When our team responded to a request for a Restorative Circle in a family where an adolescent girl had shot and wounded her father, it seemed that the offender and victim roles were fairly in line with those outlined by victims' legislation. As one piece of evidence, John, the father, had a surgery scar on his left side, where the bullet had entered near the heart. As another, Theresa, then 15, was being released from the local Juvenile Detention Centre (youth jail) where she had served time for her offense. However, as the preparatory meetings and the Restorative Circle itself unfolded, things began to appear more complex. Stories from Theresa, her younger sister Chloe, and their older cousin Meredith (who had been living with the family at that time), revealed what seemed to be an continuous pattern of verbal harassment of Theresa by her father, which included sexual teasing (e.g., comments about Theresa's developing breasts), criticism of her body (e.g., comments about her being fat and gross), public denigration of her physical abilities (e.g., derogatory comments about how slow and clumsy she was in front of her soccer teammates), and attempts at coercion related to food and exercise (e.g., withholding permission for her to join the family at dinner until she performed a certain number of abdominal exercises).

Felicia, the mother, described her own implicit support of her husband's actions and now seemed shocked and devastated to hear the effect they had been having on Theresa. Having struggled with addiction to diet pills and her own strained relationship to eating and weight, she thought she was supporting Theresa's ultimate success in life by standing by her husband's "tough love" tactics, since Theresa needed to "watch herself" more if she were to have a chance to be "popular and attractive to boys in school." Meredith admitted that she had been appalled by these family dynamics and had repeatedly urged Theresa to "not take it any more" and to "stand up for herself and fight back."

While most of us would likely agree that it was still Theresa's choice to take her father's gun and pull the trigger, and while many of us could engage in a lively debate about the proportionality of Theresa's action in relation to her experience in her family, the relevant point in this context is that many of the other people around the Circle felt co-responsible and considered themselves co-offenders in what happened. Just as importantly, many individuals in the Circle, including Chloe, the youngest (who saw Theresa as her ally and protector from their father), felt victimized by Theresa's imprisonment and of the continuation of the destructive family dynamics, which not only had not been addressed in any positive way by Theresa's time in jail but had now begun to shift onto Chloe.

Thus, for those of us who wish to go beyond the minimal "requirements" of victim-centred legislation and actually centre and support everyone victimized by "the act and its consequences," one strategy is to remain open to the possibility of multiple victimization and offer victim-centred supports and rights to as many involved parties as possible (Lyubansky & Barter, 2011; Barter, 2012).

With this expanded view, our team approached each person in Theresa's case as potentially experiencing victimhood, and in this way, supported several of the stated objectives of the EU Victims' Directive:

Dignity and Respect. We tried to express respect and acknowledgment of the underlying dignity of all involved parties by, for instance, listening to each person without expressing judgment or condemnation; asking everyone the same restorative questions in our preparation and Circle meetings (i.e., not using a different set of questions with the identified offender); offering refreshments to all parties (i.e., not offering water or snacks only to adults or only to the official victim); and facilitating the Circle conversation in a way that allowed mutual responsibility and mutual understanding to emerge among all those directly involved and impacted by the event.

Protection from Intimidation and Coercion. To help increase protection of all possible "victims" from further intimidation and coercion from all possible "offenders", we stressed the voluntariness of the process at several points along the way; talked to all participants about barriers to full participation (e.g., fear of retaliation or consequences); generated strategies that could increase participants' sense of safety (e.g., seating arrangement, location of Circle), and tried to attend to possible power dynamics in our facilitation (e.g., between parents and children) by staying "multi-partial" in our facilitation and Circle support.

Supports, Justice and Restoration. To help increase appropriate supports and access to justice and restoration for everyone experiencing victimization in the case, we made a restorative justice process available to Theresa and her family (among other options); explained the process clearly during preparatory meetings; allowed time and space for individuals to tell their stories and clarify their needs in private before the Circle meeting; provided everyone with copies of our restorative questions (so they could follow along and have the same access to our procedures as the facilitators); allowed opportunity for everyone to speak and to be heard during the Circle; and supported the co-creation of an Action Agreement that took into consideration the multiple facets of victimization and offenderhood that had been discussed, in order to help address the multiple deep needs on the table. These agreements included family therapy, individual eating-related counselling for Felicia, the reinstatement of several family practices aimed at increasing cohesion (e.g., family dinners, family game nights), and reconnection to moral actions (e.g., John and Felicia attending church more regularly). For Theresa, who was also worried about her re-integration into school, we also made plans to offer a Circle process in her classroom which would include students and teachers impacted by their knowledge of Theresa's "violent history."

Just as Theresa's example illustrates the phenomenon of social construction and attempts to illustrate the complexity of victimhood and offenderhood when maltreatment may be present, Theresa's is also a good introduction to the complexity of victimization and offenderhood within family and group systems.

Offenders as Victims of Systems

A system is a set of interacting or interdependent components forming an integrated whole. A system has recognizable behaviours which are distinct from those of its individual parts, boundaries, and substructures that govern its operations, and feedback loops that influence its functioning. Systems are found in both the natural world (e.g., forest bio systems, marine systems) and social world (e.g., families, organizations, congregations) (Pidwirny, 2006).

In the social world, systems theories provide explanatory mechanisms for how individuals interact with, and are influenced by, systems and system substructures. For instance, Bronfenbrenner's ecological systems theory (e.g., 1994) describes the way individuals interact with their family and peer systems and are impacted by social systems such as neighbourhoods, social service systems, and local policies (direct impact), and systems at the national and international level, such as culture and national attitudes, policies, and ideologies (indirect impact).

A multitude of research over many decades has shown that certain factors found across these systems (e.g., poverty, family aggression and childhood maltreatment, institutionalized discrimination based on group membership), unequally affects the chances that an individual will be cast as an offender, as well as the chances that an individual will offend. This research serves as yet another reminder that victimhood, even in cases of indisputable harmful acts, can be shared by multiple involved parties.

First, children and adolescents who have been victims of adult violence (physical and sexual) and/or parental neglect are significantly more likely to aggress against others and break the law than those who have not been maltreated (see review by Widom & Wilson, 2009).

In addition, children and adolescents are vulnerable to the presence and absence of positive peer and adult role models in their environments and to the various influences of poverty, such as absence of positive youth activities or jobs in their community (e.g., Caputo, 1987; Becroft, Te Kaiwhakawa Matua o Te Kooti Taiohi o Aotearoa, & Thompson, 2006; Loeber & Farrington, 2012; Wasserman et al, 2003). Individuals who are part of closed systems, such as families, schools, gangs, and organizations are also more likely to engage in reciprocal aggression in which acts of harm are passed back and forth among individuals (e.g., Lauritsen, Sampson & Laube, 1991). In addition, individuals within the system who do not seem to be directly involved in the harmful act are often involved in co-creating the conditions for the act to take place, or in co-creating the menu (along with other systemic realities and influences) from which the actors choose their actions (Barter, 2012). Thus, a particular criminal act of harm, in which one party is the official offender and the other the official victim, may not capture the dynamic and fluid nature of the actual victimization(s).

Structural inequity and past maltreatment also continue to disproportionately affect adult offenders. International studies of adult prisoners, both male and female, have shown them to have extensive histories of trauma and abuse (e.g., Sindicich, 2014; Arnold, Stewart & McNeece, 2001). In addition to higher levels of maltreatment in their families of origin, incarcerated individuals are more likely to have come from families living in poverty and struggling with untreated addiction and mental health issues. For instance, Crane & Heaton (2008) found that almost 75% of incarcerated individuals reported drug and alcohol addiction in their family, with over 80% reporting that drug and alcohol contributed to their offense. A 2006 study by the U.S. Bureau of Justice Statistics found that over half of all jail and prison inmates have mental health issues. Specifically, an estimated 1.25 million inmates suffer from mental illness, over four times the number in 1998, and two to four times greater than the general population (James & Glaze, 2006). Incarcerated individuals are also more likely to have parents, siblings and other adults in their life involved in the legal system. In one study, 66% of incarcerated individuals in the U.S. reported that they had family members in jail, prison or on probation (Crane & Heaton, 2008).

International data, though heavily weighted by U.S. findings due to the severity of the issue there, also show disproportionate percentages of incarcerated individuals to come from certain ethnic, racial,[3] minority or disadvantaged groups. For instance, in the U.S., African Americans make up about 13% of the general population, but 30% of arrested individuals and almost 50% of the prison population. Black men, in particular, are almost 6 times more likely to be incarcerated than White men, and men of Hispanic origin twice as likely as White men (Mauer & King, 2007). In Australia, individuals who self-identify as Aboriginal and Torres Strait Islander are about 3% of the general population but 27% of the prison population (Australian Bureau of Statistics, 2013). In the U.K., individuals self-identifying as Black make up about 9% of custody convictions, despite being 3% of the national population (Ministry of Justice, 2013), and individuals identifying as Muslim, who make up about 5% of the population, comprise 13% of the prison population, a 200% rise in the last 15 years (Berman & Dar, 2013). In other European countries, where ethnic statistics are often protected or not collected (Simon, 2007), similar trends are also seen where data are available (e.g., Albrecht, 1997 on foreign nationals in Germany; Gounev & Bezlov, 2006 on the Roma in Bulgaria). While Tonry (1997) cautions against international comparisons of criminal system responses along racial and ethnic lines, because, for instance, there are critical philosophical differences among nations regarding concepts of race, he also notes that:

> *Members of* **some** *disadvantaged minority groups in every Western country are disproportionately likely to be arrested, convicted, and imprisoned for violent, property, and drug crimes. This is true whether the minority groups are members of different "racial" groups from the majority population, for example, blacks or Afro-Caribbeans in Canada, England, or the United States, or of different ethnic backgrounds, for example, North African Arabs in France or the Netherlands, or – irrespective of race or ethnicity – are recent migrants from other countries, for example, Yugoslavs or Eastern Europeans in Germany and Finns in Sweden. Important social policy dilemmas that are seen in individual countries to be uniquely their own, such as race relations in the United States or assimilation of Aborigines in Australia, are not unique at all but are instead variations on common themes of social structure that characterize many countries.*

Though reasons for this type of over-representation of some groups are still under debate (e.g., Albrecht, 1997), studies suggest that this disproportionality in the criminal justice system results, at least in part, from legal policies and practices reflecting implicit (unconscious, unintended) and explicit biases against certain groups. That is, based on categories of social class, ethnicity, race, religion, and immigration status, justice systems are more likely to (a) cast their fishing nets within certain populations; (b) consider certain populations as offenders rather than victims; and (c) in some nations, provide harsher sentencing for individuals belonging to certain groups, even when such differential treatment is not intended.

In the U.S., these difference are thought to be due, at least in part, to the unsuccessful, but racially biased, "war on drugs" started by the Reagan administration in the 1980s (e.g., Alexander, 2010). Specifically, Alexander argues that a combination of anti-drug possession laws, monetary incentives for drug-related arrests and raids, mandatory sentencing laws, a legal system which provides people with high incomes a significantly higher level of legal defence, and policies and practices that discriminate against ex-prisoners (e.g., barriers to employment, inability to vote) has perpetuated a caste system not unlike the Jim Crow practices and laws of a century ago.[4]

Though the international examples below attempt to individuate these practices for purposes of illustration, it is important to note that they actually interact, build upon, and exacerbate each other, as in Alexander's description.

Over-fishing

As an example of legal over-fishing within certain populations, U.S. studies show significantly higher rates of police automobile searches for citizens who are phenotypically Black versus White, despite significantly smaller *percentages* (per group) of contraband being found for Black versus White citizens in those geographic locales (Lyubansky & Hunter, 2014). Similarly, in England and Wales, ten years after the changes wrought by the landmark 1993 Lawrence case,[5] the likelihood of being stopped and searched by police officers continues to be 7 times greater for individuals who are Black, and twice as likely for individuals of South Asian descent than for persons who are White (Bennetto, 2003), same as rates cited by the UK Government in 1998 (Borooah, 2001).

Other international studies also reveal racial, ethnic, and religious profiling by police and unequal rates of stopping, searching and/or arrests of citizens along ethnic lines, including France, Germany, Italy, the Netherlands, and other EU member states (Neild, 2009) and Canada (Meng, 2006; Ontario Human Rights Commission, 2003), though the underlying causes remain controversial.

Another example of potential over-fishing is found in analyses, performed by Human Rights Watch, of almost three decades of FBI data which reveal that, despite rates of drug offenses (e.g., possession, sale/manufacturing) remaining roughly equal for Blacks and Whites in the U.S., "...between 1980 and 2007, blacks were arrested nationwide on drug charges at rates relative to population that were 2.8 to 5.5 times higher than white arrest rates" and "...at rates in individual states that were 2 to 11.3 times greater than the rate for whites" (Felner, 2009, p.1). A report by the American Civil Liberties Union (Edwards, Bunting, & Garcia, 2013) looking at more recent data and focusing on arrests for possession of marijuana, which accounted for almost 50% of U.S. drug arrests in 2012, shows similarly staggering – and increasing - differences along racial lines, despite roughly equal reported rates of marijuana use among people identifying as Black versus White.[6] For example, nationwide arrest rates for marijuana possession were almost 4 times higher for people identified as Black or African American than White, with arrests of Black citizens in some counties and states being 6 to 30 times higher than those for White citizens.

Social Construction

As an example of social construction of victimhood and offenderhood along social class and racial lines, research has shown that both youth and adults who are poor and/or Black and have disabilities or symptoms of mental illness are more likely to be funnelled into the justice system, whereas individuals with the same mental health symptoms and disabilities, who are middle class and White, are more likely to be funnelled into the mental health or special education system (e.g., Tulman & Weck, 2010). Other research has shown that youth identified by police as Black are more likely to get arrested in cases of more ambiguous, not violent-crime, and that neighbourhood characteristics affect police officer discretion, such as whether to arrest a youth (Leiber & Peck, 2013). In England, the infamous Stephen Lawrence case, which produced multiple investigations and reports, found metropolitan police response to be rife with fundamental errors, such as failure to give first aid to the wounded (Black) man, and arrest-related and investigation-related errors which were later linked to possible racial motivation (e.g., Bridges, 1999).

Bias in Prosecution and Sentencing
In the U.S., the bias in capital punishment sentencing against individuals who are poor and Black is well documented (e.g., Levinson, Smith, & Young, 2014; Taslitz, 2013), with other research showing bias in non-capital prosecution and sentencing. Generally, individuals who are Black are more likely to be detained, held, prosecuted, and given longer and harsher sentences (e.g., Kutateladze, Andiloro, Johnson, & Spohn, 2014; Lynch, 2013; Sutton, 2013).[7] Other countries with prison populations which are not representational along racial lines have also begun to examine and find some preliminary evidence for racial bias in sentencing (e.g., Snowball & Weatherburn, 2007 with individuals of Aboriginal descent in Australia; Weinrath, 2007 with individuals of Aboriginal descent in Canada).

Thus, while systemic victimhood (past or current maltreatment, trauma, discrimination, and biases) does not excuse, minimize or diminish the very real negative consequences of people's acts of harm, it suggests and ethical justification for offering at least some victims' rights and supports to multiple people involved in a justice case, including the official offender. This will be illustrated by the case of Lamar in the next section.

Offenders as Victims of Their Offense

Though much research exists on the negative psychological effects of being the target of aggression, violence, and social transgression, there is also evidence that those who offend against others also suffer negative psychological consequences as a result of their actions. MacNair (2002a) examined post-traumatic stress scores in a random stratified sample of more than 1,000 U.S. veterans of the Vietnam conflict and found that self-reported post-combat trauma symptoms (e.g., nightmares, flashbacks, intrusive memories) were higher for those who said they killed others than for those who only witnessed killing, and *highest* for those who killed in "non-traditional" ways as opposed to in "traditional combat".

Similarly, an analysis of interviews with a different sample of over 350 U.S. combat veterans involved in the conflict in Vietnam revealed that those who were directly engaged in killing others reported elevated symptoms of post-traumatic stress (after returning home) compared to those who only "passively" witnessed traumatic events (Van Winkle & Safer, 2011). Another U.S. study of veterans from more recent conflicts in Iraq and Afghanistan showed that, contrary to predicted outcomes, soldiers reporting the highest levels of post-traumatic and depressive symptoms were those who *returned fire* after being attacked, as opposed to those who were attacked and did not return fire (fewer symptoms) and those who were neither attacked nor attacked others (fewest symptoms).

Based on these and other studies, MacNair coined the term "Perpetration-Induced Traumatic Stress" (PITS). In her book, on the Psychological Consequences of Killing (2002b), she reviewed evidence from studies and post-hoc analyses of those who have killed others, including combat veterans, paid executioners, police officers, individuals incarcerated for killing, and members of the Nazi party in WWII Germany. This and consequent scholarship (e.g., Papanastassiou, 2004) suggests significant traumatic and other psychological consequences (depression, suicidality) for those who have killed others.

While, understandably, homicide seems to lead to the most consequential psychological sequelae for the author of the act, it turns out that the perpetuation of other harmful acts (e.g., physical violence not resulting in death, coercion, emotional violence, social exclusion), also results in negative consequences for the "offenders." For instance, in one study of incarcerated men who had committed violent offenses, post-traumatic symptoms were found in over half of the sample, with 80% having *no prior history of significant trauma* and reporting the violent offense as the traumatic event (Pollock, 1999). Similarly, Byrne (2003) found that individuals who had committed violent acts suffered significant levels of traumatic symptoms, especially those with no prior history of violence and those whose violence was aimed at a familiar other. Gray et al (2003) also found that in a sample of individuals already suffering from mental illness (as defined by a prior diagnosis), symptoms of trauma were *highest* for those who had committed a violent offense and *most frequent* for those who expressed regret for the offense.

Negative emotional consequences also exist for perpetrators of less overt acts of harm. For instance, while many are aware that children and adolescents who are the target of continual harassment, sexual teasing, social exclusion, and physical aggression are more likely to develop symptoms of depression, anxiety and suicidality, the data also show that perpetuating these actions against others is significantly associated with many of these same symptoms (e.g., van der Wal, de Wit, & Hirasing, 2003). Showing a more direct causal effect, a recent longitudinal study of more than 1,000 fifth graders found that those who were *both* targets *and* sources of peer aggression and exclusion in fifth grade reported higher levels of depression in sixth grade than those who were only targets (Henrich & Sahar, 2014). A series of laboratory experiments also showed that social exclusion and ostracism negatively affected those who were the "perpetrators" of these behaviours (the official "offenders") as well as the official "victims" (Legate et al, 2013; Paulsen & Kashy, 2011).

To conclude, while both the targets of violence, aggression and social exclusion, and the family and loved ones of those who were killed, suffer continuous and significant harm that needs to be taken seriously by our justice responses, those who perpetuate harm are also victimized by their own actions. A broader understanding of the fluid nature of victimization would not excuse or minimize the harm, but instead, allow a fuller justice response that could lead to greater community healing and social safety for all involved.

The case of Lamar illustrates the combination of these elements (victimization caused by one's offense) and of systemic victimization discussed in the previous section.

A Life for a Life: Offenderhood and Victimhood in a Fatal Peer Shooting

Through our team's work within the local Juvenile Detention Center (JDC) we became acquainted with Lamar (aged 16), who was awaiting trial for the fatal shooting of Kareem (aged 21). Lamar and the JDC staff heard through the rumour mill that Kareem's brothers and cousins, all well known to Lamar, were planning revenge for Kareem's death as soon as Lamar was released. Since several of these young men (all African American) were familiar with Restorative Circles through our weekly restorative justice programming, they agreed to participate in a Circle when Lamar initiated one.

Some of the things that became evident as a result of this Circle were that (a) Lamar and Kareem were best friends (more like brothers), as echoed by every young man in the Circle; (b) the shooting had been an accident resulting from Lamar and Kareem's handling of the gun; (c) despite "a" and "b," the other young men still planned on a revenge killing of Lamar after he was released, as this most accurately reflected the law of the street (a life for a life); and (d) Lamar also seemed to be suffering high levels of post-traumatic symptoms as a result of the close-range and bloody killing of a close friend. This was evidenced by his recurring nightmares, flashbacks, and intrusive memories. In addition, during the Circle, Lamar went into periods of what seemed to be dissociation[8] while trying to talk about the afternoon of the shooting. Lamar also displayed signs of depression, hopelessness, and mild suicidal ideation (although the event was not recent), as evidenced by things he wrote to Kareem on the memorial poster he would later co-create with the other young men from the Circle. Finally, in our private preparation meeting, Lamar discussed his concerns for his own safety, as well as those of his family. Indeed, we created a safety plan with one of the other young men in our individual preparation meeting, to support him in not attacking Lamar during the Circle.

As we sat within the Circle, witnessing the young men trying to find their way towards honouring Kareem's death without more violence and incarceration (for them) it became painfully clear that Kareem (the deceased) and his mother and brothers were certainly not the only ones victimized by this tragic case. First, Lamar was victimized by the trauma of killing his friend at close range, as described above. Lamar was also victimized by the tyranny of chance, as both young men were handling the gun (which belonged to Kareem), and the gun went off when Lamar was holding it, rather than when Kareem had it a few minutes earlier. In addition, Lamar was a clear victim of homicidal threat. According to systems analyses, the young men who were threatening him were also, themselves, victims of their cultural heritage, community values, and absence of positive male role models (because so many of their fathers and older brothers, all African American, were in prison). This left them with the belief that the only way to honour a loved one was through revenge, even though this risked their incarceration and separation from their remaining loved ones, something they actually did not wish. Finally, in an ever-expanding circle of victimization, if the young men (some of whom had children) had carried out their revenge plans, they would likely be incarcerated, further victimizing their own families. For instance, some research has shown that mothers of incarcerated sons experience increased grief, anxiety and financial difficulties, as well as childcare burdens (having to help care for their grandchildren) (Green, Ensminger, Robertson, & Hee-Soon, 2006) and that children of incarcerated individuals also have poorer academic, psychological, and financial outcomes than children in the general population (e.g., Travis & Woul, 2003).

Again, it is important in cases like Lamar's, where the harm is serious and irrevocable, to neither minimize nor excuse the real tragic consequences of the loss for those impacted by Kareem's death. It is just as important, however, if we are to move out of the cycles of violence and injustice, to broaden our horizons and provide "offenders" like Lamar the same attention and rights as official "victims" like Kareem and his family.

Without a broader understanding of victimization, which would take into consideration not only the very real victimization of Kareem's mother, brother, cousins, friends and other loved ones, but also of Lamar and his family, our justice response would not be able to maximally attend to the real needs of everyone involved. By leaving open the possibility that everyone affected by the case was experiencing victimization (including the author of the harm and his family), and therefore, offering all members of the Circle similar levels of support, we were able to better address the needs of everyone involved. Moreover, by attending to Lamar's needs for restoration and support, we were able to better provide for the healing and restoration of others. For example, Kareem's mother, who had not been able to speak to Lamar since the shooting, had a tearful meeting with him as one action resulting from the Circle, which was healing not only for Lamar but also for her. Similarly, the memorial poster jointly created by the young men wound up being displayed in a public community space where other youths were able to add their words of grief and honour for Kareem, bringing some restoration and healing not only to the members of the Circle but to the wider community. In addition, Lamar's symptoms of grief and trauma were more directly addressed through referrals to counselling and mentoring, strategies that can only help Lamar's community as he grows into his manhood.

Moving Forward: Addressing the Paradox of Victims' Legislation

As has been clear from the introduction and numerous examples throughout, this chapter is a call for broadening our conceptualization of victimhood beyond the person directly harmed by a criminal act, and, consequently, employing increasing multi-partiality in our justice approaches. The chapter also suggests that one vehicle for addressing multiple victimizations is to offer and employ restorative justice approaches as a response to conflict and harmful acts. The EU Directive explicitly lists the availability of restorative justice (RJ) services as one of the rights of all victims, and repeatedly addresses certain safeguards in the context of offering individuals RJ options, which include attention to voluntariness, unbiased information about the RJ process, and confidentiality guidelines (European Union: Council of the European Union, 2012). As illustrated in the case studies in this chapter, these minimum requirements can greatly enhance the level of overall restoration for all parties when they are more broadly applied to multiple individuals within the conflict.

Hudson's 2004 chapter on *Victims and Offenders* in "Restorative Justice and Criminal Justice: Competing or Reconcilable Paradigms?" concludes:

> *... restorative justice is concerned with providing constructive outcomes for both victims and offenders, and is not simply part of the victim movement... Essentially, it is a way of moving forward form the 'zero-sum' approach to victims and offenders, which sees rights for one being at the expense of rights for the other, concern for one being at the expense of concern for the others. Restorative justice is envisaged as a way of dealing constructively with both victims and offenders, jumping off, rather than on, the populist bandwagon, which believes that what helps the victim must necessarily hurt the offender...*

Indeed, restorative justice allows us to attend to the needs of both the official victim and offender. However, let us stretch beyond even this laudable goal, rejecting the duality of victim-offender and see, instead, the concepts of victimization and offenderhood as more complex and fluid, even within the restorative justice field.

Facing the inherent paradox of victim-centred legislation requires us, as Rumi says, to go into that somewhat uncomfortable field beyond wrongdoing and rightdoing,[9] facing the inherent paradox of victim-centred legislature. From there, numerous strategies can be adopted to increase the multi-partiality with which all parties in a conflict are treated. What is important, according to Barter (2011), is to differentiate the victimhood of individuals who are involved in a conflict from their roles in relation to a specific act of harm. For instance, in the previous example of Theresa, the young woman who shot her father, Theresa would be understood as the Author of the act, the father would be understood as the Receiver of the act, and the mother, younger sister, and other people present in the Restorative Circle would be understood as the Conflict Community (people indirectly impacted by and/or contributing to the conflict in some way). It is important to note that, in this case, Author and Receiver are *not* synonyms for Offender and Victim, since it is understood that many – if not all – the people in this conflict feel some sense of victimhood. Instead, these designations help us orient ourselves during the process of support, protection, and restoration for which we strive.

Going beyond these important linguistic and symbolic designations, Barter's Restorative Circles take other measures (e.g., using the same restorative questions and offering the same accommodations to each individual) to help ensure that all parties experiencing victimization receive the recognition, respect, support, care and restoration intended by victims' rights legislation. What may be most important, however, is not the actual way multi-partiality is carried out, which will differ by locale, culture, and need, but that we become more open to the idea of multi-partiality as a way to go beyond the letter of victim-centred law to the heart of its spirit.

Notes

1 The 13 years of Francine's victimization by James were well documented in police reports, photographs, and witness accounts, as Francine repeatedly (though unsuccessfully) sought help and support for herself and her children, including the obtaining of a legal divorce.

2 All case illustrations have been altered to protect confidentiality and/or presented with consent from participants.

3 While scholars agree that "racial" categories are sociological rather than biological concepts, they are referred to here not as a way to support the idea of racial classification, but as a way to acknowledge the inequity and discrimination that continues to result from the use of these classifications in parts of the world where they are currently relevant social concepts. In addition, for the purposes of this paper, "Black" and "African American" are used interchangeably for the U.S. context.

4 "Jim Crow" refers to a system of laws (e.g., segregation of public schools, public transportation and public spaces by racial category) and practices (e.g., unfettered harassment, torture and homicide of African Americans by individuals and groups such as the Ku Klux Klan) which operated during the U.S. post-slavery and Reconstruction era (1870s-1960s) to create a caste system in which African Americans were held back economically, legally, and socially.

5 The racially biased murder of 18 year old Stephen Lawrence by seven White youths, and the subsequent investigation, which revealed racially biased police handling of the case, and structural racism within the department, raised public awareness of racial bias in policing and generated policies and laws to address the issue.

6 These differences are also not explained away by amounts of marijuana found in the possession of Black vs. White individuals (e.g., Dillon, 2013).

7 While there is agreement among researchers that significant racial bias exists in capital sentencing, the bias findings in non-capital sentencing are contested by some scholars (e.g., Talich, 2013; Warner, 2000).

8 Temporary emotional and cognitive disengagement from the situation as evidenced by blank stare, lack of tracking, unfocused/glazed look, emotional numbness or detachment, "blank periods" of time unaccounted for by daydreaming or attention on something else.

9 "Out beyond ideas of wrongdoing and rightdoing, there is a field. I will meet you there." - *Rumi*

References

Alexander, M. (2010). *The New Jim Crow: Mass Incarceration in the Age of Colorblindness.* New York, New York. New Press.

Albrecht, H. (1997). Ethnic Minorities, Crime and Criminal Justice in Germany. *Crime and Justice*, 21, 31-99.

Australian Bureau of Statistics (2013). *Prisoners in Australia, 2013.* Retrieved from: http://www.abs.gov.au/ausstats/abs@.nsf/Lookup/by%20Subject/4517.0~2013~Main%20Features~Contents~1

Arnold, E.M., Stewart, J.C., & McNeece, C.A. (2001). *Perpetrators as Victims. Violence and Victims*, 16 (2), 145-159.

Avnet, J. & Greenwald, R. (1984). *The Burning Bed* [Motion picture]. USA.: NBC.

Barter, D. (2011). *A restorative critique of restorative justice.* Talk given at the Mediation and Restorative Justice Commission of the Rio Grande do Sul state branch of the Brazilian Lawyers Association, Porto Alegre, Brazil.

Barter, D. (2012). Walking Toward Conflict. *Tikkun*, 27(1), pp. 21 & 70.

Bennetto, J. (2003). *Police and Racism: What Has Been Achieved Ten Years After the Stephen Lawrence Report?* Equality and Human Rights Commission. http://www.equalityhumanrights.com/sites/default/files/documents/raceinbritain/policeandracism.pdf

Becroft, A.J., Te Kaiwhakawa Matua o Te Kooti Taiohi o Aotearoa & Thompson, R. (2006). *Youth Offending: Factors that Contribute and how the System Responds.* Symposium Child And Youth Offenders: What Works.

Berman, G. & Dar, A. (2013). *Prison Population Statistics.* House of Commons Library. Retrieved from: http://www.parliament.uk/Templates/BriefingPapers/Pages/BPPdfDownload.aspx?bpid=sn04334

Borooah, V.K. (2001). Racial bias in police stops and searches: an economic analysis. *European Journal of Political Economy*, 17 (1), 17-37.

Bronfenbrenner, U. (1994). Ecological models of human development. In T. Husen & T. N. Postlethwaite (Eds.) *International Encyclopedia of Education* (2nd Ed). Oxford, England: Pergamon Press.

Bridges, L. (1999). The Lawrence Inquiry – Incompetence, Corruption, and Institutional Racism, *Journal of Law & Society*, 26 (3), 298-323.

Byrne, M. K. (2003). Trauma Reactions in the Offender. *International Journal of Forensic Psychology*, 1 (1), 59-70.

Caputo, T.C. (1987). The Young Offenders Act: Children's Rights, Children's Wrongs. Author(s). *Canadian Public Policy / Analyse de Politiques*, 13 (2), 125-143.

Christie, N. (1986). The Ideal Victim. In E.A. Fattah (Ed.) *From Crime Policy to Victim Policy: Reorienting the Justice System.* New York: St. Martin's Press.

Crane & Heaton, 2008. Handbook of Families and Poverty. New York: Sage Publications.

Dillon, M. (2013). The Black/White Marijuana Arrest Gap, in 9 Charts. *The Washington Post* (online). Retrieved from: http://www.washingtonpost.com/blogs/wonkblog/wp/2013/06/04/the-blackwhite-marijuana-arrest-gap-in-nine-charts/

Douglas, H. (2005). The Criminal Law's Response to Domestic Violence: What's Going On? *Sydney Law Review*, 30, 438-469.

Edwards, E., Bunting, W., & Garcia, L. (2013). *The War on Marijuana in Black and White.* New York, NY: ACLU Foundation.

European Union: Council of the European Union (2012). Directive 2012/29/EU of the European Parliament and of the Council of 25 October 2012 establishing minimum standards on the rights, support and protection of victims of crime, and replacing Council Framework Decision 2001/220/JHA. *Official Journal of the European Union*. Retrieved from: http://eur-lex.europa.eu/legal-content/en/ALL/?uri=CELEX:32012L0029

Fattah, E.A. (2003). Violence against the Socially Expendable. In W. Heitmeyer & J. Hagan (Eds.) *International Handbook of Violence Research.* Kluwer Academic Publishers; Dordrecht.

Felner, J. (2009). *Decades of Disparity: Drug Arrests and Race in the United States.* New York: Human Rights Watch.

Gray, N.S., Carman, N.G., Rogers, P.R., MacCulloch, M.J., Hayward, P., & Snowden, R.J. (2003). Post-traumatic stress disorder caused in mentally disordered offenders by the committing of a serious violent or sexual offence. *The Journal of Forensic Psychiatry & Psychology,* 14 (1), 27-43.

Green, K. M., Ensminger, M. E., Robertson, J. A., & Hee-Soon, J. (2006). Impact of Adult Sons' Incarceration on African American Mothers' Psychological Distress, *Journal of Marriage and Family,* 68 (2), 430-441.

Gounev, P. & Bezlov, T. (2006). The Roma in Bulgarias Criminal Justice System: From Ethnic Profiling to Imprisonment. *Critical Criminology,* 14, 313-338.

Henrich, C.C. & Sahar, G. (2014). Moderators of the Effect of Peer Victimization During Fifth Grade on Subsequent Symptoms of (Anxious) Depression: The Roles of Engagement in Bullying and Baseline Symptomatology. *Prevention Science,* January, 1-9.

Hudson, B. (2004). Victims and Offenders. In von Hirsch, A., Roberts, J., Bottoms, A.E., Roach, K. & Schiff, M. (Eds.) *Restorative Justice and Criminal Justice: Competing or Reconcilable Paradigms?* Oxford: Hart Publishing.

James, D. J. & Glaze, L.E. (2006). *Mental health problems of prison and jail inmates.* U.S. Bureau of Justice Statistics Special Report. Retrieved from: http://www.bjs.gov/content/pub/pdf/mhppji.pdf

Kinsella, C. (2012). Re-locating Fear on the Streets: Homelessness, Victimisation and Fear of Crime. *European Journal of Homelessness,* 6 (2), 121-136.

Kinport, K. (2004). So Much Activity, So Little Change: A Reply to the Critics of Battered Women's Self-Defense. *St. Louis University Public Law Review,* 23, 155-164.

Knox, C. (2001). The `Deserving' Victims of Political Violence: `Punishment' Attacks in Northern Ireland. *Criminology and Criminal Justice,* 1 (2), 181-199.

Kutateladze, B.L., Andiloro, N.R., Johnson, B.D., & Spohn, C.C. (2014). Cumulative Disadvantage: Examining Racial And Ethnic Disparity In Prosecution and Sentencing. *Criminology,* 52 (3), 514-551.

Legate, N., DeHaan, C.R., Weinstein, N., & Ryan, R.M. (2013). Hurting You Hurts Me Too: The Psychological Costs of Complying With Ostracism. *Psychological Science,* 24 (4), 583-589.

Levinson, J.D., Smith, R. J. & Young, D. M. (2014). Devaluing Death: An Empirical Study Of Implicit Racial Bias On Jury-Eligible Citizens In Six Death Penalty States. *New York University Law Review,* 89 (2), 513-581.

Lauritsen, J.L., Sampson, R.J., & Laub, J.H. (1991). The Link Between Offending and Victimization Among Adolescents. *Criminology,* 29 (2), 265-292.

Leiber, M.J., & Peck, J.H. (2013). Race in Juvenile Justice and Sentencing Policy: An Overview of Research and Policy Recommendations. *Law & Inequality: A Journal of Theory and Practice,* Summer (2), 331-368.

Loeber, R. & Farrington, D.P. (2012). *From Juvenile Delinquency to Adult Crime: Criminal Careers, Justice Policy, and Prevention.* Oxford, England: Oxford University Press.

Lynch, M. (2013). Institutionalized Bias: The Death Penalty, Federal Drug Prosecutions, and Mechanisms of Disparate Punishment. *American Journal of Criminal Law,* 41(1), 91-133.

Lyubansky, M. & Barter, D. (2011). Restorative Approaches to Racial Conflict. *Peace Review,* 23, 37-44.

Lyubansky, M. & Hunter, C. (2014). Towards Racial Justice. In E. Mustakova-Possardt, M. Lyubansky, M. Basseches, & J. Oxenberg (Ed.). *Toward a Socially Responsible Psychology for a Global Era.* New York: Springer Science + Business Media, LCC.

MacNair, R. M. (2002a). Perpetration-induced traumatic stress in combat veterans. *Peace and Conflict: Journal of Peace Psychology,* 8(1), 63-72.

MacNair, R. M. (2002b). *Perpetration-Induced Traumatic Stress: The Psychological Consequences of Killing.* Indiana: Authors Choice Press.

Mackenzie, G. & Colvin, E. (2009). *Homicide in abusive relationships: A report on defences.* Prepared For The Attorney-General And Minister For Industrial Relations.

Mauer, M. & King, R.S. (2007). *Uneven justice: State rates of incarceration by race and ethnicity.* Washington, D.C.: The Sentencing Project. Retrieved from: http://www.sentencingproject.org/doc/publications/rd_stateratesofincbyraceandethnicity.pdf

McNulty, F. (1980). *The burning bed: the true story of Francine Hughes, a beaten wife who rebelled.* California: Harcourt Publishing.

Mills, L.G. (2006). *Insult to Injury: Rethinking our Responses to Intimate Abuse.* Princeton, New Jersey: Princeton University Press.

Ministry of Justice (2013). *Statistics on Race and the Criminal Justice System 2012.* Retrieved from: https://www.gov.uk/government/uploads/system/uploads/attachment_data/file/269399/Race-and-cjs-2012.pdf

Meng, Y. (2006). Racially Biased Policing and Neighbourhood Characteristics: A Case Study in Toronto, Canada. Cybergeo: *European Journal of Geography.* Retrieved from http://cybergeo.revues.org/26165

Miller, S. (2005). *Victims as Offenders: The Paradox of Women's Violence in Relationships.* New Jersey: Rutgers University Press.

Miers, D. (1990). Positivist Victimology: A Critique. Part 2: Critical Victimology. *International Review of Victimology,* 1, 219-230.

Neild, R. (2009). *Ethnic Profiling in the European Union: Pervasive, Ineffective, and Discriminatory.* New York, NY. Open Society Institute.

Ontario Human Rights Commission (2003). *Paying the price: The human cost of racial profiling.* Retrieved from: http://www.ohrc.on.ca/sites/default/files/attachments/Paying_the_price%3A_The_human_cost_of_racial_profiling.pdf

Poulsen, J.R. & Kashy, D. A. (2011). Two sides of the ostracism coin: How sources and targets of social exclusion perceive themselves and one another. *Group Processes & Intergroup Relations,* 15, 457-470.

Papanastassiou, M., Waldron, G., Boyle, J., Chesterman, L.P. (2004). Post-Traumatic Stress Disorder in Mentally Ill Perpertrators of Homicide. *The Journal of Forensic Psychiatry & Psychology,* 15 (1), 66-75.

Pidwirny, M. (2006). *Definitions of Systems and Models. In Fundamentals of Physical Geography,* 2nd Edition. Retrieved from: http://www.physicalgeography.net/fundamentals/4b.html

Pollock, P.H. (1999). When The Killer Suffers: Post-Traumatic Stress Reactions Following Homicide. *Legal and Criminological Psychology,* 4 (2), 185-202.

Ryan, W. (1976). *Blaming the Victim.* New York, New York. Vintage Publishing.

Sahlin, I. (2004). Constructing Victims and Villains: Unintended Outcomes of Contact Prohibition Orders. *Journal of Scandinavian Studies in Criminology & Crime Prevention,* 5(1), 85-107.

Simon, P. (2007). *"Ethnic" statistics and data protection in the Council of Europe countries.* Study Report by the European Commission against Racism and Intolerance (ECRI). Retrieved from: http://www.coe.int/t/dghl/monitoring/ecri/activities/themes/Ethnic_statistics_and_data_protection.pdf

Sindicich, N., Mills, K.L., Barrett, E.L., Indig, D., Suniic, S., Sannibale, C., Rosenfeld, J., Najavits, L.M. (2014). Offenders as Victims: Post-Traumatic Stress Disorder and Substance Use Disorder Among Male Prisoners. *Journal of Forensic Psychiatry and Psychology,* 25 (1), 44-60.

Smolej, M. (2010). Constructing ideal victims? Violence narratives in Finnish crime-appeal programming. *Crime Media Culture,* 6 (1), 69-85.

Snowball, L. & Weatherburn, D. (2007). Does Racial Bias in Sentencing Contribute to Indigenous Overrepresentation in Prison? Australian & New Zealand Journal of Criminology, 40 (3), 272-290.

Strobl, R. (2004). Constructing the Victim: Theoretical Reflections and Empirical Examples. *International Review of Victimology,* 11, 295-311.

Sutton, J.R. (2013). Structural bias in the sentencing of felony defendants. *Social Science Research,* 42(5), 1207-1221.

Swan, S.C., Gambone, L.J., Caldwell, J.E., Sullivan, T.P., & Snow, D.L. (2008). A review of research on women's use of violence with male intimate partners. *Violence and Victims,* 23, 301-314.

Taslitz, A. E. (2013). Racial Threat versus Racial Empathy in Sentencing – Capital and Otherwise. *American Journal of Criminal Law,* 41(1), 2-41.

Tonry, M. (1997). Ethnicity, Crime, and Immigration: Comparative and Cross-National Perspectives. *Crime and Justice,* 21, 1-29.

Travis, J., & Waul, M. (2003). *Prisoners Once Removed: The Impact of Incarceration and Reentry on Children, Families and Communities.* Washington, D.C. The Urban Institute Press.

Tulman, J.B & Weck, D.M. (2010). *Shutting Off the School-to-Prison Pipeline for Status Offenders with Education-Related Disabilities.* New York Law School Law Review, 54, 875-907.

van der Wal, M.F., de Witt, C.A.M., & Hirasing, R.A. (2003). Psychosocial Health Among Young Victims and Offenders of Direct and Indirect Bullying. *Pediatrics,* 111 (6), 1312-1317.

Van Winkle, E.P. & Safer, M.A. (2007). Killing versus witnessing in combat trauma and reports of PTSD symptoms and domestic violence. *Journal of Traumatic Stress,* 24 (1), 107-110.

Vrij, D. and Fischer, C. (1997). The Role of Display of Emotions and Ethnicity in Judgements of Rape Victims. *International Review of Victimology,* 4, 255-265.

Walklate, S. (2007). *Imagining the victim of crime.* Philadelphia: Open University Press.

Wasserman, G.A., Keenan, K., Tremblay, R.E., Coie, J.D., Herrenkohl, T.I, Loeber, R., & Petechuk, D. (2003). *Risk and Protective Factors of Child Delinquency.* Child Delinquency Bulletin Series of U.S. Department of Justice, Office of Justice Programs, Office of Juvenile Justice and Delinquency Prevention.

Weinrath, M. (2007). Sentencing Disparity: Aboriginal Canadians, Drunk Driving and Age. *Western Criminology Review,* 8 (2), 16-28.

Will, J.A. (1993). The Dimensions of Poverty: Public Perceptions of the Deserving Poor. *Social Science Research,* 22 (3), 312-332.

Wimberly, M. (2007). *Defending victims of domestic violence who kill their batterers: using the trial expert to change social norms.* American Bar Association.

Winkel, E. W. (1991). Interaction Between the Police and Minority Group Members: Victimization Through the Incorrect Interpretation of Nonverbal Behavior. *International Review of Victimology,* 2, 15-27.

Widom, C.S. & Wilson, H.W. How Victims Become Offenders (2009). In B.L. Bottoms & B. B. Editor (Eds.), *Children as Victims, Witnesses and Offenders.* New York: Guilford Publications.

Wright, M. (1996; reprinted in 2002). *Justice for victims and offenders : A restorative response to crime.* Philadelphia: Open University Press.

RJE Training Session, delivered by IARS at Greater Manchester Probation Trust – June 2014, Manchester, UK. © IARS

Restorative Justice and Sexual Violence: Overcoming the Concerns of Victim-Survivors

*Shirley Jülich and Fiona Landon**

Abstract

Adult survivors of historical child sexual abuse described processes that could be identified as restorative justice when asked what processes might provide them with a sense of justice. However, they did not embrace restorative justice as anticipated. Instead, they raised a number of concerns regarding restorative justice as an effective model to pursue justice. This article outlines the concerns they raised and discusses the implications for restorative justice practice. It describes Project Restore, a specialist restorative justice provider that engaged with specialists from restorative justice and across the sexual violence sector to develop a model specifically to address sexual violence. The model used by Project Restore is based on the New Zealand conferencing model, expanded to include three specialists – the restorative justice facilitator, the survivor specialist and the offender specialist. Much emphasis is placed on preparation of all intending participants during which time the Project Restore develops restorative processes that specifically address the circumstances of each case. The article concludes that Project Restore's model and its use of three specialists addresses the concerns of victim-survivors of sexual violence.

Introduction

Restorative justice emerged in the New Zealand adult criminal justice jurisdiction in the mid-1990s. Inspired by the family group conference of New Zealand's youth justice system, the restorative conference became the model of choice, in which facilitators brought together a victim and an offender with their communities of care or interest (significant members of their family and social systems) to address the aftermath of crime. Restorative justice provider groups, trained and funded by government, became established providing pre-sentence restorative processes for cases referred by the district courts. It should be noted that unlike New Zealand's youth justice system, restorative justice in the New Zealand adult criminal justice system is an extra layer of justice, an extra process that victims and offenders must navigate. It does not replace the adversarial system of justice but it does aim to centre the victim in the justice process.

In the early days, referrals from the courts did not include cases of domestic violence or sexual violence. This has changed in regards to sexual violence. Project Restore, a specialist restorative justice provider, has received limited funding since 2005 from a variety of sources including government.

* Dr. Shirley Jülich (victim of crime and Senior Lecturer Massey University, Albany, New Zealand), contact Massey University, Albany, Private Bag 102904, North Shore, Auckland 0745, New Zealand, +6494140800 S.J.Julich@massey.ac.nz , Fiona Landon, Programme Director, Project Restore New Zealand.

Subsequently, restorative processes have been provided for those cases referred by the courts and also for those that have bypassed the conventional criminal justice system and self-referred direct from the community. Currently, funding contracts offered by the New Zealand Ministry of Justice, specifically allow for cases of sexual violence.

The prevalence of sexual violence varies across studies and countries. New Zealand estimates indicate that one in four women experience rape or attempted rape (Gavey, 1991) and one in seven males report being a victim-survivor of sexual violence (Fleming et al., 2007). International reports are similar, notably it is difficult to directly compare studies as definitions of sexual violence vary across studies and the questions asked vary. Yet, only about 10% of victim-survivors report sexual violence to the police (Morris & Reilly, 2003; Triggs, Mossman, Jordan, & Kingi, 2009), sexual violence which is perpetrated three out of four times by someone known to them (Morris & Reilly, 2003).

Attrition rates highlight the difficulties victim-survivors encounter in the conventional criminal justice system. A recent New Zealand study found that of those who report sexual violence to the police only 31% proceed to court with 13% of all cases resulting in a conviction (Triggs et al., 2009). Again this is not unusual to New Zealand, international reports identify similar attrition – 14% of reported rapes reaching trial in one UK study, only 8% of those originally reported resulting in a conviction (Kelly, Lovett, & Regan, 2005), and 'in no other crime is the victim subjected to so much scrutiny at trial' (HMIC & HMCPSI, 2007, p. 162).

There are all sorts of arguments and debates regarding studies and their results. Definitions and methods vary and different questions are asked prompting different responses. Such discussions are beyond the scope of this article. Suffice to say that sexual violence is significant and the majority is unaddressed in our communities. The human cost is substantial. So too is the financial cost. In 2003, the NZ Treasury (Roper & Thompson, 2006) estimated that one incident of sexual violence cost $72,130. The impacts of sexual violence cannot be addressed whilst there is a conspiracy of silence. If there were structures that addressed the harm caused by sexual violence and the underlying causes of offending, victim-survivors might be more inclined to report sexual violence. These are the aims of restorative justice; in particular these are the aims of Project Restore.

In the early days of restorative justice in New Zealand and elsewhere, facilitators had little theory to draw on to guide the development of restorative justice. They tended to do what worked best and the theory followed. From these modest beginnings there is now a substantial international body of literature describing, critiquing, evaluating, discussing the pros and cons of restorative justice and comparing it to the processes of conventional criminal justice systems. This is not the case with restorative justice that is specifically designed to address sexual violence. The literature tends to focus on restorative responses to general crime, and there many such responses internationally that use restorative justice. As yet there are very few operational programmes working specifically with adult victim-survivors and perpetrators of sexual violence. Project Restore is one of two or three programmes known to be operational internationally (Koss, 2014).

This article uses the research findings of Shirley Jülich, an author of this paper and founding member of Project Restore, to demonstrate how Project Restore overcomes the concerns raised by adult survivors of child sexual abuse. We discuss their concerns, identify the implications for practice and describe how Project Restore addresses these concerns.

Concepts and Terminology

For the purposes of this article, the term survivor is used to identify the group of adults in Jülich's research, victim-survivor refers to all others who have survived sexual violence and victim refers to those who have been victimised by crimes other than sexual violence. Perpetrator is used to denote those who have sexually victimised others, in recognition that most have not been brought before the courts. We do at times at times use the terms offender because many of the agencies Project Restore works with use this terminology. We use the term facilitator for those who facilitate restorative processes. Also, we use the terms bystanders (Herman, 1997), those who have been subjected to the same complex dynamics as the victim-survivor, and outsiders (Graham, Rawlings, & Rigsby, 1994) to describe those who have not been subjected to these dynamics. Finally, the term equality is understood as substantive equality, that is, equality of outcome as opposed to equality of access. This is in recognition that the concept of formal equality or equality of access, an underlying principle of conventional criminal justice systems, does not necessarily provide an experience of a sense of justice (OHCHR, 2009). Restorative justice is sufficiently flexible to provide substantive equality, particularly in the restorative processes developed by Project Restore.

Project Restore

Project Restore was inspired by the RESTORE programme in Arizona (Koss, Bachar, & Hopkins, 2003), the research of Dr Shirley Jülich and the frustration of victim-survivors of sexual violence pursuing justice in New Zealand's conventional criminal justice system. It was officially launched in August of 2005 after some 18 months of dialogue across the restorative justice and sexual violence sectors, that is both victim-survivor and offender support agencies. Project Restore is unique in that it has been developed by victim-survivors as opposed to restorative justice advocates or facilitators. It engages with those agencies that provide services to perpetrators and victim-survivors of sexual violence and it is positioned across community stakeholder groups who are committed to the success of the programme. Project Restore works from the perspective of understanding the gains that women have made to bring all forms of gendered violence onto the political agenda. Within this context Project Restore aims to develop and deliver safe restorative processes in consultation with victim-survivors, perpetrators and their supporters.

Project Restore did not set out explicitly to overcome the concerns of survivors in Jülich's research. Rather, a range of experts (including the two authors of this article), representing the interests of victim-survivors and perpetrators, came together and shared their expertise. The model they developed has attracted international interest. Over time Project Restore has developed significant experience delivering restorative processes for cases of sexual violence, including historical child sexual abuse. This was recognised by the Ministry of Justice who consulted with Project Restore as they developed practice standards for facilitators and community specialists working in this field.[1] These have been in place since late 2013. The Project Restore model for restorative justice is based on the New Zealand conferencing model,[2] expanded to include the following:

- A restorative justice facilitator, trained by the New Zealand Ministry of Justice to work in the court system, but whom also has an in-depth understanding of the dynamics of sexual violence.

- Two community specialists – a survivor specialist, a trained counsellor experienced in working with victim-survivors of sexual violence, and an offender specialist, a trained therapist working with those who sexually offend against children and adults. Both these specialists have an in-depth understanding of restorative justice.
- A clinical supervisor who provides professional supervision, acts as a team leader, but has no contact with the victim-survivor, the perpetrator or members of their communities.
(Jülich, Buttle, Cummins, & Freeborn, 2010)

Together these four professionals form Project Restore's clinical team. The restorative justice facilitator and the two community specialists, create a team-based facilitation approach. Referred to by Project Restore as the 'three cornered stool', this three pronged approach is reflected in all of Project Restore's activities to ensure a balanced approach to delivering restorative processes, that is a balance between restorative justice values, the justice needs of the victim-survivor and the justice needs of the perpetrator. The restorative justice facilitator's role is focussed on ensuring that the values of restorative justice are upheld. The survivor specialist and the offender specialist aim to make the process safe for all parties throughout the preparation period and the restorative process. The clinical team leader supports this process by providing objective supervision and oversight, thereby ensuring safety for all parties, both Project Restore personnel and intending participants of restorative processes.

Clinical team meetings are held weekly, new cases are reviewed, cases under preparation are reviewed and monitored, and completed cases are debriefed. The process enables risk and readiness to be assessed, which in turn, informs the decision as to when and if the case progresses to a restorative process. The case work, to date, has addressed both historical and current sexual violence. Most perpetrators have been male, there has been one female perpetrator, and victim-survivors have been both male and female. Referrals to Project Restore have come from the court system and directly from the community, that is, cases that have bypassed the conventional criminal justice system.

The work of Project Restore is based on an assumption that justice can be therapeutic, however the process provided by Project Restore is therapeutic only within the context of realising a 'sense of justice' (Jülich, 2006). Although Project Restore does not provide therapy or treatment, the work is undertaken in a therapeutic way. This approach is recognised in most responses to victim-survivors of sexual violence – for example, police and forensic medical processes follow special procedures in order to minimise harm, specialist support services are available, and the New Zealand Evidence Act makes several dispensations to provide environments that support healing rather than harm for victim-survivors of sexual violence (McDonald & Tinsley, 2011).

Satisfaction surveys of restorative justice tend to be positive. This is not surprising, given that those who engage in restorative processes are highly motivated and offenders have acknowledged wrong doing or have pleaded guilty to a crime. Participants of restorative processes are perhaps not typical of the broader cohort of victims and offenders (Latimer, Dowden, & Muise, 2005). The same is true for Project Restore: surveys tend to indicate high levels of satisfaction with the restorative processes they have facilitated (Jülich et al., 2010). In response to Daly's (2013) call for evaluators to move beyond mere satisfaction surveys, a recent evaluation of Project Restore specifically asked a series of questions about whether justice needs had been satisfied as opposed to querying satisfaction regarding the process (Jülich & Landon, 2012, 2013).[3] The first phase of the study was a desk-based analysis of 12 cases; the second was a series of surveys engaging victim-survivors, perpetrators and their communities from a total of 16 cases. All participants said that the process had attended to their justice needs. They had a voice in the process, perpetrators had demonstrated accountability by attempting to make amends or put things right, the sexually harmful behaviour was validated by perpetrators acknowledging the harm, and vindication was realised by perpetrators accepting responsibility for their behaviour. An experience of a sense of justice appeared very real for these victim-survivors and their supporters.

A Sense of Justice

Jülich (2001, 2006, 2010) investigated the relationship between recovery and justice for adult survivors of child sexual abuse. She found that among a group of 18 women and 3 men there was a reluctance to report the sexual victimisation to which they had been subjected. The same reluctance is observed in adult victim-survivors as evidenced in the statistics quoted earlier in this article. When Jülich asked survivors 'what is your understanding of justice' their replies indicated that for this particular group recovery, healing and justice were interdependent. Revenge did not appear to be a component of justice; they appeared to be more concerned that the needs of both perpetrators and victim-survivors were met, that is, addressing the underlying causes of offending and promoting healing for victim-survivors.

Confronting the perpetrator and pursuing justice seemed to be a central element of the recovery journey. Survivors were not specifically seeking apologies; they were not vindictive, neither were they vengeful. They wanted to understand what had happened to them. They wanted the underlying causes of offending addressed. They wanted perpetrators to attend some sort of therapeutic programme that would address the offending behaviour. Most importantly, survivors wanted to protect potential vulnerable victims in their family or social network. Talking about sexual violence in the family, or bringing it out in the open, is a very effective way of doing this. Jülich (2001) concluded that to experience a sense of justice, survivors need to have their stories heard by witnesses in a safe forum, in which the offender acknowledges his or her responsibility and demonstrates accountability. Survivors wanted the victimisation they were subjected to affirmed and validated by the offender, bystanders, outsiders, and their community.

Women and children are typically sexually assaulted by someone known to them. They share a community with the perpetrator and will continue to do so. Even if the perpetrator is found guilty and imprisoned, sooner or later he or she will return to the same family or social network as the victim-survivor. If offending is to stop, the perpetrator needs support, but at the same relationships must be transformed so that the victim-survivor and perpetrator can co-exist in any shared community.

A Process for Justice

In New Zealand court referrals to restorative justice services are supported by legislation. To date, these referrals have been a small percentage of the total number of eligible cases. New legislation might change this. The Victims' Rights Amendment Act 2014 aims to strengthen the rights of victims of crime and provides for increased access to restorative justice. The development of restorative processes are not mandated by legislation but are guided by best practice principles (Ministry of Justice, 2004). The recent development of restorative justice standards for sexual violence (Ministry of Justice, 2013), to which Project Restore contributed, indicates a growing awareness, in New Zealand at least, that restorative justice requires a specialist service if it is to centre the victim-survivor in the process.

While the basic philosophies and values of restorative justice might be shared internationally, the way it is achieved differs. Member States of the European Union must comply with decisions and directives of the European Parliament. Of note for victims of crime is the recent European Union Directive on Minimum Standards on the Rights, Support and Protection of Victims of Crime (Directive 2012/29/EU, 2012). Known as the Victims' Directive, it is more generally concerned with victim support in the conventional criminal justice system, except for Articles 12 and 25 that relate directly to restorative justice. The latter article focuses on the training of all those practitioners that victims are likely to come into contact as they pursue justice, which would include restorative justice facilitators. Article 12 focuses on safeguards and service delivery, requiring the victim to be safeguarded 'from secondary and repeat victimisation, from intimidation and from retaliation' (Directive 2012/29/EU, 2012, p. 69). Further, the directive requires Member States to ensure that those victims participating in restorative processes 'have access to safe and competent restorative justice services, subject at least to the following conditions' (Directive 2012/29/EU, 2012, p. 69):

a) the restorative justice services are used only if they are in the interest of the victim, subject to any safety considerations, and are based on the victim's free and informed consent, which may be withdrawn at any time;
b) before agreeing to participate in the restorative justice process, the victim is provided with full and unbiased information about that process and the potential outcomes as well as information about the procedures for supervising the implementation of any agreement;
c) the offender has acknowledged the basic facts of the case;
d) any agreement is arrived at voluntarily and may be taken into account in any further criminal proceedings;
e) discussions in restorative justice processes that are not conducted in public are confidential and are not subsequently disclosed, except with the agreement of the parties or as required by national law due to an overriding public interest.

The Victim's Directive does not specifically target restorative justice services addressing sexual violence, and is similar to New Zealand's best practice principles developed in 2004 (Ministry of Justice, 2004). An exception is the last clause of Article 12 regarding confidentiality. New Zealand does not have this protection. The directive and the best practice principles are minimum standards for the delivery of restorative justice services, which are insufficient when addressing the complexity of sexual violence.

Jülich (2001) asked survivors (those she interviewed for her research) to consider that if they had the power to change the criminal justice system, what changes they would make that firstly could provide them with a sense of justice and secondly might encourage them to report the sexual violence they had been subjected to. They described processes that could only be identified as restorative justice. Although they were excited to learn that such a system existed, without exception they did not embrace restorative justice as Jülich had anticipated. They made comments such as 'this would work for some people,' and 'it wouldn't work for me or my family.' Further, they critiqued the underlying principles of restorative justice. These were as follows:

- The involvement of victim-survivors
- Voluntary participation
- Neutrality and impartiality
- A negotiated community response
- The transfer of power to the community

The survivors interviewed by Jülich were concerned that restorative justice might not address their unique circumstances. Although this particular group of survivors had been subjected to sexual violence in their childhood, their concerns are just as valid for those subjected to sexual violence as adults. Jülich concluded that these must be addressed if restorative justice is to be effective in cases of sexual violence. Indeed, addressing these concerns would ensure that restorative justice services in Europe comply with the Victims' Directive of the European Union. Therefore, the concerns outlined in the following section and the practice implications that are subsequently identified are not only relevant for specialist restorative justice services addressing sexual violence but also are equally relevant for generic restorative justice services addressing other crimes.

The Involvement of Victim-Survivors

Perpetrators of sexual violence typically use explanations for their behaviour that deny and minimise sexual violence. These mechanisms, known as constructs of denial, in some instances are constructed and maintained over many decades and can be difficult to break down.[4] Survivors confronting perpetrators in Jülich's research said they were unable to break down these constructs of denial. Some commented that perpetrators of child sexual abuse were master manipulators and outsiders might not realise just how manipulative these particular perpetrators can be. They were afraid that both bystanders and outsiders would not recognise this. In particular, they noted that outsiders, restorative justice facilitators with limited experience of the dynamics of sexual violence, would not be able to sufficiently support and empower victim-survivors to break down entrenched constructs of denial.

Survivors were concerned that the burden of responsibility for restorative justice to proceed would rest on victim-survivors. They believed that restorative justice could proceed without the actual attendance of the victim-survivor with a spokesperson or surrogate victim-survivor attending in their place. Justice would be realised by the victim-survivor through the process of feedback. That is, feedback on the restorative conference itself and the monitoring of the conference outcomes.

Survivors queried the role of victim-survivors in restorative justice. They acknowledged that restorative justice could produce benefits for victim-survivors, perpetrators and society. They were concerned that the needs of victim-survivors to confront the offender could be exploited. They were also concerned that if facilitators lacked understanding regarding the dynamics of sexual violence, victim-survivors' truths would not be heard or understood.

Although victim-survivors might want to confront the offender and have their say, they need to be ready to do so. The dynamics of sexual violence make it difficult for victim-survivors to attend a restorative process and so the timing is crucial. Complicating this is the pre-existing relationship with the offender. It is easy for those unaware of the complexity of sexual violence to assume it is a relationship based on equality, but this is not so in sexual violence. While the power imbalance between two adults might not be as obvious as it is between an adult and a child, it can be subtle, but it is always significant (Jülich & Buttle, 2011). Accordingly some critics have argued that the adversarial system could better serve victim-survivors of sexual violence (Hooper & Busch, 1996). In contrast, others have noted that the adversarial system is just as inadequate in coping with these disparities (Carbonatto, 1995; Taylor, 2004). Facilitators need to be sure as to whose interests are being served: the victim-survivor or the perpetrator. Restorative justice aims to provide victim-survivors with an experience of justice, and while it might appear advantageous for victim-survivors to meet with the perpetrator this must never occur at their expense.

Voluntary Participation

Voluntary participation is an accepted principle of restorative justice, but when perpetrators and victim-survivors are related or known to each other, as is often the case in sexual violence, the principle of voluntarism comes under pressure. Survivors noted this point. They were concerned that victim-survivors could experience significant pressure to participate, particularly if the perpetrators' supporters believed that engaging in restorative justice could avoid imprisonment.

Facilitators need to be mindful of the dynamics of sexual violence and understand the pressure that victim-survivors might be experiencing from family members. Both victim-survivors and perpetrators need enough information about the process to make an informed decision as to whether they will participate or not. Facilitators might experience different pressures. They want people to engage. They might need to provide outcomes to satisfy funding contracts. It would be very easy to overstate the potential of restorative justice. In their efforts to encourage participation they should be careful that they are not creating unrealistic expectations.

Some survivors were so keen to confront the offender they suggested that perpetrators should be coerced to participate. It is interesting to note that some commentators such as Marshall (1998) have acknowledged that perpetrators might be uncooperative and although victim-survivors, perpetrators and their communities of support should participate voluntarily, perpetrators could be encouraged, educated and invited to become cooperative. Rather than aim for some unrealistic ideal, Marshall suggested that perhaps it is better to acknowledge the existence of pressure and coercion and debate the degree of persuasion or supportive coercion that could be applied to perpetrators without compromising the principles of restorative justice. These comments aside, it is important to note that victim-survivors must never be coerced.

Neutrality and Impartiality

Adult survivors of child sexual abuse queried the definitions of neutrality and impartiality and their role in restorative justice. They had difficulty reconciling the neutral role of a restorative justice facilitator facilitating a conference for what is defined as serious crime. The restorative justice literature appears to present a confused picture in respect to the neutrality and impartiality of restorative justice facilitators. Some writers advocated that facilitators should be neutral (Marshall, 1998), others supported impartiality (Dandurand & Griffiths, 2000), or they argued that facilitators should be sufficiently neutral so as to be perceived as fair (Bowen & Consedine, 1998). Yet others suggested that neutrality is neither possible nor desirable (Boulle, Jones, & Goldblatt, 1998). Coker (1999) argued that restorative justice has never ascribed to the ideal of a neutral facilitator.

Restorative justice in itself is not neutral, an acknowledged wrong has occurred. The process aims to generate meaningful accountability and to acknowledge the harm perpetrated against the victim. To achieve this restorative justice attempts to empower weaker parties so that their voices can be heard and their stories told. Unless weaker parties are empowered the restorative justice process might make it possible for perpetrators to maintain constructs of denial. In so doing, facilitators use a variety of interventions to support the weaker participant against the power of the stronger participant. This is not neutrality. As Coker (1999) argued, the neutrality of a restorative justice facilitator combined with the structural disadvantages women experience could ignore past injustices between the victim-survivor and the offender.

Jülich (2001) reported that when talking to restorative justice facilitators, they described their role as similar to that of a neutral third party as is seen in the mediation model. Drawing comparisons between restorative justice and models for dispute resolution is not helpful. Indeed, the language of conflict resolution did not appear to invoke images of justice for adult survivors of child sexual abuse (Jülich, 2001). Koss and Achilles (2008) similarly found that use of the term 'mediation' and reference to 'resolution of conflict' was problematic for crimes of sexual violence. The focus on 'getting to yes' (Fisher & Ury, 1983), 'win-win', 'finding the middle ground' or concepts of third party neutral facilitators (Boulle et al., 1998) are simply not appropriate for sexual violence. While sexual violence might be a conflict and crime might be disputed, reframing sexual violence as a dispute could mutualise or domesticate sexual violence (Cobb, 1997). Realities could be reframed so that victims and offenders are merely disputants.

Boulle, Jones and Goldblatt (1998) suggested focussing on distinguishing between neutrality in the sense of disinterestedness (neutrality) and neutrality in the sense of fairness (impartiality). Jülich and Buttle (2011) urged restorative justice facilitators to move beyond neutrality and impartiality and challenge inappropriate explanations for sexually harmful behaviour. In a similar vein, Howard Zehr[5] spoke of balanced partiality which he attributed to Dave Gustafson co-director of Community Justice Initiatives in British Columbia. While he did not label it as such, balanced partiality would provide a forum based on substantive equality. The victim-survivor and perpetrator might not be treated equally a process based on balanced partiality, but substantive equality (equality of outcome) is more likely to be achieved when the difference between the victim-survivor and perpetrator is recognised and accommodated. Models that ignore inequality risk replicating the societal structures that foster sexual violence and the disempowerment of victim-survivors.

Survivors were afraid that in the long term, restorative justice would merely replicate the patriarchal structures of the courts.[6] To avoid this, facilitators cannot be a third party neutral facilitator. They must be prepared to intervene and challenge all explanations for sexual offending that are gender based, victim-blaming, minimising behaviour or contributing to the construct of denial.[7] Often referred to as rape myths, these beliefs, held by many people about sexual violence, are harmful to survivors (Easteal, 1994). Some of these myths exist because of historical reasons, such as inherited societal structures, gender role expectations, and the imbalance of power in a patriarchal society (University of Minnesota Duluth, 2005). Restorative justice must not undermine the work of feminists putting sexual violence on the political agenda.

A Negotiated Community Response

Restorative justice emphasises the involvement of victims, offenders and their communities to come together, discuss the offending and negotiate a community response. While community might mean different things to different people, it can be thought of as a group of people, who share a common interest, but may or may not be living in the same geographic location. Typically, a community associated with restorative justice processes are those who have an interest in the lives of either the victim or the offender. This could include family members, friends, work colleagues and the like. A restorative justice process is an opportunity for the community of care or interest to come together, discuss the impacts of the offending, and generate some consensual solutions to address the harm. In the instance of sexual violence a community can demonstrate their condemnation for the sexually harmful behaviour, provide support and validation to the victim-survivor, and determine how relationships can be transformed so the victim-survivor and perpetrator can co-exist in a shared community.

The concept of community was an important point for survivors of historical child sexual abuse, they queried its definition and asked who would attend the restorative process (Jülich, 2001).

Without exception, they pointed out that that their communities consisted of those people who were unable to protect them in the first instance. Bystanders, those people who knew or suspected something was wrong, traditionally have looked the other way (Herman, 1997). Outsiders too, were unable to protect them. Sarah said 'I had my leg broken in the same place 6 times ... how did they not know'(Jülich, 2001, p. 185). In addition, she said she had bruising on the inside of her thighs and even though she was taken each time to the same hospital, the doctors – outsiders – said nothing. At times bystanders and outsiders demonstrated to survivors that they had little understanding of the complex dynamics of sexual violence. Sarah and other survivors had no reason to trust bystanders and outsiders; they had limited confidence in the ability of their communities to validate their experiences.

Survivors contributing to Jülich's research identified that not all communities are equal. Some communities might be able to provide more resources in relation to meeting the needs of victim-survivors and offenders, while others might have limited access to resources. Survivors were concerned that successfully completing any agreed outcomes from the restorative process might depend on the ability of the community of care to provide them. Some form of funding might be necessary to ensure that agreed outcomes are met.

Survivors discussed the negotiation of a community response not only in terms of complex pre-existing relationships between themselves and offenders, but also in terms of those that existed between the members of the community of care or interest. Survivors noted that it could be difficult for some family members to endorse outcomes that might include imprisonment. Jülich (2001) noted that entrenched intergenerational sexual violence within a family system could inhibit the ability of some community members to ensure agreed outcomes were carried out. Women in these communities might be less equipped to withstand the offender's constructs of denial and other rationalisations for offending. Consider also, that restorative justice places a '...great faith in a group of people, assembled for a single meeting, labelled a community ... to challenge structural inequality and deeply held...' patriarchal views that society itself has been unable to address (Stubbs, 1997, p. 11).

The Transfer of Power to the Community

From the 1980s, decentralisation, de-institutionalisation and devolution were sold to the public as a means of empowering the community (Kelsey, 1997). This ethos, congruent with both the restorative justice movement and neo-liberalist ideologies, is reflected in the policies of many countries across the western world. Fiscally frugal governments, such as Singapore and New Zealand, were quick to embrace restorative justice (Braithwaite, 1996), a seemingly progressive response to crime. However, as Kelsey (1997) argued, when not properly funded the rhetoric of neo-liberalism translates to 'shifting the burden from the state to primarily women "volunteers" who were assumed to have a limitless capacity for unpaid labour in "the community" or the home' (p. 292).

Survivors contributing to Jülich's research noted this point, although not in these terms. They asked who would pay and who would be responsible for the ongoing delivery of services. They were concerned that the transfer of power could ultimately mean the transfer of costs to the community and the transfer of responsibility to women. They were sceptical that restorative justice provider groups could deliver reliable and consistent services throughout New Zealand. There are some grounds for this concern. Restorative justice in New Zealand is not providing full time employment for all facilitators. There is some payment involved but as yet the payment is minimal and insufficient to live on. Often, it is a role that people take on in addition to their regular paid employment. Survivors were concerned that this could mean more unpaid work for women; not only in their involvement as facilitators, but also they were concerned that women could become the unpaid supervisors of perpetrators in their family system with the responsibility of keeping them safe. Survivors, therefore, were not supportive of the transfer of power to the community without appropriate structures in place to ensure women were not further disadvantaged.

Overcoming the Concerns of Survivors

The concerns raised by the survivors of historical child sexual abuse are addressed within the model that has been developed by Project Restore. Much emphasis is placed on the preparation stages in which the survivor specialist and the offender specialist are involved with the victim-survivor and perpetrator respectively. They aim to build rapport, identify desired outcomes, and provide a realistic picture to both parties as to what is possible. They provide sufficient information so that victim-survivors and perpetrators can make informed choices and decisions. They assess readiness and capacity to engage in the process. They educate and inform all intending participants of the dynamics of sexual offending, challenging any distortions of thinking, constructs of denial, or other potentially, harmful actions and statements by any participant.

Most participants need support to develop emotional capacity and strengthen key relationships that have been harmed by the sexual offending. In the case of historical child sexual abuse, it is our experience at Project Restore that often the relationship between the victim-survivor and the non-offending parent or parents must be repaired before they can sit together in a restorative justice process. However, if significant emotional capacity building is required, it might be necessary to complete this work in an on-going independent counselling or therapeutic relationship external to Project Restore. The role of the counsellor or therapist is distinct from the role of Project Restore's community specialists – the counsellor or therapists in treatment programmes address issues relating to the sexual violence, while Project Restore's community specialists prepare victim-survivors and perpetrators to engage in restorative processes. Project Restore's community specialists liaise regularly with the individual counsellors or therapists to ensure that the clinical team is well informed regarding risk and readiness to progress.

Perpetrators are required to undergo assessment for entry into a treatment programme and are encouraged to undertake the same if appropriate. In this way Project Restore is addressing the underlying causes of offending. Survivors of sexual violence reported that this was an important component of achieving a sense of justice (Jülich, 2006). Ideally, the restorative process would occur towards the end of any treatment programme that is being undertaken by the perpetrator. At Project Restore, we have found that this is the optimal time to maximise the perpetrator's ability to demonstrate accountability and an understanding of the impacts of their offending. Victim-survivors experience validation when the community specialists provide feedback regarding the perpetrator's development of capacity to understand his or her behaviour and the impact it has had. Timing is critical to safety and so the process tends to go as fast as the slowest person. However, this is influenced by court and treatment timeframes and may result in adaptations to what can be realistically achieved.

The community specialists work together with the restorative justice facilitator to adapt the process for each and every case so that safety is maximised and the potential for harm is minimised. Accordingly, a number of restorative responses have been developed to meet the needs of a diverse client group. These include victim-survivor only processes, shuttle mediation, victim-survivor and perpetrator only meetings, a community panel in which the victim-survivor is represented by a survivor advocate, and the restorative conference which is attended by both the victim-survivor and perpetrator together with the communities of support. If the victim-survivor does not attend the restorative process, his or her voice is brought to the conference by the survivor specialist and in turn a sense of justice is realised for the victim-survivor when he or she is provided with feedback on the process and outcomes.

During the restorative process, the community specialists intervene as required. This might include advocating or speaking on behalf of the victim-survivor or perpetrator, halting the process to allow some debriefing in separate break out rooms, deepening the dialogue to address issues, challenging constructs of denial, and providing information about common experiences, issues or impacts for victim-survivors. The power dynamics of sexual violence and the process of disempowerment complicate the provision of neutral or impartial processes. To counteract these dynamics, Project Restore practises balanced partiality and is victim-survivor driven – that is the victim-survivor is well informed, provided with choices, and is well supported throughout the entire process. Both parties are equally valued with the emphasis on shifting power structures from 'power over' to self-determination and autonomy for the victim-survivor.

Following the restorative process, Project Restore monitors any agreed outcomes. This might include attending offender treatment review meetings. The victim-survivor is informed on progress regarding agreed outcomes. Three months after the completion of the restorative process Project Restore invites all participants to complete a survey that provides feedback on the process. The clinical team debriefs regularly on cases, those that are in process and those that are completed. This dialogue contributes to not only the ongoing development of Project Restore's model but also the training and professional development of the clinical team.

The only concern raised by survivors of historical child sexual abuse in Jülich's research that has not been resolved by Project Restore is the issue of securing a consistent and reliable stream of funding. This would enable the on-going development of expertise and capacity so that the provision of restorative processes can be expanded and enable the employment of full time personnel. However, in government contracts, Project Restore has negotiated the provision of restorative processes to an agreed number of cases that have bypassed the conventional criminal justice system. This is in recognition that most cases of sexual violence in our communities go unaddressed.

Conclusion

The impacts of sexual violence suggest that the human and financial costs to victim-survivors, offenders, their families and the broader society could be substantial. Statistics not only demonstrate victim-survivors' reluctance to report to the police or other investigative authorities, but also the difficulties of securing criminal convictions. Victim-survivors are not likely to experience a sense of justice within a criminal justice system that all too often serves to revictimise and further marginalise them. They are not central to the process of justice in conventional criminal justice systems, which appear to be based on the assumption that a victim and an offender are previously unknown to each other. This is not the case with sexual violence; most victim-survivors know the perpetrator.

The informal structure of restorative justice enables creativity and flexibility in dealing with the aftermath of crime and offers hope to victim survivors of sexual violence. However, societal acceptance of restorative justice as a process to deal with the aftermath of crime is yet to be universally attained. The informality of its structure could render restorative justice powerless as it attempts to address the complexity of sexual violence. A critical analysis of the underlying principles of restorative justice – the involvement of victims, voluntary participations, neutrality and impartiality, a negotiated community response and the transfer of power to the community – highlighted a range of issues that must be overcome if restorative justice is to centre victim-survivors in the justice process and avoid their further marginalisation. Although restorative justice might aim to empower victims, this appears to be based on a premise that a condition of equality pre-existed the criminal behaviour. Sexual violence, as an abuse of power within a complex relationship, negates any notion of pre-existent equality. Complicating this disadvantage is an additional power imbalance existent between men and women. This deeply entrenched power imbalance could preclude any assurance of formal equality, let alone substantive equality.

Project Restore was founded specifically to design restorative justice processes that address sexual violence and its focus has been to develop a model that safeguards all participants, that is, victim-survivors and perpetrators and their communities of care. It has aimed to centre victim-survivors in the justice process and in so doing is victim-survivor driven. The concerns raised by survivors in Jülich's research are mitigated by the use of community specialists – the survivor specialist and the offender specialist – and a restorative justice facilitator who has an in depth understanding of the dynamics of sexual violence. Careful preparation, assessment for risk and readiness ensures that victim-survivors and perpetrators are not coerced. It should be noted that voluntary participation can mean that either the victim-survivor or the perpetrator can withdraw from the process at any time. If the case has been referred through the conventional criminal justice system it returns to the courts for sentencing. Frequently, the preparatory work alone is sufficient for victim-survivors to experience a sense of justice. Practising balanced impartiality ensures all stakeholders are treated fairly. Empowering weaker parties and challenging misperceptions of sexual harmfully behaviour provides victim-survivors with some confidence that a negotiated community response can be achieved within even the most difficult of communities. Resolving concerns regarding the transfer of power to the community is not as simple. Restorative justice must be sufficiently funded so that it is not a way of transferring costs to the community and further disadvantaging women. While restorative justice can contribute to attitudinal change, it alone cannot resolve deeply entrenched patriarchal attitudes evident in society.

Codes of ethics, minimum standards of practice and the development of best practice models are essential for consistency of service delivery and the credibility of restorative justice to address the complexity of sexual violence. Reaching minimum standards alone is insufficient. The practice model developed by Project Restore goes beyond the minimum standards that guide the development of generic restorative justice services in New Zealand. Also, it has gone beyond the Victims' Directive of the European Union. This is Project Restore's point of difference. Its practice model is victim-survivor driven thereby positioning victim-survivors at the centre of restorative justice processes so that their justice needs are met. In this way it avoids the paradox of marginalising victim-survivors while pursuing justice, as are the outcomes of conventional criminal justice systems and, it could be argued, those generic restorative justice processes that address other forms of crime. Even though it is another layer to be negotiated, a sense of justice can be achieved in a specialist restorative justice programme. Providing a sense of justice is therapeutic and enables all concerned to continue on their journeys of recovery, thereby producing positive benefits for victim-survivors, perpetrators, their families and the broader society.

Notes

1. For more information on restorative justice in New Zealand see (Ministry of Justice, n.d.). For the Ministry of Justice's standards for working with sexual violence cases see (Ministry of Justice, 2013).
2. For more information on the conferencing model, see (Morris, Kingi, Poppelwell, Robertson, & Triggs, 2005)
3. Publications are forthcoming.
4. For more information on denial see (Langton et al., 2008)
5. Personal communication.
6. For more information on the embedded patriarchy in conventional criminal justice systems see (Taylor, 2004)
7. Offenders typically use explanations for their behaviour that deny and minimise sexual violence. These mechanisms, known as constructs of denial, in some instances are constructed and maintained over many decades and can be difficult to break down. For more information on denial and minimisation see (Langton et al., 2008)

References

Boulle, L., Jones, J., & Goldblatt, V. (1998). *Mediation: Principles, process, practice.* Wellington: Butterworths.

Bowen, H., & Consedine, J. (1998). *Restorative Justice: Contemporary Themes and Practice.* Christchurch: Ploughshares Publications.

Braithwaite, J. (1996). Restorative justice and a better future. *The Dalhousie Review,* 76(1), 9-32. Retrieved from http://dalhousiereview.dal.ca

Carbonatto, H. (1995). *Expanding intervention options for spousal abuse: The use of restorative justice.* Occasional Papers in Criminology. New Series: No. 4. Institute of Criminology, Victoria University of Wellington. Wellington, N.Z.

Cobb, S. (1997). The domestication of violence in mediation. *Law and Society Review,* 31(3), 397-440. doi: 10.2307/3054041

Coker, D. (1999). Enhancing autonomy for battered women: Lessons from Navajo peacemaking. *UCLA Law Review,* 47, 1-111. Retrieved from http://heinonline.org/HOL/LandingPage?collection=journals&handle=hein.journals/uclalr47&div=10&id=&page=

Daly, K. (2013). Reconceptualizing sexual victimization and justice Retrieved August 28, 2014, from http://www.griffith.edu.au/__data/assets/pdf_file/0009/493632/K-Daly-FINAL-Reconceptualizing-Sexual-Victimization-and-Justice-6-February-2013.pdf

Dandurand, Y., & Griffiths, C. T. (2000). *Handbook on restorative justice programmes.* New York: United Nations Office on Drugs and Crime.

Directive 2012/29/EU. (2012). *Official Journal of the European Union,* L315, 57-73. Retrieved from http://eur-lex.europa.eu/LexUriServ/LexUriServ.do?uri=OJ:L:2012:315:0057:0073:EN:PDF

Easteal, P. (1994). *Voices of the survivors.* Melbourne: Spinifex.

Fisher, R., & Ury, W. (1983). *Getting to yes: Negotiating agreement without giving in.* New York: Penguin Books.

Fleming, T., Watson, P., Ameratunga, S., Dixon, R., Clark, T., & Crengle, S. (2007). *Violence and New Zealand young people: Findings of Youth 2000 - A national secondary school youth health and wellbeing survey.* Auckland: The University of Auckland.

Gavey, N. (1991). Sexual victimisation prevalence among New Zealand university students. *Journal of Consulting and Clinical Psychology,* 59(3), 464-466. doi: 10.1037//0022-006X.59.3.464

Graham, D. L. R., Rawlings, E. I., & Rigsby, R. K. (1994). *Loving to survive: Sexual terror, men's violence and women's lives.* New York: New York University Press.

Herman, J. L. (1997). *Trauma and recovery: The aftermath of violence - from domestic abuse to political terror.* London: Basic Books.

HMIC, & HMCPSI. (2007). *Without consent: A report on the joint review of the investigation and prosecution of rape offences.* London: Her Majesty's Inspectorate of Constabulary Retrieved from http://www.hmic.gov.uk/media/without-consent-20061231.pdf.

Hooper, S., & Busch, R. (1996). Domestic violence and restorative justice initiatives: The risks of a new panacea. *Waikato Law Review,* 4(1), 101-130. Retrieved from http://www.waikato.ac.nz/law/research/waikato_law_review/volume_4,_issue_1,_1996

Jülich, S. (2001). *Breaking the silence: Restorative justice and child sexual abuse.* PhD Thesis, Massey, Albany. Retrieved from http://mro.massey.ac.nz/handle/10179/2110

Jülich, S. (2006). Views of justice among survivors of historical child sexual abuse: Implications for restorative justice in New Zealand. *Theoretical Criminology,* 10(1), 125-138. doi: 10.1177/136248060 6059988

Jülich, S. (2010). Restorative justice and gendered violence in New Zealand: A glimmer of hope. In J. Ptacek (Ed.), *Restorative justice and violence against women* (pp. 239-254). New York: Oxford University Press.

Jülich, S., & Buttle, J. (2011). Beyond conflict resolution: Towards a restorative practice process for sexual violence. *Te Awatea,* 8(1), 21-25.

Jülich, S., Buttle, J., Cummins, C., & Freeborn, E. V. (2010). *Project Restore: An exploratory study of restorative justice and sexual violence Auckland:* AUT University. Retrieved from http://www.academia.edu/324795/Project_Restore_An_Exploratory_Study_of_Restorative_Justice_and_Sexual_Violence.

Jülich, S., & Landon, F. (2012). *Achieving outcomes for participants of Project Restore's restorative processes.* Auckland: Project Restore.

Jülich, S., & Landon, F. (2013). *Achieving outcomes for participants of Project Restore's restorative processes: The perspectives of participants.* Auckland: Project Restore.

Kelly, L., Lovett, J., & Regan, L. (2005). *A gap or a chasm? Attrition in reported rape cases.* London: Home Office Research.

Kelsey, J. (1997). *The New Zealand Experiment: A World Model for Structural Adjustment?* (2nd ed.). Auckland: Auckland University Press, Bridget Williams Books.

Koss, M. P. (2014). The RESTORE programme of restorative justice for sex crimes: Vision, process, and outcomes. *Journal of Interpersonal Violence*, 29(9), 1623-1660. doi: 10.1177/0886260513511537

Koss, M. P., & Achilles, M. (2008). *Restorative justice responses to sexual assault.* Retrieved January 3, 2010, from http://new.vawnet.org/Assoc_Files_VAWnet/AR_RestorativeJustice.pdf

Koss, M. P., Bachar, K. J., & Hopkins, C. Q. (2003). Restorative Justice for Sexual Violence. *Annals of the New York Academy of Sciences*, 989(1), 384-396. doi: 10.1111/j.1749-6632.2003.tb07320.x

Langton, C. M., Barbaree, H. E., Harkins, L., Arenovich, T., Mcnamee, J., Peacock, E. J., . . . Marcon, H. (2008). Denial and minimization among sexual offenders: Posttreatment presentation and association with sexual recidivism. *Criminal Justice and Behavior*, 35(1), 69-98. doi: 10.1177/0093854807309287

Latimer, J., Dowden, C., & Muise, D. (2005). The effectiveness of restorative justice practices: A meta-analysis. *The Prison Journal*, 85(2), 127-144.

Marshall, T. (1998). *Restorative Justice: An Overview.* London: Home Office, Information and Publications Group.

McDonald, E., & Tinsley, Y. (Eds.). (2011). *From "real rape" to real justice: Prosecuting rape in New Zealand.* Wellington: Victoria University Press.

Ministry of Justice. (2004). *Restorative justice: Best practice in New Zealand.* Wellington: Ministry of Justice.

Ministry of Justice. (2013). *Restorative justice standards for sexual offending cases.* Retrieved from http://www.justice.govt.nz/publications/global-publications/r/restorative-justice-standards-for-sexual-offending-cases/publication

Ministry of Justice. (n.d.). *Restorative justice.* Retrieved May 13, 2014, from http://www.justice.govt.nz/policy/criminal-justice/restorative-justice

Morris, A., Kingi, V., Poppelwell, E., Robertson, J., & Triggs, S. (2005). *New Zealand court-referred restorative justice pilot evaluation.* Wellington: Ministry of Justice.

Morris, A., & Reilly, J., (with Berry, S & Ransom, R). (2003). *New Zealand national survey of crime victims 2001.* Wellington: Ministry of Justice Retrieved from http://www.justice.govt.nz/publications/publications-archived/2003/the-new-zealand-national-survey-of-crime-victims-2001-may-2003.

OHCHR. (2009). *Convention on the Elimination of All Forms of Discrimination against Women* Retrieved November 12, 2012, from http://www.un.org/womenwatch/daw/cedaw/

Roper, T., & Thompson, A. (2006). *Estimating the costs of crime in New Zealand in 2003/2004.* Wellington: The Treasury.

Stubbs, J. (1997). Shame, defiance and violence against women: a critical analysis of "communitarian" conferencing. In J. Bessant & S. Cook (Eds.), *Women's encounters with violence: Australian experiences* (pp. 109-126). Thousand Oaks, California: Sage.

Taylor, S. C. (2004). *Court licensed abuse: Patriarchal lore and the legal response to intrafamilial sexual abuse of children.* New York: Peter Lang Publishing.

Triggs, S., Mossman, E., Jordan, J., & Kingi, V. (2009). *Responding to sexual violence: Attrition in the New Zealand criminal justice system.* Wellington: Ministry of Women's Affairs.

University of Minnesota Duluth. (2005). *List of rape myths: Sociology of Rape.* Retrieved July 3, 2013, from http://www.d.umn.edu/cla/faculty/jhamlin/3925/myths.html

Achieving Balance: Towards Rights-Centred Justice

*Anne Hayden**

Abstract

The chapter presents an international dimension along with the research on which it is based. It also adds an additional and much needed element, not only in terms of its qualitative argument for a rights based approach, but also geographically. Furthermore, exploring Māori practice is important for two reasons. First, this indigenous foundation of restorative justice must not be ignored, and second, it has been used as a model for a number of EU contemporary practices, particularly in the UK, for example the family conferencing and Thames Valley restorative justice processes.

Introduction

Restorative justice has been examined from many perspectives. A core debate is the extent to which it should be considered a victim-centred approach, in contrast to the offender-focused orientation of traditional criminal justice (Ward, Fox and Garber 2014). This chapter considers this issue by critically appraising assumptions made about victims, perpetrators and what justice is, in order to provide a basis of what a criminal justice system with a different focus could mean. While I do not disagree with there being greater focus on victims, which I consider is definitely required, in this chapter I explore the possibility of going further than a formal system that is victim-led. Instead I argue towards a 'rights-centred criminal justice system. The chapter is informed by my research into initiatives for victims of crime (1996), a case study relating to a Māori man who offended (1997) and the restorative justice conference which I coordinated and co-facilitated,[1] and my largely qualitative doctoral research about non-reporting of intimate partner violence (2010).[2]

To many professionals, academics and individuals, the criminal justice system as it is today, is not meeting their needs or values (Curtis-Fawley & Daly, 2005, (Jordan, 2004, p. 1413; Ruiz-Perez, et al., 2006; Seuffert, 1996). Quotations from the research participants (2010) below support this claim. The chapter concludes with a vision of what a rights-centred criminal justice system could be. While the intent of the existing criminal justice system is to achieve justice after wrongdoing by and harm to people, a paradox exists where, in fact, the system has been guilty of committing additional harms to those it is designed to adjudicate.

* Dr. Anne Hayden (Research Associate of the Office of the Pro-Vice Chancellor, Auckland University of Technology, New Zealand, Winston Churchill Fellows Association member), contact 30 West Street, Greytown, Wairarapa, 5712, New Zealand.
Ph: 64 6 562 4034 Mob: 64 272 300 343 Email: Anneda@orcon.net.nz

Defining the Paradox

Justice is about putting right the harms done to people after crimes have been committed, yet the focus of criminal justice system is invariably on the perpetrator. This was clearly articulated by Gerry Johnstone (2013) who described the habitual question asked after a crime had been committed, as, "What should we do when a member of the group does something wrong?" This question leads to our focus turning towards the wrongdoer and what should be done about him or her. Johnstone suggests another question should take precedence, that is, "What should we do for the victim?" something that restorative justice, in contrast to formal criminal justice systems, highlights and attempts to achieve.

A significant part of the paradox is that in many, if not most Western jurisdictions, any offence committed is officially against the state rather than the victim because state law has been violated. I will discuss this in some detail later on. The victim is often 'left out in the cold', used as witnesses and even revictimized by the legal process, with the result that their encounter with the criminal justice system is unsatisfactory and unlikely to leave them with a sense of justice having been done.

Defining Justice

Although justice is difficult to define, it is understood because most people could recognise an injustice when it occurs (Jülich, 2001). Victims, perpetrators and society have tended to use the term according to their needs, and generally speaking, what they want is fairness. Aristotle, an early Greek philosopher, provided a framework for thinking about justice which is still used today (Honderich, 1995). *Aristotle saw justice as a dual concept, both a moral or internal and a material or external concept, where the key purposes were to reduce social inequality and achieve common wealth (Artinopoulou and Gavrielides 2013).* These were described as distributive justice, corrective justice (Honderich, 1995), retributive justice and commutative justice (Fletcher, 1996). Kant was a prominent Enlightenment era thinker who talked about justice as a unitary concept, one which was understood irrespective of cultural, gender or class constructs. Therefore individuals had a moral right to live under laws that protected them from being used, against their will, to satisfy other people's desires. Accordingly, the purpose of law, according to Kant, was to prevent coercive interference with the freedom of individuals, either by other individuals or by government (Nardin, 2006).

Jülich (2001) canvassed the concept of justice in depth with adult survivors of child sexual abuse. She found that a sense of justice comprised the provision of survivors with a safe forum in which they had a voice. The processes they described which could provide them with a sense of justice were what Jülich identified as those used by restorative justice.

At present, the conventional criminal justice system does not provide fairness to all, nor is it perceived as fair by many who have experienced it. Restorative justice, on the other hand, may offer more to victims and perpetrators, particularly a sense of being treated fairly, where both parties' needs can be met (Zehr, 1990) more equitably. Restorative justice can allow participants to define justice for themselves, albeit often within the framework of the criminal justice system (Hayden 2010).

Restorative Justice in Brief

Zehr (1990) explained what restorative justice could offer, thus illustrating the ability of the community to define justice for itself. He stated "[c]rime is a violation of people and relationships. It creates obligations to make things right. Justice involves the victim, the perpetrator, and the community in search for solutions which promote repair, reconciliation, and reassurance" (p. 181). Marshall (1999) described restorative justice as "a process whereby parties with a stake in a particular offence collectively resolve how to deal with the aftermath of the offence and its implications for the future" (p. 5). McCold, Llewellyn and Van Ness (2007) put forward that there were four principles of restorative justice, namely that it is harm-focused, relational, participatory and democratic (Van Ness 2014). As well as having multiple philosophies, restorative justice comes in many forms and is practiced in a wide range of forums.

Restorative justice processes have aimed to redress the imbalance caused by the offending by holding perpetrators accountable to the victim and community. Dignity and respect are extended to all present. Thus, through balancing the power held by the parties, restorative justice processes can increase the likelihood of understanding, mutual empathy and resolution, thereby benefiting victims, perpetrators and communities (Hayden 2010).

Generally the process has involved meetings facilitated by one or more trained facilitators in a safe place. Unlike conventional criminal justice systems, restorative justice has not dealt with issues of guilt or innocence, nor has it removed prisons as a possible sanction; instead it has presented a new way of thinking when responding to crime (Young & Morris, 1998). Restorative justice does not need to be separate from conventional criminal justice systems. Notwithstanding its differences, restorative justice has often been practised alongside them, optimizing justice with greater involvement and satisfaction for victims. So how do we understand two or more forms of justice operating together, a notion called legal pluralism?

Legal Pluralism

Legal pluralism is a term indicating the existence of two or more forms of procedural justice or law. The terms 'law' and 'justice' are used as separate entities because for many people, state or formal law is not the same as justice. The term 'procedural justice' denotes a process through which justice can be sought. This model prevails over other initiatives operating to provide justice fitting special criteria or needs; the needs created by difference. Other initiatives are comparatively un-resourced and do not possess the coercive power of the dominant model. As a result they are comparatively marginalized. Some believe the state is the best and possibly the only hope for maintaining democracy, human rights and the rule of law Twining (2010).

Twining (2010) described it as similar to multiculturalism using Webster's (1981) explanation where diverse ethnic, social and cultural interests co-exist and develop together. With legal pluralism two or more individual legal orders exist in the same time and context, usually where one appears to be a dominant state law and others, non-state laws. The non-state laws take account of religious law and customary law, for example (Twining 2010). Legal pluralism challenges a view called 'state centralism' where the state is the only institution that contributes to social order. Twining explained that even though legal pluralism can be accepted in some circles, a milder form of state centralism still prevails (2010:7). This description may well apply to New Zealand, where there is some acceptance of indigenous 'lore' as opposed to the dominant 'state law', which I will illustrate later. This is, however, a delicate balance.

While there is much legal and academic discussion about legal pluralism, the most relevant concept to this chapter within legal pluralism is 'recognition', where a state accords recognition or acknowledges the existence of a non-state order without giving it legal status (Twining 2010). Instead, as will be seen in the case study, a judicial or administrative discretion is used at sentencing. As cited by Paliwala (2003), Derida (1992:39) separated law from justice, where law provides determinancy and the judge is the "calculating machine who placidly provides a good rule to a particular case". In other words, the judiciary administer the law. Fitzpatrick (1992) refers to the subordination of the law to administration, an important issue when considering judicial discretion, also discussed later on.

Notwithstanding the complexities of legal pluralism, victims and perpetrators in my 2010 research were quite straight forward in their response to my invitation to comment on the criminal justice system. Many comments were negative, including:

- *I have little faith in the jury system.* (Alice)
- *This is a huge machine that sometimes is not doing what it should be.* (Brenda)
- *It is very confrontational ... more attacking victims.* (Eileen)
- *It is unfair.* (Fraser)
- *The domestic violence court treats men like feral beasts who need to be controlled.* (Ian)
- *The family court is gender-biased.* (Lawrence)
- *The courts believed the lies of victims.* (John).

One key informant, a judge who was less than happy with the status quo, described the criminal justice system as being like a giant washing machine. He clearly saw advantages in a less formal system, and cited cases involving intimate partner violence where victims can recant. He commented:

> *We endlessly find that after a particular assault is over, in the majority of the cases, the female complainant will want to recant, in whole or in part. This can be as early as a few hours after the assault ... So, if prior to the assault, or during those hours, days even, before he appears in court, she knows that an RJ problem solving approach is the first approach to be considered, and that in the event of a positive outcome, any punitive result for him will be significantly reduced, she is much more likely to seek help in the first place.*

State law and legal pluralism is about power, in particular, macro power, which affects society from 'top-down'.

Power in Intimate Partner Violence

Power is a universal entity, affecting individuals as well as institutions. Thus, as well as working top down it also works bottom-up. Its parameters were described by Lipman-Blumen in the following way:

> *Power – seeking it, using it, abusing it, decrying it, coveting it, contesting and overthrowing it – is central to the human condition* (Jean Lipman-Blumen 1984)

This section discusses power at the macro and micro levels as it was experienced by participants in my (2010) research.

Power is integral to intimate partner violence and is typically considered to occur when one person in the relationship has, or exerts, more, power over another (Hayden 2010, 2014). As Foucault (1982) put it, power is part of our experience rather than a theoretical question. He distinguished between 'power over' and 'power to' when expanding our understanding of how both types of power work in modern society (Chesney-Lind and Pasko 2013, 136). There may be degrees of power. As Lipman-Blumen (1984) stated, once power is firmly established, where the capacity to reward or punish is clear, the powerful rarely need to resort to using it. Accordingly, if one accepts Lipman-Blumen's argument, it seems likely that continued or intermittent abuse by the abuser indicates some vulnerability of the abuser's power and/or control (Hayden 2014).

For a long time I have been interested in power, not in having it, but understanding it. While doing my doctoral research I noted that there were two broad types of power: micro and macro power. Clearly macro power involves institutions, both governmental and non-governmental agencies. Micro-power, on the other hand, concerns personal power, and power between individuals, which I called relational power. The most under-theorized type of power seemed to be 'personal power' (Hayden 2014). So I decided to interview a friend who I knew had lived with breast cancer for 24 years. If anything demonstrated personal power I thought that surely did. She was also a key informant and victim advocate as well as an actor and opera singer. Rather than having an academic or theoretical discussion I learned about her life with cancer and how she dealt with its various stages. From this discussion I concluded that personal power involved five processes. These were:

- Becoming informed about matters directly related to one's social, physical and emotional wellbeing
- Prioritising the most important aspects
- Making informed decisions about how priorities could become reality
- Taking responsibility for decisions made
- Involvement in outside/community activities (Hayden 2010, 2014).

Participants' experiences

The participants (both perpetrators and victims) in my research used power positively and negatively. Furthermore, power was exercised at both micro (relational and personal) and macro levels. One victim, Dudley told me about abusive relational power he experienced in the form of threats to his wellbeing by his same-sex partner:

> [T]*here were all sorts of threats hanging around and he would try and drive me out of my business ... he would shout and scream and abuse me whilst I was consulting.... he would equally bully and abuse my staff. He would bully me in front of clients ...* [once it got physical] *my business was at risk, my income was at risk, [and] my staff were at risk.* (Dudley)

As well as ending the relationship, Dudley used his personal power positively when he delivered important personal documents into the care of a friend one year before the relationship ended. Children were used as another form of power by both victims and perpetrators, sometimes by implementing a combination of relational and institutional or macro power. Some perpetrators experienced this in terms of custody and access to their children. How then, do we define victims and perpetrators? As well as discussing legal definitions, I list common stereotypes of these roles followed by critique which is supported by quotes and stories from participants in my (2010) research.

What is a Victim?

The New Zealand Victims' Rights Act 2002 states that a victim is a person against whom an offence is committed by another person, whether they suffer injury or not, and anyone who, through an offence committed by another person suffers physical injury, loss of or damage to property, directly or indirectly, or suffered any form of emotional harm. The definition of the victim also includes a person who has suffered emotional harm as a result of an offence, to enable them to have treatment and access to services (Ministry of Justice, 2009). *Directive 2012/29/EU of the European Parliament and of the Council (2012) in Article 2, specifies that a victim means: a natural person who has suffered harm, including physical, mental or emotional harm or economic loss which was directly caused by an offence, and family members of a person whose death was directly caused by a criminal offence and who have suffered harm as a result of that person's death.*

Taking a wider perspective of 'victim', Van Ness (2014) named four types of victims – direct and secondary victims, members of the community, and the State or public victim. As Strang (2012:5) citing Joutsen (1994) commented, "Inevitably the victim and the state hold different perspectives about the nature of the offence and the way it should be dealt with. To the victim it is a personal matter requiring repair of the harm suffered ....To the state it is a violation of criminal law."

What is a Perpetrator?

The literature on intimate partner violence and the criminal justice system refers to people who have committed one or more acts of intimate partner violence in a variety of ways. The terms *offender* and *perpetrator* appear to be used most frequently. Less frequently used are the terms *abuser, defendant* (a person who has been prosecuted)[3] and *suspect*. In New Zealand, an offender is a person convicted of a crime or offence that has affected a victim, and includes a person found guilty of, or who pleads guilty to, that crime or offence as per the New Zealand Victims' Rights Act 2002. Offending or wrongdoing under the Domestic Violence Act 1995 requires there to be violence from one person to another; however, it does not define victim or offender. There must, nevertheless, be a perpetrator of violence against a victim before there is a protection order issued by the Family Court.[4] Very serious intimate partner violence, such as common assault or male assaults female, is dealt with in the Criminal Court (Hayden 2010). Some examples provided below may show that the definition, in reality, is not so clearcut, especially when the fact that male assaults female is a more serious charge than common assault is taken into account. In other words, if a woman is found to have assaulted a man, she faces a lesser charge than a man who has assaulted a woman.

What are Some Common Assumptions about Victims and Perpetrators?

Stereotypical victims are regarded as usually they:

- Are weak
- Did nothing wrong
- Did not cause the wrongdoing
- Are innocent
- Want their perpetrators to be imprisoned or punished
- Are women in cases of intimate partner violence and sexual violence
- Do not want to influence outcomes
- Are not interested in restorative justice
- Have no power
- Do not use power negatively against the perpetrator
- Have no interest in the judicial process and outcome
- Need protection from information which may traumatise them
- Need decisions made for them
- Do not want to meet perpetrators, and,
- Do not include the family of the perpetrators.

A good example of a victim stereotype is Goodmark's (2014) statement that much of the literature about intimate partner violence paints a picture of "a subordinated woman in need of salvation"(2014: 2) where there is an assumption that all women subjected to abuse want or should want to separate from their partners.

Yet, when discussing restorative amnesty processes, Mallinder (2014) referred to Brewer's comments (2010) who stated that when space is made for dialogue between victims and offenders, encounters can show how victim and offender identities are "politically complex and overlapping" (154). Victims can and do become repeated aggressors in the same way former perpetrators can become victimized (Mallinder 2014).

Turning again to stereotypes, perpetrators are usually considered to be:

- Men
- Bigger and stronger than their victim
- Evil
- Unable to understand what it is like to be a victim
- Have no remorse
- Incapable of feeling anything
- Are angry
- Unable take responsibility
- Incurable or recidivist offenders
- Always to blame
- Always initiating the crime, and,
- Are more powerful than their victims.

I turn now to the data from my 2010 research. As stated above, victims are frequently regarded as weak and powerless. Before she separated, Gayle, a mother of two adult children might have been judged in this way. She stated

> [I]*t was more threats, intimidation, emotional abuse, verbal abuse ... If there had been a lot of real physical violence, then it [would have] been different. You know sometimes I'd think, you know, give me a good punch, I['d] have the scar, the black eye, the broken nose, whatever, and then I could go, you know?*

But was she weak and powerless? Certainly she was unaware of the parameters of the actual definition of intimate partner violence. However, she had also made a personal decision to remain with her children's father because she felt that was what was best for her children. Thus she had exercised her personal power in making that decision.

> *All along I tried to do what I thought was the best thing for the kids* [and] *that was to stay ... he does love the kids and he's spent huge amounts of time with them. Disrupting their whole lives ... seemed terrible.*

Another victim, Eileen, the mother of a seriously ill child, could also have been seen to be helpless. Again she had not identified what was happening to her which was unsurprising given her preoccupation with her ill child. Fortunately the medical team identified the abuse and referred her to the domestic violence team in the same health facility.

> [The domestic violence team] *really just told me how to deal with someone that's bullying and controlling ... they gave me strategies for dealing with text bullying and the emails ... and then we got the lawyers involved.*

Eileen made the decision to accept the advice given to her, thereby being assisted onto a path of independence, while still caring for her child. In other words, once she was informed she exercised her personal power and became proactive dealing with the abuse.

Heeni, a Māori woman who had had three children by her partner, a gang member addicted to methanphetamine, told me she did not report the violence because:

> *I hoped he won't do it. He's more verbal, very verbal ... it's like, we'll let him cool down and he'll be right after that. It's just one of his outbursts....* [If] *I was to make a call and say, "he is abusing me, come around." All those details would come out. "You rang the police on me." You might not get it right then, but eventually you're going to get it. It might not happen at that time, but down the track it's going to come back on you.... There's always been threats. "I'll kill you, cut you up, stab you." All of that. It's all there ... At the time you get told, "I'll poke you full of holes ...* [I]*n the back of your mind you know he's capable of it ... because knowing his history in his gang, it's like, "Yeah, you're capable of doing it" ... I could even be put in the boot and taken somewhere. I know that's possible because he carries a knife with him and has access to guns.*

Was Heeni weak and powerless? Although Heeni was very afraid of the consequences of reporting the violence to the police as well as the fact that it took her over twenty years for her to "take a stand", somehow she retained her self-worth, attained and enjoyed a very good job. She fed, clothed and raised their family on her salary and is still with her partner, some 25 years later. I cannot see this as weakness, rather more I interpret this as endurance or personal strength.

Another assumption about victims of intimate partner violence is that they are generally females. However, the most vulnerable victim in my research was Fraser. This was Fraser's second marriage and he had really wanted to it to work. But his second wife turned out to be abusive. He had been married to her for 24 years, during which time she abused him physically and psychologically. He explained her behaviour was due to her being sexually abused as a child.

On these occasions she rang the bank and credit card company and told them that she'd lost her credit cards, twice saying Fraser had stolen them. Basically, she controlled the purse-strings. His salary was put into her account. He was given $60 per week pocket money and she took $100. She needed more than him because she needed to buy makeup. Fraser had agreed to this arrangement as he did everything he could to please her.

Fraser's wife had other strategies of abuse. On four occasions, she rang the police and informed them she was being abused. When this happened she told Fraser what she'd done. He would wait for the police outside his house at the roadside. When they came, he showed them in, telling them they were coming in response to a call from his wife. After interviewing each party separately the police left, recording the case as an M1, involving a mentally unstable person (referring to his wife). On numerous occasions their two daughters were present but the police never considered them at risk of any abuse. This was despite them sometimes witnessing the altercations. To add to his distress, Fraser later learned that this contravened the provisions of the Domestic Violence Act 1995, by allowing the children to witness the abuse. Although there is no universal definition of child abuse, by definition, it involves the person who is entrusted with protecting a child, violating their position of power (Gavrielides 2012). Although Gavrielides was discussing child sexual abuse, the failure of Fraser and his wife to prevent their children witnessing her abuse to him was a violation of their position (see Gavrielides and Coker 2005). Although Fraser had a full-time job he was expected to cook dinner when he returned in the evenings. This was because his wife was busy homeschooling the children. If he was more than five minutes late due to heavy traffic she'd be furious. When he tried to explain this to the police, he advised, "[T]hey looked at me as though I was some sort of wimp".

Once *he* tried reporting the abuse to the police. In response to questioning, he advised that he was not in fear of his wife. The disbelieving policewoman responded, "You be a man, leave the house". No further support or advice was offered to him.

When Fraser finally left home, he suggested that he and his estranged wife go for mediation and/or counselling in order to come to an arrangement for access to his children. In response to this request, she took out a protection order against him, accusing him of violent behaviour. This was a means of preventing him from seeing the children. The application (which took 109 days to be heard, and cost him $17,000) was declined. No costs were awarded. Furthermore, according to Fraser, his wife alienated the children against him. He had not seen them for 299 days at the time of interview (Hayden 2010).

Fraser's story, which I have set out in more detail, illustrates a number of myths about victims and perpetrators in situations involving intimate partner violence. These are:

- Women are less abusive than men
- Men are stronger than women
- Previous victimhood is an excuse to become an abuser
- All allegations to the police are truthful
- Women never use power (macro or micro) against their partners
- Police assumed children witnessing abuse by a woman is not bad for them
- Intimate partner violence is physical and sexual abuse only
- Psychological abuse doesn't damage
- Men as victims do not need the same help as women
- The police and courts are fair and just.

Victims are usually regarded as innocent of any wrongdoing, or of having done something which led to the offending. This is especially so in intimate partner violence, where it is assumed that it concerns the actions of one person against another. A different perspective on this was discussed by Muftic, Bouffard & Bouffard (2007), where violence could occur when the victim acted as a direct precipitator of the crime, in other words, victim precipitation. They cited Wolfgang who in 1967 reported on his study of 588 homicides, to find that in 26% of these, the victim had been the first to use physical force. While the saying 'It takes two to tango' is out of favour, sometimes it is true. Heeni told me:

> *I couldn't help but be negative towards him. So I probably encouraged a backlash, caused us to fight more and the kids would see it.... And it was the kids who said, 'Mum, why do you do that?' and I said, 'It pisses me off Dad's on that shit again!'*

The context of the offending is important but is seldom adequately examined in the criminal justice system. In fact one key informant, a restorative justice practitioner, pointed out the need for judges to be more informed before making a referral to restorative justice:

> *I don't think the judges would have sufficient information re each person's reason for wanting restorative justice. Whether or not they are genuine and whether or not there has been coercion.*

The difficulty here is that the restorative justice process followed by a full report would probably be a better way for a judge to gain further insight into this and other issues such as the context of the offending and what the victim's wishes were. This is illustrated in the case study, Harawira, discussed below.

Another victim, Christine, relayed the incident which led to major violence from her partner. They had arranged to meet in the large carpark at the casino after work. Although she had searched for him in the carpark and the casino thoroughly for about 45 minutes, he was not to be seen. She decided to drive home. He was extremely angry to see she had already left and had to take a taxi. On his arrival he lashed out at her. She subsequently called the police. Around the time of interview she was arranging to take out a protection order against him. As a result of taking this action she said:

> *"And I felt SO in control, I was absolutely removed from him and there was no emotion left in me.... I think it unnerved him a little bit because he was used to being so in control, and now I was totally in control and absolutely pulling the strings."*

Accordingly, even though she had precipitated the offending, as the victim of violence she reported his violence towards her. This was very empowering. Of particular interest was her account that the policewoman who visited her gave her 24 hours to decide whether she still wished to press charges without advising her either way. This was also empowering as the police did not decide for her. Interestingly, my research showed that the variations in power and its applications at either macro or micro levels by victims and perpetrators, or, indeed, a combination of these, supported the concept of victim precipitation (Muftic, Bouffard and Bouffard (2007).

The one victim, Alice, who was completely opposed to the use of restorative justice for intimate partner violence stated,

> *The support's there, but once you leave that controlled situation, what happens when you go home with the person? ...* [If restorative justice] *was something that was a matter of course ... that if someone* [was aggressive] *towards someone, they saw* [restorative justice] *as, "Well, if I'm repentant, this system will see me through without a severe penalty ... All I have to do is make the right noises and I'll come out the other end."*

This poses a necessary challenge to practitioners to ensure that their assessment and preparation of participants is sound (see Hayden, 2012).

A common understanding about intimate partner violence is that it is usually violence against women by men. Barnett, Miller-Perrin and Perrin (2011: 46-7) explained this in part when they described the patriarchal nature of the US anti-violence movement, where men hold the greater power and privilege in the social hierarchy than do women. Similarly, Chesney-Lind and Pasko (2013) pointed out that in general, men have been able to exert greater structural power than women whereas women have tended to exercise more power in relational and transformative ways. Barnett et al, however, also cited Heggen 1996, saying that the socialization of acceptance of male dominance unfortunately contributes to a certain moral disengagement about females who abuse. We women, therefore, are not always the passive victims some would have us believe. But our acknowledgement of this has some way to go.

People are classified within the judicial process as being either victim or perpetrator, yet there are situations where it is not clear who is the victim and who is the perpetrator, or even when their designated role is wrong. Included in my perpetrator group of participants was an Iranian man called Kaveh. His wife physically fought back because he insisted they separate. She had hit him and he responded by holding her wrists up against the wall so that she could not hit him again. Within 24 hours she laid a complaint to the police that he had abused her. He spent thousands of dollars defending himself in both the Family and Criminal Courts and even though the case was dismissed in the Criminal Court, he still lost unsupervised access to his daughter. Kaveh's case was, as far as I could tell from hearing only one side of the story as well as viewing relevant documentation, an abuse of power. This case highlights the need for greater information being available to decision-makers after offending has occurred. Even though Kaveh was officially in the perpetrator group of participants, he was really a victim in more ways than one.

As far as perpetrators being evil is concerned, another man in the perpetrator group, Zeddy, admitted that he had been abusive to his partner and described his abuse in detail. However, by way of apology to his partner he attended an anger management group, where he learned about the impact of his violence. He then decided to become a leader in a similar group. As well as being a member of my perpetrator participants group I allocated him into my key informant group. His qualitative data only was used in this category. With his first hand experience as an abuser his contributions were particularly helpful. When discussing good practice for restorative justice processes, in particular the need to have support people for both the victim and perpetrator he made the following observation about screening all participants, including support people. He stated:

> *I'd be concerned the support person wouldn't know how to support, you know? One of the things we tell men when they're taking time out, and you need to leave the house, you don't go and talk to your mates.... No. it's the last thing you do. Because you'll all start, she did this, she did that. He'll start supporting that and you don't need extra support around that.*

This showed a remarkable transformation where he had taken responsibility for his own abusive behaviour and was instrumental in helping others take responsibility for theirs. His remorse could not, I believe, have led to a more proactive outcome.

A frequent counter-argument to the use of restorative justice for intimate partner violence is that victims do not want to face their partner again and are likely to be revictimized by their abuser. However, half of the eight victims believed that the availability of restorative justice would increase reporting and most wished they had known about the possibility of using restorative justice in the earlier stages of the abuse. Furthermore, an Asian woman, Brenda, commented that restorative justice would offer more to ethnic families, where the emphasis was on the family, rather than on the individual. She stated:

> *I think restorative justice is a very good platform, especially in the Asian culture because the thing is ... the shame aspect of it. You report the man, the woman gets chastised and criticized by the community because the community thinks, "This woman doesn't know ... she brings shame to the family." So if you have a process like restorative justice, where you have trained people who can equalize the power ... and make it a safe environment ...*

Although the New Zealand criminal justice system attempts to meet cultural needs, for example, by using translators, culture is deeper than language alone. The following case study illustrates this, along with the system's difficulties dealing with the indigenous traditions. In 1998 Arthur Harawira was involved in a serious event.

The Harawira Incident

A man from a high profile Māori family named Arthur Harawira claimed that a group of medieval martial arts practitioners engaged as part of a book launch threatened the honour of his ancestors. This led him to take steps to prevent this from occurring. Despite his attempts through official channels to persuade the organisers not to hold an enactment on Narrow Neck Beach, Auckland, Harawira was unable to effect a change of plan. The beach had a *rahui* on it, meaning it was sacred because the bones of his ancestors or *tupuna* were being washed up on its shores. His only recourse, in his view, was to physically prevent them from landing on the beach.

In the meantime the practitioners playing the role of the Spanish newcomers had no inkling of these events and concerns. They found themselves in a situation they could not have predicted, that is, being assaulted by two Māori men armed with *taiaha* or long hardwood weapons.

The event led to considerable involvement of both the criminal justice system and restorative justice service providers. A number of charges were made and court appearances were frequent and highly publicised. Initially Harawira was recorded as having pleaded 'not guilty'. Refusing to recognise the authority of the court over the issue, he wanted a culturally suitable venue and the matter to be heard by his peers rather than the judiciary (Tie, 1999: 1). His 'not guilty' plea was withdrawn, and a restorative justice conference was suggested and agreed to by the court. The restorative justice conference took place on a *marae* or meeting area (Ryan 1997) at the suggestion of the victims and concluded with agreed resolutions. Harawira apologised for his actions after explaining in detail his reasons. His explanation was understood and his apology accepted. Harawira undertook to refund expenses for equipment damaged in the incident and to conduct regular classes about Tikanga Maori for the victims who wished to learn more.

Upon reporting back to the court after the restorative justice conference a 'guilty' plea was not entered until immediately prior to sentencing, when Harawira admitted he was "guilty of defending the honour of his *tupuna*". Even though the police sought a deferred sentence, the judge discharged Harawira under section 19 of the Criminal Justice Act, on the grounds that "All ...the parties seem to have resolved the outstanding issues between themselves" (Police v Harawira (CRN 7044015290-98)) noting that had resolution not occurred a sentence of imprisonment would have been involved.

To summarise then, a Māori man challenged the dominant criminal justice system stating the matter needed to be dealt with in an environment appropriate to his indigenous needs. Although Harawira was by no means the first to do this, the resolution, the means by which it was attained and confirmed by the formal system of law, was significant. It provided an example of legal pluralism, and how accommodations can be made between models of law and/or procedural justice.

Harawira as an Example of Legal Pluralism

As stated earlier in this chapter, formal or state law often finds itself accompanied by alternative forms of procedural justice, which have different priorities and foci. The most prominent in New Zealand are *marae* justice and restorative justice. The former relates particularly to Harawira's indigenous identity as Māori, the second to a community-based alternative form of procedural justice. These have potential to work instead of, alongside or within the criminal justice system.

The Harawira case illustrates the potential of alternative initiatives to meet needs of cultural identity and tradition and how they can be seen to, on the one hand, challenge formal law, and on the other, enhance it. Their roles can be described as 'counter-hegemonic'.[5] Both *marae* justice and restorative justice epitomise the development or resurrection of ideological movements and each provide for difference.

Not surprisingly, New Zealand's history as a British colony is a crucial element in the Harawira case, along with the relationship between the law and administration of this country. The Westminster System derived from Britain is to provide checks and balances through the separation of three powers or components; the Legislature, which has the power to make laws; the Executive, which includes the Cabinet, politicians with the power to vote in law to be signed by the Queen; and the judiciary who are subordinate to the law, but not to Cabinet. When considering the needs of the indigenous people like Harawira, it is necessary to examine the most relevant normative structure to Harawira's culture, *'tino rangatiratanga'*, or 'full chieftainship' over their tribal land (Orange 1987: 154).

Meaning more than possession, and including the exercise of power, authority and jurisdiction, *tino rangatiratanga* had been used in the 1835 Declaration of Independence to refer to New Zealand's independence as it was acknowledged by the British (ibid.:154). Orange reports that Māori agreed to sign the Treaty of Waitangi mainly because it guaranteed their *rangatiratanga* over their lands, forests, fisheries and "other prized possessions" (for example independence to manage their own disputes). The Native Land Purchase Ordinance of 1846, however, was described as the first step in the negation of the Treaty, indicating government firmness in its dealings with Māori, presumably to bring them firmly within the compass of British law (ibid.: 105-6). Accordingly, Māori believing they had retained their rights of chieftainship or authority over their own when the Treaty was signed, soon discovered that this was being taken away from them.

Case law concerning present day challenges to the Court by Māori stating they "...have a customary right to be tried by their own people according to their own law and in accordance with *tikanga*" (The Queen v Knowles CA 146/98), has shown little encouragement for such claims. This is because the New Zealand Constitution Act 1852 (UK) which allowed for customary rights provided the Queen sent written patents to support this, was apparently never endorsed. The same Act was repealed by the Constitution Act 1986 and rendered more powerless by the Statute of Westminster 1931 (The Queen v Knowles CA 146/98). Subsequent amendments to the 1852 Act have bestowed upon the New Zealand Parliament the power to make laws, under which people, including Māori, are charged. Almost one hundred and fifty years from the enactment of the New Zealand Constitution Act, 1852, the Harawira incident occurred, and Harawira made another attempt by Māori to effect change, and to claim back what he considered was a customary right.

At this juncture I will bring the discussion back to my question of what was being challenged by Harawira, the law or the state. To address the first part, *tino rangatiratanga* as it has been explained previously, shows that it was not simply the law of the land being challenged; it was the state or that entity that had diminished the *rangatiratanga* (or in this case, 'prized possession' of independence in dispute management) of his people. *Tino rangatiratanga* would have provided a situation where the spirituality aspects of the incident could be understood, considered and a fair outcome achieved. Turning now to the second issue, Fitzpatrick noted that "for all the limits on law's ability to subordinate administration, it does retain a capacity to do so but one that is not testable" (Fitzpatrick, 1992: 157). This, he argued, is because the legal terms in which "control" of administration is effected are indefinite, characteristically taking the form of "open judicial discretion" (ibid.:157).

The grey area implicit in Fitzpatrick's writing seems to transform into black and white in case law. In Warren v the Police, AP 133/99, among seven firm principles contained in legal precedents on this issue, the following were most relevant to Fitzpatrick:

> *" [d] The Courts of New Zealand must uphold the legislation enacted by the New Zealand Parliament;*
> *[e] The Courts of New Zealand are subservient to the Parliament of New Zealand."*

That there is an element of compulsion and judicial subservience to Parliament is clear (Tie (1999). Significantly, Harawira's sentencing notes by the judge made no comment about the Treaty of Waitangi, even though, according to Tie (1999: 1) Harawira refused to recognise the authority of the court. It could be argued that the judge made a decision based on common sense. The matter was resolved. From this one must ask whether the omission of the Treaty of Waitangi was a deliberate omission which allowed the Judge to bypass case law, exercising his discretion instead. I now turn to Tie's interpretation of the tensions apparent in the courtroom at the time of sentencing. Tie stated;

> *To this end, the Harawira case was ultimately dominated by the police's adjudication of the tension that had developed between the mediation and judicial processes and, more specifically, by its adjudication in favour of judicial power. The former had been initiated to resolve the conflicts surrounding the offending incident while the latter had, itself, initiated the mediation process in order to de-escalate the challenge which the case mounted to the constitutional authority of law. It is not surprising that the police, as the key institution through which New Zealand's liberalist political and economic power functions, retained the charges, thereby marking the offending incident as a crime committed by a pathological individual against society rather than as an expression of long-standing inter-ethnic division...exemplif(ying) the manner in which policing institutions play a significant role in determining the fortunes of alternative forms of law.* (Tie, 1999: 258-9).

My analysis differs from Tie's, and it rests on the identity of the parties to the tension Tie ascribed to the mediation and judicial processes. It is true that tension was present, however not between the judicial process and the restorative justice process (which he called mediation). The restorative justice group was represented to assist the court with further information over and above the report, as required. The judge congratulated the group and everyone involved on the manner in which the incident was resolved. Furthermore on page 2 of the sentencing notes the judge stated:

> *"The Police seek a deferred sentence. With all respect to Inspector ... I do not know what that is going to achieve. All of the parties seem to have resolved the outstanding issues between themselves.... Had this matter not been resolved in this way it is quite likely that a sentence of imprisonment would have been involved but it is far better that the healing process that has been undergone was adopted and has been successful. I do not see the need for any further action on the part of the Court."* (Police v Harawira CRN 7044015290-91).

The foregoing judgement paints a different picture, rather that the tension was between the state, represented by the inspector and the potential for judicial discretion which did not support the state's point of view. In Fitzpatrick's terms, the state opposed the "law's ability to subordinate administration" (Fitzpatrick, 1992: 157) or the juridical power being exercised by the judge. The "open judicial discretion" (ibid.:157) was being challenged by the state representative because Harawira was testing the state, rather than formal law, as has already been discussed. Because the judge's discretion appeared likely to favour the resolution obtained through the restorative justice process, tension was extended from the state representative to the restorative justice practitioners present in the Courtroom. It became a matter of the power of the 'uniform' of the state within the judicial setting, versus the facts portrayed by the counter-hegemonic restorative justice group. Defending the territory of the state, the inspector's opposition to the restorative justice group representatives who were partly instrumental to the resolution, he probably enhanced the likelihood of judicial discretion being exercised. For obvious reasons, the inspector's approach to the judiciary, although pragmatic, was couched with more deference.

Did the restorative justice group, as a counter-hegemonous entity take the role as supportive of the formal law of the state, or did it oppose it? In my opinion it was supportive rather than oppositional for the following reasons: the restorative justice group was asked by Harawira's legal representative of the day to explore the possibility of a restorative justice conference and the court agreed to this; the conference was able to provide more social information to the court to enable it to make its decision in a more informed way; and finally, the court, as quoted above, praised the participants for a good outcome and a "de-escalat(ion) (of) the challenge which the case mounted to the constitutional authority of law" (Tie, 1999: 258-9).

Arguably the incident at issue and Harawira's challenge to the state became secondary to what could be described as a double threat to the state, of 'insubordination' by both the judicial discretion and the restorative justice group. This raises another conjectural but significant question. In sociological terms is 'judicial discretion', which is not within the control of the state and is independent, a structured form of counter-hegemony? If so, is this form of counter-hegemony a tool for maintaining the checks and balances as summarised under the overview of the Westminster System discussed above? Is this also a potential tool for a more balanced and fair criminal justice system?

Less positive about one counter-hegemonic concept, Tie expressed concern restorative justice has the potential to marginalize those who wish to promote the Treaty of Waitangi as a political reality rather than a legal one. He described a third "class of actors (that) vies for the power to specify the relationship of the Treaty to the constitution"[6] supporting "the judicial view that the force of the Treaty lies beyond law" (Tie, 1999:256). Marginalisation, he states, will prevent New Zealand's law from being reconfigured in keeping with the cultural beliefs and norms of the third class (ibid.:256-8). He used Harawira as an example of this, stating that the critical issue became the status of the formal charges (ibid.:259). This was in contrast with the refusal to accept the jurisdiction of the court. Accordingly, the Harawira case supported Tie's marginalisation argument.

The Harawira case warrants closer examination of this concern, in ways somewhat different to those stated by Tie. As stated earlier, the Harawira sentencing notes made no acknowledgement of the political nature of Harawira's stance. It could be argued that the restorative justice conference made this omission possible, arriving as it did, at a resolution the Judge found satisfactory and warranting the use of his discretion. This certainly exemplifies Tie's suggestion of marginalisation of Treaty issues, of the politics behind Harawira's refusal to accept the jurisdiction of the court. However, it also lends itself to an argument that the notion of the judicial discretion can be used to assist cultural needs being met under, beside or in cooperation with formal law. Obviously this is provided judicial discretion is accepted as an instrument of counter-hegemony, itself a political concept. In Harawira, judicial discretion played a role as a 'check and balance' of the formal legal system's handling of the case. This is not to negate the thrust of Tie's expressed concern of marginalisation, rather it is to show that other ways exist already, to meet indigenous needs. It is important to acknowledge, however that they are not of an overt political nature as desired by the "third class", instead the judicial discretionary process is more subtle and unpredictable.

Harawira demonstrated that legal pluralism is a reality in New Zealand. An event of spiritual significance to Harawira, and criminal offending according to the formal legal system led to a situation of encroachment of the formal law. The encroachment took place as a result of counter-hegemony. This was represented in two, possibly three forms: by an indigenous individual refusing to acknowledge the authority of the court over the issue, by a group offering a different form of justice, restorative justice, and possibly by an example of judicial discretion which took precedence over the wishes of the state representative, and, indirectly previous case law. However, Harawira demonstrated the power of judicial discretion and how restorative justice and judicial discretion are instruments for dealing with difference. The case also showed how the needs of difference can be met by counter-hegemony in an environment of social change.

The word 'difference' is relevant to justice and fairness. Broadly speaking, the ideal posed by this book is a different criminal justice system, one which deals with victims first or at least is led by the interests of victims. 'Difference' also relates to different understandings of what or who are victims and perpetrators. Clearly Harawira, as well as being a perpetrator, was a victim, a man deeply distressed by the idea of his *tupuna* being dishonoured. He had tried using legal means of preventing this from happening. One could also argue that he was victimised by colonialism, through the loss of his right to be accountable through customary process or lore. The police charges gave no quarter to either of these issues. Furthermore, his cousin who was the other party in the incident was a victim, along with other members his *whanau*/family affected by the media frenzy. Some recognition of his victim status was possibly reflected in use of judicial discretion, although the judge did not acknowledge this in sentencing. How could 'recognition', another important word previously discussed in my discussion about legal pluralism, occur and what could its impact be? A possibility is a criminal justice system with another focus from being offender-centred, that is, rights-centred. This is not the same as a victim-led criminal justice system, however it includes victims' rights as a group deserving of recognition of their human rights.

Human Rights

I will briefly set out the provision of one of the many international instruments promoting human rights, before addressing key legislation from New Zealand. One of the purposes and principles of the United Nations Charter, in Article 1(3) provides for the:

> *promot*[ion] *and encourag*[ment of] *respect for human rights and for fundamental freedoms for all without distinction as to race, sex, language, or religion.*
> (http://www.un.org/en/documents/charter/chapter1.shtml)

Another important instrument is the European Convention on Human Rights (ECHR). This international treaty was formed to protect human rights and fundamental freedoms in Europe and came into force in 1953. The Convention established the European Court of Human Rights ((ECtHR), which is an avenue for anyone who feels their rights have been violated under the Convention to have them dealt with at the Court. Although rarely used, State parties can also take other State parties to the Court (Wikipedia). http://en.wikipedia.org/wiki/European_Convention_on_Human_Rights (see also Gavrielides, 2012)

New Zealand has a Commission for Human Rights where Commissioners are required to promote understanding of measures to ensure equality, of indirect discrimination, to promote education, including a better understanding of the Treaty of Waitangi and their relationship with domestic and international human rights law (Human Rights Act 1993 5 (2) (c) and (d)). Commissioners are also required to promote and encourage understanding and compliance with the New Zealand Bill of Rights Act 1990. Among other things, this Act provides for freedom from discrimination (section 19) and relevantly, the rights of minorities (section 20) which states:

> *A person who belongs to an ethnic, religious or linguistic minority in New Zealand shall not be denied the right, in community with other members of that minority, to enjoy the culture, to profess and practice the religion, or use the language of that minority.*

The New Zealand Victims Rights Act 2002 requires that victims be treated with courtesy and compassion; and their dignity and privacy respected (Part 2, 7 (a) & (b). The same legislation also provided that victims may participate in decision-making processes.

Each of the above human rights provisions gives certain guidance to human rights which require consideration in the development of a rights-centred criminal justice system.

What could a Rights-centred Criminal Justice System look like?

A rights-centred criminal justice system should adopt the human rights principles cited above in conjunction with the principles of justice. Recognition of difference must be an integral part allowing for indigenous or non-state processes for other cases such as has been illustrated by the Harawira case. Stated objectives of the criminal justice system should include:

- Decisions to charge, convict or discharge a perpetrator should be made on *full* information to the court or its officers
- Full information about options for victims and perpetrators should be made readily available, including information about restorative justice, or culturally appropriate forums
- The resolution of issues or conflict to be prioritised over retribution
- The use of judicial discretion to be used as a counter balance to the autocracy of the state, and,
- As with perpetrators, victims should have access to state-funded legal advice.

Relevant legislation should include a phrase which amends the definition of a victim or a perpetrator to state that they are victims irrespective of their gender, age, class or ethnicity, and should include families of perpetrators as possible victims. Anyone who uses force or violence, including psychological violence, whether or not they present as the victim, needs to be considered a perpetrator. Perhaps when offending involves both parties they should be acknowledged as co-perpetrators, for example in situations like intimate partner violence where the violence is mutual. Similarly they can be categorized as co-victims. In such cases restorative justice by appropriately skilled service providers should be given serious consideration.

Because of the gatekeeping role of police,[7] initial interviews of the offending party and the victim could each be conducted by a police representative accompanied by a community representative such as a restorative justice facilitator, social worker, counsellor, friend of the court or psychologist. Taped recordings should also be taken of each account of the incident(s). This would also allow for both accounts of context related to the offending to be available when decisions are made whether to charge someone, as well as to gain an awareness of safety, accommodation or other needs of either or both parties. As part of this interview and as appropriate, it would be useful to request an indication from each as to what they hope the outcome to be. It could also be appropriate to allow each party from 24 hours or longer, as fitting, to confirm or change their mind. Like perpetrators, victims need to have state funded legal advice (Hayden 1996)[8] and representation as necessary.

Police and court personnel need to be trained to be prepared for the unexpected, to not look for stereotypical responses or situations, and to treat all people carefully and respectfully. In other words to be aware of the grey aspects of human nature, rather than seeing the black and white of stereotypes in regard to gender and who did what to whom and why. The same personnel and others working in the field must ensure that all parties are told, without bias, about restorative justice or other culturally appropriate forums as possible means of reaching a resolution.

To provide monitoring and accountability of the criminal justice system, a Commissioner of Criminal Human Rights should be appointed who shall:

- Promote a culture of reasonableness and resolution in the criminal justice system
- Ensure publicity about human rights in criminal settings is freely available possibly through the use of volunteer friends of the court
- Resource allocation is reviewed and monitored on the basis of submissions received from government on non-governmental agencies
- Ensure all funding allocated to each of the victim and perpetrator groups is used for its designated purposes[9]
- Investigate any complaints by victims, perpetrators, their representatives or any personnel relating to a criminal justice process where there is a perceived violation of human rights.

As stated above, Harawira illustrated the subtlety and power of judicial discretion for catering for difference, or in his case, the act of allowing him (albeit to a limited extent) the freedom to use a more culturally appropriate forum to address his behaviour. Therefore I believe the use of judicial discretion should be broadened to include the following criteria:

- That both victims and perpetrators have had their say about the incident and how they feel about outcomes proposed and/or agreed to
- That the judge can have a meeting with both or either party as necessary
- That any *full* restorative justice or community meeting report about a conference is taken into account
- That there are reasonable consequences for each party as appropriate
- That the judge ensures no stereotypical view is part of his or her motivation for using judicial discretion.

On that idealistic note I will conclude this chapter.

Conclusion

When I started writing this chapter I was committed to writing about a victim-led criminal justice system. It seemed to be a great idea. However as I proceeded, it became clear that what was necessary was balance, an objective restorative justice endeavours to attain after a crime has been perpetrated and referral received. It seems to me that to revert from a offender- led criminal justice process to victim-led system is not going to create balance; instead it could simply reverse the scales, still leading to dissatisfaction, but from a different quarter. The discussion about stereotypes, with examples, shows that it is not always straight forward as to who is the victim and who, the perpetrator. Zeddy, Fraser, Heeni, Gayle, other participants in my research (2010) and Harawira, showed how accepting stereotypes as a given is, or can be, damaging to individuals, the community and as a result, the State. It is necessary therefore, to be aware that there are occasions when an individual can be both victim and perpetrator during the presenting incident or historically. Therefore prioritizing one party, the victim, could easily lead to an exacerbation of the situation, especially in matters involving intimate partner violence.

One key informant in my research, a restorative justice facilitator and a lawyer, told me he thought restorative justice "should not be anyone centred". This makes sense. To take this further, what is necessary is a people focus, or as I have argued, a rights-centred criminal justice system. Judicial discretion is a powerful tool which could be used to ensure that human rights are met. This should be reinforced by the appointment of a Commissioner for Criminal Human Rights. All this is unashamedly idealistic, but without ideals, necessary societal changes for the better cannot take place.

Notes

1 I was a member of *Te Oritenga* Restorative Justice Group, the first contemporary restorative group in New Zealand.

2 All participants' names, except Arthur Harawira, are pseudonyms to protect their privacy. Harawira's case was highly publicised, making his story identifiable.

3 Personal communication with Catherine Gardner, New Zealand Police, 12 March, 2010.

4 Personal communication from Judge David Mather, 16 March, 2010.

5 'Hegemony' is explained in Marxist terms as the "ideal representation of the interests of the ruling class as universal interests" (Marshall, 1998). Thus, counter-hegemony opposes or challenges the dominance of the ruling class.

6 The word "constitution" as far as New Zealand is concerned has two meanings in the present context. The first is a literal meaning, where it is depicted as non-existent in New Zealand eg. "Like other states using the Westminster system, New Zealand has no written constitution per se. Two important documents are the Treaty of Waitangi and the Bill of Rights Act" (NZGO website http://www.govt.nz/nzgovt/parli.php3). The second is one of common usage where there is a body of laws known as the constitution of New Zealand. Another common phrase is "constitutional law".

7 See Hayden (2013) in *Reconstructing Restorative Justice Policy* edited by Gavrielides, Artinopoulou. Ashgate, Surrey.

8 In my Winston Churchill Fellowship report (1996) I made the following recommendations, inter alia: 15. Procedures are developed for the implementation and monitoring of sound briefing of victims, including any legal right they might have to veto proposals, prior to any form of restorative justice ... 37. State-funded legal counsel for victims is appointed to courts (Hayden 1996).

9 As part of my Churchill Fellowship research I returned with an impressive Homicide Survivors Information Pack from the UK. I gave it to a senior police inspector with a view for it being a precedent for a NZ version. This never happened, and the following year I learned that several million dollars had been returned to Government from the Victims budget, unused.

10 See also Gavrielides 2012.

References

Artinopoulou, V. and Gavrielides, T. 2013. *Aristotle on restorative justice: Where the restorative justice and human rights movements meet in Reconstructing Restorative Justice Philosophy* edited by T. Gavrielides and V. Artinopoulou. Ashgate Publishing: Furnham, UK, 25-47.

Barnett, O., Miller-Perrin, C. and Perrin, R. 2011. *Family Violence Across the Lifespan*. Sage, 3rd edition, California.

Brewer, J. 2010 *Peace Processes: A Sociological Approach*. Cambridge, Polity.

Chesney-Lind, M. and Pasko, L. 2013. *Girls, Women and Crime: selected Readings*. Sage, 2nd edition, California.

Curtis-Fawley, S., & Daly, K. 2005. Gendered violence and restorative justice: The views of victim advocates. *Violence Against Women*, 11(5), 603-638.

Derrida, J. 1992 *Force of Law: The Mystical Foundations of Authority*. trans. Mary Quittance In Cornell.

Fitzpatrick, P. 1992. *The Mythology of Modern Law: Sociology of Law & Crime*. Routledge: London.

Fletcher, G. P. 1996. *Basic concepts of legal thought*. New York: Oxford University Press.

Gavrielides T. and D. Coker 2005. Restoring Faith: Resolving the Catholic Church's Sexual Scandals through Restorative Justice, *Contemporary Justice Review*, 8:4, 345-365. ISSN 1028–2580 (print) /ISSN 1477–2248 (online).

Gavrielides, T. 2012. Bridging Restorative Justice and Human Rights for Youth Justice, in *Rights and Restoration within Youth Justice*, edited by T. Gavrielides. de Sitter Publications, Whitby.

Gavrielides, T. 2012.. Clergy Child Sexual Abuse & the Restorative Justice Dialogue, *Journal of Church and State*, 55 (4). 617 – 639.

Hayden, A. 1996. "There is light at the end of the tunnel: Initiatives for victims of crime at a local, national and statutory level." Winston Churchill Fellowship Report,: Winston Churchill Memorial Trust Board, Wellington.

Hayden, A. 2000. Harawira: How Significant was This Case in Legal Pluralistic Terms? Unpublished essay.

Hayden, A., 2010. *Why Rock the Boat? Non-Reporting of Intimate Partner Violence*. PhD Thesis, Auckland University of Technology, Auckland.

Hayden, A. 2012. Safety issues associated with using restorative justice for intimate partner violence in *Women's Studies Journal*. Vol.26. No 2. Women's Studies Association of New Zealand, December 2012: 4-16.

Hayden, A. 2013. Gatekeeping in Restorative Justice and Related Research in *Reconstructing Restorative justice Philosophy*, edited by T. Gavrielides and V. Artinopoulou, Surrey, Ashgate Publishing, UK.

Hayden, A. 2014. Falling Prey to Power, Gatekeeping and Violence. Paper presented at Restorative Justice, Responsive Regulation and Complex Problems, University of Vermont, Burlington, Vermont, 15-18 July 2014.

Heggen, C. 1996. Religious Beliefs and Abuse. In *Women, Abuse and the Bible: How Scripture can be Used to Hurt or Heal*, edited by C. C. Kroeger and J.R. Beck. Baker Books Grand Rapids, MI, 15-27.

Honderich, T. 1995. The Oxford companion to philosophy. New York: Oxford University Press.

Joutsen, M. 1994. Victim Participation in Proceedings and Sentencing in Europe. In *International Review of Victimology*, 3: 57-67.

Johnstone, G. The Teachings of Restorative Justice, in *Reconstructing Restorative justice Philosophy*, edited by T. Gavrielides and V. Artinopoulou, Surrey, Ashgate Publishing, UK.

Jordan, C. 2004. Intimate partner violence: An examination of the interface. *Journal of Interpersonal Violence,* 19(12), 1412-1434. doi:10:1177/0886260504269697

Jülich, S. 2001. *Breaking the silence: Restorative justice and child sexual abuse* (PhD). Massey University, Albany, New Zealand.

Lipmen-Blumen, J. 1984. *Gender Roles and Power.* Prentice-Hall Incorporated.

Mallinder, L. 2014. Amnesties in Pursuit of Reconciliation, Peacebuilding, and Restorative Justice, in *Restorative Justice, Reconciliation and Peacebuilding*, edited by J. Llewellyn and D. Philpott. Oxford University Press, New York.

Marshall, G. 1998 *Oxford Dictionary of Sociology.* 2nd Edition. Oxford University Press, Oxford

Marshall, T. 1999. *Restorative justice: An overview.* London: Home Office.

McCold, P. Llewellyn, J. and Van Ness. 2007. *An Introduction to Restorative Peacebuilding.* Working Party on Restorative Justice, Alliance of NGOs on Crime Prevention and Criminal Justice. New York.

Ministry of Justice. 2009. *A focus on victims of crime: A review of victims' rights.* Wellington: New Zealand Government.

Muftic, L. R., Bouffard, J. A., & Bouffard, L. A. 2007. An exploratory analysis of victim precipitation among women arrested for intimate partner violence: Violent women or violent resistance? *Feminist Criminology,* 22(6), 753-774. doi:10.1177/0886260507300756

Nardin, T. 2006. International political theory and the question of justice. *International Affairs,* 82(3), 449-465.

Orange, C. 1987 *The Treaty of Waitangi.* Bridget Williams Books Limited, Dept of Internal Affairs, Wellington.

Paliwala, A. 2003. *Irresolutions of Modernity, Law, Nation and Empire: A Reading of Fitzpatrick's Modernism and the Grounds of Law in Conjunction with Hardt and Negri's Empire.* Law, Social Justice & Global Development.

Ryan, P. 1997. *The Reed Dictionary of Modern* Māori. Reed Publishing (NZ) Ltd.

Ruiz-Perez, I., Mata-Pariente, N., & Plazaola-Castano, J. 2006. Women's response to intimate partner violence. *Journal of Interpersonal Violence,* 21(9), 1156-1168.

Seuffert, N. 1996. Lawyering for women survivors of domestic violence. *Waikato Law Review: Taumauri* 4(1), 1-38.

Strang, H. 2002. *Repair or Revenge: Victims and Restorative Justice.* Clarendon Studies in Criminology, Oxford University Press, NY.

Tie, W. 1999. *Legal Pluralism: Toward a Multicultural Conception of Law.* Dartmouth: England.

Twining, W. 2010. Legal Pluralism 101. May 12. http://www.ucl.ac.uk/laws/academics/profiles/twining/Legal_Pluralism_101_2010.pdf

Van Ness, D. 2014. *Accountability in Restorative Justice, Reconciliation and Peacebuilding,* edited by J. Llewellyn and D. Philpott. Oxford University Press, New York.

Webster, M.1981. The Oxford English Dictionary.USA.

Wikipedia European Convention on Human Rights. http://en.wikipedia.org/wiki/European_Convention_on_Human_Rights[32]

Wolfgang, M. 1967. Victim-Precipitated Criminal Homicide in *Studies in Homicide* edited by M.Wolfgang, Harper & Row, New York. 72-87.

Young, W., & Morris, A. 1998. *Reforming criminal justice: Reflecting on the present and imagining the future.* Joint Augural lecture. Victoria University of Wellington. Wellington.

Zehr, H. 1990. *Changing lenses: A new focus for crime and justice.* Ontario: Herald Press.

Legislation

Constitution Act 1852 UK
Criminal Justice Act 1985
Constitution Act 1986
Human Rights Act 1993
New Zealand Bill of Rights Act 1990
New Zealand Victims Rights 2002

Sentencing Notes:

Police v Harawira (CRN 7044015290-98)
The Queen v Knowles (CA146/98)
Warren & Police (AP 133/99)

PART II:
SAFEGUARDING VICTIMS & EMPOWERING PROFESSIONALS: FIVE COUNTRY CASE STUDIES

RJE Training Session, delivered by IARS – June 2014, Bulgaria. © IARS

The Victims' Directive and the project Restorative Justice in Europe: Safeguarding Victims and Empowering Professionals: An overview

*Theo Gavrielides**

Abstract

By November 2015, all EU member states will need to have demonstrated that they have modified their domestic laws to give effect to the Directive 2012/29/EU "Establishing minimum standards on the rights, support and protection of victims of crime" (Victims' Directive). For the first time, restorative justice is explicitly regulated at the EU legal level, as the Victims' Directive aims to establish a baseline for its safe implementation across member states. This chapter aims to provide an overview of the Victims' Directive, while introducing the reader to the EU funded programme Restorative Justice in Europe: Safeguarding Victims and Empowering Professionals (RJE). RJE was carried out between December 2012 – November 2014 and it aimed to generate scientific results that will facilitate the implementation of the restorative justice related articles of the Victims' Directive in the five participating RJE countries (UK, Greece, Germany, Bulgaria and the Netherlands) and across the EU.

Introduction

According to the European Commission (EC), around 30 million crimes are committed in the European Union (EU) every year.[1] The fundamental EU principle of free movement suggests that independently of their location, EU citizens must be protected consistently across the Union. It also means that minimum standards must be applied in the provision of appropriate victim services once a crime has been committed against them. And yet, this consistency has not been achieved.

However, this is not surprising given that traditionally, the victim has occupied a marginal position in criminal proceedings independently of whether these are carried out under the inquisitorial or adversarial traditions.[2] Schafer claimed, "if one looks at the legal systems of different countries, one seeks in vain a country where a victim of crime enjoys a certain expectation of fully restitution for his injury" (1970: 117). According to Gavrielides (2011), victims were not always marginal in the pursuit of

* Dr. Theo Gavrielides (Founder and Director of Independent Academic Research Studies, Co-Director of the Restorative Justice for All Institute, Visiting Professor at Buckinghamshire New University and Adjunct Professor at Simon Fraser University, School of Criminology), Unit 14, Dock Offices, Surrey Quays Road, Canada Water, London SE16 2XU, UK, T.Gavrielides@iars.org.uk +44(0)20 7064 4380.

justice and that they lost their place in the system of criminal justice only during the second period of the Middle Ages. This change is documented in Geis' work (1977). There, he used historical examples to show that it was during the Middle Ages, when kings established their power and took the conflict-solving process away from the parties involved by creating a firm 'State'-controlled criminal justice system. For instance, in the Anglo-Saxon hemisphere, after the division of the Frankish Empire by the treaty of Verdun in 843 AD, restitution was replaced by a fine payable not to the victim, but to the king. Pollock and Maitland said that one justification that was used for these changes was: "The wrong done to an individual extends beyond her own family; it is a wrong done to the community of which she is a member; and thus the wrong-doer maybe regarded as a public enemy" (1898: 47). Barnett (1977) also seems to agree that it was the increasing power of kingships as trans-local and trans-tribal institutions that repositioned the victim in criminal justice. This is mainly because they united the tribes and large areas, changing in this way the structure of societies from 'communitarian/tribal' to 'hierarchical/feudal'. Barnett (1977) claimed that what helped this to happen was the ecclesiastic law of that time. This claim is also supported by Tallack (1900), who noted that the ecclesiastical powers of the time aimed to exact a double vengeance upon the offenders by taking their property, and by applying corporal punishment or imprisonment, ignoring victims completely.

Founded upon the principles of "respect for human dignity, freedom, democracy, equality, the rule of law and respect for human rights" (Article 2, EU Treaty), in 1999, the EU progressed legislation in favour of victims so that they are gradually repositioned in the criminal process while aiming for minimum protection across members. The aim was simple and that was to make it explicit that victims are individuals whose basic human rights must be respected in the pursuit of justice. Given that victims remained in the margins of the criminal justice system since the Middle Ages, EC reforms that would move them to a more central position were expected to be difficult in their implementation.

According to the European Commission, people falling victim to crime have a range of needs, varying from victim to victim. To meet these individual needs, the Commission acknowledges that it is necessary that all victims are treated individually. However, the Commission proceeds to identify five broad categories of victims' needs:

- **respectful treatment** and **recognition** as victims, both within the justice system and more widely by society;
- **protection** both from intimidation, retaliation and further harm by the accused or suspected and from harm during criminal investigations and court proceedings, such as by avoiding repeated interviewing of the victim;
- **support**, including immediate assistance following a crime, longer-term physical and psychological assistance and practical assistance during proceedings to help victims understand, participate and to reduce their distress;
- **access to justice** to ensure that victims are aware of their rights and understand them both linguistically and legally, are able to provide additional information and to participate in proceedings; and
- **compensation** and **restoration**, whether through financial damages paid by the State or by the offender or through mediation or other form of restorative justice that allow victims to face the accused, with a view to reaching a voluntary agreement between them on how to repair the harm to the victim.

With the purpose of meetings the aforementioned needs and also in the hope of achieving consistency in victims' rights protection across the EU, in 2001, the Commission passed the Council Framework Decision 2001/220/JHA on the standing of victims in criminal proceedings. This provided for minimum rights, but it did not go far enough to protect victims' rights. Furthermore, due to the non-legislative nature of Framework Decisions, it was not able to grant rights that are enforceable in member states' jurisdictions. Almost 15 years later and we can safely claim that the Decision's intention for consistency in the implementation of victims' rights was not achieved.

Recognising this challenge, in 2009, the Stockholm Programme was adopted by the EC recognising that a coordinated and long-term strategy was needed under the leadership of the Commission so that members' national legislation is improved for victims' rights across the EU. This included a package of legislative proposals. In 2011, the EC passed a Resolution on a roadmap for strengthening the rights and protection of victims in criminal proceedings (the "Budapest Roadmap"). The Roadmap stated that the 2001 Framework Decision was out of date and that new legislation needed to be implemented to protect victims' rights. This resulted in the development and passing of the Directive 2012/29/EU of the European Parliament and of the Council establishing of minimum standards on the rights, support and protection of victims of crime ("Victims' Directive"). Once the transposition date of November 2015 has passed, member states must have implemented at least the Directive's minimum standards.

Since the passing of the Directive, the EC invested a considerable amount of resources in order to prepare member states for November 2015. This included the award of grants to EU-wide projects aiming to help with the Directive's implementation. This edited collection uses findings from one of these projects titled "Restorative Justice in Europe: Safeguarding Victims and Empowering Professionals" (RJE).[3] The project is led by the international UK-based think-tank Independent Academic Research Studies (IARS), and is carried out in 5 EU countries (UK, Germany, Bulgaria, Greece and the Netherlands). The four European partners are: Restorative Justice Nederland (Netherlands), Institute of Conflict Resolution (Bulgaria), European Public Law Organization (Greece), and University of Applied Sciences (Germany).

The purpose of this introductory chapter for Part II of the book is twofold. First, it will provide an overview of the Victims' Directive placing an emphasis on the restorative justice related articles. Subsequently, the chapter will give a descriptive account of the RJE project without getting into the methodological details and results of the individual country projects. This will be done in the subsequent chapters of Part II of this book.

The Victims' Directive: An Overview

The Directive 2012/29/EU of the European Parliament and of the Council of 25 October 2012 establishing minimum standards on the rights, support and protection of victims of crime, replacing Council Framework Decision 2001/220/JHA (the 'Directive') was published in the Official Journal of the European Union on 14 November 2012 (Victims' Directive). According to the EC, the general objective of the Directive is "to improve the real, day-to-day situation of millions of victims of crime across Europe to the greatest extent possible". Put another way, the core objective is to deal with victims' needs in an individual manner, based on an individual assessment and a targeted and participatory approach towards the provision of information, support, protection and procedural rights.

According to Article 27, all EU Member States must bring into force the laws, policies, practices, regulations and administrative provisions that are necessary to comply with the Directive by 16 November 2015. These measures will need to take into account existing good practices in the field of assistance and protection for victims. Obligations imposed on the Member States stemming from the Directive will demand transposition by a legislative instrument, while practical and technical implementation to achieve these objectives might be ensured by appropriate non-legislative measures.[4]

Furthermore, member States are expected to put in place a specific legal framework to enable individuals to recognise clearly their rights and obligations under this Directive. This framework will not exist in a vacuum, but must be constructed taking into account the general principles of EU law (e.g. equality and non-discrimination) and the Charter of Fundamental Rights. Moreover, it is necessary to recall the positive obligations and existing case-law standards of the European Court of Human Rights, which contains various references to victims' rights (e.g. access to justice, due process). Finally, a number of relevant international standards on victims' protection that have been developed by the United Nations and by the Council of Europe must also be considered.[5] The Directive aims to achieve two objectives:

- **1st**: To introduce new rights and obligations
- **2nd**: To strengthen rights and obligations that existed through the Framework Decision.

Table 1: New rights and obligations under the Victims' Directive

Family members of deceased victims are defined as victims and benefit from all rights in the Directive; family members of surviving victims have the right to support and protection. Family members are widely defined and include also non-married intimate partners.
Accessible and understandable information – All communication with victims must be made in a way that victims understand (linguistically or otherwise); an emphasis is made on child-sensitive communication.
Access to victim support – Member States must ensure access for victims and their family members to general victim support and specialist support, in accordance with their needs. The Directive specifies the basic level of services that need to be provided. Support is not dependent on the victim having reported the crime. Member States must facilitate referrals from police to victim support organisations.
Specialist support services must as a minimum provide shelters and targeted and integrated support for victims with specific needs, such as victims of sexual violence, victims of gender based violence and victims of violence in close relationships, including trauma support and counselling.
Review decision not to prosecute – Victims have the right to be informed about a decision not to proceed with prosecution of the offender and will also have the entirely new right to have such decision reviewed.
Individual assessment to identify vulnerability and special protection measures – All victims will be individually assessed to determine whether they are vulnerable to secondary or repeat victimisation or intimidation during criminal proceedings. If they have specific needs, a whole range of special measures will be put in place to protect them.

In its first article, the Directive makes its objective clear to all. The Directive aims to ensure that victims of crime receive appropriate information, support and protection and are able to participate in criminal proceedings equally, safely and fairly. Furthermore, in all contacts with victim support or restorative justice services, victims must be treated in a tailored, respectful, sensitive and non-discriminatory manner. The Directive makes it explicit that contrary to what has been the practice across the EU, the victim must now have a key role in criminal proceedings. Arguably, moving the victim from the margins to the centre of the criminal justice system is one of the most ground-breaking elements of this EU law and indeed an ambition that will be tested in time.

Table 2: Strengthening rights and obligations in the Victims' Directive

Information rights – Victims will receive a range of information from first contact with authorities. Victims will also receive information about their case, including a decision to end the investigation, not to prosecute and the final judgment (including the reasons for such decisions), and information on the time and place of the trial and the nature of the criminal charges.
Interpretation and translation - During criminal proceedings, victims with an active role have the right to interpretation and translation to enable their participation. Victims can challenge a decision not to receive interpretation and translation. All victims will receive a translation of the acknowledgement of their complaint.
Protection of all victims is reinforced – The privacy of victims and their family members must be respected and contact with the offender avoided (all new court buildings must have separate waiting areas).
Restorative justice safeguards –Victims who choose to participate in restorative justice processes (referred to as mediation in the Framework Decision) must have access to safe and competent restorative justice services, subject to some minimum conditions set out in the Directive.
Training of practitioners has become an obligation and emphasis is also put on cooperation between Member States and at national level and awareness raising about victims' rights.

Definitions and Conceptual Agreements

Definitions can be artificial and run the risk of becoming obsolete very quickly, particularly if they refer to continuously evolving concepts such as restorative justice. Therefore, our purpose here is merely to allow the consistent use of key terms throughout the book. It is also important to reflect on the research data as these were collected for the RJE project, using terms that are agreed here.

Restorative justice

A glance at the extant literature will render a number of definitions for restorative justice (e.g. see Marshall, 1999; Braithwaite, 2002; Gavrielides, 2008). Morrison (2006) argues that restorative justice has been conceived in two broad ways. One is a *process conception*; the other is a *values conception*. The process conception is characterized by a process that brings together all parties affected by harm or wrongdoing. It is generally accepted that RJ practices consist of direct and indirect mediation, family group conferences, healing/sentencing circles and community restorative boards (Bazemore & Walgrave 1998; Crawford & Newburn, 2003; Gavrielides, 2007). The values conception, on the other hand, is characterised by a set of values, or principles, that distinguish RJ from traditional punitive state justice.

For the purposes of this book, we will accept the definition of the Victims' Directive. "Restorative justice is any process whereby the victim and the offender are enabled, if they freely consent, to participate actively in the resolution of matters arising from the criminal offence through the help of an impartial third party" (Article 2, para 1.d).

Given what was stated above regarding the victim's journey and what led to its marginalisation in the criminal justice system, restorative justice seems to be offering an opportunity for equal participation that sits outside both the inquisitorial and adversarial criminal justice objectives. The role of the modern state and the hierarchical/ feudal systems of top down structures of justice are all reconsidered through these "new lenses" (Zehr, 1990).

Victim

According to the Victims' Directive, victim means: (i) a natural person who has suffered harm, including physical, mental or emotional harm or economic loss which was directly caused by a criminal offence; (ii) family members of a person whose death was directly caused by a criminal offence and who have suffered harm as a result of that person's death.[6]

'Family members' are the spouse, the person who is living with the victim in a committed intimate relationship (i.e. same - or different-sex), in a joint household and on a stable and continuous basis, the relatives in direct line (i.e. parents and children), the siblings and dependants of the victim (i.e. other than dependent children). The criterion 'committed intimate relationship, in a joint household and on a stable and continuous basis' presupposes close emotional ties and financial interdependence between two persons. In transposing and implementing the Directive, Member States should use inclusive definitions of 'family members' when it comes to the victim's partners. Interestingly, definitions should include spouses, as well as unmarried partners, regardless of whether the partners are in a registered civil partnership under its national laws on the recognition of unmarried couples, same-sex couples and same sex marriages.[7]

The application of the Directive in a non-discriminatory manner also applies to a victim's residence status. Therefore, rights set out in the Directive are not made conditional on the victim having legal residence status on their territory or on the victim's citizenship or nationality.[8] In relation to the cross-border compensation of crime victims (Directive 2004/80/EC) the definition of a victim is limited to a victim of an intentional violent crime.

Victim Support Services

The right to access victim support services (Article 8) is at the core of the Directive. The Directive defines them to include the provision of information, support and advice in relation to the victims' role in criminal proceedings including preparation for attendance at the trial. The services can be public or private, voluntary or professional. They must be provided to all victims free of charge, before, during and for a period after the criminal proceedings. It is important to note that these services must be provided even where there are no criminal proceedings underway. This ensures that victims who choose not to report a crime to the police can still access support services. The Directive stresses that advice and information should also be provided on specialist support services available, emotional and psychological support, and financial and other issues.

According to the Directive, victim support should be available from the earliest possible moment after a crime has been committed, irrespective of whether it has been reported. Victims may also require support during proceedings and for an appropriate period thereafter. For the first time, referrals to victims support services are formalized while they become a legal obligation for all member states. The EC acknowledges that the absence of a referral system is often a bottleneck for victims requiring proper support. Furthermore, victim's access to support is neither dependent on having made a formal complaint, nor conditional on the authorities launching a criminal investigation. This is particularly helpful for victims of domestic violence, repeat violence and hate crimes.[9]

Therefore, victims must remain free to choose whether to report a crime. This should not impact on the services they received and thus for referrals of victims and to facilitate reporting, a sound channel of cooperation between victim support services, police and judicial authorities is essential to create trust and efficient ways of collaborating. Not surprisingly, most victim support services in the EU are provided by NGOs working on a voluntary basis. Provisional information based on recent mapping of existing services shows there are general VSO services in 20 Member States[10] and only support for specific types/groups of victims in 8 Member States.[11]

Restorative Justice in the Victims' Directive

The main section covering restorative justice within the Victims' Directive is Article 12. Unlike what many within the restorative justice movement may have expected, this article does not intend to promote restorative justice. Its key objective is to introduce a right to safeguards in the context of restorative justice. In fact, when the article was being debated in the European Parliament, a number of NGOs and restorativists made submissions asking for a more positive approach towards restorative justice.[12] The primary concern remained the re-victimisation of the victim in the restorative justice process. More importantly, the Article does not oblige Member States to introduce restorative justice services if they do not have such a mechanism in place in national law. Indeed, the Court of Justice of the European Union (CJEU) has confirmed that Member States are not obliged to use mediation/restorative justice for all offences.[13]

It is worth pointing out that the article covers restorative justice whether this is attached to, running prior to, in parallel with or after criminal proceedings (pre-trial and post-trial). Furthermore, it may be available in relation to certain types of crime or only in relation to adult or child offenders and include for example victim-offender mediation, family group conferencing and sentencing circles.

The Directive encourages restorative justice practitioners to work closely with psychologists, psychiatrists, debt counsellors and child protection specialists acknowledging the holistic approach that restorative justice should take to restoring harm. Primary significance is given to the ability of the parties to give free consent, be duly informed of the consequences of restorative justice process, issues of confidentiality, access to impartial/neutral advice, the possibility to withdraw from the process at any stage, the monitoring of compliance with the agreement and the competence of practitioners. We must stress that the Directive assumes that any restorative justice process must also safeguard the fundamental procedural rights of the offender. Finally, similar to the expectations of creating referrals for victim support services, the Directive expects member states to establish referral arrangements for victims looking to participate in restorative justice measures. Again, these will need to be adapted to national circumstances.

One of the key ambitions of the Directive is to drive standards and quality in the delivery of victim services and of the criminal justice system including restorative justice. Therefore, Article 25 explicitly aims to regulate the training of practitioners who come in contact with victims including police, court staff, prosecutors, lawyers, judges, victim support and restorative justice services. According to the Directive, types of training include:

- For police officers and court staff, training on victims' rights and needs to become part of their basic training
- For lawyers, judges and prosecutors, victim awareness training should form part of the basic curriculum in law or bar school
- For all staff/volunteers within victim support and restorative justice services, victim awareness training must be provided. In fact, the Directive introduces a requirement for specialised victim awareness training to form part of the funding or service delivery agreement between the State and individual support organisation(s)
- Specialised courses regarding the rights and needs of victims of crime should also be offered as part of on-going professional development. Professionals could be encouraged to take part in training courses, including cross-disciplinary training, if, for instance, taking and completing specific victim awareness courses were a requirement for professional promotion and specific judicial positions.

The project Restorative Justice in Europe: Safeguarding Victims and Empowering Professionals

RJE's general objective was to produce scientific and practical results that will be directly used by victims, decision makers, policy makers and practitioners in their national implementation of the Victims' Directive. It was intended for the produced material to be evidence-based, reflecting the needs and wishes of victims and professionals. RJE's scientific and practical results were produced in English, Bulgarian, German, Dutch and Greek. In particular, RJE aimed to create an evidence base that can be used to:

- develop, pilot and implement protocols and guidelines for providing restorative justice in the interest of the victim and the offender with the aim of improving victims' safeguards in restorative justice services, and the consistent implementation of minimum standards throughout Europe
- develop, pilot and implement training materials and programmes for professionals (e.g. prison and probation staff, police, prosecutors, victim support workers) with the aim of improving their skills and knowledge on how they treat and interact with victims
- develop, pilot and implement best practice guidance that will enhance multi-agency, cross-sector cooperation among restorative justice / victim services and national agencies with the aim of minimising the risks of secondary and repeat victimisation when interacting with victims.

RJE's activities were organised into 5 workstreams (WK) following a clear and methodological order.

- WK 1 (Review & Theoretical Development) looked at existing evidence from the participating countries and internationally.
- WK 2 (Fieldwork) conducted action research in the participating countries with victims, offenders and professionals to collect new knowledge.
- WK 3 (Production) used the evidence base from WK 1&2 to produce Protocols and Guidelines for victims' safeguards, Training Programmes for professionals and Best Practice Guidance for multi-agency cooperation.

- WK 4 (Pilot & Implementation) piloted the Protocols/Guidelines/Training Programmes/Best Practice Guidance in various institutions and contexts in the participating countries (e.g. in prisons, police, probation, the community).
- WK 5 (Dissemination – Cooperation – Awareness Raising) disseminated widely RJE's scientific and practical results. Actions were also taken for their wider implementation across Europe.

Learning from the Extant Literature

As part of Workstream 1, each partner completed a review of their native literature (Greek, Dutch, Bulgarian, English and German) concerning victims and the restorative justice process, and then produced a summary of their report in English. The native language literature reviews and English summaries are available online on the RJE Project Resources site, via RJ4All.

Among a number of objectives, the review constructed the policy framework within which the new Directive as well as the RJE project were placed. For instance, it reminded partners that in addition to the Directive, member states are also committed to a variety of Council of Europe Recommendations.[14] The first major Recommendation surrounding the role of the victim in the criminal justice process was agreed in 1985,[15] while a 1987 Recommendation[16] encouraged trials between victims and offenders. The 1999 Recommendation on mediation, however, was the first that related directly to restorative justice and highlights the importance of training for facilitators, informed consent prior to commencing the process, and the principles of confidentiality and voluntarism. It also establishes that parties should be aware of possible outcomes and that these outcomes should contain only reasonable obligations.

In 2001, the EU recommended[17] that Member States should promote mediation for appropriate offences and to avoid partial solutions that may cause secondary victimisation. It also encouraged states to establish safeguards to stop this occurring and victims being pressured into the process. This recommendation is similar to the Resolution on restorative justice[18] passed by the Conference of European Ministers of Justice in 2005, which again encourages states to promote the application of restorative justice. It also specifies a need to design different strategies for the specific needs of vulnerable victims and offenders who require additional safeguards.

At the international level, the aforementioned states are also subject to UN agreements on restorative justice, particularly the UN Economic and Social Council Resolution of 2002.[19] This reflects Council of Europe Recommendations by stating that restorative justice requires the free and voluntary consent of the victim. It also states that the victim and offender must agree on the basic facts of what happened prior to the meeting and that the safety of all parties must be considered when undertaking a restorative justice process. Furthermore, it instructs facilitators to factor potential power imbalances between the parties in to their decision whether to commence.

Victim Awareness of Restorative Justice

In each country that carried out a review of the literature, it was noted that there was limited and sporadic awareness of restorative justice and possible restorative options among victims. This was commented on by all researchers and the UK research demonstrated that staff who work with victims were themselves sceptical of offering restorative justice due to their own lack of knowledge and experience of what the process entails. Similarly, the German literature calls for greater awareness training and in Bulgaria restorative justice programmes are still at a very early stage and so not widely publicised. The Greek literature also showed that many initiatives were at the local level, which had led to inconsistent national coverage. In each of the reviews it was evident that victims are not always being offered available restorative justice measures.

Relationship between Victim Support Groups and Restorative Justice

A common debate in each country is that of the role of victim associations or support groups in restorative justice. In Bulgaria, victim groups have criticised the process for being too offender-focused, as it is perceived to concentrate on offender rehabilitation. The review shows, however, that this is the result of a failure to adhere to good restorative justice practice rather than an inherent flaw. It is also explained that victim support groups produce most of the Bulgarian literature aimed at supporting victims in restorative justice. The Dutch 'Victim in Focus' scheme facilitates informal victim-offender mediation but, perhaps due to similar scepticism, the amount of referrals from Victim Support has remained at a lower level than expected.

In both Germany and Greece there are ongoing debates about the relationship between victim support groups and victim-offender mediation groups. In Germany, there is no legal relationship between them, although academics have proposed that victim associations should control victim-offender meditation training and awareness raising so that it remains in the interests of victims. In Greece, there is general cooperation between both parties but no best practice guidance to enhance this and minimise repeat victimisation. In the UK, Victim Support is supportive of restorative justice as long as it is voluntary and in the interest of the victim. Victim Support is now a partner of RJE, emphasising their commitment to a victim-led approach to restorative justice.

Victim Satisfaction

In Bulgarian and German literature there are criticisms of current restorative processes as being too focussed on the offender, at the risk of ignoring the needs of the victim. Despite this, however, surveys in Germany have found high satisfaction rates with the process. Likewise, in Netherlands the vast majority of victims and offenders report very positive experiences of restorative justice, although they did note that hardly any research has been carried out on victims' experiences and satisfaction of restorative practices in custody. Although victim satisfaction rates have also been estimated to be 85% in the UK, case studies have also demonstrated that facilitators can become pre-occupied with targets instead of focussing on the victim. Furthermore, the victims have not been consulted in the design of this evaluation process, so what we mean by 'victim satisfaction' may not accurately reflect the real needs of victims in restorative processes.

Type of Crime

The type of crime that restorative justice is used for also varies by country. Bulgarian schemes have had success with juvenile and adult offenders in mediation schemes and although they have usually been used for low-level crime, there is also evidence that they work with serious crimes. Restorative responses are available for a broader range of crimes in Germany, where property offences, arson, private disputes, civil or commercial disputes may be resolved through mediation. RJE researchers did comment, however, on the lack of available training manuals for using restorative justice in different contexts, risking a one-size-fits-all approach. Within the English-speaking literature there were a range of theories as to what was an appropriate case for restorative justice. Women's Aid, for example, strongly opposes its use with domestic violence cases as it could replicate power imbalances and lead to re-victimisation. This debate extends to other types of crime and there is now research to suggest that it can be used with a range of offences, including hate crime. Although this debate is still ongoing, Germany and the UK have had successful trials with domestic violence cases and found them to be empowering for the women involved.

Restorative Justice in Secure Institutions

The use of restorative justice within secure institutions such as prisons has also been debated by academics (Gavrielides, 2011). In the last 15 years, the Netherlands has attempted to develop victim-offender mediation within youth prisons, but this has only been successful in a fraction of cases. In this setting, the emphasis is often initially on restoration of the offender and restoration of the offender with their family or network. This research has been furthered recently by the Mediation and Restorative Justice in Prison Settings (MEREPS) project. In the UK, Gavrielides found that a lot of services that claim to be restorative only involve the offender (preparatory), and that although 'delivery practices' involving victim-offender mediation take place within prisons in the UK there is no information as to how victims feel in this environment and if they have particular concerns. This gap is to be addressed, however, by the new EU-funded project 'Restorative Justice at the Post-sentencing Level: Supporting and Protecting Victims'. RJE will therefore work closely with this research project and share results and information.

National Training and Practice Standards

Although many restorative programmes are community-led or local projects, there is a differing degree of national standards, guidelines, training and accreditation in each country. In Bulgaria, there is training for mediators, judges, prosecutors and other professionals. This is all carried out by NGOs. There are limited written materials, with only basic manuals, flyers, brochures and protocols aimed at supporting victims. In Germany, despite the self-regulatory national victim-offender mediation guidelines, there are no national training manuals for facilitators. The role of the mediator in Greece, however, is defined by law and states that they must be a lawyer, accredited by a licenced institution of training in mediation that operates as a non-profit and is supervised by the Ministry of Justice, Transparency and Human Rights.

While these formalities are stipulated by law, there is no legislation concerning the content of training, the purpose and practice of restorative justice or reference to any guidelines or training materials, nor are there set registration requirements. A survey of practitioners in the UK found that they felt there was a lack of consistency in training courses as there is no national standard. Despite this, it is not clear that a singular, unified training course would necessarily lead to consistent delivery and practice, and this project will approach this issue with caution. It has also been suggested that the absence of set standards has led to a prolificacy of practices and expertise, and so any standards must endeavour to incorporate this ground-level knowledge.

Victims' Perspectives and Input

The literature reviews demonstrated considerable academic debate concerning how to best protect victims during restorative justice. Furthermore, in some states, such as the UK, although there are no national standards or training programmes there is a variety of best practice guidance, protocols, guidelines and training manuals available. However, in the Netherlands, it is recognised that much of the social and academic discussions on victims and restorative justice have quite an ideological character and are not based on solid research on the actual needs of victims of crime. Similarly, despite increasing amounts of legislation pertaining to restorative justice, Greek legal provisions have not been based on pilot programmes and practitioners have not received any official training.

Article 12 of the Victims Directive requires Member States to carry out restorative justice in the interests of the victim at all times, which cannot be done without asking victims for their input. In the UK, implementation of restorative justice programmes appears to have accelerated with the Government launching the new Restorative Service Standards and Restorative Justice Quality mark, and it is vitally important that this takes into account victims' perspectives on what they want from a restorative process and what makes it successful. The UK Victims Code, which sets guidelines for all organisations and professionals working with victims, is also currently under review, creating a further opportunity for victims' voices to be heard and adopted into government policy. The gap in victims' input is also noted in Bulgaria, where this user-led project is deemed to be timely and important.

Challenges in the Implementation of RestorativeJustice in the Interests of Victims

The review has shown that there are considerable differences in the provision of restorative services both within and between EU member states and much academic debate about how to proceed. From all of the individual literature reviews it is also evident that there is a lack of victims' perspectives when considering how best to safeguard victims during a restorative justice process.

One of the main perceived faults in Bulgarian restorative justice services is the discrepancy between legislation, proposed policy and practice. Although the Support and Financial Compensation to Crime Victims Act allows for restitution and reparation, this is a lengthy procedure and there are no efficient procedural mechanisms for how to implement these rights. Despite the National Strategy for the Support and Compensation of Crime Victims 2006 envisaging victim-offender mediation as a victim protection measure, this has never been enacted. Moreover, the Bulgarian Penal Procedure Code of 2005 does not specify what types of cases are appropriate for mediation. To enable this to be introduced on a national scale, it is essential that victims' voices are heard to provide an evidence base for safeguarding them at all stages of the process. In all of the reviews there was ambiguity in defining which types of crime are suitable for a restorative justice process. This was evident in the New Zealand Ministry of Justice guidelines, which stipulate that the limitation of its use to 'appropriate cases' without explaining what this constitutes. There is also no English-speaking victim-led analysis of the effects of restorative justice on victims of different types of sensitive and complex cases.

German legislation and Victim-Offender Mediation standards establish similar principles for restorative justice as the new Victims Directive. However, reflecting a gap in the current literature, these national standards also explicitly stress the need for future standards to contain a greater focus on victims' perspectives. As well as this, these standards are targeted at victim support workers, whereas the new Victims Directive calls for general and specialist training for all staff that encounter the victim throughout the restorative justice process, such as police, prosecutors and lawyers.

From the Greek literature review it was evident that while there are currently training manuals and best practice guidance available for restorative justice professionals, there are a lack of materials reflecting the differing needs of victims and necessary safeguards in different contexts. This is echoed in the English review, which demonstrates that while there is evidence that restorative justice may vary according to the crime, the victim and the offender, there is little empirical work that suggests how to respond to this in practice. In Germany, it is also noted that the literature only contains standards of practice, which are not specifically training materials for professionals working with victims.

To establish a more structured relationship between victim support groups and mediators, the German literature also calls for the development of criteria and best practice guidance for multi-agency cooperation. Furthermore, it has been suggested that to maximise the options available to victims there need to be alternative routes of access to victim-offender mediation rather than solely referrals. There is a necessity for research into which routes empower the victim the greatest and give them the most options and control of the process.

Generating New Evidence

Following the literature review, workstream 2 focused on collecting primary data. The methodologies, context and environments that were to be applied varied from partner to partner and from country to country. It was important that each partner applied their intended methodology. Therefore, they were left to design, deliver monitor and report freely. However, it was also important that each country project contributed to the overall RJE objectives.

In order to achieve both the above objectives all country projects kept four core questions. These were based on the common themes that emerged from the literature review of workstream 1 and they were:

1. What do victims want from restorative justice?
2. What do victims understand by "victim satisfaction" from justice procedures?
3. What do victims think are the best and safest ways to implement restorative justice?
4. What are the best ways for enforcing the Victims' directive?

Depending on each partner's agreed sampling methodology, the answers to the above questions either came directly from victims or indirectly from their representatives or people with direct experience having worked with them. Some country projects also include the views of offenders, while others were focused on specific environments. This chapter will not go into the details of the methodology and findings relating to each country that participated in the RJE. This is done in detail in the subsequent country specific chapters of this book. It is worth mentioning here that as the coordinator, IARS also proposed some non obligatory questions that arose from the literature review. These were split into two groups and again partners were left free to decide which to include in their fieldwork:

General Questions

1. How can RJ be provided in a way that is not, and is not perceived to be, offender focused?
2. How can victims be made more aware of their restorative justice options?
3. Is there a best way to initially approach victims, i.e. is a letter too impersonal?
4. How can offenders be best equipped with the social and apology skills for a meeting?
5. How much focus should be on post-meeting follow-up sessions with both parties? What should a facilitator do if victim is re-victimised?
6. Is there any research from the partner countries that explores the use of restorative justice with sensitive and complex cases or vulnerable victims?
7. Are there any best case studies from the partner countries where restorative justice is implemented safely and with adequate satisfaction rates for victims?
8. How relevant are materials from other countries / how applicable in different national context?

9. Will practitioners in different institutions be interested in workshops/training on RJ?
10. Will key professionals find training materials, protocols, guidelines & best practice guidance useful when applying RJ in different contexts, services & agencies?
11. What do victims of crime that have participated in RJ think about the RJ services, what are their needs and (good and bad) experiences?
12. What knowledge and skills do professionals that work with victims, lack and/or need / ask for?
13. What tools do professionals that work with victims, need to create better safeguards for victims?
14. Should the state finance RJ?
15. What are the advantages or disadvantages of legislating restorative justice?
16. How much victims know about restorative justice?
17. If victims were to know more about restorative justice would they opt for it?
18. At which stage of the criminal justice system (police, prosecution, courts, post/ pre sentence, prison, probation, ALL) do victims think restorative justice is most appropriate?
19. What do restorative justice practitioners need to implement restorative justice safely and according to the Victims' Directive?
20. What are the key challenges for criminal justice agencies for implementing restorative justice?
21. What do professional think will be the key challenges in implementing the Victims' Directive?

Country-specific Questions

- **UK** - How can we ensure that the UK implementation of the EU Minimum Standards Directive utilises the views of users of the criminal justice system and the community-based knowledge that has already been established?
- **Bulgaria** - How can NGOs and criminal justice system cooperate better?
- **Germany** - Which method should we choose for our survey?
  How can they reach maximum associations and victims and ensure a high uptake for survey?
- **Netherlands** - What knowledge and skills do prison staff that work with victims lack to enable them to work with victims in a sensitive way to prevent secondary victimization of victims? How is restorative justice in (juvenile) prisons implemented, what are the strengths and weaknesses of the current implementation, what are the concerns about the safeguards for victims and how can these be addressed? What tools (protocols, guidelines, best practices and/or other tools) do providers of RJ services, victim support agencies and other relevant professionals that work with victims in prisons want and need, to create –better- safeguards for victims within a prison context?

Capacity Building and Piloting

The subsequent chapters of Part II of this book will present the country specific findings from the fieldwork. These findings were brought together under one roof to construct capacity building material that would help with the implementation of the Victims' Directive. The target audiences for these materials can be grouped into two broad categories:

- Professionals such prosecutors, judges, lawyers, police officers, prison and probation staff, restorative justice practitioners, third party key workers and anyone who is working directly with victims of crime and their families.

Table 3: Sampling and Research Methodology for the RJE project

Country	Sample contacted (original)	Sample reached (final)	Research Method employed
UK	39 victims	24 victims	In-depth interviews (qualitative)
	54 offenders	28 offenders	In-depth interviews (qualitative)
	5,240 contacts	107 victims and offenders	Online survey (quantitative)
	51 experts	24 experts	Focus Group (qualitative)
Germany	245 victims and institutions	53 victims and 30 institutions	Quantitative Survey
	466 victims and institutions	20 victims and 4 institutions	Quantitative Survey
Greece	100 victims	20 victims	In-depth interviews
	10 professionals	10 professionals	In-depth interviews
Bulgaria	10 victims	10 victims	In-depth interviews
	22 professionals	22 professionals	Focus groups (x5)
Netherlands	197 practitioners/ professionals	75 practitioners/ professionals	Attitudinal survey (qualitative)
	197 practitioners/ professionals	75 practitioners/ professionals	Fact finding survey (qualitative)
	20 stakeholders/ experts	20 stakeholders/ experts	In-depth interviews
	10 offenders (juveniles)	10 offenders (juveniles)	In-depth interviews
	20 experts	20 experts	Mini conference
	2 case studies (juvenile prisons x 5)	2 case studies (juvenile prisons x 5)	In-depth observation

- Victims of crime and their families as these are defined by the Victims' Directive.

The outputs can again be grouped into two broad categories:

- Face-to-face capacity building, which included:
  - A face-to-face training session
  - A training manual
  - Best practice case studies
  - Protocols and Guidelines

- Group exercises and self-assessment tools
- Other background reading material including the Victims' Directive and associate official guidelines.

- Online capacity building, which included:
  - An e-learning course
  - Online reading material
  - A self-assessment toolkit
  - Follow up telephone and email support.

The outputs were tailored to the two key audiences and thus a separate face-to-face and online capacity building programmes were produced one targeting victims and their families and one targeting professionals. All outputs were translated into the participating country languages i.e. English, Greek, Bulgarian, Dutch and German. The content of the courses for professionals was independently certified as conforming to universally accepted Continuous Professional Development (CPD) guidelines (20 CPD learning points – Intermediate level).[20]

In total, 27 pilots were carried in the five participating countries reaching 1,131 individuals and 383 organisations. Table 4 provides a summary of the pilots that were conducted face to face in the participating countries as well as a description of the organisations that were reached. The online

Table 4: RJE face-to-face pilots

Country	Partner	Pilots	Delegates	Organisations	Types of Organisations trained
UK	IARS	10	145	71	Prison Staff, victims and families, NOMS, Ministry of Justice, victim support staff, local authorities, university staff, probation staff, civil society, independent practitioners, Youth Offending Teams, policy makers
Greece	EPLO	5	621	15	Civil society orgs, victim support staff, police, lawyers, judiciary, university staff, mediators, probation staff, ex-prisoners, independent practitioners, social workers
Nether lands	RJN	5	54	20	Civil society orgs, victim support staff, public sector
Bulgaria	IARS	3	49	20	Independent practitioners, university staff, civil society orgs, mediators, prosecutors, human rights activists, lawyers, students
Germany	Bremen Universtiy	4	262	257	Victim-Offender Mediation services staff, public sector, criminal justice services, lawyers, judiciary, victim services staff, civil society orgs
TOTAL	–	**27**	**1131**	**383**	

course for victims was downloaded 200 times whereas the CPD accredited course for professionals was downloaded 50 times. The online capacity building programme was hosted on the RJ4All website whereas the piloting for the face to face capacity building programme was delivered by each country partner with the exception of Bulgaria where IARS took responsibility for the delivery. As with the findings from workstream 2, it is not the intention of this chapter to present the feedback from the pilots. These are presented in detail in the subsequent country chapters.

Awareness Raising

A key objective of the project was to raise awareness about the Victims' Directive. The target groups included professionals, victims and their families as well as the general public, the media, politicians, decision makers, policy makers and funding bodies. These target groups spread from local, national and EU wide platforms and were reached through various methodologies which included:

- An international launch event that was held in December 2012 at the UK Ministry of Justice. This involved all participating countries and was endorsed by the UK Justice Minister who gave the opening speech
- An international closing event that was held over two days in November 2014. This involved all participating countries as well as several other EU member states, representatives from Australia, the US, South Africa and Canada. It was endorsed by the Head of Unit Directorate General Justice – European Commission, the UK Justice Minister for Victims as well as the UK Director of Public Prosecutions who were all speakers
- Various press releases (e.g. just in the UK twelve press releases were produced)
- A dedicated website which was split into the following pages
    - Project page http://www.rj4all.info/content/RJE
    - Partners page http://www.rj4all.info/content/RJE_partners
    - Project resources page http://www.rj4all.info/content/RJEresources
    - Independent Advisory Group page http://www.rj4all.info/content/RJE-IAG
    - A Photo Gallery page http://www.rj4all.info/rje-photo-gallery
    - The final book page http://www.rj4all.info/content/RJEbook
    - A page for the e-course of professionals http://www.rj4all.info/content/RJE-etraining
    - A page for the e-course for victims and their families http://www.rj4all.info/content/victimscourse
- Presentations at international and national conferences
- Radio and TV interviews as well as coverage in the print and social media
- E-Newsletters disseminated to over 3,000 organisations on a monthly basis for the duration of the project.
- Country specific campaigning activities that were carried out either online or through face to face platforms. Examples include:
    - The UK based online campaign during international restorative justice week 2013
    - A Greek based face to face campaign during international restorative justice week 2013
    - A Bulgarian based online campaign.

Again, it is not the intention of this chapter to analyse the impact of these awareness raising activities at the national and EU levels. This is done in detail in the subsequent chapters.

Peer Review and Research Ethics

Consistent with IARS' research ethical standards, the RJE introduced a peer review process throughout its duration through two separate methods. Firstly, and Independent Advisory Group (IAG) was set up specifically for the project with the aim of providing feedback, guidance and independent scrutiny to the RJE Principal Investigator, Dr. Gavrielides. The IAG consisted of six individuals (1 victim, 1 ex offender, 2 academics, 1 victim support manager and 1 civil society/ policy executive).[21] They were from various countries including the UK, Hungary and Canada.

Secondly, the IARS Editorial Board was consulted particularly in relation to peer reviewing the RJE publications (e.g. the literature reviews, the training material) as well as scrutinising the research ethics of the RJE fieldwork. The Editorial Board is a standing independent committee consisting of 22 equality and criminal justice experts from around the world including the UK, Canada, Greece, the US, Hungary, Cyprus and India.

IARS has applied for COPE membership (see: http://www.publicationethics.org). COPE provides advice to editors and publishers on all aspects of publication ethics and, in particular, how to handle cases of research and publication misconduct. This means that IARS Publications adheres to high ethical standards in publishing. IARS staff and representatives who carry out research on behalf of the organisation and which involves vulnerable groups are expected to apply for Research Ethics Approval from the IARS standing Editorial Board. Approval must be obtained in advance of the research.

Furthermore, the following structures were employed for research ethics and legal compliance: (1) IARS Research Ethics Handbook (2) Data Protection Law (3) Confidentiality & Consent Forms where appropriate (4) User Engagement Policy (5) Lone worker policy.

In addition to being evaluated as a programme in its entirety, specific outputs (e.g. face-to-face training, online training, conferences, events) were monitored and evaluated through evaluations forms and online surveys that were completed by the participants. The data were analysed by IARS and fed into an evaluation report to the European Commission relevant Directory.

Notes

1 http://ec.europa.eu/justice/criminal/victims/index_en.htm (accessed April 2014)

2 The adversarial system is described as "a contest between two equal parties, seeking to resolve a dispute before a passive and impartial judge, with a jury ('the people') pronouncing one version of events to be the truth" (Jorg et al. 1995: 42). The system is based on the "fight theory" of justice, mainly described by its adversarial principles, whereby parties "fight out" their case in front of a jury and an impartial tribunal. That is why criminal justice in the adversarial model is treated as a 'contest'. On the other hand, the inquisitorial system is described as "the investigation of an event, and the persons involved, by the State with a view of establishing the truth" (Jorg et al. 1995: 42). The truth in such a system must be discovered in the investigative procedure. Therefore, the criminal process is seen as an "inquest" (further in Gavrielides, 2005).

3 The project website page is http://www.rj4all.info/content/RJE (accessed September 2014).

4 According to Case 96/81 of the European Court, the State's freedom to decide on the manner of implementation of a Directive "does not release it from the obligation to give effect to the provisions of the Directive by means of national provisions of a binding nature …Mere administrative practices, which by their nature may be altered at the whim of administration, may not be considered as constituting the proper fulfilment of the obligation deriving from that Directive".

5 Including: the UN Convention on the Elimination of All Forms of Discrimination against Women (1979), Declaration of Basic Principles of Justice for Victims of Crime and Abuse of Power (1985), Basic Principles on the Use of Restorative Justice Programmes in Criminal Matters 2002/12, Guidelines on Justice in Matters involving Child Victims and Witnesses of Crime (2005), Draft UN Convention on Justice and Support for Victims of Crime and Abuse of Power (2006), Council of Europe Recommendation (1985)11 on the Position of the victim in the Framework of Criminal Law and Procedure, Council of Europe Recommendation (2006) 8 on Assistance to Crime Victims, the 2011 Guidelines of the Committee of Ministers of the Council of Europe on child-friendly justice, the 2005, Convention on Action against Trafficking in Human Beings and the 2011 Convention on preventing and combating violence against women and domestic violence and the Treaty on the European Union.

6 Victims of crime under international law are not specifically mentioned in the Directive.

7 The Directive gives the freedom to Member States to limit the number of family members who may benefit from the rights and to determine which family members should have priority. This is to avoid that the definition gives rise to disproportionate demands on criminal justice actors, since all the rights in the Directive apply to all family members of deceased victims and the rights to support and protection apply to family members of surviving victims.

8 Thus, third country nationals and stateless persons who have been victims of crime on EU territory should benefit from these rights. This may be of particular importance in the context of racist and xenophobic hate crime, crime against undocumented migrant women and girls who are particularly exposed to various forms of gender-based violence (such as physical violence, sexual exploitation and abuse, female genital mutilation, forced marriages and so-called 'honour crimes') and trafficking in human beings.

9 It is worth noting that Article 8 of the Council Framework Decision 2008/913/JHA requires that investigations into or prosecution of the racist and xenophobic hate speech offences shall not be dependent on a report or an accusation made by the victim.

10 Austria, Belgium, Czech Republic, Croatia, Denmark, Estonia, Finland, France, Germany, Hungary, Ireland, Luxembourg, Malta, Netherlands, Poland, Portugal, Slovakia, Spain, Sweden, UK.

11 Bulgaria, Cyprus, Greece, Italy, Latvia, Lithuania, Romania, Slovenia.

12 See for instance http://www.iars.org.uk/content/restorative-justice-new-eu-directive-victims-concerns (accessed September 2014).

13 CJEU rulings in cases C-205/09 Eredics34 and Joined Cases C 483/09 and C 1/10 Gueye/ Sanchez35 interpreting Article 10 FD on mediation.

14 A COE Recommendation is issued by the Committee of Ministers on matters for which they have agreed a common policy. They are not binding on Member States. See http://www.llrx.com/features/coe.htm#Committee of Ministers

15 Recommendation No. R (85) 11 of the Committee of Ministers to Member States on the position of the victim in the framework of criminal law and procedure.

16 Recommendation No. R (87) 21 of the Committee of Ministers to Member States on assistance to victims and the prevention of victimisation.

17 EU Council Framework Decision 2001/220/JHA of 15 March 2001 on the standing of victims in criminal proceedings.

18 Resolution No. 2 on the social mission of the criminal justice system- restorative justice. Passed at the 26th Conference of European Ministers of Justice in 2005.

19 United Nations Economic Social Council (ECOSOC) Basic principles on the use of restorative justice programmes in criminal matters, ECOSOC Res 20012/12.

20 CPD Certificate of Completion awarded by Independent Academic Research Studies through The CPD Certification Service

21 See http://www.rj4all.info/content/RJE-IAG (accessed September 2014)

References

Barnett, R. (1977) 'Restitution: A New Paradigm of Criminal Justice', *Ethics: An International Journal of Social, Political, and Legal Philosophy* 87(4), 279-301.

Bazemore, G. & L. Walgrave (1998). *Restorative Juvenile Justice: Repairing the Harm of youth Crime,* Monsey, NY USA: Criminal Justice Press.

Braithwaite, J. (2002) *Restorative Justice & Responsive Regulation,* Oxford: Oxford University Press.

Crawford, A. and Newburn, T. (2003) *Youth Offending and Restorative Justice: Implementing Reform in Youth Justice,* Cullompton, Devon: Willan Publications.

Gavrielides, T. (2008) "Restorative justice: the perplexing concept. Conceptual fault lines and power battles within the restorative justice movement" 8:2 *Criminology and Criminal Justice Journal*, pp. 165-183.

Gavrielides, T. (2011). "Restorative Practices: From the Early Societies to the 1970s". *Internet Journal of Criminology* ISSN 2045-6743 (Online).

Gavrielides, T. (2011). *Restorative Justice and the Secure Estate: Alternatives for Young People*, IARS: London

Geis, G. (1977) 'Restitution by Criminal Offenders: A Summary and Overview', in J. Hudson and B. Galaway (eds) *Restitution in Criminal Justice*, Lexington, MA: Lexington Books.

Marshall, T. (1999) *Restorative Justice: An Overview*, London: Home Office, Research Development and Statistics Directorate.

Morrison, B. (2006). "Restorative Justice and Civil Society: Emerging Practice, Theory and Evidence", *Journal of Social Issues* (special issue 62(2).

Pollock, F. and Maitland, F. W. (1898) *The History of the English Criminal Law Before the Time of Edward I*, Cambridge: Cambridge University Press.

Schafer, S. (1970) 'Victim Compensation and Responsibility', *Southern California Law Review* (43), pp. 55-109.

Tallack, W. (1900) *Reparation to the Injured and the Rights of Victims of Crime Compensation*, London: Wertheimer.

Zehr, H. (1990) *Changing Lenses: A New Focus for Crime and Justice*, Scottdale, Pennsylvania Waterloo, Ontario: Herald Press.

From the Margins to the Centre: A Victim-focused Criminal Justice System for the United Kingdom

*Grace Loseby**

Abstract

The Victims' Directive has brought much promise and weight to the rights of victims within the European Union. Member states, such as the United Kingdom, are at a turning point in their treatment of victims and with this Directive the message is clear - whatever this direction may take, the role of victims in the Criminal Justice System must change. This position, with its obvious opportunities and challenges, form the basis of this chapter and act as a tool for reflection on the findings generated by the Restorative Justice in Europe project. Firstly, we will explore the current literature and research; this will include important developments of the last twelve months in relation to the position of the victim in the national and European context. Secondly, we will analyse the fieldwork of questionnaires, interviews and the expert seminar. Thirdly, we discuss in significant depth the training section that includes highlighting concerns from the field. Lastly, recommendations and best practice will be explored and will seek to evaluate the possibility of a victim-led criminal justice system in the United Kingdom.

Introduction

> *'It has been stated that restorative justice should be accessible and something that victims feel comfortable and confident requesting at any stage of the criminal justice system. That this process should be led by the victim and be on their terms. Further, that if it doesn't work for the victim, then it should not happen.'* (Restorative Justice Action Plan, Ministry of Justice, 2012).

In the Ministerial Foreword of the Restoration Justice Action Plan for the Criminal Justice System 2012 the message was clear. Restorative justice was to be available to any victim on their terms. This position is not just a shallow rhetoric with the potential to fade come next national political election. However, it is enshrined in the Victim's Directive. This declares a minimum standard of rights, support and protection for victims is supported by European Commission legislation. Both political and legislative approaches are important as they signify the shifting nature of victims in the criminal justice system. Rather than seeing them as experiencing individualised harm and with individual needs, it has been argued that victims had been treated as a homogenous group and that their purpose was purely in providing evidence in the application of state punishment. These new approaches point to a clear evolution of the relationship between the state and harmed persons, a wanted change that has long

* Grace Loseby, IARS Projects' Coordinator (Justice), Unit 14, Dock Offices, Surrey Quays Road, Canada Water, London SE16 2XU, UK, +44(0)20 706 44380, g.loseby@iars.org.uk

been championed by national and international restorative justice enthusiasts and victim advocacy groups alike. The Directive is thus one of the most important pieces of legislation with regard to victims and restorative justice in the United Kingdom to date.

Beginning with a national overview of current literature in relation to victim's rights, including the political and economic issues in providing services to victims, this chapter will offer perspectives upon the evolving position of the victim within the United Kingdom. Theoretical analysis will be offered alongside commentary of the political, thereby offering an example of how restorative justice is realised in practice. This section will also highlight the current approach to European legislation and how this position affects the implementation of the Directive. Next, the fieldwork will be discussed. Fieldwork constituted of questionnaires, semi-structured interviews and an expert seminar. We will then go onto to discuss the training section for the United Kingdom- this includes both face-to-face and online training. For the research team it was important to engage a range of practitioners and users in the training, from Police Crime Commissioner's and Ministry of Justice to victims themselves. The reason for this was due to an important aspect of empowerment, we have called this the 'Victim's Initiative' and aids the promotion of reflective learning and practice. This, as we suggest, helps victims to realize their rights in the justice system, leading to the development of a rights-based restorative justice that is individualised to each victim and their needs resulting from harm. Although, this is somewhat of an encouraging prospect we go on to discuss concerns from the field regarding the empowerment of the victim and what this could mean for the criminal justice system. Finally, we consider a victim-led criminal justice system for the United Kingdom.

The time span of the project offers an insightful snapshot into the changing approach to the 'victim voice'. Due partly to the last political year of the current government and in the run up to the next general election, this has become somewhat of a political currency. It is not down to chance. With the rise and prominence of victim advocacy, victims are becoming more readily noticed and usually to the detriment of the government, social and criminal justice agencies. Examples from recent years in the United Kingdom highlight the mistreatment of victims and a disregard for their needs particularly within racial and child abuse cases. These have highlighted the lasting effects of crime on victims, including secondary victimisation. The voice of the victim that has been previously disregarded suddenly needs to be listened to and considered in attempt to meaningfully engage them within the justice system. The victim is therefore recognized, along with their emotional need and necessary access to advocacy. Thus restorative justice is an attractive initiative by being an emotionally intelligent practice- satisfying victims' needs and holding offenders to account.

Many of the issues that have come to light from the project will not come as a surprise to both, supporters and skeptics of restorative justice. Their questions include: How can restorative theory translate to practice? Does legislative and political support help or hinder its traditionally communitarian ethos? How do we navigate the changing landscape of justice and the position of the victim within this process? A constant, often daily struggle, in holding true to restorative values is not a new one. As highlighted in the chapter, predictions from restorative justice scholars are still relevant today as they were in their original conception. Depending on the next steps and the mobilisation of victims and the wider the community, the possibility of a truly victim-led criminal justice appears somewhat of a utopian pipe dream- preserved in theory and outside the political and economic arena.

The argument in this chapter focusses on a central paradox. While a restorative practice grows which regards victims at its centre, rather than directly addressing their rights and needs, there is simultaneously an increasing emphasis on utilizing the victim to rehabilitate perpetrators as part of the machinery of alternative disposals. Cumulatively, this chapter will argue, that there is a danger that this central paradox and the dichotomy in the treatment of victims will continue and that if there not is sufficient reflection and research on the gravitas that the Directive brings, there will be no change in culture- a change that has long been awaited.

Reviewing the Extant Literature

Our research began with a literature review and initial mapping exercise of restorative justice services in relation to their efforts of safeguarding victims' rights. Previously, Gavrielides and McKenna (2013) highlighted that the current political and legal framework did offer certain safeguards and protection measures for victims but they found that there was no particular reference to rights. They went on to discuss the implication issues for the Directive in regards to access, preparation, physical safety, on-going support for victims of crime, training issues and restorative justice in prisons. This chapter will offer an update; In particular relevant updates including the position of EU legislation and the commission of victim services.

Recently, the U.K is witnessing growing animosity towards membership of the E.U. This was not always the case considering the long history and relationship of the UK with EU institutions. At present, the leading party in the U.K exemplify this position by stating their intention for an E.U membership referendum; the Conservative Party European Election Manifesto 2014 includes under the title of 'real change we will deliver'; an in-out referendum on Britain's membership of the E.U. This has been coupled with the rise of Euro-sceptic parties, such as the United Kingdom Independence Party who received the greatest number of votes of any British party at 27.49% in the 2014 European Elections (BBC News, May 2014). The 'will we, won't we' debate gives an unpredictable future for E.U membership and its affiliated legislations. Additionally, as the Directive is an opt- in, the position is somewhat unstable in relation to the connection of the U.K with its E.U partners. The true extent of this will not be known until the next year and the coming months in anticipation of the general election. Although E.U membership is diminishing in political popularity, their view of the victim belonging to a group with insufficient political attention grows.

During the last two years, strategic decisions have been made by reorganising government departments and their ministers in the lead up to the next national political election. The Victim's Minister (previously Helen Grant MP) has now become part of the Minister of State for Policing, Criminal Justice and Victims (now Mike Penning MP). These decisions for a pro victim agenda have also been seen in the creation of the Victim's Commissioner (currently Baroness Newlove). Where, as in the Domestic Violence, Crime and Victims Act 2004, the Commissioner's role is summarised as: "promoting the interests of victims and witnesses, encouraging good practice in the treatment of victims and witnesses and keeping the operation of the Victims' Code under review" , a year into the role, the Victim Commissioner's plans for the future include 'Restorative Justice- my aim is to find out more about the potential benefits and risks of RJ. I want to secure a better understanding about where it should and should not be used and ensure victims are genuinely aware of their choices to participate or not' (2014, p.8). In her report the 'victim's voice' was cited as an important element within the criminal justice system and the justice system more widely. Although her position is an independent voice within government, it signifies the importance and onus the current government has put on the needs of victims.

The government's support of victim's rights does not just come in the physical presence of ministers and officials abut also in accompanying policy frameworks. The Code of Practice for Victims of Crime (Victim's Code) was launched by the Ministry of Justice in December 2013 with the headline of; "Victims put first in the criminal justice system". This documented entitlement to Victim Personal Statements, referrals to victim services and communication tools such as assistance with writing Impact Statements. Chris Grayling, Justice Secretary opened with this statement; "Victims deserve the best possible support to cope and recover from the effects of crime...I want to create a fairer criminal justice system where victims have a louder voice and those who break the law are more likely to go to prison for longer" (Ministry of Justice, 2013). This nod to the emotional needs of victims and the 'power to be heard', whilst holding offenders to account is also witnessed in the growth of restorative justice services.

The process of nationally embedding restorative justice and the commission of victim services by the Police Crime Commissioners[2] is underway as support documents state that services need to be in place by April 2015, these will supports the emotional recovery of victims with the assistance of restorative justice (Ministry of Justice, 2012). An update provided by Restorative Justice Action Plan for the Criminal Justice System (2013) reported on several areas of progress; provision by Crime and Courts Act 2013 and National Offender Management Service (NOMS) have provided by one-off funding to Probation Trusts (Kent, South Yorkshire and Thames Valley) which enable them to develop local models for the delivery of pre-sentence restorative justice in magistrate's courts known as 'pathfinders'. Restorative Solutions has formed delivery partnerships with Victim Support to establish pre-sentence restorative justice pathfinders in 10 Crown Courts across England with expected capacity to deliver 100 interventions, per area. In the outsourcing documentation National Offender Management Service 'Service Specification for Deliver Victim-Offender Conferencing (Restorative Justice)' (2014) explicitly stated that the Victim's Directive and its safeguard requirements to prevent secondary and repeat victimisation, intimidation and retaliation. It states that such services should therefore have as a primary consideration the interests and needs of the victim, repairing the harm done to the victim and avoiding further harm.

Although these changes are encouraging, there is a growing concern, previously explored by Zehr (1990), and most recently by Gavrielides of the 'McDonalisation' of restorative justice. Gavrielides (2013); "Restorative justice must be more than a programme within the current system- it must be a new paradigm for responding to harm and conflict with its own philosophical and theoretical framework. Facilitating this shift requires a re-thinking of the assumptions around punishment and justice, placing emphasis instead on values and relationships". It is suggested that by the outsourcing and creeping commodification of restorative justice there is a danger of being outcome focussed and with significant distance from core principles and objectives - where punishment takes the place of restoration and shared rehabilitation. This is illustrated in the Justice Secretary's announcement of the Victim's Code - coupling the emotional need of victims and harsher punishments for offenders. This highlights the on-going rhetoric of the criminal justice system where victims and their needs are seen parallel to the retributive punishment of offenders rather than the need of the victim in feeling safer from further crime by having a say in the offender's rehabilitation. Thereby, despite articulating a victim-led system, the paradox actually continues. As explained in the original literature review for the RJE project (Gavrielides and McKenna (2013, p.5), 'evaluation of how successful a restorative process has been also problematic as some staff felt that they were focussing on targets rather than providing full support for the victims'. As we come to the end of the two-year project there are signs that this problem prevails and that a restorative re-thinking and emphasis has not taken place, thereby the process becomes another programme within the current system.

The dangers of outcome-focussed work are well documented and can leave victims feeling pressured to participate in the restorative justice process (Bazemore and Schiff 2005; Choi and Gilbert 2010; Daly 2002, 2003). Furthermore, Choi et al. (2012) suggests a possibility that victims and their needs can easily be marginalized, and in some cases, even re-victimised by the process. In highlighting previous studies victims were dissatisfied with the process because of; coercion, professional capabilities, poor practice, inadequate planning, lack of understanding about restorative justice requires among service providers, feeling their needs were not met, lack of preparation and being pressured into accepting the apology. Due attention to these theoretical positions needs to be paid, as Choi et al (2012) highlights in their study of unsatisfactory restorative justice for victims, it is where little attention was paid to the process and more focus on developing suitable outcomes for offenders. In the UK, Victim Support is supportive of restorative justice as long as it is voluntary and in the interest of the victim. Although, victim satisfaction rates have been estimated to be 85% in the UK, case studies have also demonstrated that facilitators can become pre-occupied with targets instead of focussing on the victim. Furthermore, the victims have not been consulted in the design of this evaluation process so what we mean by 'victim satisfaction' may not accurately reflect the real needs of victims in restorative processes. Zehr (2005) highlights the need to redress our principles before implementation "Such an effort is important at this time. Like all change efforts, as restorative justice has developed and spread, it has sometimes lost its way...like the criminal system it aims to improve or replace, restorative justice may become primarily a way to deal with offenders" (p.5).

Despite the increasing ambiguity of E.U membership and its eventual impact on the UK, it has been highlighted that has been a change to include the victim more within the justice system. This has been signified by growing political, legislative and economic support. However, as introduced in the initial literature review, how safeguards and protection measures are realised in practice and how more importantly they remain wholly restorative is not spelled out. The fear of restorative justice shifting away from principles in terms of victims' needs was supported in our interviews with staff that worked directly with victims, who were themselves sceptical of offering restorative justice due to their own lack of knowledge and experience of what the process entails. This was particularly true of those who came from primarily 'offender' focussed organisations and roles such as probation and police.

New Evidence

In the second stage of U.K research, we conducted quantitative and qualitative field research; an online questionnaire, semi-structured interview and an expert seminar. There were a total of 183 participants involved in the research and this was made up of victims, offenders and criminal justice practitioners (see Table 1. overleaf).

The questionnaire that was conducted online showed that out of the 23% of victims who were offered restorative justice in our research, 79% of them agreed to take part in the process. Satisfaction levels among those who participated ranged on an average of 85%. The most popular reason for them taking part was "To stop it happening again to anyone else" followed by, "To have your say and explain the impact of the offender's actions" and "To feel that the offender was working to change their behaviour and stop offending". This is compared to the most important reason for those who choose not to take part was

Table 1: Methods and sample sizes of the UK RJE Research

Research tool	Original sample	Final sample	Response rate
In-depth interviews	39 victims	24 victims	61.53%
In-depth interviews	54 offenders	28 offenders	51.85%
Online survey	Undefined, emailed widely	107 (67 victims and 40 offenders)	N/A
Focus group	51 experts	24 experts	47.05%

which that they "Doubt offender's sincerity", "physical safety concerns", sincerity of the process, the referral agency and the practitioner. The majority of victims felt that all victims should be offered the chance to choose restorative justice over the traditional criminal justice process. However, there were conditions attached to this and most of them were covered by the expectations included in the Victims' Directive. Some victims said that it should not be up to the court to decide whether a restorative justice intervention should take place or not. Of the 22% offenders who were offered restorative justice the vast majority undertook it in prison settings. The key reason for not taking part was "inconvenience" followed by "lack of information" and "being too traumatic". Additionally, research highlighted that victims are not always the most vulnerable in the restorative justice processes. So, safeguards needed to protect both sides. There was also consensus that there is no evidence to believe that restorative justice would not be appropriate with certain crimes. Again, concerns expressed included the need to first change the criminal justice culture before the Victims' Directive can be genuinely implemented.

On Monday 23rd September 2014 in London, the annual expert seminar brought together practitioners and experts from the field of probation, prison, charity and users in a discussion regarding the national readiness for the Directive and its implications. It was held in the formation of a traditional restorative circle, whereby every member of the circle had the opportunity to contribute when holding a 'talk piece'. Most importantly, it involved hearing from practitioners and the dangers of bad practice that is at risk of becoming more prevalent in the current market and highlighting the clear need for safeguards. Most risks were associated to the out-sourcing environment with targets and expectations to meet. There was also a discussion about the victim, how is that quantified and how is it experienced. Again, there were obvious concerns. The Directive provides a framework for minimum safeguards but the research and data that emerges from it does not have clarity in suggesting how the power structure within the UK restorative justice movements can be managed in order for it to be successfully implemented. Despite good intentions it was felt that the E.U is still not convinced that change has taken place in member states, which would eventually reposition the victim in the criminal process. Consequently, current practice that is being developed may serve victim's needs but the agendas of the gate keepers and those who are in position to dictate, when, how and for which crimes restorative justice should be offered (Gavrielides, 2014).

There are currently plenty of adequate legislative and institutional arrangements for the protection of victims in the criminal justice and restorative justice process. Nevertheless, it was highlighted that there is a considerable gap in the implementation of these intentions. Restorative justice is provided both within the criminal justice system and outside and this includes partnerships with community organisations who seem to have taken the principal role in the implementation and innovation of restorative justice. In fact, it appears that the UK constitutes an example where restorative justice takes meaning principally in the hands of its community although there is no indication that its delivery by criminal justice agents and within formal structures will necessarily be hampered. Related to the above is the lack of awareness and capacity among professional of the victims Directive.

Although the standards within the Directive are included in other relevant UK documents such as the Victims Code, the Best Practice Guidance and the Government's 2012 Restorative Justice Action Plan, their implementation and enforcement mechanisms are absent. Most victims who took part in the research were from complex and serious cases. There was no indication that restorative justice was not deemed appropriate. Those who did not undergo restorative justice showed interest in the research and indeed participated because they wished they had been offered the option and thus wanted to know more through their engagement with the project.

It is questionable whether legislation alone can help with the implementation of restorative justice according to the Victims' Directive. In fact, attempts, efforts and resources directed into legislative initiatives may detract from the actual issue which revolves around enforcement. There are strong power structures within the victims and restorative justice movement that make victims and offenders suspicious of restorative justice processes. Gatekeepers often treat victims in a patronising or tokenistic manner despite the existence of guidance and regulations. There are fears that this deterioration will continue as funding is being rolled out to mainstream restorative justice too quickly and without consideration of its complex, local and fluid nature.

More information is requested from victims, offenders and professionals, but not necessarily in the form of printed material. Case studies and real live examples were thought the best way to increase awareness while online material, email and the use of videos and audio were all recommended. The majority of victims felt that they should be offered the chance to choose restorative justice over the traditional criminal justice process. However, there were conditions attached to this and most of them were covered by the expectations included in the Victims' Directive. There seems to be a strong rhetoric around the implementation of restorative justice which does not reflect real practice. Compared to other EU countries, there are a considerable number of practices labelling themselves as restorative justice. However, actual encounters between victims and offenders are extremely rare as most practices involve indirect ways of resolving conflict while most are of preparatory nature. As Gavrielides (2013) underlines, successful restorative justice at a political level requires a shift in focus and different emphasis on the victim and their needs. Therefore, it is not only the outsourcing of restorative justice that needs to occur but wider victim awareness with an aim to truly recognise the victim's voice and its importance in the restorative process.

Capacity Building: Learning from the Pilots

Following the literature review and fieldwork, ten pilot training sessions were held with a wide range of participants including Ministry of Justice, Police, Prisons, Probation, RJ practitioners, victim support organisations and victims themselves. We called the training 'Victims' Voices and Restorative Justice in the new EC Directive', as we felt it encapsulated the ethos of the training and overall project. It was important for the research team to be training in different parts of the country so training was held in London, the North East, North West and the Midlands. Training was twofold- both face to face and online. Both cover the same information in relation to the Victim's Directive, detailing the applicable restorative justice Articles (mainly 12 and 24). However, it should be noted that the online training includes two pathways- practitioner and victim. As mentioned, it was important for the project to directly empower victims through training so as to support our own position in the need to directly inform and empower victim in regards to their rights. We will begin with a discussion about the face to face training.

To promote internal and external reflective practice in the training sessions we kept the training agenda open and flexible but grounded it in experiential learning. The learning experience went in four stages and reflected Kolb's experiential learning theory which involves a cycle of experiencing, reflecting, thinking and acting (Kolb, 1983). These reflections are then assimilated (absorbed and translated) into abstract concepts with implications for action which the person can actively experiment with, which in turn can enable the creation of new experience. Specifically, in the training- we had an introduction to the session and information on the Directive, a victim awareness exercise, a discussion in how to apply this experience to the Directive with the assistance of case studies and then a concluding exercise to concrete this learning and integration into own work. Following a four-stage cycle-; 1. Concrete experience, 2. Reflective observation, 3. Abstract conceptualisation, 4. Active experimentation.[3] It was important for training to be reflective in its conception and application and thereby reflecting the shift in practice and placing value in learning, experience and relationship as guided by restorative principles.

The victim awareness exercise or reflective observation was prompted by Kubler-Ross and Kessler (2005,1) "They are responses to loss that many people have, but there is not a typical response to loss, as there is no typical loss. Our grief is as individual as our lives". By using the 'On Death and Dying-process of recovery and change' adapted from Kubler-Ross 1989 (See Graph 1) We entered into a group exercise named the 'process of recovery', choosing from their own experience or from a case they had good knowledge of. It was important for the practitioner to begin this exercise with their own experience of being a victim. Experiences ranged from minor to serious crimes, however they all differed in their recovery time and mostly agreed with the 'process of recovery' as suggested by Ross. This exercise was done so that participants could take off their 'organisational hat' and begin 'thinking like victims'. This was particularly important to assist in cultural change by stimulating dynamic thinking, especially in the implementation of restorative justice and the need for cultural shift in line with restorative principles including emotionally intelligent way of working. Presentations also highlighted that criminal justice agencies can contribute to the length of time for the process of recovery; in some instances this can go so far as inflicting secondary victimisation.

It was discussed that Stage 3 'acceptance and integration' was the most conceptually problematic stage and so was the term 'restorative' in understanding these two terms. The diagram is used often in restorative justice training and can sometimes lead to the false illusion of the practice with the idea that it would lead to full recovery and the end result of being 'restored'. However, it was discussed that there is a possibility that the victim is never truly 'restored', adding to the false hope and unrealistic expectations of restorative justice. One practitioner commented that the term 'restorative' was very

Graph 1: Kubler-Ross, E. (1969) On Death and Dying- process of recovery and change

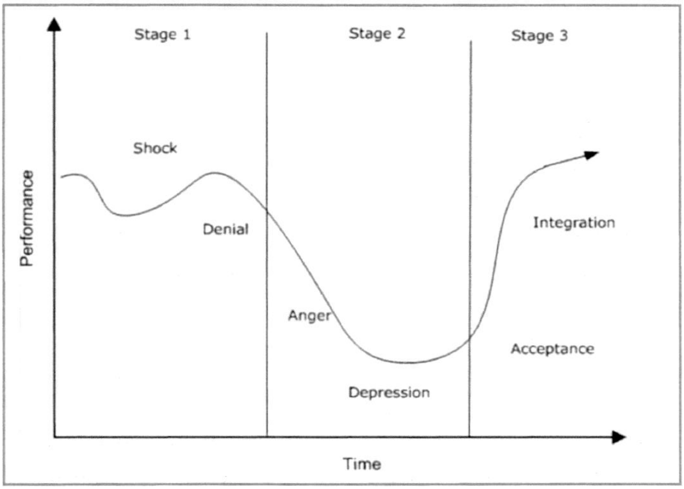

optimistic. This reflective observation was then encouraged with the use of case studies, therefore applying the Directive and lived experience of being/the 'victim' to specific examples. It was here that participants really began to 'think like victims'.

After the victim exercise, the abstract conceptualisation was introduced- this was called the Victim's Initiative. The research team named it as an 'initiative' because of the definition; 'the ability to assess and initiate things independently...the power or opportunity to act or take charge before others to' (Collins English Dictionary, 2011). In restorative justice this standpoint is often compared to the adversarial nature of the traditional criminal justice system whereby decision-making is insisted of hierarchy. Rossner (2013: 16) highlights that part of reintegrative shaming allows for non-hierarchical and participatory nature of the conference, instilling a sense of legitimacy into the proceedings and leading victims and offenders to believe that the criminal justice system is just and fair. It was important for us to make part of the training about the awareness of needs and for this to be the vehicle of choice and empowerment (see Diagram 1) with the assistance of legal weighting. Empowerment is essential to the restorative justice process. Wormer (2004:5) highlights that the approach to counter victimisation is the gaining of a sense of personal power, assuring responsibility for recovery and change which may entail helping others, 'of special relevance to criminal behaviour and without which change is unlikely, is the taking of personal responsibility for one's actions and one's life'. Similarly, Pranis (2001) points to theory and practice that gives 'ordinary folks' the capacity to identify and solve their own problems. Therefore, as highlighted by a victim early on in the training, restorative justice is a way of regaining control and increase understanding that was lost during and after the crime. However, how empowerment is encouraged and quantified, as a successful outcome is problematic.

To assist the victim in their initiative; 'The Victim's Guide' was designed to ensure that the problems of the criminal justice system are not reciprocated in the restorative justice process and work to empower victims. The Victim's Guide is designed as leaflet/booklet in layman's language about the purpose of the Directive and how it can assist victims in the restorative process. As Zehr (1990, p.12)

Diagram 1: An illustration of the Victim's initiative used in training presentations

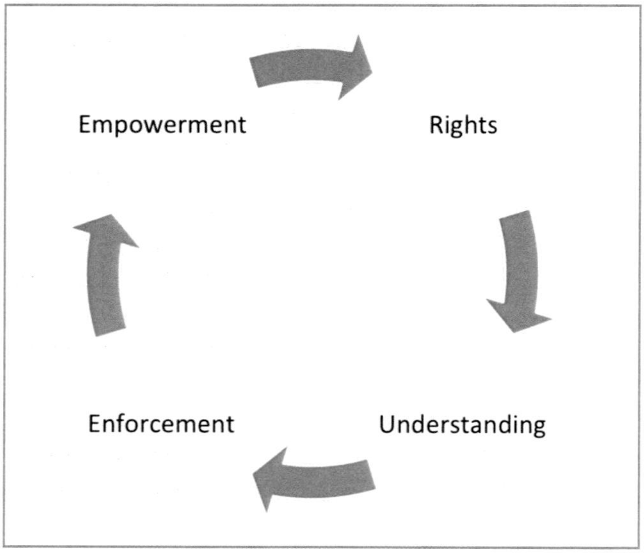

highlights "Victims often feel ignored, neglected, or even abused by the justice process". Therefore by equipping victims with knowledge of rights and minimum safeguards, this knowledge works to encourage participation and empowerment. Additionally, as highlighted by Rundell (2007) a principle of restorative practice involves respecting and encouraging individuals and communities to participate in their own decision-making. Furthermore, for Pranis (2001) direct participation and the exercise of power in decisions affecting one's life are essential elements of a just social order and are at the centre of restorative justice. This concept is not new, as Moore (2008) developed in a 'Rights-Based Restorative Practice: Evaluation Toolkit'. Supporting the victim before and during the restorative process further develops our version.

The fourth part of the training was shaped as active experimentation. This was where the Victim's Guide was played out as a role-play, with participants working in groups of two- one the restorative justice practitioner and the other as a victim of crime. The scenario was that the practitioner has gone to the see the victim who is interested in restorative justice. The victim then asks questions under the following headings; Information, The Restorative Justice Process, Informed choice, My wishes and needs, Confidentiality and Consent agreement. Questions included, what information has been given to me about the restorative justice process? Is this in writing and I have a copy? Have I been asked formally whether I agree to take part in a restorative process?. It is interesting to note that these have been developed in relation the minimum rights and safeguards of the Directive. However, this exercise was received with mixed feedback by participants- where some found it a useful tool to adequately prepare their restorative dialogue with victims, others believed it would be too challenging for the victim and could potentially dissuade them from participating.

The application of free and informed consent was discussed especially in relation to the funding of restorative justice is determined by outcomes and targets. Practitioners openly admitted to the difficulty of implementing this when faced with prescriptions of successful outcomes. Confidentiality issues were also discussed and in particular the 'client/solicitor' relationship was articulated. This was of particular concern as practitioners began to internally change their approach to victims in a more professional manner, thereby beginning to see them as a customer in the justice journey with outcomes equally successful and unsuccessful. In pre-trial restorative justice it was asked if confidential issues were shared then would these be mentioned to the Courts, especially if it may change the outcome of the case. This would take away the very essence of restorative justice as an emotionally intelligent response to crime and assimilating it with the traditional justice system. On numerous occasions the research team attempted to engage legal practitioners in the dialogue regarding disclosure of information in the restorative process. However, on these occasions those involved were unable to comment on predicted behaviours. Seemingly, as restorative justice is consumed by the formal criminal justice system, decisions and positions will be made on previous cases and subjective tests being applied to confidentiality. We wait with eager anticipation about the results of the pre-trial pathways in relation to these developments.

Many of the training participants were unsure of how the Directive would be enforced especially in relation to the uncertainty of European membership and legislation. Although a reasonable concern, the research team highlighted that these are the reasons why it is important to equip victims with the necessary knowledge so that they can enforce their own rights- embodying the radical shift in culture. Training, including the Victim's Guide is available online. The online training package was demonstrated at the face-to-face training; again this was received with a mixed response. Some felt that the training would not be accessible to victims, in particular to young people. Others were enthusiastic that the training was available for all with independent information so that they could instruct their victims to go on the training and that would then satisfy the Victim's Directive requirements. Thus, as highlighted by Rundell (2007), practises like empowerment, cooperation, and involvement toward the goals of responsibility, reparation, and reconciliation and the development of social competency uses interactional dialogue and fair process challenges to mainstream expert knowledge. We employed this for both trainings and it is our hope that victims will use the guide to further challenge, leading to a cultural change from the bottom-up.

The Possibility of a Victim-led Criminal Justice System in the UK

As predicted by Rossner (2013, p.16) "Restorative justice has been offered as an antidote to all that ails criminal justice. It has been pregnant with promise since its inception". Those involved in restorative justice have an enormous task on their hands. This small-scale study highlights the difficulties in changing the approach to justice in becoming restorative.

As Zehr (1990, p.22) highlights, victims lack empowerment from the formal justice process, "Victims often feel like control has been taken away from them by the offense control over their property, their body, their emotions, their dreams. Involvement in their own case as it goes through a justice process can be an important way to return a sense of empowerment to them". This does not just mean the conference, but also the process. Inserting agency is paramount for victims to regain control in the present and future. Rundell (2007: 54) highlights this in the principled restorative practice- 'many of us are used to serving others by doing things "for", "to" or "against" them. Continual awareness and reflection are required to work "with" people'. This means employing emotionally intelligent ways of working and applying them to practice, clear on what emotional processes should be addressing. The challenge in relation to commodification of restorative processes is that it is difficult to recognise and quantify. The consideration here is then, how do we confront this paradox?

Part of the solution is in recognising victims as individuals, close to our own individualised needs and their own ability to exert these. In its purest form, restorative practice helps us to do this. What the Directive offers is a point of reflection and as highlighted by Moon (2013, p.15) 'For reflection to be meaningful, it must be an honest examination of learning through questioning and investigation, which leads to the development of informed decision making and understanding'. What the reflective review promotes is the restorative processes. This is not only in restorative outcomes but restorative approaches to work. As Choi et al (2014,p.40) highlights, when restorative justice works well, it is the process, not the desire to attain an outcome that make it work. If restorative justice is emotionally intelligent then so the application of the Directive should be and this should be reciprocated in the approach to outsourcing of restorative and the need for successful outcomes. However, emotionally intelligent approaches must be open to vulnerability. As Gavriedlies (2013: 1) writes "It is not a soft option. It entails pain; not just for the offender, but also the victim and their communities". This involves a degree of vulnerability of communities. To allow for better working, this can also sometimes involve vulnerability and openness by state agencies and thus, signalling a collective redress and the opportunity to view crimes differently.

It is recognised by the U.K research team that with European uncertainty; change of providers and an overhaul of services, it is difficult to ensure restorative processes against real world pressures. It is therefore paramount to make victims aware of their rights through community initiatives and not to 'win' against the offender for punishment but for restoration. As suggested by the Victim's Initiative and Moore's suggestion of a rights-based restorative justice and that the reason to evaluate restorative practises is to ensure 'authenticity'- restorative practice is authentic, when actions are harmonious with participants' voices and experiences, and the goals and principles of restorative programming'. Priorities need to align and be made restorative, whereby the political system will allow for the victim to have a voice and this against the noise of commodification and private companies with the danger that this may not be a successful outcome. If this fails, the voice of the victim is again side-lined, with the state taking the loudest platform and dictating the needs of its users, primarily offenders.

Conclusion

This chapter started with the ministerial foreword on the intention for restorative justice in U.K. This position is reflected in the Victim's Directive in that restorative justice should be available to all victims, if wanted, and that this process should be safeguarded. The Directive comes into force as a wider agenda of victims' rights is being addressed in the U.K. This is not an accident but symbolic of the attempt to include users within the wider political agenda. It has been suggested that there are several reasons for this shift in emphasis. Many of these relate to where victims were not respected or listened to when reporting crimes, especially for child or racial abuse crimes. This has demonstrated, more than ever, a representation of the ignorance of the state and criminal justice in relation to victims' needs and harm.

Therefore there is a clear need to change the position of the victim in the criminal justice system.

This policy has been introduced as listening to the 'victim voice'. This chapter has documented the reasons why the government has chosen this position, presenting a clear break from previous justice systems. The new direction for the UK government has come at a time of uncertainty both politically and economically where the possibility of reconciling restorative outcomes is bleak. However, it is full steam ahead for victim services with various forms of political and legislative backing. Part of this involves outsourcing, including localised approaches to restorative justice but also available throughout the criminal justice system with both a pre and post-trial focus. It is probable that more developments are to come. We are at the tip of the iceberg for restorative justice provision in the UK, where restorative justice could be seen as a successful addition to the justice system offering a new outlook to our idea of punishment or as another out of court disposal with limited impact on the needs of victims.

For the research team at IARS, a user led and user focused NGO, it was paramount that the victim's voice was identified and encouraged in the Directive. It was also important to have a training element to the project, the aim of which was not only to promote the research with concrete information on the Directive but also to promote victim awareness in the increasing use of restorative justice. Our contribution to this new direction of restorative justice is to campaign for an emotionally intelligent and needs focused approach to implementing the Directive. More widely we suggest that in successfully implementing the Directive it is important to re-evaluate the practices and direction that enable a culture for restorative experiment. There is also a need for a constant reflective review, realigning practice. This means not just asking about the priority of meeting targets but internally examining the responsibilities of this practice against outcome focus and providers situated within offender-focused agencies. It is here that we highlight the need to include victims and practitioners in this reflective practice and direction. We must properly address victims' concerns, needs and trauma with respect to their human rights to truly implement this much-needed change of culture.

The Lord Chief Justice Thomas (2011) (previously President of European Network of Councils for the Judiciary 2008-2010) spoke to this task in addressing the implementation of the Directive;

> *"The most important task is to change culture...it seems to me that this cultural change will also involve the adoption by those bodies responsible for the governance of the police, the prosecution and the judiciary of their own responsibility for ensuring that the rights of victims are properly observed. This is not only a question of bringing about major cultural change, but there should be regular evaluation of what has been achieved by the bodies responsible for the governance of the police, prosecutors and judges"* (p.4).

Notes

1 41 Police and Crime Commissioners (PCCs) were elected across England and Wales on the 15th November 2012. When PCCs took office on the 22nd November 2012 they became responsible for a combined police force area budget of £8 billion. The role of the PCCs is to be the voice of the people and hold the police to account. They are responsible for the totality of policing (APCC, 2014)

2 Please note that only specific elements of the training have been highlighted. For full presentation visit www.rj4all.org.uk/projectresources (Last accessed 13/9/14)

References

Association of Police Crime Commissioner's (2014) *Role of the PCC*, Available online: http://apccs.police.uk/role-of-the-pcc/ [Last accessed 15/09/14]

Bazmore, G. and Schiff, M. (2005) *Juvenile justice reform and restorative justice; Building theory and policy from practice*, Oregon, Willan Publishing

BBC News, May 2014 Vote 2014: *UK European election results*, BBC News 26th May 2014 Available online http://www.bbc.co.uk/news/events/vote2014/eu-uk-results [Last accessed 15/09/14]

Choi, J. J., G. Bazmore, and M.J. Gilbert. (2012) Review of Research on Victims, Experiences in *Restorative Justice: Implications for Youth Justice Children and Youth Services Review*, 34 (1): 35-42

Choi, J.J. and Gilbert, M. 2010) *Joe Everyday, People off the Street: A qualitative study on mediators' roles/skills in victim offender mediation*, Contemporary Justice Review, 13 (2), 207-227

Collins English Dictionary (2011) Edition 11. Bishopbriggs, HarperCollins Publishers

Conservative Party European Election Manifesto (2014), Available online: http://www.conservatives.com/europe/~/media/Files/Downloadable%20Files/MANIFESTO%202014/Euro%20Manifesto%20English.ashx [Last accessed 15/09/14]

Crime and Courts Act 2013

Daly, K. (2002) Restorative justice: The real story, *Punishment & Society*, 4 (1), 55-79

Daly, K. (2003) The limits of restorative justice in Sullivan, D. and Tifft, L. (Eds) *Handbook of restorative justice : A global perspective*, New York, Routledge

Domestic, Crime and Victims Act 2004

Gavrielides, T. (2013) *The McDonaldisation of community-born and community-led ethos*, RJ4all. Available online: http://www.rj4all.info/content/mcdonaldisationRJ [Last accessed 15/09/14]

Gavrielides, T. and McKenna, P. (2013) *Victims and Restorative Justice in the UK: An overview*, RJ4all. Available online: http://rj4all.info/library/RJEUKwk1 [Last accessed 15/09/14]

Kolb, D. (1983) *Experiential Learning: Experience as the Source of Learning and Development*, London, Prentice Hall

Kubler-Ross, E. and Kessler, D. (2005) *On Grief and Grieving; Finding the Meaning of Grief Through the Five Stages of Loss*, London, Simon & Schuster

Lord Chief Justice Thomas (2011) *PROTECTING THE VICTIMS IN THE EU: THE ROAD AHEAD, Presented in Budapest, March 2011 Working Group on Access to Justice Strengthening The Victim's Role in Criminal Procedure Lord Justice John Thomas*

Ministry of Justice (2012) *Restorative Justice Action Plan for the Criminal Justice System*. Available online https://www.gov.uk/government/uploads/system/uploads/attachment_data/file/217311/restorative-justice-action-plan.pdf [Last accessed 12/09/2014]

Ministry of Justice (2013) *Restorative Justice Action Plan for the Criminal Justice System-Report on Progress One Year On*. Available online https://www.gov.uk/government/uploads/system/uploads/attachment_data/file/259832/restorative-justice-progress-report-2013.pdf [Last accessed 12/09/2014]

Moon,J. (2013) *A Handbook of Reflective and Experiential Learning: Theory and Practice*, London, Routledge

Moore, S.A. (2008) *Rights-based restorative justice*, University of Minnesota, Human Rights Center

National Offender Management Service (2014) *Service Specification for Deliver Victim-Offender Conferencing (Restorative Justice) Service Specification Document*

Pranis, K. (2001) Restorative justice, social justice, and the empowerment of marginalized populations in Bazemore, G. & Schiff, M. (eds) *Restorative community justice*, Ohio, Anderson

RJ4all (2013) *Restorative Justice in Europe: Safeguarding Victims and Empowering Professionals, Summary report: The English, Bulgarian, Dutch, Greek and German literature on restorative justice and victims* (work stream 1) Available online http://rj4all.info/sites/default/files/files/WK1_RJE _Final _Report_0.pdf [Last accessed 12/09/14]

Rossner, M. (2013) *Just Emotions: Rituals of Restorative Justice*, Oxford, Oxford University Press

Rundell, F. (2007) *"Re-story-ing" Our Restorative Practice Reclaiming Children and Youth*, 6 (2), 52-59

Sharpe, S. (2011) *WALKING THE TALK: Developing Ethics Frameworks for the Practice of Restorative Justice*, British Columbia, Community Justice Initiatives Association

Strang, H. (2001) Justice for victims of young offenders: The centrality of emotional harm and restoration in Maxwell, G. and Morris, A. (Eds) *Restorative Justice for juveniles*, Oxford, Hart Publishing

Ministry of Justice (2013) *The Code of Practice for Victims of Crime, Ministry of Justice*. Available online: https://www.gov.uk/government/uploads/system/uploads/attachment_data/file/254459/ code-of-practice-victims-of-crime.pdf [Last accessed 15/09/14]

National Offender Management Service (2014) *Service Specification for Deliver Victim-Offender Conferencing (Restorative Justice) Service Specification Document*, Available online: https://www.gov.uk/government/uploads/system/uploads/attachment_data/file/317466/2014-06-03-RJ-Spec-P1-0.pdf [Last accessed 15/09/14]

United Nations Office for Drugs and Crime (2006) *Handbook on restorative justice programmes*. Criminal justice handbook series. New York, United Nations

Victims' Commissioner for Victims and Witnesses (2014) *Commissioner for Victims and Witnesses: Report for the Secretary of State for Justice 2013-14*

Wormer, V. (2004) Restorative justice: A model for personal and societal empowerment *Journal of Religion & Spirituality in Social Work*, 23 (4) 103-120

Zehr, H. (1990) Changing Lenses: A New Focus for Crime and Justice, in Zehr, H.and Toews, B. (eds) *Critical Issues in Restorative Justice*, Pennsylvania, Herald Press

Zehr, H. (2005) Evaluation and Restorative Justice Principles in Elliot, E. and Gordon, R. (eds) *New Directions in Restorative Justice: Issues, Practice, Evaluation*, Cullompton, Wilan Publishing

Zehr, H. (2002) *The Little Book of Restorative Justice*, Intercourse, Good Books

Marie Schmidt discussing the Victim's Directive with mediators, Victim - Offender Mediation Forum, May 2014, Trier, Germany © IARS

The Victims' Directive and Restorative Justice in Germany

*Arthur Hartmann and Marie Haas**

Abstract

The chapter deals with the impact of the EU Victims´ Directive in Germany and its implications for restorative justice services. It reviews the reality of restorative justice in Germany, which is still dominated by victim-offender-mediation. This reality is reflected in the light of the Directive. The definition of "victim" in the Directive and restorative justice theory are also analysed. The first part of the chapter indicates some paradoxes, which evolve when analysing the Directive. The second part of the chapter presents the contribution of the German partner to the RJE project. A Europe wide online victim survey was developed and piloted. Issues of research methods as well as the actual results and implications of this pilot study are discussed. Furthermore, the legal environment of restorative justice in Germany is reviewed taking the Directive into account. The paper pays particular attention to the German Criminal Code, the Mediation Act and existing mediation standards and their compatibility with the Victims' Directive. Finally, the chapter looks at the opportunities and threads surrounding the Victims´ Directive for restorative justice services in Germany positing recommendations for improvement.

The Victims´ Directive and Restorative Justice in Germany

The Victims' Directive ("Directive of the European Parliament and Council, establishing minimum standards on the rights, support and protection of victims of crime, and replacing Council Framework Decision 2001/220/JHA")[1] became effective one day after it has been published in the Official Journal of the European Union on the 15th of November 2012. As a Directive, member states have to implement its regulations into their national law. For the citizens no rights or duties can be directly derived from the Victims´ Directive. Member states have three years, which is until the 16th of November 2015, to implement the regulations into national law (Art. 27 I EUVD).

As the new Victims´ Directive comprises 72 considerations and 32 articles, we will and cannot dwell on every single content in particular here. We will however instead on such considerations and articles which are relevant for restorative justice (RJ), although even in this matter we do not seek completeness either. Hence this paper introduces a subjective selection of regulations which to us seem to be the core messages of the Victims´ Directive relating to RJ. For this matter we will in a first step introduce the Victims´ Directive, in a second step amplify the implications of the Victims´ Directive for RJ and in a last step compare these implications with the recent legal situation in Germany.

* Professor Arthur Hartman, contact University of Applied Sciences in Public Administration Bremen, Doventorscontrescarpe 172C, 28195, Bremen, Germany, Arthur.Hartmann@HfOEV.BREMEN.DE and Marie Haas, (Research Associate at Institute for Police and Security Research (IPOS))

During the legislative procedure of the Victims´ Directive the *European Forum for Restorative Justice* started a signature campaign. Background of this campaign was the phrase "and replacing Council Framework Decision 2001/220/JHA" which meant the cancellation of duties in relation to RJ as art. 10 of the Framework decision from 2001 bounds the member states to

- promote mediation in criminal affairs and to
- consider agreements between victims and offenders in the criminal procedure.

Table 1: Article 10 of the Framework decision 2001/220/JHA

Penal mediation in the course of criminal proceedings
1. Each Member State shall seek to promote mediation in criminal cases for offences which it considers appropriate for this sort of measure. 2. Each Member State shall ensure that any agreement between the victim and the offender reached in the course of such mediation in criminal cases can be taken into account.

This was the foundation for the fact that in all member states basic legal regulations for the mediation in criminal affairs had been implemented and efforts had been undertaken to actually promote those. The new Victims´ Directive initially did not contain any respective regulations. The signature campaign and further interventions of the *European Forum for Restorative Justice, Independent Academic Research Studies (IARS)* and many other institutions and private persons have been undertaken as a reaction to this. Probably only through these interventions the respective obligation to acknowledge and support mediation in criminal affairs into the Directive has been incorporated.

As a first core message we can therefore register that in eleven years during which article 10 of the framework decision from 2001 was effective, Europe did obviously not succeed in promoting RJ as a matter of course in the criminal justice system even though this had been evaluated as a necessity in European politics. Although politicians stated the importance of RJ over and over and it is seen as a story of success, which is a judgment that we happily affiliate to, paradoxically we also have experienced that the wind blows head-on if one tries to promote RJ, at least in Germany.

The central regulation concerning RJ is article 12 of the Directive. Looking at this article closely as a second core message one can obviously note, that the EU Victims´ Directive under the overall impression of art. 12 par. 1 EUVD adopts a rather sceptical position towards RJ despite the signature campaign of the European Forum for Restorative Justice. With art. 12 par. 2 EUVD the state of the framework decision from 2001 is kept: the member states are obligated to facilitate the referral of cases. For that however they shall establish procedures and guidelines that naturally have to respect the provisions of art. 1 and 12 EUVD.

A similar paradox position can be observed when looking at the "Convention on preventing and combating violence against women and domestic violence" (Istanbul Convention) of the Council of Europe from 11th of May 2011, which is recently in the ratification procedure.[2] In art. 48 the convention forbids mandatory alternative dispute resolution processes or sentencing in cases of violence against women and domestic violence. These official positions of a convention of the Council of Europe on the one hand and an EU Directive on the other hand raise the question, whether RJ practice or theory gives reason to these paradox.

The Victims´ Directive and Restorative Justice Theory

Whilst in practice victim-offender mediation (VOM) is still predominant in Germany the full concept of "restorative justice" and the respective ideas and protocols ("settings") are lately getting more and more attention. The journals *TOA-Infodienst* and *TOA-Magazin* edited by the *Servicebüro für Täter-Opfer-Ausgleich und Konfliktschlichtung*[3] have dedicated a whole series of articles to this matter and by that substantially contributed to the dissemination of those ideas.

According to No. 46 EUVD, RJ services are for example "victim-offender-mediation", "family group conferencing" and "sentencing circles". By that the Victims´ Directive emphasizes clearly the variety of established RJ concepts and not only the concept of mediation. However, the theory of RJ goes beyond this concept and sets up a ranking of the named settings in terms of which are more or less restorative. According to the theory completely restorative are only those settings, in which all those concerned ("stakeholders") are represented. Besides victims and offenders the community is frequently also affected by criminal offences. Only those settings can therefore be seen as completely restorative, which involve representatives of the community, thus only family group conferencing and sentencing circles but not mediation between victim and offender only (*McCold / Wachtel 2001*; regarding German literature see *Hagemann / Lummer 2012*).[4]

Furthermore, the Victims´ Directive acknowledges victims and others affiliated by the offence. Opposite to the concepts of "stakeholder" and "community", these terms defined clearly in art. 2 No. 1a EUVD. As others affiliated art. 2 No. 1b EUVD only mentions family members: "family members" are the spouse of the victim, the person, who has been living with the victim in a permanent, stable and intimate partnership and shares a household, as well as direct relatives, siblings and dependents of the victim.

However, the definition of a victim of a criminal offence can fall within a broader circle of people. If for example a youth gang terrorizes another gang or e.g. an apartment building through threats, vandalism etc., according to the Victims´ Directive all those are victims who suffered a concrete physical, psychological, emotional or economic damage as a direct consequence of the offence. But a general victimization of the community as a consequence of common uncertainty or other common expenses which can be affiliated to the criminal offence(s) does not count according to the Victims´ Directive. The broad "stakeholder" concept, which legitimates the general involvement of the community into the RJ process, is not provided by the Victims´ Directive. Instead the Victims´ Directive emphasizes on the contrary the special role of the victims who are directly concerned and secures their special rights compared to other interests and also those of the community. Therefore a shift of emphasis, maybe even a conflict line between the Victims´ Directive and RJ theory – not necessarily in the practice too – seems to be recognizable.

With regard to a ranking of appropriate RJ settings we can find regulations in art. 4, art. 6 par. 4 and art. 12 EUVD. According to art. 4 par. 1j EUVD the victim is already to be informed about available RJ services when having the first contact with a competent authority. Thus, if there are a variety of possibilities it has to be informed about all of them. According to art. 6 par. 4 the wish of the victim to receive information or not is insofar compulsory. Consequently, RJ service providers or the further interest of the community may be decisive, but the extensively informed victim decides which setting seems to be most restorative and suitable in his or her case. Because of the voluntariness the same is true for the offender.

The authorities and providers of RJ services, according to art. 12 par. 1 EUVD, have to be concerned to safeguard the victims (as defined in art. 2 No. 1a EUVD) within the RJ setting from secondary and repeated victimization, intimidation and retaliation. Insofar the involvement of others to support the victim within the framework of a conference can be both, beneficial and critical. Central aspect naturally here too, is to safeguard the concrete victim. Community interests, like for instance with regard to reintegration, improvement of the social climate etc. have to stand back behind this. A shift of emphasis from established RJ theory therefore exists also in this aspect. In practical terms this means, that victims and offenders are to be involved not only into RJ processes but also in the precursory step, the selection of an appropriate setting (mediation, conference, circle) and that their preferences are to be considered. The relevance of this is directly apparent when looking at the relatively high number of cases of domestic violence RJ services in Germany are dealing with. The Victims´ Directive does not indeed dictate, that various settings are available for selection, in the sense of the Victims´ Directive it would however be defined as more or even completely restorative if the victim would have such a choice.

Against this background, a development which leads to the clear distinction of the providers of mediation, conferences and circles would not be desirable and the approach of an "expanded victim-offender-mediation" ("erweiterten Täter-Opfer-Ausgleichs"),[5] in which different settings can be seen as a continuum on which the individual optimum setting can be chosen by victims has to be regarded as preferable and "most restorative" in respect to the Victims´ Directive. One cannot exclude the possibility that the broad concept of victims in RJ theory that includes any stakeholders in a conflict contributes to the above mentioned sceptical position of the Victims' Directive and the Convention of the Council of Europe because there is some danger that the actual victims of a crime in the sense of Art. 2 EUVD became second rate in relation to the needs and interests of the many stakeholders and problems, which should be served and targeted by RJ according to far reaching theoretical concepts. Therefore it is important to address the aforementioned paradox through empirical evidence in order for victims' rights and interests are best served.

New Evidence: Europe-wide, Online Victim Survey

During the duration of the RJE project (December 2012 – November 2014), an EU wide, online victim survey was prepared, designed, piloted, implemented and analysed. The key aim of the survey was to offer victims an easy way to judge and assess the services they had received from their criminal justice systems. The continuous control of the quality of services and victims´ satisfaction with these services has become available literally for any restorative justice and victim support scheme in Europe on an easy to handle and low cost basis. So far no other continuous quality control of restorative justice and victim support schemes regarding victim satisfaction had been implemented in European countries. The aim of our contribution was to change this. This instrument could also be useful in relation to art. 28 of the Directive, which requests data that shows how victims can access their rights deriving from the Directive.

Even though it was planned to conduct the survey not only in the area of RJ but also in the victim supporting field, we soon had to note, that each area has its very individual characteristics and that to acknowledge these would demand the development of an individual research design. We therefore decided that we would conduct one survey after another. The obvious advantage of this was that we would be able to learn from the experiences in the first survey and use this knowledge for the other survey. As we are more experienced in the field of RJ, we decided to conduct the first survey in this area.

Based on the RJE findings from workstream 1 (review and theoretical development), we developed a questionnaire based on Avedis Donabediens (1980) categories. Amongst others, Altweger & Hitzl (2001) point to their usefulness in this research area. Therefore, we structured and phrased the questions based on Donabedian´s categories (structure, process and outcome). Further we considered the challenges that are demanded by the legal and formal regulations (see chapter 1a and b in the WS2 interim report) and the findings of recent research, especially the results from Bindel-Kögel & Karliczek (2013). Our intention to implement the survey online to reach as many people as possible and to ensure the highest level of anonymity was further supported by Fischelmanns (2006) who shows that online interviews are compared to other methods of questioning indeed recommendable when targeting victims. For more information about the theoretical background please consider the interim report.

Methodology and Implementation

The development of the questionnaire

In May 2013, we started to design the questionnaire. For that we did not only consider the aforementioned theoretical findings, but also gathered information about other questionnaires that have been implemented successfully in a similar concern. The first draft of the questionnaire consisted of 12 pages and 43 questions and was then discussed repeatedly during our internal project meetings and edited respectively. We also asked a psychologist to check the questionnaire from a psychological view. The feedback from this angle was very positive and she had only a few very useful remarks which we discussed and then have been adapted to the draft. Finally the draft was sent to experts in the field of RJ in July 2013. Due to the summer holidays we only had responses in August 2013.

The feedback was very positive in general, most of the experts however stated that they thought the questionnaire might be too long which might affect the quantity of responses. We therefore tried to shorten the questionnaire as far as possible but were not able to reduce the number of questions but only the answering categories. We then translated the questionnaire into English and sent it out to our project partners for more feedback. The feedback from them was very positive too so that we started to prepare further translations and to put the questionnaire online with the programme SoSci Survey[6] (Leiner, 2013) in September / October 2013. In the end we were able to offer the questionnaire in 10 different languages: German, English, Portuguese, Greek, French, Spanish, Polish, Dutch, Italian and Swedish.[7]

Going Online

To create a low-threshold access to the online-questionnaire we first planned to design a splash screen / website which could be accessed via a simplified web-address. This plan however would have assumed that we design such a splash website in all languages and this again would have meant that each splash screen requires an own web-address. Unfortunately we could not go through with this plan time- and resource-wise.

We created the online-questionnaire with the software *SosciSurvey*[8] (Leiner 2013) which already had proven its usefulness in other projects. This software is freeware when used for scientific, non-commercial research and has been developed by the University of Munich in cooperation with the University of Zurich. It is at public´s disposal since 2006. The respective server and the further development of the software can be financed through commercial users since 2013.

The questionnaire can be accessed online in the internet and with an individual access code, which can only be used once and is meant to prevent misuse and guarantee the anonymity of the interviewees. We generated 20.000 individual access codes. A further helpful feature of the software is the possibility to monitor the response in real time. While *SosciSurvey* only collects the data, the further analysis of the data is done with *IBM SPSS Statistics*.[9] The online version of the questionnaire has first of all been created in German and as one standard and one mobile version, which optimizes the layout of the questionnaire for mobile devices. A little later the other language versions have been put online as well and also in each language as a standard and a mobile version.

Researching the Institutions and Implementing Mailing Lists

Our aim was on the one hand to develop an instrument which enables victims to evaluate RJ services and on the other hand to provide RJ services with the possibility to be evaluated. For this matter we had to find RJ services that would be willing to try our tool by asking victims who had been using their service to evaluate the service. The only safe way to only reach such victims was therefore to go over the institutions which meant that we had to research RJ institutions all over Europe. The only criteria for us were that the institution provides any form of RJ service (mediation, conferencing or circles) in criminal cases.

The research of institutions which offer RJ services in the 28 EU member states was mainly done through the internet (e.g. search engines such as Google). From our project partners we also received contact data of institutions in Bulgaria, the Netherlands, United Kingdom and Greece. The EPLO (Greece) however asked us not to conduct our survey with the Greece institutions as this would have interfered with their own research there. Every search, besides naturally those for Germany and Austria, was made in English with the following keywords plus the name of the country (e.g. Sweden): restorative justice Sweden; restorative justice service Sweden; family group conference Sweden; victim offender mediation Sweden; victim offender Sweden; mediation criminal Sweden.

We were able to identify some useful country-specific information, for example about how RJ services are called, what kind of RJ services are offered, the development of RJ, since when RJ has been offered, which target group is common and finally and most important for us, who offers RJ services. In most cases at that point we already found contact data of relevant RJ institutions. As coverage and to reach a preferably high completeness of the data we then however, under consideration of what we already had found, further researched in the respective national language. We therefore translated the keywords via an online dictionary dict.cc and Google Translate and started the research again.

After the substantial research in all member states of the EU in October 2013 740 potential institutions could have been gathered in our data base. Parallel to the research the cover letters and the questionnaire have been translated into Portuguese, Greek, French, Spanish, Polish, Dutch, Italian and Swedish by external staff. After the translations into English, Greek, Portuguese, Spanish and Italian have been completed the first approach to institutions was made on the 28th of November 2013. As for the different language versions and national languages in the different countries diverse mailing lists had to be implemented for this matter:

- One mailing list per language, which contains all countries in which the respective language is spoken (Cyprus, Portugal, Spain, Italy, United Kingdom, Ireland, Germany and Austria).
- One mailing list for Poland, France, Belgium, the Netherlands and Luxembourg, who received the material in English but with the hint that we are working on the translation of the material into their national language.
- One mailing list for each of the Associate Partners (Cyprus and Hungary) asking to forward the email request to relevant institutions and / or to inform us about the state of affairs in the country.
- One mailing list for the remaining EU-countries, who received the material in English but with the remark that we would try to provide them with a translation in their national language in the case they would want to participate.

Altogether, 10 mailing lists were accrued. Further mailing lists have been installed when further translations were completed, so that in January 2014 new mailing lists for francophone countries (France, Luxembourg, Belgium), Poland, the Netherlands (and Belgium) and Sweden could be implemented and approached again.

Approach

It was planned that we contact the researched RJ institutions / services, inform them about the project and our survey and ask them to participate. To participate meant for them that they would have to estimate the number of cases they would complete during the survey period respectively the number of victims that they would be able to contact in this period of time and hand out a cover letter from us to them.

To pre-empt compatibility problems, we produced a PDF file which contained a cover letter for the institutions and for the victims with detailed information about the survey and background as well as the questionnaire. The email itself only contained a few introductory lines and the request to look into the attached PDF file. The *cover letter for institutions* contained general information about the RJE project and the EU Victims´ Directive. Furthermore, it explained the aim of the project and especially the Europe wide web-based victims' survey, introducing the Institute for Police and Security Research (IPoS). Also it contained links to the RJ4all and the IPoS Website. The *cover letter for victims* contains overall some less information. It explained why we applied to them, what the survey is about, that it is an online interview and what the survey aims for. Finally, it also contained information about the Institute for Police and Security Research (IPoS) and links to the RJ4all and the IPoS Website and naturally refered to the anonymity and confidentiality of the data. After sending out the emails we received 168 fault reports due to wrong or problematic email contacts, most of which we were able to correct after further research. In the end only 29 emails, most of them personalized could not have been delivered, which makes a final number of 711 emails respectively institutions in 28 countries that have been asked to participate.

Initial Response Rates

We received a couple of answers with a positive response concerning the participation in the survey. Altogether the answers we received were mostly helpful and even if they were not responsible for RJ we often received brief information about the situation of RJ in the countries. Most positive responses we got from German institutions, which could have been expected. As for Croatia we were informed that there has been a pilot project in the field of VOM between the years 2006 and 2009. The central office which is responsible for RJ services in Croatia was still carrying out an evaluation of this project. Because of that we were told that it would not be advisable to start a second survey in the same field, but we were offered to use their findings for our research. From Portugal we received the information that since 2011 RJ services no longer exist in Portugal. They however showed much interest in the survey and project and offered to support us in the area of victim assistance. In the case of Finland, we had to cancel the cooperation due to excessive administrative obstacles.

In the end, 30 German, 2 Swedish, one Belgian and one British institution agreed to participate in the survey. Altogether that makes 34 of 711 institutions, which have been contacted, representing 4 out of 28 countries.[10] This equals a response rate of 4.8 %.

The institutions which were willing to participate received the requested number of sealed envelopes from us containing a cover letter for the victim of which each includes an individual access code. When sending out these envelopes we again described the procedure and contents of the envelopes in a brief cover letter for the institutions. In this cover letter we also asked the institutions to respect the following to conditions: to hand out an envelope only to those victims which completed a RJ process during the period 1st of February and 30th of April 2014 AND/OR to send out the envelope to victims who have been completed the process some time before this period but also contact them with the envelope only during the named period. Altogether we sent out 1.879 envelopes.

Due to the very low response rate, after some weeks within the survey period (~10 interviews) we met with one institution to discuss the probable causes with the result that we decided that it could be helpful to shorten the cover letter. We therefore replaced the envelopes containing the old cover letter by envelopes containing the new and much shorter cover letters for this institution (400 envelopes). Further we sent incentives in the form of chocolate to two other institutions (100 envelopes). As these measures didn´t seem to have much of an impact on the response, we decided to extend the survey period until the 31st of July and informed all participating institutions via Email. As an additional measure to enhance the response rate we also decided to implement an open version of the survey which could be accessed without an access code and sent out another German email to all German and Austrian institutions and another English Email to all other institutions that we had researched.

Final Response Rate and Results

Within the prolonged survey period from the 1st of February until the 31st of July 2014 (6 months) the questionnaire has been activated 73 times, 40 times with an access code and 33 times without an access code. The questionnaire has mainly been activated in German (see Table 1).

On closer examination of the data, 41 of the 73 activated questionnaires were at least partly filled in which is therefore the size of the sample (that is the number of interviews) we will present selected results of in the following. Of the 41 interviews only four have been accessed without an access code. 34 of the interviewees used the German version, three the Dutch and two the Swedish version and the English and French version haven been used each once.

Planned and conducted as a Europe wide quantitative victim's survey this small number of interviewees does not meet our expectations and above this does not fulfil the criteria to represent victims from different RJ schemes and with different national backgrounds from all over Europe. For that the total number is simply too small and above this the sample mainly consists of victims having

Table 1: Language of the activated questionnaire (n =73)

	N	%
German	53	72.6
Swedish	6	8.2
English	4	5.5
Dutch	3	4.1
Portuguese	3	4.1
Greek	2	2.7
French	1	1.4
Polish	1	1.4
Total	73	100

Figure 1: Did you already know of VOM? (n= 41)

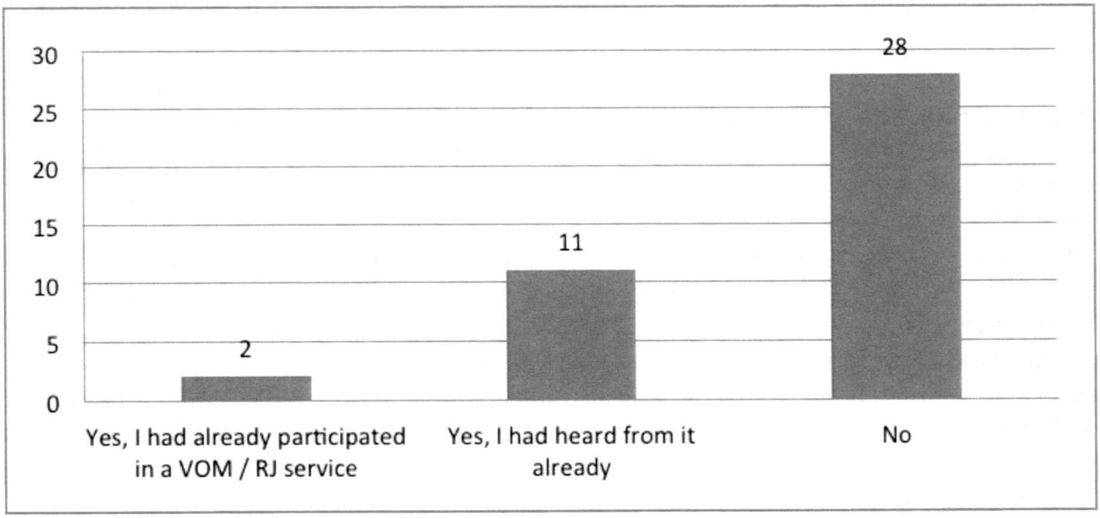

participated in German schemes (probably VOM). As this survey has been a pilot and the feedback has been good overall despite the very low response, in the following we will give a small insight into the sample anyway. In a second step we will try to derive what can be learned by this experience and especially what can and must be improved to have more success with such a survey in the future.

Results (n = 41)

As an introductory question and to find out more about the popularity of VOM / RJ services we asked the interviewees whether they knew the VOM / RJ service before they became a victim.[11] Figure 1 shows that almost 70& of the interviewees did not know of or hear from VOM / RJ services before.

As Bindel-Kögel & Karliczek (2013) found out in their recent research about VOM, how the victim becomes a victim that is the context of the offence plays a role in how VOM is undergone. We therefore

Figure 2: Context of the offence (n= 41)

asked the interviewees to *"Please evaluate the following statements concerning the offence."* Figure 2 shows that the majority of the victims either have been actively involved in the conflict or became a victim by accident.[12]

Further we asked the interviewees about the severity of their damages.[13] Concerning the sample the damages of the crime the interviewees became a victim of and which then have been dealt with within the VOM / RJ service have been materially in 43.9 percent, physically in 72.9 percent and emotionally in 80.5 percent of the cases. In most of the cases the harms have been minor or medium, but some have also been severe, especially emotionally (see Table 2).

Table 2: Damages, in % (n = 41)

	materially	physically	emotionally
minor	19.5	34.1	19.5
medium	17.1	24.2	36.6
severe	7.3	14.6	24.4
prefer not to say	22	7.3	4.9
not applicable	34.1	19.5	14.6
Total	100	100	100

The EU Victims´ Directive, amongst others, requires from the VOM / RJ services many structural suppositions, which is why we asked for a number of related aspects in the questionnaire (see questionnaire in the WK2 summary report).[14] In 85.4 percent of the cases the first connection between the VOM / RJ service and the victim was made by the RJ service via a cover letter or phone and more than 90 percent have evaluated this contact as informative and helpful. 78 percent of the interviewees received information material which has also been evaluated positively by the majority. Above this the VOM / RJ in general (accessibility, infrastructure, equipment etc.) as well as the atmosphere have mainly (by at least 60 percent of the interviewees) been evaluated positive.

The Directive further expects from the VOM / RJ services to inform the victim about a number of relevant facts, which therefore have also been enquired in the questionnaire. Table 3 summarizes the positive answers and shows that in this sample the requirements of the Victims´ Directive have been met almost completely.

Table 3: "I have been informed (about)…" (n = 41)

…the voluntariness of the participation	40
…that I am free to quit at any time	38
...that a written agreement only comes into being if you approve to the contents	40
…the confidentiality of the contents	38
…my rights as a victim	37

The interviewees were also asked whether they had a mediation dialogue with the offender or not.[15] Of the 41 cases a mediation dialogue directly with the offender took place in 29 cases and in 15 cases a mediation dialogue took place without the offender (indirect communication). This probably means that in some cases mediation dialogues have taken place with AND without the offender. Altogether not more than 29 of the interviewed victims have met their offender. 34 of the interviewees (83 percent) have been altogether satisfied with the mediation dialogue(s), regardless of whether they have met their offender directly or not.

When asked about their expectations concerning VOM / RJ services, the interviewees gave the following answers, illustrated in figure 2. In a second step, we also enquired whether these expectations have been met during the process and illustrated the answers in Figure 3 (overleaf).

It is clear that most of the expectations could have been more or less met during the process. Especially the expression of demands, issues and troubles could in most cases be realized during the VOM. Some expectations have however been belied, as for example 34 victims had hoped to change the offender and only 21 actually thought that they were able to do so. Also to find closure was expected by more victims (30) than actually have found closure in the end (23) and what seems alarming / problematic: only 24 interviewees actually thought that their damage had been acknowledged and less than half (17) stated that they saw the offenders remorse.

At the end of the questionnaire, we asked victims to *"please evaluate the following statements regarding the outcomes of the VOM/RJ procedure."* The following table gives an overview over the answers and these are overall very positive. For example 32/35 victims would recommend others to participate in a VOM / RJ service.

Figure 3a: "I thought it would be... / I wanted (to)..." (n= 41)

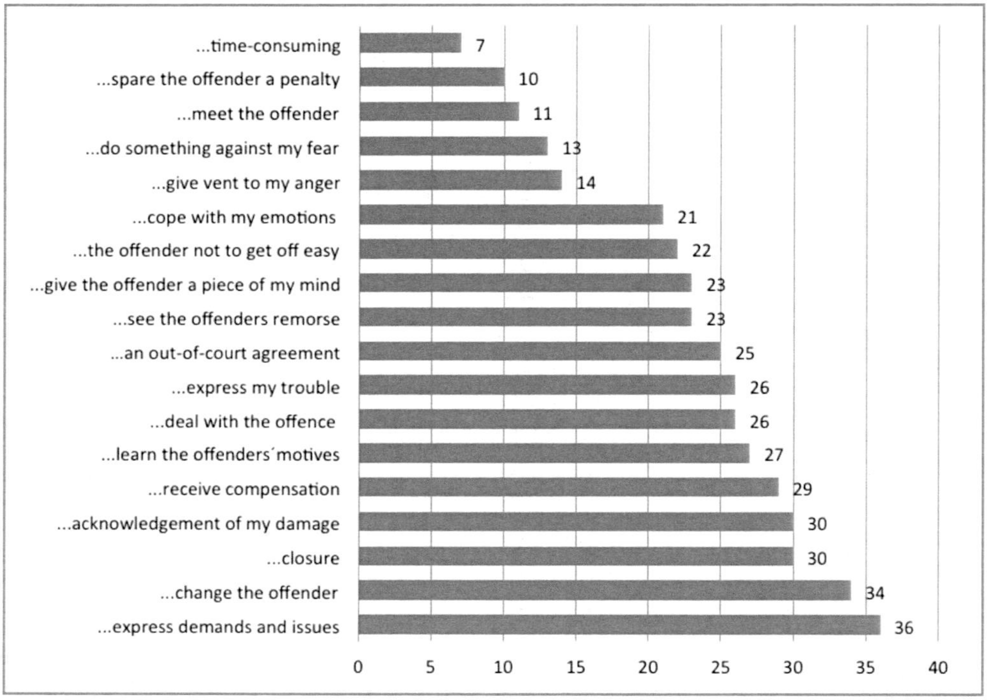

Figure 3b: "I could actually ... / It was ..." (n= 41)

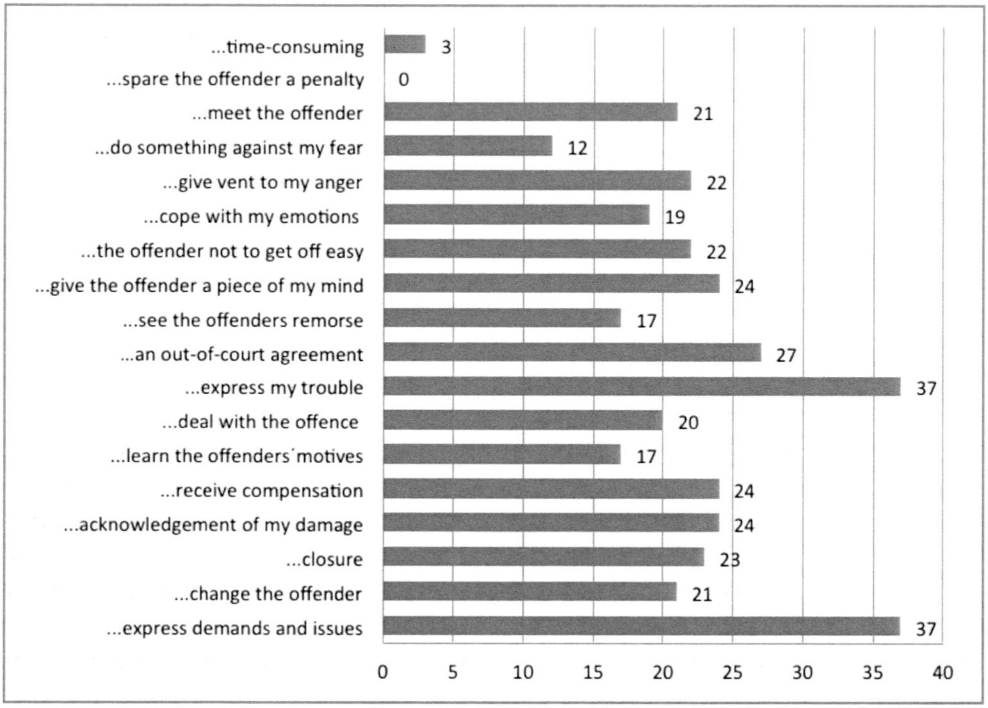

Table 4: Outcomes of the VOM / RJ service (n = 41)

	Strongly agree / Inclined to agree	Neither agree nor disagree
"I found help accomplishing the consequences of the offence."	21	5
"I was supported and strengthened with regard to my victims´ rights."	28	4
"I would do the VOM/RJ service again if I was in the same situation."	31	4
"The adduced compensations were appropriate with regard to the damage made."	21	6
"I would refuse a VOM/RJ service now."	2	6
"I would recommend others to participate in a VOM/RJ service."	32	3
"I think that the result of the RJ is not fair."	2	5
"I feel safe again."	19	10
"The information given in the preliminary interviews was proven wrong."	0	3
"The facilitator(s)/mediator(s) did not sufficiently consider my interests."	31	3
"I regret having participated in the VOM/RJ service."	2	1
"Overall, I am satisfied with the outcome of the RJ."	31	4

Finally, the interviewees were asked about some legal aspects of their case. According to this sample, penal proceedings have been commenced in 22 cases, but only half of the victims (11) have been informed about the outcome of the proceedings, which is not in accordance with what the EC Victims´ Directive requires. When asked, "How would you generally rate the penal reaction to the offence?" the following answers have been given (Table 5).

Table 5: Rating the penal reaction (n = 41)

way too soft	too soft	adequate	too strong	n/a
4	7	26	1	3

Implications

Overall, the data paint a positive picture of RJ services from the victims view both in subjective terms and in terms of what the EU Victims´ Directive requires. The caveat of our small sample size, however, must be kept in mind. Nevertheless, the results support our original hypothesis that RJ schemes in Germany (as most of the interviewees have been German) already meet most, if not all, preconditions of the EU Victims´ Directive. This is probably affiliated with the fact that the VOM standards, which contain high quality standards for VOM, are spread and used by those schemes even though they are not legally binding. The results also give support to the idea of improving our survey on the basis of the experiences in the RJE project.

Follow up Research with Victim Support Services

To follow up our findings, a supplementary survey with victims who have been participating in a victim support schemes is being carried out. With correlation analysis we filtered the answering options in terms of which ones tend to say the same or are at least very similar in their content. By this, we have been able to shorten the questionnaire drastically, so that it now contains only 26 questions on 7 pages.[16] We also met with an expert in this area and discussed the questionnaire with him. At the moment we are looking for institutions that are willing to support us by participating in the survey.

The Recent Legal Situation in Germany and the Requirements of the Victims' Directive

Article 12 EUVD speaks of "restorative justice services" (in German "Wiedergutmachungsdiensten"). This can be deemed a bold and unusual translation of the concept of „Restorative Justice". The difficulties of translating "Restorative Justice" into German have been discussed in the *TOA-Infodienst* (as an example, see *Hagemann / Lummer 2012*) from diverse perspectives, which is why we will not go into details here. But these difficulties bias also the implementation of the Victims' Directive into German law.

The central definitions of "restorative justice" for the purposes of the Directive can be found in Art. 2 and are also explained in Consideration No. 46 EUVD. Following consideration no. 46 of the Victims´ Directive, especially three procedures have to be understood as Restorative Justice: Victim offender mediation, Family group conferences and Sentencing circles.

The central norm regarding RJ in Germany is section 46a German Criminal Code (GCC), which defines "Täter-Opfer-Ausgleich". The same definition can also be found in sec. 10 par. 1 no. 7 Juvenile Court Act (JCA). "Täter-Opfer-Ausgleich" usually is translated with "victim-offender-mediation", because the term "Täter-Opfer-Ausgleich" is used for victim-offender-mediation in German language. But the legal definition of "Täter-Opfer-Ausgleich" in sec. 46a GCC and sec. 10 JCA has a different meaning.

From a comparison of the definitions of the Victims' Directive and sec. 46a GCC we can see: Restorative Justice ("Wiedergutmachung") according to art. 2 EUVD is

- a procedure
- in which victim and offender can voluntarily and actively
- and assisted by an impartially third party
- contribute to the regulation of a criminal offence.

"Täter-Opfer-Ausgleich" according to Section 46a No. 1 German Criminal Code in comparison is any effort to achieve reconciliation, which can be considered by the court, if restitution has been given to the victim or the offender has at least honestly tried to give restitution. Thus art. 2 EUVD means a procedure, in which an impartial third party is involved. Section 46a GCC on the contrary does not say anything about the procedure and especially does not mention the necessity of an impartial third party. Section 46a German Criminal Code is not procedure but output oriented. The result, restitution or at least earnest efforts to give restitution are regulated as preconditions of the legal effect the mitigation or discharge of a sentence. Art. 2 of the Victims´ Directive on the opposite only speaks of the active involvement in the regulation of the consequences of the offence. Whether this actually is achieved and what it contains is not relevant for the definition of the procedure.

This conceptual difference between procedural and output-oriented definitions and regulations is also important and controversial in RJ theory (Walgrave 2010). Art. 2 of the Victims´ Directive does not speak of legal consequences itself but further regulations concerning RJ are drawn on in art. 2. Section 46a GCC thus regulates, when and how the result of efforts to restitution can be considered in the assessment of penalty whereas art. 2 of the Victims´ Directive defines, what is to be understood by Restorative Justice services like for example by a mediation in criminal affairs (for more details see *Hartmann / Steengrafe 2012; Hartmann 2013*).

The following diagram illustrates the above explained similarities and differences. It shows that a mediation in criminal affairs which leads to an amicable agreement (reconciliation) generally has to be acknowledged as a "Täter-Opfer-Ausgleich" according to Section 46a GC Code.

Diagram 1: Legal definitions by comparison

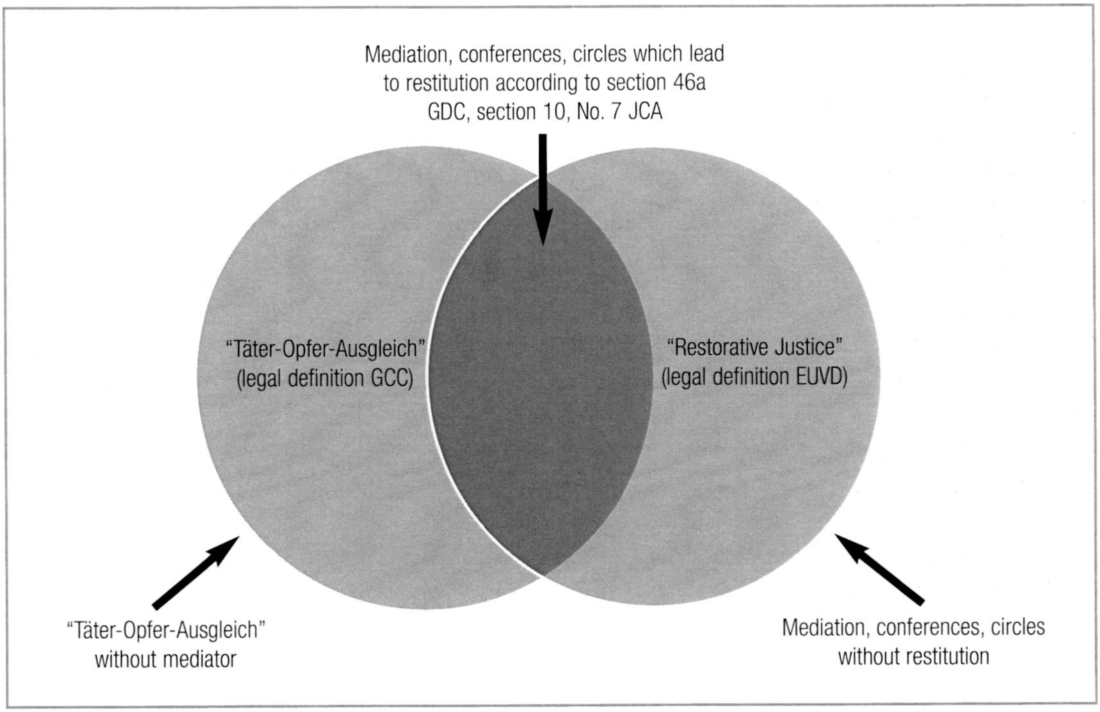

The image shows that a mediation in criminal affairs which leads to an amicable agreement has to be acknowledged as a "Täter-Opfer-Ausgleich" as per Section 46a German Criminal Code. However, "Täter-Opfer-Ausgleich" and RJ (e.g. mediation in criminal affairs) are not completely congruent. This becomes clear when looking at the cases of "Täter-Opfer-Ausgleich" on the left, which proceeded without the assistance of an mediator and on the right with the mediations that did not lead to a restitution and therefore cannot result in the mitigation of the penalty according to section 46a GCC. Hence section 46a GCC und art. 2 of the Victims´ Directive are distinct but have simultaneous meaning, as they serve different assignments.

Independently of these general conceptual differences between "Täter-Opfer-Ausgleich" and Restorative Justice services ("Wiedergutmachungsverfahren"), according to the Victims´ Directive we have analysed which implications the Directive has for the legal situation in Germany. For this matter we considered in addition to sec. 46a GCC the most important regulations for RJ in Germany, which can be found in the German Criminal Code, the German Code of Criminal Procedure (GCoCP), the Mediation Act (MA) and the above mentioned VOM Standards of the *Bundesarbeitsgemeinschaft Täter-Opfer-Ausgleich* and the *Servicebüro für Täter-Opfer-Ausgleich*. The following table gives an overview of the results of this comparison.

Table 6: Comparrison Results

EU Victims´ Directive	Laws and Standards in Germany
Art. 2 No. 1 d Restorative justice: • voluntary; • help of an impartial third party • participate actively	Section 155a, 3 **GCoCP** • Against the explicit will of the victim an agreement must not be assumed / supposed. Section 1 **MA** • Voluntarily and independently • Assistance of one or more independent, neutral persons without decision-making power Cypher 1.2 **VOM Standards** • voluntarily • active participation • abandonment of presettings from the legislation
Con. 46 Restorative justice services • Mediation between offender and victim • Conferences and Circles ...	Section 2 par. 4 **MA** • Third parties can be involved if all parties agree. **VOM Standards** • Designed only for mediation, further participants are not ruled out. Concrete regulations for conferences and circles are missing.
Art. 12 par. 1 Safeguards • Secondary victimisation • Repeat victimisation • Intimidation • Retaliation • Safe and competent restorative justice services	Section 155 b **GCoCP** • Protection of the personal data of those affected Section 2 par. 3 **MA** • The mediator ... ensures, that the parties are involved in an appropriate and fair manner into the mediation.

EU Victims´ Directive (continued...)	**Laws and Standards in Germany** (continued...)
	Section 5 **MA** • Initial and further training of the mediator, certified mediator Cypher 1.2, 5.5 **VOM Standards** • A repeated victimization is to be prevented. Cypher 2.1, 4.1 und 4.3 **VOM Standards** • Requirements to the provider, the qualification of the mediator, the design of a non-violent dialogue with the aim of a non-violent future.
Art. 12 par. 1, a • based on the victim's free and informed consent	Section 136 par. 1,4, 163a par. 4,2, 155a,2 **GCoCP** • link to RJ in the sense of section 46a GCC. Police, prosecutors and courts shall consider in every stage of a criminal procedure, whether a reconciliation between victim and offender is possible and they shall work towards it in appropriate cases. Against the explicit will of the victim a reconciliation must not be assumed. Section 2 par. 2 und 6 **MA** • the mediator makes sure that the parties have understood the principles and the procedure of the mediation procedure, participate voluntarily and make agreements only with knowledge of all facts. Cyphers 1.2, 4.4, 5.2, 5.3 und 5.4 **VOM Standards** • voluntariness and transparency, extensive information in the preliminary talks, unaffected decision-making
Art. 12 par. 1b • Extensive information about mediation procedures, the possible consequences and measures to monitor and guarantee the fulfilment of agreement	Section 2 par. 2 **MA** • No regulations concerning monitoring and fulfilment of the agreement (section 2 par. 6 MA) Cypher 5.6 **VOM Standards** • Control / monitor the fulfilment of the agreement…
Art. 12 par. 1c • The offender has acknowledged the basic facts of the case;	Section 46a **GCC** • The Federal Supreme Court (BGH) requires a confession in cases of (severe) assault and sexual offences. Cypher 1.3 **VOM Standards** • Basic condition is that the offender take responsibility for their behaviour.

EU Victims´ Directive (continued...)	**Laws and Standards in Germany** (continued...)
Art. 12 par. 1d • any agreement is arrived at voluntarily and may be taken into account in any further criminal proceedings;	Section 46a **GCC** • consideration of reconciliation and compensation between offender and victim
Art. 12 par. 1e • confidentiality • not subsequently disclosed, except with the agreement of the parties or as required by national law due to an overriding public interest.	Section 155b **GCoCP** • ensuring data protection Section 155b par. 2, 3 **GCoCP** • duty of the mediators to report relevant details to the prosecution or court. Section 4 **MA** • extensive obligation to confidentiality, clause of the *ordre public*. Based on that a right to refuse to give evidence according to section 383 par. 1 Cypher. 6 Code of Civil Procedure in civil cases. Cypher 5.3 **VOM Standards** • reference to missing right to refuse to give evidence for the mediators (in criminal cases).

We do not want to go into every detail here, but would like to highlight the three following points:

1. According to art. 2 No. 1d EUVD RJ has to be voluntary and assisted by an impartially third party. As within the frame of section 46a GCC no procedure is regulated, section 155a GCoCP consequently refers to the result: "Against the explicit will of the victim an agreement must not be assumed." Naturally it makes sense to already design the mediation process in a way that guarantees the voluntariness from the beginning. Such regulations are phrased in section 1 MA and in the VOM Standards.

2. Art. 12 par. 1 requires to safeguard the victim from secondary victimization. Section 155b GCoCP only refers to the protection of personal data. Respective regulations are again to be found in the Mediation Act and the VOM Standards.
   The same applies to the guarantee of safe and competent RJ services and the initial and further training of the mediators, which according to art. 24 par. 4 of the Victims´ Directive are explicitly designated. Respective regulations could for instance eliminate hesitations that exist towards traditional mediation services which are ethnically or religiously related and are discussed intensively repeatedly (*Hartmann 2013*).

3. Art. 12 par. 1e EUVD requires confidentiality. According to section 4 MA an extensive obligation to confidentiality and based on that, a right to refuse to give evidence in civil proceedings exists.

The existing regulations of the GCC, the GCoCP and the JCA concerning VOM do therefore in our eyes not meet the numerous requirements that derive from the obligation of the member states to take measures to ensure safe and competent RJ services and to develop respective protocols and guidelines. If one however also considers the Mediation Act and the VOM Standards, the requirements of the Victims´ Directive would be met mostly.

Hence RJ services which have the respective seal of quality probably do already today satisfy what the Victims´ Directive requires. It is disputed whether the MA is applicable for mediation in criminal affairs. We have demonstrated the applicability elsewhere (*Hartmann / Steengrafe 2012*), but in order to meet the requirements of the Victims´ Directive, the German legislator should explicitly regulate that the MA has to be observed also in criminal cases and not only for mediation but also for other RJ settings like conferences etc.

The VOM Standards are not legally binding. Hence we think that the German legislation cannot do otherwise but support and make sure the implementation of the Victims´ Directive with additional legal regulations. We do not believe that the EU will be satisfied with the fact that a voluntary seal of quality (according to the VOM standards) exists as long as only a minority of RJ services have this seal. The comparatively small number on the opposite highlights the necessity to arrange compulsory standards.

Professionals in Germany: Learning from the RJE Piloting

From the feedback to our piloting and dissemination activities for the RJE project, we were able to gain an insight of the different views and expectations that exist German-wide amongst practitioners and professionals on the EU Victims´ Directive. Furthermore, we received feedback on the training materials that were produced within the RJE project and which we disseminated to around 250 RJ institutions. At the VOM-Forum in Trier, which can be assessed as the most important national event with regard to the Victims´ Directive and RJ we had the possibility to present the project and the training material during one of five theme cafés, which was part of the conference programme. Besides the many face-to-face discussions that took place in this context we mostly did the dissemination via Email. Overall the training material has been highly valued and appreciated by everybody who we talked to.

Professionals' opinion about the EU Victims´ Directive is generally positive especially in relation to the many chances the Victims´ Directive states concerning the further (legal) implementation of RJ. On the other hand, some discussions showed that the Victims´ Directive's tone is critical and vague towards RJ. Only time will show the actual impact of the Victims´ Directive on RJ practice and standards. Conclusively, our impression is that practitioners are willing to learn more about victims and victims´ rights and that the material produced in the RJE project are valued by German practitioners who deemed them suitable for awareness raising and learning.

The German VOM Standards (which are however not legally binding) already conform with the Victims´ Directive. This was stated by many practitioners we talked to. Formally however the German law does not implicitly cover what the Victims´ Directive requests (see above). Therefore to make the Victims´ Directive really change something (for example "Täter-Opfer-Ausgleich" organised outside RJ schemes) the German government needs to consider changes of the German law and only then the Victims´ Directive would have direct impact to the practitioners and maybe would request further training. If the German legislator will implement the regulations of the Directive respectively and by that strengthens RJ practitioners and by that RJ services, this would enable them to improve their services not only for victims but all parties involved in the process.

Concluding Thoughts

Due to the new Victims´ Directive, the German legislator must further regulate RJ services (mediation, conferences, and circles) in Germany. This means a number of threads and opportunities for the restorative justice movement in Germany.

For instance, due to this change, we anticipate that the "Täter-Opfer-Ausgleich" (mediation in criminal affairs, a conference or a circle) becomes distinguishable from a "Täter-Opfer-Ausgleich", that the defense attorney suggests last minute right before the judgment of the court. This typically concerns those cases in which offenders try to defend themselves, and only in the moment when the evidence is oppressive the victim restitution is offered, (see Hartmann, 2013). This last-minute VOM is criticized with good reason and is starting to affect the image of "Täter-Opfer-Ausgleich" negatively in the public. It also damages the reputation of RJ services in Germany. The label "Täter-Opfer-Ausgleich" is now known and introduced, but can become a trap for RJ services, if the different qualities are not marked with different labels.

One of the threads that we anticipate is that the German legislator may follow the sceptical attitude of the Victims´ Directive and according to art. 12 par. 2 EUVD create very narrow provisions for the selection of cases which can be referred to RJ services. This would mean that the lights would go out in many RJ services in Germany.

The expansion of RJ settings going beyond mediation would be very welcome in Germany. As argued, "most restorative" according to the Directive is not a broad coverage of any stakeholder interests in restorative processes but only the best service to the victims in the narrow sense of art. 2 EUVD. This should also have a clear impact to RJ practice. Preferable are not schemes that offer only one specific service like conferencing or victim-offender-mediation but schemes that are willing and able to adjust the settings and procedures to the specific needs and informed decisions of the actual victims and offenders. Fortunately the trend in Germany is going in this direction. Established VOM schemes are opening for a broader spectrum of settings (conferencing, circles, etc.), which they can offer to victims and offenders. As we have shown above this kind of flexible setting would meet the requirements of the Victims´ Directive.

Unfortunately, RJ in Germany is not walked by its own dynamics. Regions with high numbers of cases are confronted with extensive RJ deserts. Paradoxically after years of good practice, RJ still has not convinced. Therefore, reliable and approved data are decisive in the public debate. The RJE findings can serve as a step towards this direction. This is also reflected in art. 28 of the Victims´ Directive, which obliges the member states to deliver data about the utilization of the guaranteed rights by the victims. Offender-related data concerning RJ is not sufficient for that. The national statistics for VOM (*"Bundesweite Täter-Opfer-Ausgleich-Statistik"*)[17] is one of few statistics that collects respective data also victim-related and does not extend the mostly offender-dominated view of the judiciary into the data. The German national ministry for justice and consumer protection (*"Bundesministerium der Justiz und für Verbraucherschutz"* (BMJV)), that plays a central role when it comes to the implementation of the Victims´ Directive, trusts the national statistics for VOM, because it funds these statistics since many years and publishes the data under its own editorial.

Analysis of the satisfaction of victims attest RJ very good results in numerous countries. But in Germany and also in other European countries such analyses have only been implemented few and far between. By that a big chance has been left unexploited. Within the frame of the project "Restorative Justice in Europe – Safeguarding Victims and Empowering Professionals" (RJE) we tried to correct this with the aforementioned Europe wide online-based victim's survey.

We argue that the EU Victims´ Directive and the "Istanbul Convention" of the European Council have a somewhat paradox position regarding RJ services. They are supportive and at the same time sceptical about RJ. This sceptical position may, among other reasons, also be affected by predominant RJ theories or approaches. In contrary to restorative justice theory, the Victims´ Directive contains a rather narrow definition of victims and requires that restorative justice services should have as a primary consideration the interests and needs of these victims. As a consequence services have to give them priority in regard to other stakeholders. RJ services have to ensure that victims of crime receive appropriate information and are able to participate in criminal proceedings. Participation in RJ processes has to be based on the victim's free and informed consent. According to our view this regulation includes that the victim is among other points also informed about different RJ settings and can influence with his or her consent, which kind of RJ setting (VOM, conferencing, circles etc.) will be applied. From this perspective RJ services that are able and willing to offer a variety of RJ processes are preferable to services that offer only VOM or conferences.

Regarding the legal situation we demonstrated that the German Criminal Code and the German Code of Criminal Procedure do not regulate RJ services in a way that complies with the Victims´ Directive. But if the German Mediation Act and the VOM Standards are included the most if not all requirements of the Directive are met. The Problem here on the one hand is that it is controversial if the Mediation Act can be applied in criminal cases and that on the other hand the VOM Standards are not legally binding. Therefore we suggest that the German legislation regulates RJ services in compliance with the Directive. In doing this the legislation can and should resort to the Mediation Act and the VOM Standards.

Regarding RJ practice in Germany, we face a paradoxical situation. On the one hand, we have a wide spread practice of VOM and a growing number of schemes that offer conferences and circles. According to the results of our survey and the findings of the RJE project, these RJ schemes practise the requirements of the Directive as part of their professional ethics that tend to be informed mainly by the VOM Standards. On the other hand, there is also a practice of "Täter-Opfer-Ausgleich" outside these known RJ schemes. This is possible, because the legal definition of "Täter-Opfer-Ausgleich" does not regulate the process of reconciliation ("Ausgleich"). There is some evidence that the requirements of the Directive presumably are not met in many of these cases. As both practices are indistinguishably labelled as "Täter-Opfer-Ausgleich" in German language the absence of legally binding safeguards regarding RJ processes is a growing problem.

In order to overcome the somewhat paradox positions of the EU Victims´ Directive and the Istanbul Convention of the European Council, we developed and implemented an Europe wide victim survey. With that instrument we wanted to give the victims a voice as well as an opportunity to practitioners, professionals and decision makers to evaluate whether the requirements of the Victims' Directive are met in practice. By that we gave member states first-hand information in order to comply with their reporting duties from art. 28 EUVD. Both, the number of RJ schemes participating and the response from victims were disappointingly small in the pilot. Nevertheless we are convinced that victim satisfaction should be measured on a constant and broad basis. This is necessary to ensure the quality of RJ services and their compliance with the Victims' Directive. In our opinion this is an inevitable element to overcome the somewhat paradox positions of European legislators and other stakeholders in this field. Therefore we are trying to learn from the pilot survey and by that will soon be able to offer an improved and revised version of the instrument.

Notes

1 OJEU 2012 L 315, pp. 57-73 from the 14th of November2012.
2 http://www.coe.int/t/dghl/standardsetting/convention-violence/default_en.asp
3 http://www.toa-servicebuero.de/magazine
4 The problems that derive from using the concept community ("Gemeinschaft") and it's use within the frame of RJ theory will not be further discussed here (on this discussion see Vanfraechem 2012; Hartmann 2007).
5 As far as we know this concept has been developed in Schleswig-Holstein.
6 https://www.soscisurvey.de/index.php?page=info
7 http://195.37.102.112/sosci/opferbefragungoffen/
8 https://www.soscisurvey.de/index.php?page=info
9 http://www-01.ibm.com/software/de/analytics/spss/products/statistics/
10 As for Germany 10 of 16 federal states have been represented at this point.
11 "Did you know the VOM/RJ service before becoming the victim of that offence?"
12 We summarized the answers "inclined to agree" and "strongly agree"
13 "In your opinion, how severe have the damages caused by the offence which was subject to the VOM, been?"
14 Both reports are available at http://www.rj4all.info/content/RJEresources
15 Two questions: "Have, in your case, mediation dialogues with the offender, taken place?" and "Have, in your case, mediation dialogues without the offender (in terms of an indirect mediation/dialogue/communication) taken place?"
16 See WK2 summary report available at http://www.rj4all.info/content/RJEresources (accessed September 2014).
17 http://www.bmjv.de/DE/Ministerium/Abteilungen/Strafrecht/KriminologieKriminalpraevention/_doc/Taeter_Opfer_Ausgleich_Bundesjustizministerium_legt_neuen_Bericht_zur_TOA_Statistik_vor_doc.html

References

Altweger, Andrea; Hitzl, Evelyn (2002): Außergerichtlicher Tatausgleich. Kundenzufriedenheitsanalyse der Geschädigten. In *Sozialarbeit und Bewährungshilfe* 24 (1), pp. 17-22.

Bindel-Kögel, Gabriele; Karliczek, Kari-Maria (2013): *Außergerichtliche Konfliktschlichtung als opferstützendes Instrument*. Camino gGmbH; Friedrich-Ebert-Stiftung. Potsdam, 28/05/2013.

Donabedian, Avedis (1980): *The Definition of Quality and Approaches to Its Assessment, Explorations in Quality Assessment and Monitoring. Band 1*. Health Administration Press, 1980.

Fischelmanns, Frank (2006): Die Onlinebefragung als Methode für Opferbefragungen. In Rebekka Salome Henrich, Veronika Kesoglou, Juletka Schulter-Ostermann (Eds.): *Praxis, Forschung, Kooperation: gegenwärtige Tendenzen in der Kriminologie. Sammelband zu der Tagung: „Im Gespräch. Zur Aktualität der Kriminologie"*. Frankfurt [am Main]: Verlag für Polizeiwissenschaft., pp. 89-108.

Hagemann, Otmar; Lummer, Ricarda (2012): Restorative Justice - auch das Unübersetzbare braucht klare Begriffe. In Servicebüro für Täter-Opfer-Ausgleich und Konfliktschlichtung (Ed.): *Infodienst. Rundbrief zum Täter-Opfer-Ausgleich* (45). Köln: JVA Druck + Medien, Geldern, pp. 28-35.

Hartmann, Arthur (2007): Täter-Opfer-Ausgleich – Restorative Justice – Soziale Mediation, *Perspektive Mediation (pm)*, 2007/4, pp. 25-29.

Hartmann, Arthur (2013): Täter-Opfer-Ausgleich in der Entwicklung. In: Boers / Feltes / Kinzig / Sherman / Streng / Trüg, *Kriminologie – Kriminalpolitik – Strafrecht, Festschrift für Hans-Jürgen Kerner, Mohr Siebeck,* Tübingen 2013, pp. 591-603, 592 f.

Hartmann, Arthur / Steengrafe, Felix (2012): Das Mediationsgesetz und der Täter-Opfer-Ausgleich. *TOA-Infodienst* 43, 2012, pp. 27-32.

Leiner, D. J. (2013). *SoSci Survey* (Version 2.3.05-i) [Computer Software]. Available at https://www.soscisurvey.de

McCold, Paul; Wachtel, Ted (2001): Restorative Justice Theory Validation. In: Elmar G.M. Weitekamp and Hans-Jürgen Kerner, *Restorative Justice: Theoretical Foundations.* Devon, UK: Willan Publishing, pp. 110-142.

Vanfraechem, Inge (2012): Community, society and state in restorative justice: an exploration. In: Mackay, Bosnjak, Deklerck, Pelikan, von Stokkom, Wright, Images of Restorative Justice Theory, *Verlag für Polizeiwissenschaft,* Frankfurt a.M., 2012, pp. 73-91.

Walgrave, Lode (2010): Restorative Justice potentials and key questions. In: Ministry of Justice and Law Enforcement Republic of Hungary (ed.). *European best practices of restorative justice in the criminal procedure.* Budapest, 29-45.

RJE Training Session, delivered by EPLO at the Police Training Academy, April 2014, Athens Greece. © IARS

RJE seminar delivered by EPLO at Panteion University, March 2014, Athens, Greece. © IARS

Empowering Restorative Justice in Greece: One Step Forward for Victims

*Vasso Artinopoulou and Iro Michael**

Abstract

This chapter is based on the scientific and practical results which were produced within the framework of the EU funded project "Restorative Justice in Europe: Safeguarding Victims & Empowering Professionals" (2012-2014), in which Greece participated via the partnership of the European Public Law Organisation (EPLO). Restorative Justice has developed in Greece during the last decade. The implementation of restorative practices is based on laws and informal initiatives. Taking into account the literature review, field-work research and practical results of RJE work streams, the needs, views and expectations of victims and professionals are described regarding the implementation of the Directive 2012/29/EU and Restorative Justice. While the implementation of restorative measures and practices in the Greek Justice System and on informal level meets operational, organizational and financial obstacles, there seems to be opportunities for restorative justice to progress to a greater extent. The chapter ends through a critical thinking about the current and future progress of restorative justice in Greece, while the authors suggest recommendations which reflect the victims and practitioners needs, and aim to support the application of restorative practices and the Victims' Directive.

Introduction and Project Objectives

The debate on Restorative Justice (RJ) counts almost thirty years now. Theory, research and practice on RJ are getting more and more mature; putting RJ practices either in the core or the periphery of the criminal justice systems. The EU Directive on 'establishing minimum standards on the rights, support and protection of victims of crime, and replacing Council Framework Decision 2001/220/JHA' (2012/29/EU) reinsures the victims' rights and promotes the implementation of RJ schemes. However, the values of RJ are to be addressed in a certain context and the philosophy(ies) of RJ to be emerged.

Historically, the development of RJ in Greece is not based on a general or overarching scheme. Instead, independent and fragmented programmes and initiatives are taking place at various time intervals. The RJ schemes in Greece are based on both law and practice, but meet a number of organizational, operational and financial obstacles that hinder the implementation and development of restorative practices. The current situation is positive, but both the need to develop a wider dialogue on RJ and its practices as well as the need for better coordination and operation of existing practices and measures are significant.

* Dr. Vasso Artinopoulou (Professor of Criminology, f. Vice Rector, Panteion University of Social and Political Sciences, Athens, Greece. Co-Director of the Restorative Justice for All Institute, London, UK E-mail: vasiliki.artinopoulou@panteion.gr), Iro Michael Criminologist – Mediator; Senior Project Officer, Restorative Justice for All Institute, London, UK; PhD candidate, Panteion University, E-mail: iromichael@panteion.gr

The protection of victims has been addressed by Greek Law, while Greece is often called upon to incorporate relevant European binding documents into national legislation (see also Lambropoulou, 2005; Artinopoulou, 2010a). On academic and scientific levels, the writings of Greek criminologists in the field of research of victims are relatively rich, which reflects their long involvement in the field of victimology since the '70s, covering a wide range of themes regarding victims of crime (Artinopoulou 2010a; Artinopoulou and Petoussi 2011; Labropoulou 2005; Αρτινοπούλου, 1995, 2001, 2006; Αρτινοπούλου και Μαγγανάς, 1996; Αρτινοπούλου και Παπαθεοδώρου, 2006; Δασκαλάκη κ.ά., 2000; Δημόπουλος και Κοσμάτος, 2006; Ζαγούρα, 2007; Καράμπελα, 2001; Κουράκης, 2007; Λάζος, 2002; Μαγγανάς, 1996; Πανούσης κ.ά., 1994; Πιτσελά, 2004). In Greece, the implementation of programmes to support victims' rights is usually targeted at vulnerable groups or groups at increased risk of victimization in specific crimes (e.g. victims of interpersonal violence, victims of trafficking, child abuse etc). Such programmes aim mainly to record the quantitative and qualitative characteristics of victims, or enhance and strengthen the work of professionals working in victim services. Various NGOs play a vital role in protecting and supporting victims and defend their rights.

In the field of RJ, RJ in contemporary Greece has developed mainly over the last decade. Yet the idea of RJ can be traced already in ancient Greek philosophy. Indeed, Aristotle's "epanorthotikon dikaion" (Greek phrase for "restorative law") as this is already clearly defined in his "Nicomachean Ethics, Book V", the participation of citizens in doing justice, the implementation of mediation schemes and arbitration by the "Tessarakonta" (Greek work for "Forty")[1] and the Public referees are all exemplary of RJ practices in ancient Greece (Artinopoulou 2010a). However, the restorative practices and ideas in ancient Greece differ from the RJ schemes encountered today. Nowadays, the development of RJ in Greece is based both on laws which introduce RJ practices as complementary and alternative methods to traditional procedures of the Greek Justice System (GJS), and through independent and fragmented programmes and initiatives which take place informally outside the criminal justice framework.

This chapter is based on the scientific and practical results which were produced within the framework of the EU funded project "Restorative Justice in Europe: Safeguarding Victims & Empowering Professionals" (RJE) (2012-2014), in which Greece participated via the partnership of the European Public Law Organisation (www.Eplo.eu). Taking into account the literature review, fieldwork research and practical results of RJE work-streams, the needs, views and expectations of victims and professionals in Greece are described regarding the implementation of Directive 2012/29/EU (Victims' Directive) and RJ. The project aimed to produce scientific and practical results that will be used by policy and decision makers, and practitioners in the EU. Specifically for Greece, the RJE project intended to contribute to the development, piloting and implementation of protocols and guidelines, training materials and programmes, and best practice guidance for professionals, including providing safeguards for victims in RJ services, respecting the interest of the victims and offenders, improving the skills and knowledge of professionals, and enhancing multi-agency, cross-sector cooperation among RJ/ victim services and national agencies, with the aim of minimising the risks of secondary and repeat victimisation. In relation to these, several research questions were raised during the progress of the project.

The chapter addresses the literature review on RJ in Greece, the key findings of the original research on crime victims and stakeholders, the training for professionals and the critical issues raised by the two year project implementation. Overall, over 700 people participated during RJE work-streams' implementation in Greece. Target groups included victims, external stakeholders, the public, academia, and policy makers. Particular attention was paid to vulnerable victims (due to their age, gender and type of crime) and high-risk contexts and their effect on victims.

Restorative Justice in Greece: The Framework and the Literature

RJ practices in Greece can be found in the legal and social contexts. The national laws are introduced either as result of European binding documents or in an effort to improve and speed up the administration of justice. Additionally, RJ is promoted through various programmes at social level and is further promoted in academic and research level. Overall, the introduction of mediation is central to these developments as it has been a very important legislative step for the GJS and an evolving practice in other social contexts.

In legal settings, provisions that promote conciliation and mediation between victims and offenders are found in criminal and civil law and the law for juvenile offenders. These provisions are mainly observed at the stage of prosecution.[2] However, they can be more or less observed in all stages of criminal proceedings throughout formal and semi-formal practices (Lambropoulou, 2010; Artinopoulou 2010b) and are applied to petty offences, misdemeanours, and felonies, as well as in civil and commercial matters.

In the context of the Greek Criminal Justice System (GCJS), the introduction of criminal mediation in domestic violence cases (Law 3500/2006) came into full force in 2007 and was the result of the harmonization of the Greek legislation with the EU Framework Decision on the standing of victims in criminal proceedings (Council Framework Decision 2001/220/JHA). Law 3500/2006 "On Confronting Domestic Violence and other provisions" introduced victim offender mediation (Articles 11 to 14) to cases of misdemeanours of domestic violence, allowing the prosecutor to suggest to parties the possibility to resort to mediation before criminal prosecution or before trial (see also Artinopoulou, 2010b). The option for the offender and the victim to resort to mediation is given under conditions that have to do with the offender's willingness and his promise that he/she will not commit any act of domestic violence in the future, he will accept to reside elsewhere beside the family residence for a reasonable period (if the victim suggests it), he will attend a therapeutic counselling programme provided by a public health institution, and he will restore any harm or damage caused by his acts and provide fair compensation to the victim. The process of penal mediation takes place only if both the victim and the offender agree to participate.[3] If the parties reach a final agreement and the offender complied with the terms of that agreement for three years, then the case is closed. Otherwise, the prosecutor may open the case and proceed with the conduct of criminal proceedings.

In practice, the cases of mediation in domestic violence misdemeanours are referred to the National Centre for Social Solidarity (E.K.K.A. 2012). The Penal Mediation Programme of E.K.K.A. is implemented only in Athens and Thessaloniki in cooperation with the Prosecutorial offices of Athens, Piraeus and Thessaloniki. Even though the introduction of mediation in domestic violence cases has been widely accepted, it has been criticized as to its suitability in this type of crimes, raising issues of transgender inequality and imbalance of forces, while the lack of appropriate structures and sufficient training of the authorities in order to conduct the mediation process are also mentioned (Artinopoulou 2010a: 112-113; Artinopoulou 2010b: 182-184.).

More recently, penal conciliation (article 308B of the Greek Penal Procedure Code - GPPC) was introduced for certain felonies against property by Article 17 of the Law 3904/2010 on "Rationalization and improvement of the administration of criminal justice and other provisions". According to Article 17, the prosecutor, acting at the request of the accused and after having press charges in certain cases of felonies against property, may invite the defendant and the victim or their lawyers to conciliation. The achievement of conciliation is taken into account in the next stages of the proceedings, and if the accused is found guilty, the sentence will not exceed three years. Furthermore, articles of the Greek Penal Code propose the discharge of the accused from any penalty for crimes against property (Art. 375-374, 375-377, 381, 382, 386-406 Penal Code), arson, explosions, etc. (as reformed by Law 3904/2010 and Law 3160/2003), as long as the offender with his/her own will fully restores the harms or damages caused to the victim and/or reduces the risk caused by his/her acts, within the deadlines specified by the law and depending on the severity of the crime.

Especially for juvenile offenders (see also Lambropoulou 2010; Αρτινοπούλου 2010a: 98-108; Πιτσελά, 2004), Law 3189/2003 on the "Reform of penal legislation for juveniles and other provisions" is a major breakthrough in the treatment of juvenile offenders, as it restated the educational and therapeutic measures for the reformation of juvenile offenders and increased penal non-age at the age of 13 years old. A range of educational measures are included in the legislation, including conciliation between the juvenile offender and the victim, in order for the offender to express apology, manage the consequences of his/her act and settle the case out of court; community service; attendance social and psychological programmes in relevant public or private agencies or services; and other measures that have to do with the lifestyle or upbringing of a juvenile. Law 3189/2003 was reformed by Law 3860/2010 on "Improvements on penal legislation for juvenile offenders, prevention and treatment of juvenile victimization and delinquency" which increased the limits of penal nonage at the age of 15 years old and set the imposition of custodial sentences only when is proved thoroughly that the educational or therapeutic measures are not sufficient in each case.

The scheme of conciliation between the juvenile offender and the victim is conducted under the supervision of the Juvenile Probation Services,[4] where juvenile probation officers undertake the role of the mediator. Despite the lack of statistical and empirical research on the implementation and effectiveness of the legal framework for juveniles, stagnation has been observed, to some extent, in the change of the judicial practice as well as a limited use of the measure of victim-offender conciliation scheme, reflecting the lack of resources, training of professionals and appropriate structures. It seems that Juvenile Probation Officers face mediation with some ignorance and suspicion and do not seem to trust the process enough, nor have received any relevant training; so they usually avoid it (Lambropoulou 2010: 143-147; Αρτινοπούλου 2010a: 100-101).

Mediation in civil and commercial matters was introduced in 2010 (Law 3898/2010 on mediation in civil and commercial matters), while judicial mediation was more recently introduced in cases of private disputes (Law 4055/2012).[5] Moreover, article 214A[6] of the Greek Code of Civil Procedure (GCCP) provides amicable settlement outside of courts in cases of private disputes, with the participation of the lawyers of the parties or any other third person of common choice.

In all the above legal provisions, each law specifies certain preconditions in order for the parties to resort to the RJ measures and other provisions regarding the procedural steps of carrying out the RJ practices, all of which concern mainly the integration of the RJ processes in the current procedural and substantive law, rather that the development of the RJ principles and the essential development of guidelines for providing RJ in the interest of the victim and the offender and for improving victims' safeguards in RJ services. This top-down approach in implementing mediation seems to be more offender-focused than victim-led, since there is lack of provisions on safeguarding victims, while the laws refer mainly to the offender. Moreover, there is lack of provisions regarding the actual RJ process in each case. This indeterminacy seems to be an obstacle for the practitioners who are called to apply RJ schemes without any further support. Generally, there is cooperation among the RJ/ victim services and national agencies. However, there is lack of best practice guidance that will enhance multi-agency, cross-sector cooperation among RJ/ victim services and national agencies. Moreover, there is lack of training manuals and manuals for the implementation of RJ in different contexts. As a result, it appears that there is a level of lack of trust towards RJ and its benefits.

On the contrary, RJ is promoted on social level through various mediation programmes, especially school mediation (e.g. Αρτινοπούλου, 2010b; Artinopoulou et al., 2012; Θάνος, 2011). Such initiatives are based on the bottom-up approach which includes initiatives of active citizens and on the community-driven model on developing projects and initiatives, while they are carried out on local level (e.g. communities/municipalities, schools) in order to strengthen social ties, raise awareness and inform citizens and socially vulnerable groups (children, immigrants). However, the development of these informal programmes is sporadic rather than constant and systematic; a fact which is probably due to the recent growth of these initiatives and the lack of networking.

NGOs have vital role in protecting and supporting victims and defending their rights, and in promoting the practice of RJ. Some NGOs in partnership with lawyers-mediators aim mainly to raise awareness of legal practitioners on the institution of mediation, to provide training in mediation (for the accreditation of lawyers as mediators under Law 3898/2010), and to promote mediation in the business and commercial world.

RJ is also promoted on academic and research levels. The avocation of Greek criminologists with the subject of RJ is relatively limited but has been rapidly growing (e.g. Alexiadis, 1992; Αλεξιάδης, 1996, 2007; Αρτινοπούλου, 2008, 2010a, 2010b, 2010c, 2011a, 2011b, 2012, Artinopoulou, 2010b, 2012, 2013; Artinopoulou & Gavrielides, 2012a, 2012b; Artinopoulou et al., 2012˙ Gavrielides & Artinopoulou, 2013; Giovanoglou, 2008˙ Lambropoulou, 2010˙ Pitsela & Kastanidou, 2013). These texts study mostly the development of RJ theory, the relationship of RJ with other theoretical models of justice, the relationship of RJ with human rights, and the practice of conciliation and mediation as applied in Greece. RJ has now become a permanent topic in conferences and workshops organized by criminological and legal associations, developing a fruitful scientific dialogue. Of particular importance has been the realization of the International Symposia on Restorative Justice which are held in Skopelos Island (Greece). The Symposia are organized by the Restorative Justice for All (RJ4All) Institute, and are the result of cooperation of Prof. V. Artinopoulou with Dr Th. Gavrielides (founders and directors of RJ4All). Moreover, RJ is subject of study and courses in Greek universities, such as courses at the Sociology Department of Panteion University of Social and Political Sciences, the School of Law of Aristotle University of Thessaloniki, and the Faculty of Law of the National and Kapodistrian University of Athens. Equally important is the contribution of some doctoral dissertations in promoting RJ in academic and research level.

The Original Research Methodology and Key Findings

In WK 2 "Action Research & New Data", the research team conducted a qualitative research project through fieldwork focusing on victims who may had experienced RJ practices (20 interviews), and criminal justice professionals who are involved in the process of delivering RJ to victims and offenders and as well as victim support workers (10 interviews). The interviews were conducted during June and July 2013. Interesting findings and the need for further research came up.

The selection of key-professionals was based on their formal or informal involvement in the implementation of RJ procedures in Greece or their involvement in victims' services. The interviews with professionals were conducted in time and place that served their working hours. Regarding professionals' profile (see also Table 1), all of them have an average of 10 years working experience.

Table 1: Key-Professionals Profile

No	Affiliation	Years Of Working Experience	Training In RJ	RJ Practice & Duration
1	Psychologist at EKKA	1994-2009 as Social Worker, 2009-present as Psychologist	No	No
2	Head of Directorate for Crime Prevention and Juvenile Correctional Treatment, Ministry of Justice	22 years	No	No
3	Juvenile Probation Officer	12 years as Juvenile Probation Officer	No	Victim-Juvenile Offender Conciliation. About 5 cases/month
4	Juvenile Probation Officer	12 years as Juvenile Probation Officer	Basics, as part of her studies abroad	Using mediation, conciliation, & compensation in every case with juvenile victim & juvenile offender
5	Clinical Psychologist & psychotherapist at EKKA	Sep. 2008 (5 years) EKKA, 12 years generally	No	Systemic perspective on couples counselling in the context of mediation (pilot in Athens EKKA). Once/15-20 days, for 1.30 hours. Since 2008 over 20 cases
6	Social worker at EKKA	11 years EKKA, 21 years in total	No	No
7	Social worker & family psychotherapist at EKKA	Since 1998, 15 years in total, since 2001 at EKKA	Not officially	Mediation. About 6 cases the last months
8	PhD Law, Lawyer	10 years	No	Conciliation and mediation. Once/month
9	Policewoman	7 years	Only in dealing with migration issues	Approach the victim, creating a climate of safety in all stages of the process. Daily contact with citizens
10	District attorney	11 years	No	Mostly mediation and conciliation where provided

Only one professional said that she received elementary education in RJ during her studies, although seven professionals said that they implement often a RJ practice (mediation, conciliation). In addition, eight professionals have or had some involvement in services supporting victims, while five of them had some involvement in services supporting offenders, either departmental or via programmes or NGOs.

Searching for victims was a difficult process and encountered some obstacles. The initial aim was to identify victims who had participated in any of the RJ procedures offered by the GCJS. However, further communication with the victims is not maintained in any case. Thus, the interviews with victims concern victims who were mostly identified by personal contacts of the researchers or of the other victims (snowball sampling). Interviews with victims were also conducted in time and place of their

Table 2: Victims' Profile

No	Gender	Nationality	Age	Type of crime	Harms Suffered	CJS stage reached
1	F	Greek	24	Burglary and theft	Stealing various items and some of sentimental value. Psychological Consequences (Fear)	Just reported to police. Had to pay 100 euro if progressed in lawsuit
2	F	Greek	39	Theft, more than one time (repeat victimization)	Various material damages every time	Reported to police almost all the times. Low level of satisfaction
3	F	Greek	24	Theft	Material damages	No action. The item was returned
4	M	Greek	41	Burglary and theft	Damages to the house, PC, etc. carjacking. later extortion	Reported to police. There was a dystocia. The car was found. Not asked for another testimony to the prosecutor
5	F	Greek	27	Domestic violence	Psychological effects, Injuries	Reach the court (3-year suspended sentence to the offender). High level of satisfaction
6	M	Greek	29	Burglary and theft	Damage to the home, theft of personal belongings. Psychological effects (insomnia, fear, anger, despair)	Reported to police. No satisfaction
7	F	Greek	53	Scam - issuance of a false or fraudulent proof cab fare	(The participant did not answer this question)	Reported to police. Low level of satisfaction. Incident not recorded. Referred to the 4-digit number of complaints

Table 2: Victims' Profile *(continued...)*

No	Gender	Nationality	Age	Type of crime	Harms Suffered	CJS stage reached
8	M	Greek	24	Violation of property	Material damage, disappointment	No action
9	F	Greek	45	Car Theft	(Did not answer the question)	Reported to police. Standard procedure and fingerprinting
10	M	Greek	29	Theft	Material losses	No action
11	F	Greek	44	Handbag theft	irritability, feelings of injustice, loss of money and small items, engagement with the bureaucratic system	Reported to police. Briefing by the police regarding the arrest of the offender upon other criminal acts. Not interested about the sentence
12	F	Greek	23	Attempted Rape - Robbery with use of weapon	(Did not answer the question)	No action
13	M	Greek	28	Robbery with attempted murder	Injury Hand-knife, stolen wallet and jacket	Reported to police. No satisfaction. Never filed lawsuits for theft and beating
14	F	Greek	34	Assault, attempted rape	Insecurity, fear walking alone at night	Reported to police, Average satisfaction. Mobilization to identify perpetrators decoy policewomen (large number of complaints)
15	M	Greek	34	Theft	Material damages, theft briefcase with PC and working papers, anger	Reported to police, low level of satisfaction
16	F	Polish	42	Intimate partner Violence	Physical damage severely, Psychological Effects	No action
17	F	Cameroun	32	Trafficking victim	Effects on health, psychology and welfare	Reached prosecution, average level of satisfaction. Offender is free
18	F	Greek	49,5	Psychological violence within marriage	Psychological Effects	No action. In divorce (conflict, courts)

Table 2: Victims' Profile *(continued...)*

No	Gender	Nationality	Age	Type of crime	Harms Suffered	CJS stage reached
19	F	Greek	42	Sexual harassment	Psychological Effects	No action
20	M	Greek-Cypriot (univ. student from CY)	28	Burglary and theft	Material damages, identity & passport theft	Reported to police. High level of satisfaction

choice. The victims' profile (see also Table 2) covers a range of ages and both sexes, as well as a wide range of crimes of varying severity, including crimes against life, physical injuries, crimes against sexual orientation, against property, and crimes of economic exploitation of sexual life. Most victims reported the incident to the police, but only three victims participated in the next GCJS stages, mainly due to the arrest of the offender.

The researchers prepared an interview guide. The guide contains general information about RJE, information about the Victims' Directive and information on RJ in Greece. Finally, the guide contains questions which are based on the common research objectives and common core questions of the project as well as suggested questions (incurred by national reports of WK1) for WK2, which were sent by the coordinating partner organization IARS.

Specifically for Greece, a draft of the interview guide was produced. Eventually, the guide consists of two sections with questions relating to personal information of the participants and open-ended questions on RJ and the Victims' Directive. Each of the sections contains separate questions for victims and professionals. The Guide was piloted in the first interviews.

Methodology and data analysis

In WK2, the victims' and professionals' interviews were analysed based on qualitative methodology. The first set of questions was designed just to gather personal information of participants. These data were only recorded in Excel tables in order to create a short profile of the participants. For the data collected in the second set of questions, the method of Grounded Theory (G.T.) was selected for the data analysis. G.T. is valid and suitable for primary qualitative material for which there is none prior research. In the case of Greece, RJE WK2 fieldwork is the first research which studies the opinion of both the victims and the professionals concerning the application of RJ and Victims' Directive. Moreover, it is a method easily used without the need of a computer programme; given the narrow timeframe that did not allowed the purchase and learning of such a programme.

The analysis of the interviews was layered in order to extract the final conclusions. Each interview was analysed vertically using G.T. for the analysis of each individual case of victim or professional. Case theories for each participant were extracted from the analysis. Thereafter, the interviews were analysed horizontally in order to extract overall conclusions for each key research question. The horizontal analysis was based on the initial coding of the interviews and the case theories. In this way, it was considered that the research results would be much more useful and reliable for the project's needs. Twenty (20) case theories of victims and 10 case theories of professionals resulted from the analysis of interviews. All theories were based on central codes and central categories raised by coding each interview.

Limitations

RJE project is the first research study which examines the opinion of victims and practitioners regarding the implementation of RJ and Victims' Directive in Greece. Yet some limitations can be identified concerning WK2 participants and the methodology which was used. Firstly, the small number of participants in the WK2 does not leave much room for generalization of the results of the interviews, as is unknown the degree of representativeness of the target groups, especially the victims. Finding participants was difficult, particularly in relation to the victims, mainly for two reasons, the time constraints of to practitioners who were interviewed during working hours, and the suspicion of the victims to talk about their victimization.

Moreover, qualitative methodology was used for the data analysis. WK2 data were analysed using the method of G.T.. G.T. is a valid method and appropriate for primary qualitative material. However, it should be noted that the positivist basis of G.T. perceives the material as indisputable source of knowledge, and the relationship of the researcher with the object of study tends to be ignored. On the other hand, it can ensure a high degree of objectivity of the data analysis. Nevertheless, the fact that, as we will see below, all work-streams' results mutually agree, increases the generalizability of research.

Key Findings

This section presents the main results and conclusions as they emerged from the field-work qualitative research which was conducted in Greece as part of RJE WK2 aiming to study the victims' needs and satisfaction during the CJS and RJ procedures. As it is shown below, RJ in Greece is rapidly developing. Overall, there was a significant agreement among the literature review and the research and practical results. Yet, many operational and organizational needs will have to be addressed in order to implement the Victims' Directive efficiently.

Victims' Needs and Views[7]

A victim-led criminal justice system (CJS) aims to give voice to the victims to express their needs and feelings during the procedures, and receive the necessary support to recover physically, emotionally and mentally from the harms of the crime that they suffered. To this end, RJ practices aim to repair the damage caused by the crime and satisfy victims' needs while safeguarding their interests.

Victims' satisfaction emerges not only from the outcomes of the CJS processes, but also from their interaction with CJS stakeholders during the procedures. The arrest of the offender is only a first step towards satisfaction. As two victims pointed out, the punishment of the offender is not always the goal, and it does not mean the victims' catharsis:

> *" The victim does not always aim to prosecution and punishment."* (Victim 7)

> *"The punishment will not be telling me something. I would feel remorse ... perhaps that he went to prison for me .. I do not know .. I would feel weird. Maybe it was someone who was in need .. The*

punishment would not offer me anything. I think that another way .. maybe with RJ, that we are talking about, by seeing that regretted for what he did, to see that he understood the damage that he caused." (Victim 1)

On the contrary, the most common answers regarding the victims' satisfaction as to the outcomes of CJS procedures included not only the punishment of the offender through imprisonment or enforcement measures, but also the (financial, moral, social) compensation and the restoration of harms (e.g. through return of stolen property), and the protection of the victim.

Moreover, the interaction and communication of the victims with CJS agencies seems to play an important role. The attitude (interest, sensibility, and respect towards the victim) of CJS professionals seems to be a key factor in victims' satisfaction. The participants reported that victims' satisfaction is also influenced by: the degree of information and participation of the victim at all stages of CJS, the support provided to the victim, the focus of procedures to the victim, the immediacy/speed of procedures, the flexibility and clarity of procedures and avoidance of bureaucracy, cooperation between authorities, concentration of processes and avoidance of duplication of testimonies and of exposure to the media. Professionals, based on their experience, added some important comments. As reported, the victims wish to be recognized and vindicated through the CJS processes. However, their satisfaction depends on the type of crime, their involvement in it, and their general intentions.

Indeed, depending on the type of crime, the participating victims suffered various physical, physiological and psychological damages. Most victims reported the incident to the police, but the majority of them felt no or little satisfaction. Only three victims participated in the next CJS stages, mainly due to the arrest of the offender, with their satisfaction ranging on an average level. Overall, it was concluded that the needs of victims in Greece during the CJS proceedings can be summarized as shown below:

- Recognition and support of victims by allowing them to express and participate in the processes, through the consent of the parties, the individualized approach, and the (legal, psychological) victim support.
- Better treatment on behalf of the agencies: neutral attitudes of the professionals, an improved attitude (more friendly, polite, sensitive, showing interest and respect for the victim) of the CJS professionals, awareness-raising of stakeholders, and non-exposure of victims.
- The protection and sense of security is an important factor in ensuring the rights of victims.
- Informing the victims: raising awareness of victims and professionals, informing stakeholders about their role, awareness and participation of victims at all stages of CJS.
- The implementation of procedures by qualified personnel: the involvement of an impartial third person, and the training and qualification of professionals seems to be, according to the participants, the most secure way of implementing RJ processes, while developing an interdisciplinary approach.
- The speed and immediacy of the processes and avoidance of the bureaucracy, through less traumatic legal progresses (avoiding repetitive processes, flexibility and clarity of procedures).
- Satisfaction and vindication of victims through understanding and restoring the damage, victim compensation, prudent/conformity of the offender and prevention of recidivism.
- The existence of an institutionally organized civic framework, structures, and mainly their

networking with public authorities and institutions of the CJS: the organization of services, their financial support and sustainability, the need for supervising the procedures.

Especially concerning RJ practices, only six of 20 victims responded that they have some knowledge about RJ, while the other victims said they knew nothing or this was the first time they heard this term. Yet, half of the victims said that victims, including themselves, would choose RJ if they knew more. Some other victims expressed some mistrust and doubts, highlighting the need to inform victims and the importance of the type of crime. Two victims said that victims, including themselves, will not choose RJ if they knew more; while two other victims reported that they would not feel safe in any way. At the same time, all the professionals were optimistic that the victims would choose RJ, but stressed that this would depend on the type of crime and the severity of the injury, on the victims' profile, and generally, on the development of a relevant culture.

Professionals' needs and views[8]

The interaction and communication of the victims with the CJS and other victim support professionals was proven an essential element of victims' satisfaction. To this end, as part of WK2 field research, ten practitioners were interviewed and expressed their own needs and views regarding the Victims' Directive and RJ.

Depending on their profile, professionals mentioned a range of needs – educational and awareness-raising, structural and operational. They suggested their further education in crisis management, psychology, victims and offenders profiles, in the therapeutic relationship (empathy, trust), RJ (methodology, techniques, interview guides, code of conduct) and generally more specialized knowledge. Also, they reported that they want information about vocational rehabilitation of victims, about good practices, and generally on legislative developments and their role. In addition, they expressed a need for supervision and personal psychotherapy. In this context, it is important that a legal framework, an institutional system and structures are developed, operating based on interdisciplinary cooperation and continuous feedback. One professional also pointed out the need to adapt the Victims' Directive. However, while it was expected at least for the professionals to know of the existence of the Directive, only six of the 10 professionals had heard about the Directive and knew enough. To this end, all professionals demonstrated an interest in seminars/trainings, training materials, protocols, etc. on the Victims' Directive and RJ.

Indeed, the professionals' need for further information, training and education on the Victims' Directive and RJ was also expressed during the WK4 training seminars. The attendants were particularly interested in the Directive and especially the challenge that it creates to their Services and Organizations. They expressed their questioning about its implementation, mainly because of financial difficulties, lack of knowledge and expertise on this field and the general "culture" of the GCJS which is concentrated on the needs and rights of the perpetrators rather than the victims. They mentioned though the importance of a victim-oriented new criminal justice system, – a perspective missing from the Greek legal system- as a challenge that the Victims' Directive creates.

Several advantages and disadvantages of legislating RJ were identified by professionals both in WK2 field research and WK4 trainings. Operational advantages include the discharge of the courts, the speed in the administration of justice and the immediacy of procedures, and the economic benefits in operating expenses and for those involved. Moreover, they identified several advantages for the victims and the offenders, like the offenders' conformity, the victims' compensation, priority and needs' coverage of victims, and the avoidance of trial and suffering for those involved. Finally, they mentioned that securing the safeguards and rights of stakeholders is also an advantage. All the professionals agreed that follow-up meetings are very important for the safety and protection of victims. Two professionals said that re-victimization means partial failure of the professional and the process. In the case of re-victimization, professionals should explore the victims' profile and environment, and report the incident, explore re-commitments and refer the victim to a specialist for psychotherapy and guidance. The victims' and offenders' assessment before and during CJS and RJ processes, were identified by the trainings' participants as key tools in avoiding re-victimization.

Generally, the project's participants agreed that RJ promotes accountability and self-regulation of conflicts, developing a culture of reconciliation:

> *"..Now in relation to the very mentality that exists in Greece... (RJ) will help in developing a culture of reconciliation and dispute resolution in the social environment without recourse to the Criminal Justice System"* (Professional 4)

> *"...the perspective of self-regulation in the community that could lead gradually (especially in interpersonal disputes, in minor delinquency offenses), to the decongestion of the criminal justice system"* (Professional 10)

However, a professional stressed the lack of a RJ culture and the lack of political will in Greece, while others reported the lack to provide good practices for application. Also the practitioners mentioned several other disadvantages, like shifting the model of law from prison to work, the obligingness and process automation, the lack of structures and the long waiting list, as well as a potential deceit of the offender, pressure on the victim, the risk of not securing the rights of the offender.

Overall, most participants supported more or less the application and availability of RJ at all CJS stages. Yet, some practitioners mentioned that RJ is not necessary to be applied within the CJS. The implementation of RJ within CJS should be individualized, depending on the type of crime and the severity of injuries, taking into consideration the victims' and offenders' consent. The participants also stated the need for safeguards and security to ensure the dignity of the victim, an assurance process, specialized services, and awareness of stakeholders, trained professionals, and reliable support system for victims. A professional stressed the need for political will in the implementation of RJ within CJS. Moreover, all professionals argued that RJ should be funded by the State. However, a professional added the need for funding other structures as well.

More generally, as is clear from the interviews of professionals, the implementation of RJ practices (within CJS) requires the management of operational and organizational needs. Overall, the need for adequate training of the agencies, the need for organized and reliable system and proper structures with trained personnel, the need of financial support and staffing services were highlighted; needs that require political will, informing and awareness- raising of the agencies, victims and general population, in order to develop a culture that reflects more the RJ values and principles.

Training and Capacity Building: Learning from the Pilots

After addressing the problems of the implementation of RJ through the research findings, we implemented pilots in different contexts, using the evidence-based victim safeguards and protocols, and the training and capacity building material for professionals working with victims and offenders in the context of RJ. EPLO's training seminars were held during the trimester March to May 2014, under the scientific supervision of Professor Vasso Artinopoulou, Scientific Coordinator of the Greek working team of the project. The seminars' trainers were Prof. V. Artinopoulou and Ms. I. Michael, while guest speakers were also invited.

Overall, five training seminars were conducted with different target groups, and almost 783 professionals participated, such as stakeholders, police officers, lawyers, criminologists, professionals in the field of social care and health, probation officers, representatives of the Ministry of Justice etc. More specifically, 23 new sociologists and graduates of the Sociologist Department of Panteion University attended the first seminar. The second seminar was attended by 250 postgraduate students of the Police Academy, men and women. 290 graduates and students of the Departments of Psychology, Sociology, and Anthropology attended the third seminar. The forth seminar's participants consisted of 50 lawyers, mediators, criminologists and, students and professors of the Law School of National and Kapodistrian University of Athens. Finally, 18 professionals participated in the fifth seminar. The participants consisted of a representative of the 'Ministry of Justice, Transparency and Human Rights', probation officers, practitioners working at EPANODOS (NGO under the Ministry of Justice for the reintegration/rehabilitation of ex-prisoners), lawyers, sociologists and law students, and a school teacher. Overall, the seminars' participants have experience as practitioners in the fields of victim support and community services (voluntary or professional work at relevant NGOs), while many of them were policy and decision makers.

Training and capacity building material was produced as part of WK3 regarding RJ and the Victims' Directive, aiming to support victims and practitioners. The material is derived from WK2 field research, providing to professionals detailed knowledge of the Directive from the perspective of the victim and helping victims to empower themselves through the process. The purpose of the training material is to be used by professionals when assessing victims, based on the guarantees required by the Victims' Directive, by following check points in order to prepare the victims' assessment and evaluation report. The training material includes information on the victims' rights, definition of RJ, a victim's assessment guide and toolkit, and case studies which reflect safeguarding issues; equally suitable for professionals and victims. The questions are for the most part open-ended, so that the victims have the opportunity to speak freely, reflecting their needs and concerns.

The training materials produced by IARS were translated and adjusted for the Greek audience (practitioners and victims). The produced material is evidence-based and used the research data in order to reflect the needs of victims and practitioners in Greece. To this end, information on RJ in Greece and the victims' needs, based on the literature review and the field work which were conducted in Greece during previous phases of the project, is included in the training material.

The seminars used WK3 training and capacity building material and were related to a summary presentation of the Directive 2012/29 EU and more specifically of the articles regarding the implementation of RJ and the individual assessment of victims, as well as results of the research carried out within the framework of the RJE. The participants in the seminars evaluated the training material. To this end, qualitative data (comments, questions, opinions etc.) were collected from activities and feedback during and at the end of seminars, including a self-evaluation of the trainers. However, the evaluation of WK4 seminars is lacking, as non-specific evaluation tool was used due to the large number of participants, the lack of time and the limited cost coverage. This means that the measurement of the effectiveness of the seminars and the material might be problematic. Yet, the seminars seemed to be well received, as the massive participation of professionals and non-professionals expressed the need for public awareness and for practitioners' training regarding the Victims' Directive and RJ.

Dissemination and awareness activities shared the project results with Local Greek authorities and other stakeholders, Members of the European Group of Public Law (EGPL), Libraries and other institutions all around the world; by disseminating through EPLO activities, such as conferences, seminars, workshops and trainings.

What we Learn from the Project Implementation – Challenges and Expectations by the EU Directive

The implementation of the Victims' Directive and RJ in Greece may encounter various challenges involving organizational and practical considerations. The expectations of victims and professionals regarding the Victims' Directive and RJ implementation are very high. These expectations largely reflect the victims' needs in the CJS proceedings.

Through RJ processes, victims appear to wish mainly the speed and immediacy of procedures and avoidance of bureaucracy through a less traumatic legal route. The victims also stated that they wish to be recognised and supported, have the ability of expression, protection and better treatment, while RJ is implemented by qualified personnel. Moreover, victims appear to want mostly the (moral, emotional) satisfaction and vindication through the understanding and restoration of damages from the offender and compensation of victims, compliance of the offender and less recidivism. In addition, some victims may wish to reconcile with the perpetrator in order to repair the damage or just for a more peaceful communication between them. However, there were also some more punitive answers, in which victims reported that they wish to punish and sentence the perpetrator via RJ, indicating that an apology is not enough, and to diffuse responsibility over them.

During the interviews and the trainings, several challenges were identified by the participants regarding the implementation of the Victims' Directive and of RJ, and concern both the organization of services and the practical application of procedures. The actual implementation and integration of the Directive is the very first challenge, while some professionals argued that the actual implementation of RJ is a challenge, as well as the effectiveness of its implementation. The management of the role of judicial and prosecutorial authorities which have discretion in decisions is an additional and important challenge. A need for ideological change is considered of paramount importance.

Moreover, the development of a reliable system, of structures, networks and services, and their financial support, were identified as organizational challenges. The sustainability of the structures and services is essential. In practice, the exact definition of victim, the criteria for referral to RJ practices, the lack of personnel, the waiting list, the specialized training of professionals, the victims' consent and the voluntary accession of offenders in the processes, the interests to be served, balancing the rights of victims and offenders, the protection of victims, conducting appropriate inquiries, are some more challenges.

To this end, the participants suggested the concentration of processes and avoidance of duplication of procedures, speed of procedures, flexibility and avoidance of bureaucracy, and cost savings. A victim noted the need to focus on the early stages of CJS in a way that the victim should not detract, while another victim suggested the improvement of the filing system of folders and legislation, as well as a more rational system of data assessment. Furthermore, participants suggested the improvement of behaviour (more friendly, polite) of CJS professionals, to inform them about their role, the development of interdisciplinary approach and better education. A victim also mentioned the need for evaluation. Additionally, the agencies' awareness-raising, the improved information for victims and professionals, the (legal, psychological) support for victims, the non-exposure of victims, were also mentioned.

Some participants observed that generally, CJS is more focused on the offender. A victim support service is needed indeed. According to WK2 participants, the victim support service is expected to provide psychological, legal and social support, help to meet victims' needs (housing, shelters, food, job placement, assistance to foreign victims, etc.), guide and inform, and protect victims. Also, some victims suggested that it could offer out-of-court settlement of cases, preventative policing, and even service for sanctioning the perpetrator. They further suggested the support of victims at all stages, individualized, depending on the type of crime, and including follow-up. The service should also be networked with other agencies (e.g. CJS, hospitals) and have trained and qualified staff. A victim noted that the service should have a strong opinion in the society.

Especially regarding the RJ implementation, WK2 victims and professionals suggested good and safe ways of both organizing and implementing RJ processes, as well as regarding those involved in the proceedings. Victims suggested ways in which RJ can be victim-focused. The participation of a third impartial person and the training and expertise of professionals seems to be the safest way of implementing RJ. Furthermore, the protection and safeguard of the rights of victims, the coverage of victims' needs, their consent, information and support of victims, a personalized approach, the recognition and management of their emotions, the safety of those involved from psychological collapse, the distribution equilibrium of justice, the objectivity of agencies / procedures and the neutral attitude of professionals, were also reported. An important role seems to be played by the existence of an institutionally organized civic framework, of structures and especially of networking with public authorities and CJS institutions, as well as for supervising procedures. Of particular interest, some victims suggested the implementation of RJ under a judicial umbrella that will provide all the judicial guarantees and prestige to the victim, or the presence of a police officer, or legal representation. Additionally, two victims reported the existence of safety distance and escape routes during RJ procedures.

Almost all victims and practitioners stressed the need to inform victims about RJ, on a general level of public awareness (e.g. campaigns in the media, advertising, internet, states' events, workshops/seminars, dedicated telephone line or special service) and on a special level focused on awareness of victims (by CJS and agencies serving victims – e.g. hospitals, by specialists). The presentation of proofs of RJ's effectiveness and of victims' satisfaction could be beneficial.

Critical Thinking and Recommendations

Restorative Justice aims to bridge the gap between the values of justice and the realities in the traditional criminal justice systems. Furthermore, RJ comes to restore the missed trust of European citizens in the criminal justice systems and law implementation. RJ includes a value based perspective that involves community, citizens and policy makers in an open ended dialogue (Artinopoulou, 2013).

The practices, measures and initiatives that promote RJ in Greece are still at early stage. The introduction of victim – offender mediation and other restorative measures in more and more laws, the hitherto implementation of formal and informal local programmes and initiatives and the promotion of research and knowledge about RJ in social, educational and academic contexts, are neither trivial nor insignificant. Yet, the implementation of the Victims' Directive and RJ may face various challenges involving organizational and practical factors. Such factors have been identified in the literature (e.g. Lambropoulou, 2010˙ Ζαγούρα, 2007). The results of WK2 interviews and WK4 trainings confirm and corroborate the conclusions that emerged from WK1 literature review. In general, it is observed that victims' responses and the responses of professionals converge on many points.

The development of RJ in Greece is not based on a general or overarching scheme, while the introduction of RJ legal measures is often the result of European directives or of the efforts to improve and speed up justice, without further developing of the RJ theoretical framework and values on a unified base. Generally, as it is observed in practice, the application of RJ measures and practices in the GJS and on informal level meets operational, organizational and financial obstacles that hinder the wider application and development of RJ in Greece.

Despite the considerable efforts to introduce official RJ schemes in GJS, these schemes have a top-down character, since they are imposed during the regular criminal justice process and are usually applied under the control of prosecutors or court authorities, or of lawyers, demonstrating the strong legal tradition of the country, but also a weakness of the GJS to be released from the strict legal-centric and paternalistic system of crime control and punishment (Artinopoulou & Petoussi, 2011), maintaining the control of RJ measures within its limits. Moreover, victim-offender mediation is not effective because offenders often commit more offences until they account in court for a single act, as cases reach the courts with a delay of approximately 12-18 months.

Furthermore, it is confirmed that the only source of information for citizens and professionals are the very laws which do not explain the background of RJ measures and practices, their aims and objectives, creating the risk of incorrect and inappropriate implementation of RJ practices and of developing uncertainty amongst the public, legal professionals and other stakeholders as to the effectiveness of RJ (European Forum for Restorative Justice, 2008: 14). Indeed, offenders and victims often receive the character of RJ schemes as "punitive" and victims tend to demand high monetary compensation. "Reintegrating shame" and the "symbolic character of compensation" as central principles of RJ processes are overshadowed. A degree of mistrust in the implementation and effectiveness of RJ processes is also observed.

The gap between theory and practice (Gavrielides, 2007) does exist in the case of Greece. The treatment of victims in the GCJS is facing operational and organizational problems identified during RJE work-streams, and which consequently appear to affect the application of RJ practices. In general, there is lack of protocols and guidelines for the development and implementation of the current RJ practices in Greece, in terms of developing genuine RJ processes and safeguarding victims in RJ services. Pilot programmes were not conducted before the implementation of the current legal provisions, while none official training was offered to the practitioners appointed by the laws. Overall, the main reasons for the limited use of RJ practices is the lack of training of competent services to the purposes and practices of RJ, the lack of appropriate structures (e.g. mediation centres) with qualified staff to carry out the RJ procedures, the lack of guidelines and training materials, the lack of (financial) resources, and the workload of services; reasons which in turn are consequences of the lack of a wider dialogue on RJ and its practices.

Indeed, all these reflect the need to develop a broader dialogue on RJ and its practices (Αρτινοπουλου, 2010a: 100-102, 112-114· Artinopoulou 2010b: 182-183· Lambropoulou, 2010: 144-147). Despite the lack of realization of national programmes on RJ, an increasing trend of Greece's participation in EU funded research programmes that promote the implementation of RJ practices in the Member States, is observed over the past years. The current situation is on a positive course, but the need for a wider debate on RJ and the need for better coordination and operation of the existing RJ practices and measures require immediate attention. Nevertheless, the developments exhibit encouraging progress for the implementation of the Victims' Directive, since beyond the country's participation in the RJE project, there has already been established a special legislative committee to integrate the Victims' Directive into Greek law, consisting of professionals involved in the administration of justice and support for victims. The committee has been in constant contact with members of the RJE Greek working group while the RJE has been supported by the Greek Ministry of Justice under the development of national policy for the support of victims.

Taking into consideration the needs expressed by the victims and the professionals, as well as the needs identified during WK1 literature review, several recommendations can be suggested regarding the application of RJ and the Victims' Directive in Greece:

- A balanced approach regarding the rights of victims and offenders is an essential element for the proper functioning of the criminal justice system. A victim-led criminal justice system is a very promising development, but it does not exclude the respect of the rights of the offenders.
- Educational materials, guides, protocols, and brochures for professionals and victims, which will describe the principles and benefits of RJ, ways of good and safe application, good practices and ways of implementing the Victims' Directive and RJ focused on the victim, presenting evidence of the efficiency of RJ processes (surveys, real stories, experiences documentation), need to be produced.
- More training seminars and raise awareness of police, prosecutors, judges and other professionals who staff the existing bodies currently responsible for implementing RJ measures, need to be carried out, aiming to better familiarize them with the principles, techniques, good practices and methodology of RJ. The practitioners should be trained and sensitized on the rights of victims and RJ processes.
- Supervision programmes for professionals who come into contact with victims, but also apply RJ practices, should be established.
- The organization of national programmes in collaboration with relevant NGOs, state institutions, academia and other scientific agencies could be beneficial in order to implement RJ practices in all areas of society (community, schools, workplaces, justice system, academic and scientific community) and raise awareness of citizens and stakeholders.
- Mediation should be promoted as an immediate alternative for reconciliation and conflict resolution, while RJ services should be expanded beyond the court system, to other social services, in order to decongest the CJS and the implementation of additional RJ practices.
- Efficient assessment and preparation for offenders and victims should be provided by experts

trained in restorative practices as well as psychologists and social workers. Complete and impartial information should be given to victims and offenders about the processes before taking part in RJ.

- A central (governmental, semi-governmental, academic or non-profit) entity for the coordination, organization, promotion and research of RJ and its practices, and a national database for RJ in Greece should be created. This way will develop an integrated and organized system of RJ.

To this point, RJE project has proven to provide great support to victims and professionals. The paradox in relation to the system's treatment of victims was addressed throughout the project by identifying the gaps and needs that exist. Based on the Victims' Directive, the victims' rights were highlighted during the work-streams, while a stronger voice of the victims is eventually growing in the GCJS. During WK4 seminars, RJE materials were proven to be good tools for practitioners, policy and decision makers. The development, piloting and implementation of training materials, protocols and guidelines as part of RJE, respect the interests of the victims and the offenders, while promoting multi-agency, cross-sector cooperation among RJ/ victim services and national agencies. The RJE project empowered RJ in Greece and gave impetus to a new approach for a victim-led criminal justice system.

Notes

1 This institution consisted of forty citizens whose role included the provision of mediation services in cases of physical violence and other disputes.

2 Based on the Continental tradition, the stages of the criminal justice process in Greece are: prosecution, preliminary examination, trial and implementation/execution of penal decision. The Prosecutor supervises the whole process as well as the actions of the rest of the authorities (police, prisons and the officers in the justice system); during these stages he/she acts as an independent judicial authority in the name of the State to ensure both the Constitutional Rules and the proper operation of the application of the Law. Moreover, the Prosecutor conducts the penal prosecution and the preliminary investigation and is responsible for checking the imposition of the decisions of the court.

3 If either or both of them refuse, then the criminal proceedings take place without any substantive or procedural negative consequence.

4 Juvenile Probation Services and Child Protection Services deal with the treatment of juvenile offenders out of court and provide support to juveniles to whom the court has imposed educational or therapeutic measures. See Ministry of Justice, Transparency and Human Rights, follow Prevention and Control of Crime (in Greek).

5 In accordance with Article 214B of GCCP, judicial mediation is voluntary and confidential, and is offered in the case of private disputes. The parties with their lawyers can rely on separate and joint hearings and discussions with the judge-mediator who can propose non-binding recommendations to resolve their differences.

6 Originally introduced by Act 2298/1995 and later amended. See Ministry of Justice, Transparency and Human Rights: www.ministryofjustice.gr Follow Codes, Code of Civil Procedure (in Greek).

7 These data were collected as part of RJE Work-stream 2 "Action Research & New Data". The full report in Greek and a summary in English of WK2 can be found: http://rj4all.info/content/RJEresources

8 These data were collected as part of RJE WK2 "Action Research & New Data" and further verified during WK4 "Pilot & Implementation".

References

Greek

Αλεξιάδης, Σ. (1996). «Η συνδιαλλαγή θύματος – δράστη». Στο Β. Αρτινοπούλου και Α. Μαγγανάς (Επιμ.), Θυματολογία και Όψεις Θυματοποίησης, σελ. 195-204. Αθήνα: εκδ. Νομική Βιβλιοθήκη.

Αλεξιάδης, Σ. (2007). «Η Αποκαταστατική Δικαιοσύνη: Μια άλλη αντιμετώπιση του 'εγκληματικού φαινομένου'», Στο Τιμητικός Τόμος για τον Ιωάννη Μανωλεδάκη, τομ. II., σελ. 991-1017. Αθήνα – Θεσσαλονίκη: εκδ. Σάκκουλας.

Αρτινοπούλου, Β., (1995). Αιμομιξία: θεωρητικές προσεγγίσεις και ερευνητικά δεδομένα, Αθήνα: Νομική Βιβλιοθήκη.

Αρτινοπούλου, Β., (2001). Βία στο σχολείο. Έρευνες και πολιτικές στην Ευρώπη. Αθήνα: εκδ. Μεταίχμιο, Β' έκδοση 2007.

Αρτινοπούλου, Β., (2006). Ενδοοικογενειακή κακοποίηση γυναικών, Αθήνα: Νομική Βιβλιοθήκη.

Αρτινοπούλου, Β., (2008). «Οι γκρίζες ζώνες της αποκαταστατικής δικαιοσύνης», Ποινικός Λόγος, 6/2008, εκδ. Αντ. Σάκκουλα

Αρτινοπούλου, Β. (2010a) «Επανορθωτική Δικαιοσύνη: Η πρόκληση των σύγχρονων δικαιικών συστημάτων», Αθήνα: Νομική Βιβλιοθήκη.

Αρτινοπούλου, Β. (2010b). «Η Σχολική Διαμεσολάβηση. Εκπαιδεύοντας τους μαθητές στη διαχείριση της βίας και του εκφοβισμού» (Συνεργασία: Χρ. Καλαβρή, Η. Μιχαήλ). Αθήνα: Νομική Βιβλιοθήκη.

Αρτινοπούλου, Β. (2010c). Αποκαταστατική Δικαιοσύνη και Κοινωνικό Φύλο. Η περίπτωση της ενδοοικογενειακής βίας. Στον Τιμητικό Τόμο Καλλιόπης Δ. Σπινέλλη, Εκδόσεις Αντ. Ν. Σάκκουλα, σελ. 545-558.

Αρτινοπούλου, Β., (2011a). «Οι «γκρίζες ζώνες» της αποκαταστατικής δικαιοσύνης», στο Τιμητικός Τόμος για τον Καθηγητή Ιάκωβο Φαρσεδάκη, τόμος I (επιμ. Α. Χαλκιά), Αθήνα: Νομική Βιβλιοθήκη, σελ. 755-774.

Αρτινοπούλου, Β. (2011b). Από τη θεωρητική στην εφαρμοσμένη εγκληματολογία- Το παράδειγμα της αποκαταστατικής δικαιοσύνης. Στο «Εγκληματολογία: Διδασκαλία και έρευνα στην Ελλάδα. Πρακτικά επιστημονικού Συνεδρίου» (Επιμ. Ν. Κουράκης, Χρ. Ζαραφωνίτου, Χρ. Τσουραμάνης, Ε. Χαϊνας), σελ. 325-348. Εκδόσεις Αντ. Ν. Σάκκουλα.

Αρτινοπούλου Β. (2012). Αποκαταστατική δικαιοσύνη και ανθρώπινα δικαιώματα, Στο «Ο δρόμος προς τη Δικαιοσύνη. Συνέδριο προς τιμή του ομότιμου καθηγητή Στέργιου Αλεξιάδη» (επιμ. Α. Γ. Πιτσελά), σελ. 3-18. Αθήνα – Θεσσαλονίκη: εκδ. Σάκκουλα.

Αρτινοπούλου Β. – Μαγγανάς Α. (Επιμ.), (1996). Θυματολογία και Όψεις Θυματοποίησης. Αθήνα: εκδ. Νομική Βιβλιοθήκη.

Αρτινοπούλου, Β., Παπαθεοδώρου, Θ.Π., (2006). Σεξουαλική παρενόχληση στην εργασία. Αθήνα: Νομική Βιβλιοθήκη.

Αρχηγείο Ελληνικής Αστυνομίας (2005). «Η Αντιμετώπιση της Ενδοοικογενειακής Βίας». Τυπογραφείο Ελληνικής Αστυνομίας.

Δασκαλάκη, Η., Παπαδοπούλου, Ρ.Δ., Τσαμπαρλή, Δ., Τσίγκανου, Ι., Φρονίμου, Ε., (Επιμ.), (2000). Εγκληματίες και θύματα στο κατώφλι του 21ου αιώνα, Αθήνα: Εθνικό Κέντρο Κοινωνικών Ερευνών.

Δημόπουλος, Χ. – Κοσμάτος, Κ., (2006). Κώδικας Δικαίου Θυμάτων, Αθήνα: Νομική Βιβλιοθήκη.

Ε.Κ.Κ.Α. (2012). Ε.Κ.Κ.Α. Απολογισμός Λειτουργίας 2011. Αθήνα, 2012.

Ζαγούρα, Π. (2007). «Ο Ανήλικος Παραβάτης στο Σύστημα Ποινικής Δικαιοσύνης». Παρουσίαση σε συνέδριο, Ανακτήθηκε από: www.welfareaction.org/uplds/File/ZAGOURA.doc

Θάνος, Θ.Β. (επιμ.), (2011). «Η Διαμεσολάβηση στο Σχολείο και την Κοινωνία», Αθήνα: εκδ. Πεδίο.

Καράμπελα, Λ., (2001). Οι βιαστές και τα θύματά τους. Αθήνα: Νομική Βιβλιοθήκη.

Κουράκης, Ν., (2007). Τοπικά Συμβούλια Πρόληψης της Παραβατικότητας. Αθήνα: εκδ. Σάκκουλας.

Λάζος, Γρ., (2002). Πορνεία και Διεθνική Σωματεμπορία στη Σύγχρονη Ελλάδα, τόμ.1: Η εκδιδόμενη, τόμ.2: Ο πελάτης, Αθήνα: εκδ. Καστανιώτη.

Μαγγανάς, Α., (1996). Ειδικά θέματα που αφορούν την κακοποίηση παιδιών: η περίπτωση του Καναδά και των Η.Π.Α.. Αθήνα: Αντ. Ν. Σάκκουλα.

Μαγγανάς, Α. (2006). «Εναλλακτικές μορφές απονομής της ποινικής δικαιοσύνης», Ποινική Δικαιοσύνη, 3/2006, σελ. 298-304.

Πανούσης, Γ., Δημόπουλος, Λ., Καρύδης, Β., (1994). Θυματολογικά Κείμενα, Αθήνα: Αντ. Ν. Σάκκουλας.

Πιτσελά, Α. (2004). Δίκαιο Ανηλίκων, 5η Εκδοση, Θεσσαλονίκη: Εκδόσεις Σάκκουλα.

English (most written by Greek experts)

Alexiades, S. (1992). 'Victim Offender Reconciliation Schemes in the Greek Justice System', in Messmer, A. and Otto, H.V. (eds.), *Restorative Justice on Trial: Pitfalls and Potentials of Victim - Offender Mediation – International Research Perspectives*. Dordrecht, Kluwer Academic Publishers, 309-316.

Aristotle (n.d.), The Nicomachean Ethics

Artinopoulou, V., (2009). "Victim-offender mediation in family violence cases—the Greek experience", Στο «Εγκληματολογία και Ευρωπαϊκή Αντεγκληματική Πολιτική. Προσφορά τιμής στην Αγλαΐα Τσήτσουρα» (επιμ. Μ.Π. Κρανιδιώτη), σελ. 369-380. Αθήνα: εκδ. Σάκκουλας.

Artinopoulou, V., (2010a). "Victims of crime in Contemporary Greece". Στο «Εγκληματολογικές Αναζητήσεις. Τιμητικός τόμος για τον Καθηγητή Στέργιο Αλεξιάδη» (Επιμ. Α. Γ. Πιτσελά), σελ. 71-90. Αθήνα-Θεσσαλονίκη: εκδ. Σάκκουλας.

Artinopoulou, V., (2010b) "Victim Offender Mediation in Cases of Domestic Violence – The Greek Experience". In *European Best Practices of Restorative Justice in the Criminal Procedure*, Conference Publications. Budapest: Ministry of Justice and Law Enforcement of the Republic of Hungary, pp. 177-186.

Artinopoulou, V. (2012). Restorative Justice and Young Females in custody in Greece. In Gavrielides, Th (ed.), *Rights and Restoration within youth Justice*. DeSitter Publications, Canada.

Artinopoulou, V. (2013) Restorative Justice in Greece. In A. Pitsela & E. Symeonidou- Kastanidou (eds) *Restorative Justice in Criminal Matters. Comparative Research in 11 European Countries*. Sakkoulas Publications, Athens Thessaloniki, pp 101-124.

Artinopoulou, V. & Gavrielides, Th. (2012a). Human Rights-Based Restorative Justice for Violence against Young Women; Experiences from Greece and the UK. In Th, Gavrielides (ed.), *Rights and Restoration within youth justice*. DeSitter Publications, Canada.

Artinopoulou, V. & Gavrielides, Th. (2012b). Restorative Justice and Violence against Women: Comparing Greece and United Kingdom, *Asian Journal of Criminology*, DOI 10.1007/s11417-011-9123-x

Artinopoulou, V., Michael, I., Kalavri, Ch., (2012). "Formal and Informal Restorative Justice Practices for Juveniles in Greece; Difficulties and challenges in practice". *Youth Voice Journal*, vol. 3(1), pp. 5-18.

Artinopoulou, V. & Petoussi, V. (2011), 'Legalism and paternalism in Greece: Powerful trends in the reification of risk and the treatment of juvenile offenders'. In François, A., Massin, V., Niget, D. (eds) *Violences juvéniles sous expertise(s), XIXe-XXIe siècles/Expertise and juvenile violence, 19th-21st century*, Presses Universitaires de Louvain – UCL, pp. 157-185.

Council of European Union (2001), *Council Framework Decision of 15 March 2001 on the standing of victims in criminal proceedings* 2001/220/JHA. Official Journal of the European Communities. L 82/1. 22 March. Downloaded: http://eur-lex.europa.eu/smartapi/cgi/sga_doc?smartapi!celexapi!prod!CELEXnumdoc&lg=EN&numdoc=32001F0220&model=guichett

Department of Juvenile Justice (Italian Ministry of Justice), (2010). *Restorative Justice and Crime Prevention. Presenting a theoretical exploration, an empirical analysis and the policy perspective* (Final report of the European project 'Restorative Justice and Crime Prevention'), http://www.euforumrj.org/projects/previous-projects/restorative-justice-and-crime-prevention

European Parliament and Council (2008), *Directive 2008/52/EC of the European Parliament and of the Council of 21 May 2008 on certain aspects of mediation in civil and commercial matters,* Official Journal of the European Union, L 136/3, 24 May. Downloaded: http://eur-lex.europa.eu/LexUriServ/LexUriServ.do?uri=OJ:L:2008:136:0003:0008:En:PDF

Gavrielides, T. (2007). *Restorative Justice Theory and Practice: Addressing the Discrepancy.* Helsinki: Heuni.

Gavrielides, Th. & Artinopoulou, V. (eds) (2013). *Reconstructing Restorative Justice Philosophy,* Ashgate publications.

Giovanoglou, S. (2008). *"Prosecutors as mediators in domestic violence cases: the Greek legislator's choice"*, Paper at fifth conference of the European Forum for Restorative Justice, 17–19 April 2008. Italy: Verona

Lambropoulou, E., (2005). Crime, Criminal Justice and Criminology in Greece, *European Journal of Criminology,* vol. 2(2), pp. 211-247.

Lambropoulou, E., (2010). "Alternative Dispute Resolution and Restorative justice Schemes for Juvenile Offenders in Greece – Potential Limitations and Open Questions". In *European Best Practices of Restorative Justice in the Criminal Procedure,* Conference Publications. Budapest: Ministry of Justice and Law Enforcement of the Republic of Hungary, pp. 136-151.

Papadopoulou, P. (2006), "Victim-Offender Mediation for Minors in Greece", *Newsletter of the European Forum for Restorative Justice,* vol. 7(1), pp. 1-3.

Pitsela A. & Symeonidou- Kastanidou E. (eds) (2013). *Restorative Justice in Criminal Matters. Comparative Research in 11 European Countries.* Athens-Thessaloniki: Sakkoulas Publications.

Websites

Εθνικό Κέντρο Κοινωνικής Αλληλεγγύης (ΕΚΚΑ): www.ekka.org.gr

Ελληνικό Κέντρο Διαμεσολάβησης και Διαιτησίας: http://www.hellenic-mediation.gr

Κέντρο Διαμεσολάβησης Δικηγορικού Συλλόγου Θεσσαλονίκης: http://www.dsth.gr/kdth

Κέντρο Διαμεσολάβησης Πειραιώς: http://kedip.gr

Υπουργείο Δικαιοσύνης, Διαφάνειας και Ανθρωπίνων Δικαιωμάτων: www.ministryofjustice.gr

3E-RJ-MODEL: http://3e-rj-model.web.auth.gr

Safeguarding Victims and Empowering Professionals in the Netherlands: State of the Art and Vision for the Future

*Anneke van Hoek and Gert Jan Slump**

Abstract

In this chapter Restorative Justice Nederland (RJN) presents the key findings of their review of Dutch literature and field research in the Netherlands. Based on the Dutch findings more general conclusions and recommendations can be drafted. Two pan-European tools that are developed by Restorative Justice Nederland are presented: a Maturity Grid Restorative Practices for Judicial Organisations and a Five Step Implementation Plan for national policy makers. Recommendations include professional development (through a combination of online and off line education), much needed cultural and organisational change within judicial organisations to avoid patriarchal attitudes and instrumentalization of victims and a plea for less ideology and more evidence based practice. Finally the authors state that the ideal vision for the future isn't a victim-led criminal justice system but a well-balanced system in which the interests and rights of both victims and offenders are safeguarded.

Introduction

The project Restorative Justice in Europe (RJE) consists of five work streams. The aim of *work stream 1* is to generate an overview of the already existing knowledge base. RJN has done this by reviewing existing relevant Dutch literature.

The purpose of *work stream 2* is to generate new research data. To answer the various research questions RJN has amongst others held more than 20 in-depth interviews and executed both qualitative and quantitative surveys. The evidence base that was developed in this way was used in *work stream 3 and 4* to develop, pilot and implement the following products:

1. Protocols and guidelines for providing RJ;
2. Training materials and programs for professionals;
3. Best practice guidance that will enhance multi agency, cross sector cooperation among RJ/ victim services and national agencies.

IARS as lead partner developed these training materials, protocols and best practices. The materials were subsequently tailored to the Dutch context by RJN and piloted and implemented through face to

* Anneke van Hoek (Consultant, Restorative Justice Netherlands), contact anneke.vanhoek@gmail.com
and Gert Jan Slump (Consultant, Restorative Justice Netherlands)

face training workshops and an interactive E-training that was especially developed by RJN for Dutch professionals. RJN also developed and produced the following specific additional products:

- A Five Step Implementation Plan for policy makers and other relevant stakeholders on national level
- A self assessment tool for detention centres and other judicial organisations called "Organisational Maturity Grid Restorative Practices for Judicial Organisations"
- An advisory report about how victim oriented and restorative practices can be brought to the next level within juvenile detention centres.

These three specific products, which form appendices to this chapter, are presented and integrated in the work stream 2 report of RJN and piloted later before a national and international audience.

All throughout the 2-year period of the project relevant project results and products were disseminated (*work stream 5*) in various ways through:

- Monthly updates and country project pages on the dedicated project website (www.rj4all.info/RJE)
- Different social media outlets of RJN and the RJE-partners
- Speeches and presentation at several national and international conferences

Next to the official launch of the RJE project and the closing conference in London, two national seminars were organized by RJN in the Netherlands (in 2013 and 2014) and a "training & gaming workshop" was held during the biennial conference of the European Forum for Restorative Justice in Belfast in June 2014. Also a presentation was held with prof. Marc Groenhuijsen at a Crime Conference in November 2013 at the University of Tilburg.[1]

- Publications in scientific journals, such as the journal of the Flemish restorative justice organisation Suggnomè,[2] the journal of the British Restorative Justice Council,[3] the Dutch-Flemish Journal for Restorative Justice[4] and the Dutch Journal 'Sancties'.[5]
- Meetings with policymakers, decision makers, practitioners and other stakeholders.

More than 40 bi-lateral meetings were held. On top of this the results of the fieldwork in the Netherlands (work stream 2 report) were presented and discussed at a management team meeting in which all directors of juvenile detention centres were present.

Research Methodology

In the work stream 1 report[6] an overview of relevant Dutch and Flemish literature is provided and discussed.

The Dutch part of the RJE-project had a special focus on Restorative Justice in the post-sentence phase and more specific on victim oriented and restorative practices within juvenile detention centres. Therefore the literature review zoomed in on these topics.

Research questions

The questionnaire used by RJN during 20 in-depth interviews had six main topics:

- General questions
- What do victims want/expect from restorative justice
- Bottlenecks and minimum safeguards for a victim oriented restorative justice
- Procedures, guidelines and protocols for victim oriented restorative justice services
- The need for training
- Multi-agency cooperation
- The implementation and enforcement of the Victims' Directive

Each topic was operationalized into several questions. The full questionnaire and other research tools are annexed to the Dutch report of work stream 2. Next to these questions, that all partners needed to include in their fieldwork, Restorative Justice Nederland added quite some extra research questions in their national research in order to produce an advisory report about how to implement RJ in Custody for young offenders and victims, including restorative ways to deal with internal crimes and conflicts.

Depending on each partner's agreed sampling methodology, the answers to the main research questions that were developed by IARS came either directly from victims or – as was the case in the Netherlands - indirectly from their representatives or people with direct experience having worked with them. In the Netherlands also the views of offenders were included through a qualitative survey. Additional fieldwork was aimed at victim oriented and restorative practices in juvenile detention centres. The fieldwork formed a combination of qualitative and quantitative research. Restorative Justice Nederland executed the following *qualitative* research activities in the framework of work stream 2:

1. Twenty in-depth interviews with staff of Victim Support Netherlands, restorative justice providers, academic victim experts and other relevant practitioners and stakeholders that work frequently with victims, who collaboratively can give a clear picture of victims' needs and opinions. RJN is well connected to Dutch experts and organisations in the field of victim oriented and restorative practices, so it was not difficult to identify the main 20 stakeholders and experts in this area. To make sure that we didn't overlook some important key persons, we used the snowball methodology: we asked each interviewee who we should not forget to interview in the framework of our research. This resulted in a list of 20 key experts.
2. A mini conference for 20 experts in the field of restorative justice in custody, to present and critically discuss the preliminary results of the field work of RJN within (juvenile) detention centres. Since Belgium has some best practices in this area also Flemish experts were invited.
3. Five in-depth interviews, observations and desk research in two juvenile detention centres in the frame work of a case study around the (restorative) handling of internal crimes and conflicts. The selection of these two juvenile detention centres was based on the fact that they both had good practices in this field while other detention centres had not.
4. A qualitative survey of 10 juvenile offenders who were detained in a juvenile detention centre. In this way the perspective of young offenders could be included and added to the research findings.
5. A national conference (with 75 participants) to present, discuss and enrich the final findings of the Dutch fieldwork on victim oriented and restorative practices in juvenile detention centres.

The following *quantitative* research activities have been executed:

- An attitudinal survey for practitioners who work in juvenile detention centres.
- A fact-finding survey for practitioners who work in juvenile detention centres.

For practical reasons both surveys were combined. These surveys were held in four of the ten currently still existing juvenile detention centres. These four detention centres were selected because we had learned from relevant stakeholders that these detention centres had experience with victim oriented and/or restorative practices. Since it wouldn't be effective to include juvenile detention centres with hardly any experience in this field, this seemed a logical selection methodology. In collaboration with the directors of the four juvenile detention centres the right type of employees were selected for the survey.

Decided was to approach employees who would have knowledge of or experience with the topic, which resulted in four types of employees: treatment & care, group leaders, management and spiritual care. The total amount of relevant employees in the four centres was 747 people. Three juvenile detention centres created a sample in such a way that all four types of employees were represented adequately. One detention centre (de Hunnerberg) approached all employees who fell into the four designated categories. In this way 197 employees received an invitation for the survey. The overall response was 38%: 75 people filled in both (combined) surveys, which resulted to quite reliable overall statistics.[7] Table 1 gives an overview.

Table 1: Sample methodology of the quantitative survey in four juvenile detention centres

Juvenile detention centre	Amount of invitations sent out	Amount of filled in questionnaires	Respondents Percentage
Hartelborgt	17	4	24%
Hunnerberg	64	26	41%
Rentray Lelystad	53	21	40%
Teylingereind	63	24	38%
Total	**197**	**75**	**38%**

The results of the Dutch qualitative and quantitative fieldwork is presented in a report that consist of two parts: the first part answers the research questions that IARS had developed for all five RJE-partners. In the second part the results of the specific Dutch research in juvenile detention centres is presented.

IARS has developed training materials in the framework of work stream 3, which RJN has further enriched and tailored to the Dutch context.

These materials were piloted in two ways through:

- *Face to face training workshops for professionals*

  These workshops of 3 hours were offered to relevant organisations and practitioners that work within the criminal justice system and/or offer restorative justice services or victim support.

Nine workshops have been delivered to in total 63 professionals in the period April to September 2014.

- *E-trainings for professionals*
  Two E-training pilots were organized for in total 38 participants. The first pilot took place from early July until early August, the second pilot from end of August until end of September 2014.

For a description of the tailored materials, the structure of the (E-) trainings and the lessons learned we refer to the paragraph further below: 'Empowering professionals in the Netherlands'.

What we Already Know from Existing Literature

One of the aims of the review of Dutch and Flemish literature was to identify the needs of victims of crime as voiced by the victims themselves. These needs are many fold, but can be divided into six categories (Ten Boom & Kuypers, 2008). The first category are *emotional needs*: recognition of the victim and of what happened, restoration of relations, apologies, direct emotional support, aftercare, specific care, certain characteristics of the emotional support (quick, available, easy accessible, in your own language etc.).

Secondly there is the *need for information*. Information about the criminal justice system, the role of the victim in the criminal justice procedure, the offender (background, motives, crimes), prevention and the process of healing. Then we can distinguish the *need for practical support*: help with paperwork, procedures, medical support, crisis management, transport etc. and the *need for financial compensation* (financial compensation by the offender, support with financial procedures etc.). There is the *need for safety and security*: creation of immediate safety (sometimes by providing a shelter / new home), prevention of re-victimisation etc.. And last but not least there are *specific needs in relation to the criminal justice system*. These include the need to be treated respectfully and with care by criminal justice officials, a swift reaction by the police and other criminal justice professionals that they come in contact with, the need to have legal assistance, to have a strong legal position and the possibility to be heard and give input into the criminal justice procedure (procedural justice), the satisfaction that the output of the criminal justice process gives (the sentence/sanction), the need that the offender becomes aware of the consequences of his own behaviour and will refrain from crime and the need to get into contact with the offender.

Other findings from the Dutch literature review can be summarized as follows:

1. The new EU Victim's Directive and other international rules and regulations in the field of victims and restorative justice have a stimulating effect on national legislators and policymakers.
   In the Netherlands this has resulted in the insertion of a new article in the Penal Procedural Code (art. 51h) on mediation in penal matters, and the first draft of a policy paper on mediation in penal matters. It has also led to the implementation of legislation that empowers the position of victims of crime.
   In the last two years appeals have been made from the Ministry of Justice to the police, public prosecutors, judges, prisons and other criminal justice partners to develop a vision for their organisation on victim led practices. This has resulted in several organisational vision papers.

2. Victim's need vary. The criminal justice system doesn't meet all needs of different victims. Sometimes the criminal justice system even creates extra damage to victims (secondary victimization). The same goes for restorative justice processes and practices. Developing safeguards for victims is therefore crucial.
3. Most restorative justice projects in the Netherlands have been evaluated. Nearly all evaluations indicate that the vast majority of victims (and offenders) are very positive about their experiences with these restorative practices.
4. Despite positive evaluations a lot of the existing restorative justice projects were terminated after some time which resulted in an ad hoc policy and practice.
5. Since 2006 the national restorative justice provider Victim in Focus facilitates victim offender talks nationwide. These talks up to now are not formally connected to the criminal justice procedure and are primarily meant to address the emotional and psychological needs of victims in a setting outside of the criminal justice system.
   Although these victim offender talks are primarily set up as a provision for victims, the vast majority of referrals come from offender oriented organisations.
6. In the recent 15 years quite some awareness raising activities and projects have been developed within Dutch (youth) prisons. In only a minority of cases this leads to actual meetings between victims and offenders.
7. Within the culture of prisons different thresholds exist that need to be overcome before restoration towards victims can become a realistic option within this context.
8. Restorative justice in prisons can limit and/or prevent so called detention damage that the prison system normally causes to inmates.
9. The existing religious / spiritual care within prisons forms a fertile ground on which restorative justice in prisons can flourish.
10. Several Dutch and Flemish academics and practitioners have published their ideas about how to bring restorative justice in prisons to the next level (among others Jansen-Van Driel (2004), Blad & Pauwelsen (2003) and Wolthuis (2012)) . These models are summarized and reviewed in our work stream 1 report and used as base of a new innovative tool that RJN has developed and tested, the so called 'organisational maturity grid restorative practices' for (juvenile) prisons and other judicial organisations.
11. Hardly any research has been executed on victim's experiences and satisfaction of restorative practices in custody. Existing research in this field focusses mainly on the effects of these restorative practices on the inmates and to some extent on the culture within prisons.

Conclusions and Critical Reflections

1. Existing research doesn't provide sufficient insight in victim's need for restorative justice. There is quite some national and international research that provides an overview of different needs that victims of crime express. However, if victims are not informed or aware of restorative justice options (which will be the case in most instances), they cannot express their need for such restorative options.
2. Victims of crimes are represented, nationally and internationally, by four different social movements, who each use their own 'image' of victims and accentuate different needs of victims (Pemberton, 2012).

The Victim Support Movement focusses on the practical and emotional needs of victims, the Victim's Rights Movement on a stronger legal position of victims within the Criminal Justice System, the Restorative Justice Movement on the need of victims of restoration, reconciliation and participation in alternative processes of conflict resolution and the Women's Movement on empowerment of minorities.

3. Social and academic discussions on victims and restorative justice have quite an ideological character and are not always based on solid empirical research on the actual needs of victims of crime.
4. Restorative justice in prisons ideally aims at different levels of restoration:
   a. restoration of the offender/inmate,
   b. restoration of the relationship between the offender and his/her family/network,
   c. restoration towards the victim
   d. restoration towards the community.
5. In reality mainly the first two levels of restoration are addressed. Often restoration on these two levels are however a prerequisite to achieve restoration towards the victim and the community.
6. Restorative Justice in prisons in the Netherlands finds itself not in the initial starting phase. A lot of knowledge and experience is available on which can be build to bring restorative justice in prisons to the next level(s).
7. The current tendency to stimulate victim led practices within judicial organisations in the Netherlands creates an opportunity to develop restorative justice in prisons further and develop and implement safeguards for victims.

New data: Key Findings of the Fieldwork

The four research questions that all RJE partners needed to answer in the framework of work stream 2 (the collection of new data) were:

1. What do victims understand by 'victim satisfaction' from justice procedures?
2. What do victims want from restorative justice?
3. What do victims think are the best and safest ways to implement restorative justice?
4. What are the best ways for enforcing the Victims' Directive?

These questions will be addressed in the paragraphs below.

RJN also executed elaborate research on restorative justice in juvenile detention centres. For the results of this specific part of the Dutch fieldwork we refer to part II of our work stream 2 report and our upcoming publications in two Dutch journals.[9]

Victim's Needs and Satisfaction from Justice Procedures

Asked about victims' satisfaction from justice procedures the 20 key persons we interviewed stated that victims are satisfied with the criminal justice system if their *specific needs in relation to the criminal justice system* are met and if also their general *basic needs* are met.

Basic needs of victims that are voiced most often by victims seem to be (most experts were in agreement about this) emotional support, the need for information, the need for safety and protection, the need to be heard and recognized as a victim, the need for compensation and other forms of (immaterial) restoration and the need for justice.

Offender related needs of victims are compensation, restoration, healing, (procedural) justice, the process of awareness of the offender, contact with the offender and information about the offender (motives, crime, personal background).

Related to theories of basic human needs these needs are mainly: security, positive connection with the other, self realisation, understanding of the world/reality, positive identity, control and justice.

But then: not all victims may have all these needs. And some victims might have other specific needs that are not yet listed above.

All interviewees therefore stressed the need to *ask each victim what their needs are*.

It's crucial *not to think for the victim*, not to assume you know beforehand what (certain types of) victims need, based on your experience, practical or academic knowledge or other assumptions. It was stated that this was done far too often by criminal justice professionals.

So one of the first things judicial professionals have to learn is to actively inquire about the exact needs of an individual victim, to listen carefully and become sensitive to victim's individual needs and wishes. This implies that criminal justice professionals need to shift their focus from the offender to include the victim.

Another issue is that the needs and rights of victims need to be balanced with the rights of offenders and the needs and regulations of the criminal justice system. That means that not all victims needs can be met within the legal framework of the criminal justice system. For example the need for control is for a large part lost by the victim as soon as he or she reports the offence to the police. The criminal justice system takes over leaving little victim control over the procedure. The need for control may be better met by a restorative justice process.

What Victims Want from Restorative Justice

Victims of crime have the same needs, whether entangled in a criminal justice process or participating in a restorative justice procedure. Next to that victims expect that restorative justice procedures meet certain criteria like:

- participation is voluntarily;
- safety while participating;
- accessibility;
- the offender takes responsibility;
- the victim receives timely objective, clear and full information about the process, the consequences of participation, the possible results and how the results can be enforced and can fully understand the consequences of the type of participation;
- the mediator is neutral and independent;
- the mediator is well trained and meets certain professional standards;
- victims can actively participate in the procedure, ask questions directly to the offender, voice opinions etc.

Victims hope and expect that participation in a restorative justice procedure will benefit them, especially emotionally. They hope to become less scared and anxious, to get answers to some burning questions that might help them on their path to healing and closure, to get empowered and able to go on with their lives. They would like to see 'the monster in the eye', to experience what kind of person the offender is, to understand why the offender has committed the crime and why it was directed (on purpose or by accident) to them. Victims also like to get apologies and other forms of restoration to compensate for the suffering the crime caused. Another need they may have is that the offender will learn something from the confrontation with the victim, that awareness is raised and future crimes might be prevented.

The Best and Safest Ways to Implement Restorative Justice

Based on our research, we can conclude that the implementation of restorative justice has to meet the basic needs of victims and take into account the special needs and criteria victims have voiced for restorative justice procedures. Because different opinions seem to exist about how these needs and criteria should be concretely implemented and enforced some of these needs and criteria were discussed in more detail with our interviewees.

Safety and Protection of Vulnerable Victims

The Victims' Directive demands assessment of victims, to identify vulnerable victims that might require special safeguards and care. The idea is to prevent re-traumatisation and re-victimisation of the victim.

According to our respondents vulnerable victims that demand special attention within a restorative justice setting are:

- *Minors*
  RJ with minors requires a different kind of preparation since most minors are not able to oversee the consequences of participation as easily as adults.
- *People with mental disabilities*
  These people can be more easily influenced and often suffer from an more limited empathic capacity. This requires special skills of the mediators and a tailored preparation process. Here the advice is to involve support persons.
- *Victims of stalking*
  One has to be careful not to facilitate the stalker in his wish to have contact with the victim, since the motive of the stalker can be to re-establish contact with the victim in order to continue the stalking.
- *Victims of lover boys*
  Dependence and a big power difference in the relation between the victim and the lover boy can create extra risks.
- *Victims of (repeat) domestic violence*
  Differences in power and dependence often play a role, so part of the mediation is to find out how this can become better balanced during the meeting.
- *Victims of notorious scammers*
  In this case there is a high risk that the offender will not pay financial compensation that has been agreed upon during the restorative justice procedure.

- *Victims of group crimes*
  Peer pressure requires in these cases extra attention
- In general all cases where power imbalance, dependence and suggestibility of victims play an important part.
- *Traumatised victims that suffer from PTSD*
  People with PTSD have an increased risk of re-traumatization. Possible contact with the offender is best discussed and prepared with the therapist of the victim. A therapist could also play a supportive role during the restorative justice procedure. Especially when restorative justice is offered in a post-sentence phase when the offender is detained and/or in cases of severe violent or sexual crimes or homicide one has to be aware of this risk..

The interviewed experts agreed that the fact that a victim is extra vulnerable should not lead to the conclusion that such victims should be excluded from a restorative justice procedure. This means that the procedure and the preparation should be tailored to the specific needs of these victims and that extra safeguards should be created. All victims should be informed about the risks and the ways these risks can be redressed so they can make their own informed decision about whether or not to participate in restorative justice.

Another issue is that many judicial professionals, but also other stakeholders (even volunteers from Victim Support) still have too much of a *patriarchal attitude*: they feel they should protect vulnerable victims from this decision and therefore don't inform these victims about the option to choose for a restorative justice procedure. In that way these victims are not given the chance to get empowered and to experience any of the other benefits that a restorative justice procedure can have.

The Interest of the Victim

Victim experts mention the risk that victims become *instrumentalized* by judicial professionals once restorative justice becomes an integrated part of the criminal justice procedure. The motivation of judicial professionals to refer to restorative justice providers can be quite instrumental: it's quicker, it's cheaper, it reduces the workload of the criminal justice system etc. Tensions can arise between the criteria and procedures that must be met in the framework of a criminal justice procedure and the criteria and procedures that should be met in the framework of a restorative justice procedure. The legal setting of a criminal justice procedure can be quite compulsory e.g. when it comes to the amount of time that's available for a certain stage in the process. The speed that is wanted from the perspective of judicial professionals can be detriment to the quality of the restorative justice procedure.

The inherent risk is that not the needs and wishes of victims are leading but the demands of the criminal justice system and the needs and wishes of it's professionals.

Access

Another consequence of the fact that the motivation of judicial professionals to refer victims to restorative justice providers can be quite instrumental, is that not all victims have equal access to restorative justice.

The judicial professionals create referral criteria, which might have more to do with the interests of the judicial professionals and the criminal justice system than with the interests of the victims. This can prevent accessibility of restorative justice procedures for all victims. Therefore critical attention has to be given to create referral procedures that put the needs of victims in the centre and not organisational needs.

Another bottleneck for access for victims to restorative justice procedures is the *financial* aspect of it all. At this point some restorative justice services in the Netherlands are for free while others are not.

Since the fall of 2013 pilots with new forms of restorative justice that are integrated in the criminal justice procedure are executed. Part of the evaluation of these pilots concerns the financial aspects of the pilots and based on the evaluation outcomes the Ministry will decide which forms of restorative justice will be subsidized and therefore will be freely available to victims and which forms not. And also which types of victims can have access to these restorative justice services.

The ideal for the future is that all victims that are in need of restorative justice can have access to different forms of restorative justice without being restrained by financial aspects.

Another condition to create access is that victims should be informed about the option to participate in a restorative justice procedure. We will discuss this below.

Information

Victims can be informed about the possibility to participate in restorative justice by public information about restorative justice. Right now no public information campaigns are being held in the Netherlands. There is a TV program in the making about restorative justice in juvenile detention centres and every now and then there are TV- or radio programs that highlight some restorative justice cases on an *ad hoc* basis.

Restorative justice providers distribute leaflets in a limited way, but for the rest no public information is available about (the different forms of) restorative justice. So this is an urgent need that must be addressed in a more systematic way to inform the public independently.

Another way to inform victims is through the professionals that victims encounter after being victimized and who inform them about the possibilities of participating in restorative justice. If people become a victim of crime they can come into contact with several professionals. First and foremost with judicial professionals and victim support staff.[10] It's therefore crucial to stimulate that judicial professionals and victim support staff inform victims adequately and systematically about restorative justice. This requires organisational changes and tailored professional education.[11]

Voluntary Participation

Some experts notice that judicial professionals aren't always aware of the fact that their communication with victims can create the feeling that participation in restorative justice procedures is compulsory. For example: if a public prosecutor sends a letter to a victim stating that the victim is invited for a meeting at a certain date, a lot of victims might feel that they are obliged to go to this meeting that is organized by such an authority. Criminal justice professionals should therefore explicitly state in their communication with victims that victims are free to participate and can stop the restorative justice procedure at any time they like.

The Implementation and Enforcement of the European Victims' Directive

Based on the interviews we held with different stakeholders and experts we can conclude that the best way for implementing and enforcing the Victims' Directive is the following Five Step Plan:

Step 1. Ensure that all required national legislation is in place.
Step 2. Ensure that all required national policy is in place (victim policy restorative justice policy).
Step 3. Ensure that the legislation and victim policy is enforced by the organisations within the criminal justice system.
Step 4. Ensure that the national services for victims (Victim Support, restorative justice services) are meeting the criteria that are set in the Victims' Directive.
Step 5. Stimulate multi agency cooperation between national services for victims and judicial organisations, among others to create adequate referral protocols and practices.

This Five Step Plan can help national policy makers to implement and enforce the European's Victim's Directive. This tool can be useful not only for national policy makers in the Netherlands but also in all other European countries that face the same challenge.

Many of the experts we interviewed stated that the Netherlands are a best practice when it comes to the implementation of the Victims' Directive. Although some of the legislation and policy is quite new, recent developments in the field of victim oriented justice is quite encouraging.

Step 1: National Legislation

For many years the social and political climate in the Netherlands has been very positive for victims. The result is that over the years step by step new national legislation has been developed to improve the legal position of victims. The Figure 1 (on page 173) gives an overview of both national and international legislation.

The most recent law has come into force in 2010: the Law Improving the Position of Victims improves the legal position of victims in various ways.

One of the things that is on the legal agenda of the Ministry of Justice for the coming period is the right of victims to receive victim support.

Beside this the focus is not so much on creating new rights for victims, but on effectively implementing and enforcing the already existing victims' rights.

When it comes to legislation and policy in the domain of restorative justice the state of the art is as shown in Figure 2 on page 174.

In the Netherlands a diversionary form of restorative justice is applied by the police. It's called HALT ('the alternative') and its target group is young first offenders of not too serious crimes. This form of restorative justice has been regulated for many years through legislation, special policy frameworks, and a standardized working methodology and clear protocols for among others the referral process.

Next to this form of diversion another form of restorative justice is quite well established in the Netherland: victim offender talks that are executed by the organisation Victim in Focus, financed by the Ministry of Safety and Justice. These victim offender talks are available for all victims that want to have indirect or direct contact with his/her offender. These talks can happen in any phase of the criminal procedure (before the trial, during the criminal justice procedure and post-sentence). The aim of the talks is emotional support and restoration. The results of the talk are not taken into account by the public prosecutor or judge. This therefore is a form of RJ that is not linked to the criminal justice procedure.

In January 2012 however a new article was included in the Criminal Procedure Code (art. 51h Sv) that provides a legal base for forms of restorative justice that are directly linked to the criminal justice system.

Figure 2: National and international rules/regulations, national policy and implementation of victim oriented practice

A. International and national rules/regulations

European Framework Decision (2001)
European Victim's Directive (2012)
Law on Strengthening Position of Victims (2010)

↕

B. Policy Ministry of Safety and Justice

National policy on victims since 1980's onwards
Policy paper 'Doing Justice to Victims' (2013-2017)

↕

C. Implementation of national policy by judicial organisations and partners

– Improving and streamlining provisions for victims support and care (a.o. initiation of so called victims desks)
– Developing vision on victim oriented practices and policies by judicial organisations
– Elaborating and describing working methods and processes in protocols a.o.
– Improving expertise (training a.o.)
– Programmes on culture change

This sparkled quite some discussion between people who were in favor of this type of restorative justice and people who were against such judicial forms of restorative justice because of the risk that offenders would 'use' the victim to get a lower sentence.

In general most experts are in favour of this legalization and the opportunities it provides for new forms of restorative justice, but only unless these practices meet certain criteria and the satisfaction of the victims is monitored.

Step 2: National Policy

The current victim policy in the Netherlands is explicitly based on the main basic needs of victims. It also states that safeguards should be put in place to protect extra vulnerable victims. Additional budget is provided to support these vulnerable victims in a way that's more tailored to their needs.

Recently the need for restoration has become an explicit part of the national victim's policy. And this includes not only material restoration and compensation but also the need for restorative justice procedures. For the first time in Dutch history restorative justice is framed as part of the policy for victims which implies that restorative justice is (also) in the interest of victims (under certain

Figure 2: National and international rules/regulations, national policy and implementation of restorative practices

A. International rules and regulations

Art. 10 European Framework Decision (2001)

Art. 12 European Victims Directive (2012)

Art. 51h Penal Procedural Code (2012)

B. Policy Ministry of Safety and Justice

Policy on HALT (revised 2014)

Policy on victim-offender talks (2006/2007)

Concept policy framework on restorative mediation (2013)

Pilots on restorative mediation, evaluation, final adoption policy framework (2013-2015)

C. Implementation of national policy by judicial organisations and partners

– Further improvement and diversification of restorative provisions and variants

– Developing vision, restorative practices and policies by judicial organisations

– Elaborating and describing working methods and processes in protocols a.o.

– Improving expertise (training a.o.)

– Programmes on culture change

conditions). This is a shift from earlier days, when there was not a sound social and political base for restorative justice, since restorative justice was mainly seen as being in the interest of the offender.

In the spring of 2012 a draft policy framework was created to establish the criteria under which different forms of restorative justice that are linked to the criminal justice system (as meant in the new art. 51h of the Criminal Procedure Code) can be implemented.

In the fall of 2013 several pilots started with new forms of restorative justice that are integrated within the criminal justice procedure. During the pilots good practices, protocols for referral and uniform working methodologies will be developed, tested and determined.

Based on the results of these pilots a final policy framework for mediation in penal matters will be set in 2015.

The criteria that form the base of the current draft policy framework are totally in line with the criteria set in the Victims' Directive and other relevant international legislation.

Most experts feel that it's positive that this policy framework is being established and it can become a solid base for the implementation of new forms of restorative justice.

We can conclude that the Dutch national legislation and policy for victims is more or less already in line with the Victims' Directive. The policy framework on mediation in penal matters however is still a work in progress and should be enacted in 2015.

Step 3: Enforcement by Judicial Organisations

The organisations within the criminal justice system need to implement and enforce the rules and regulations that are set in the national legal and policy framework.

This means that judicial organisations need to develop their own organisational vision and policy, create the necessary organisational conditions (budget, staff, training etc.), culture and working methodologies to implement the intentions that are put on paper.

Implementation can have an ad hoc character and can be driven by only a couple of passionate individual pioneers that implement it within a limited context or it can have a more solid base within the organisation and can be implemented more systematic or even holistic. In other words: an organisation can be less or more 'mature' when it comes to the implementation of victim oriented and restorative practices.

Restorative Justice Nederland has developed an 'organisational maturity grid restorative practices for judicial organisations' to illustrate these different organisational implementation stages.

The grid is based on literature, interviews and experience of the project manager of RJN with developing maturity grids for organisations.

In the maturity grid five development stages are distinguished, stage 0 being the stage where there is no interest at all in restorative justice in all the five core aspects of the organisation that are distinguished. In step 1 the organisation starts orienting itself on restorative justice. In stage 2 restorative justice is more developed and described. In stage 3 restorative justice is integrated in most of the core aspects of the organisation. In the final stage the whole chain of criminal justice organisations and relevant third parties work in an integrated restorative way. This maturity grid is presented as Table 1 overleaf.

RJN has also developed a similar maturity grid for victim oriented practices. Both organisational maturity grids can be used Europe wide by organisations within the criminal justice system:

- to establish how far they have proceeded in implementing victim oriented and/or restorative practices within their organisation.
- to identify what the next steps are if they want to get to the next implementation level.

We applied the maturity grid to research data of post-sentence judicial organisations (probation, detention centres), which were collected in work stream 2, to see whether this tool adds value to the data-analysis. And it did. We also tested the grid before an international audience during the conference of the European Forum for Restorative Justice that was held in June 2014 in Belfast. The participants came from a variety of countries like Hungary, Scotland, Ireland, France, the Netherlands and the U.S.A. The feedback from these participants was very positive, so we dare to conclude that we've developed an effective pan-European self-assessment tool that can be used by judicial organisations in all European countries.

Step 4: National Provisions for Victims

Victim support is organized very well in the Netherlands.

Table 1: Organizational Maturity Grid Restorative Practices within judicial organisation (cocept, RJN, March 2013)

Activity	Stage 0: No interest	Stage 1: Orientation	Stage 2: Definition & description	Stage 3: Organisational integration	Stage 4: Chain wide integration
Vision & Policy	Absent	Ad hoc	Some defined areas	Holistic and fully integrated in and supported by the organisation	Internally and externally fully integrated and supported
Working method	Absent	First initiatives by individual pioneers	Description of restorative methodologies, guidelines, protocols, etc.	Restorative practices are integrated in daily working procedures and all required preconditions are present.	Integrated in chain wide working procedures
Expertise	Absent	Individual pioneers have some knowledge of restorative practices	Some experience with and knowledge of restorative practices at some departments /functions	Adequate and up-to-date expertise of restorative practices by all employees within the organisation	Adequate and up-to-date expertise within the whole chain of restorative and judicial organisations
Culture	Absent	Restorative attitude by some individual pioneers	Restorative attitude at some departments/functions	The organisation as a whole sufficiently supports the restorative culture within its own organisation.	All organisations within the chain sufficiently support the restorative culture within their own organisation and beyond.
Collaboration with third parties	Absent	Ad hoc	Good practices	Structured working relationship with qualified RJ providers according to set protocols	Structured working relationship with all third parties within the chain according to set protocols.

The police and public prosecutors cooperate in a systematic way in this field and have created judicial victims counters in all districts.

Beside this judicial victim support the NGO Victim Support Netherlands delivers services to 150.000 victims on a yearly base including tailored support (case management) for victims of serious violent and/or sexual crimes and for partners and family members of victims of homicide. Adequate monitoring and quality control systems are in place and victims are invited to collaborate on further improvement of victim services.

In this respect the Victims' Directive is by and large already implemented, since safe and competent provisions for victims are well in place. The development of safe and competent provisions for restorative justice are however in a different stage of development.

HALT, a form of diversion through RJ for young first offenders, is very well established and is a good practice. In fact Halt is developing further in the direction of an even more restorative organisation nowadays aiming at the increase of face-to-face mediation between (juvenile) first offenders and victims.

Victim offender talks, a form of mediation for victims of crime that is (most of the time) not directly linked to the criminal justice system, has been transformed from a project to a structural provision that is financed by the Ministry of Justice. New forms of RJ directly linked to the criminal justice system are being developed right at this moment in pilots already mentioned. Mediators and family group conference coordinators, who normally work outside of the criminal justice system (in the field of welfare, care or education or in other legal sectors than criminal justice) start working within the context of the criminal justice system, which is (partly) new to them. On the other side criminal justice professionals start working with new forms of restorative justice that they aren't familiar with yet. So although there is a solid legal and policy framework, the development of these forms of restorative justice is still in its earlier stages.

Step 5: Multi Agency Cooperation

Multi agency cooperation between Victim Support Netherlands and the different judicial organisations is going quite well, although some points still can be improved. In general this cooperation can be seen as a good practice in European perspective.

The cooperation between HALT and the judicial organisations is also well established and can be seen as a good practice too. In European perspective HALT is however a typically Dutch invention, so it will be more difficult for other European countries to learn from this.

The providers of the new forms of restorative justice that are linked to the criminal justice system are only starting now to cooperate with the judicial organisations. This means multi agency cooperation in the field of these forms of judicial restorative justice is still in it's infancy.

Empowering Professionals in the Netherlands

Face to face workshops

Based on the materials produced by our lead partner IARS we developed a Dutch version of the workshop. The workshop 'Victim oriented and restorative practices' was delivered to nine groups of professionals, both restorative justice providers, victim support workers, representatives of victim services delivered by the public prosecution office and police officers.

The content of the face to face workshop was tailored to the professional practice of the participants and consisted of four parts. After an introduction core instruction was delivered by the trainers, firstly on working with victims and restorative justice in relation to the EU-Victims directive and secondly on regulations and policies in the Netherlands concerning victims and restorative justice. After this educational part of the training a learning dialogue was started around the RJN organisational maturity grid or other relevant topics or tools that were relevant to the different target groups.

Dutch Interactive E-training

IARS had developed an E-module in English that could be used by all five project partners. RJN developed an additional interactive E-training especially for Dutch professionals, tailored to the Dutch context. This Dutch E-training was also highly interactive and included various ways for people to participate actively in the training and communicate with each other. The need to create such a highly interactive E-training was accentuated during interviews RJN had with both participants and designers of E-trainings that are offered by the International Institute of Restorative Practices (IIRP).[12]

This resulted in a Dutch E-training that consisted of eight assignments that required a total investment from the Dutch participants of 10 to 12 hours. This was a lot more than the 40 minutes of listening that was demanded of the participants of the IARS training.

So in various aspects the E-training of RJN and IARS turned out quite different. The Dutch E-training was developed with the software of LearningStone,[13] which gives the opportunity to tailor the E-training to the specific needs of the participants. It was the first time RJN used this software so also technically this E-training was a pilot. The structure and content of the Dutch E-training was as follows:

- Introduction about the RJE project
- Summary of the E-training
- Technical instructions
- Assignment 1: Profile creation and introduction to other participants
- Assignment 2: Study of reader and powerpoint presentation
- Assignment 3: Reflections on the reader and the powerpoint presentation
- Assignment 4: Reflections on opportunities and threats for victim oriented and restorative practices within own working environment
- Assignment 5: Selection and discussion of one of the presented cases
- Assignment 6: Feedback on case discussion of one of the other participants
- Assignment 7: Final reflection and pitch on victim oriented and restorative practices
- Assignment 8: Evaluation

The Dutch E-training was offered twice during the project period to in total 38 participants. One of the things we experienced is that there is a vivid interest in Dutch E-trainings in this field, since both pilots were fully booked within a week after publication.

Lessons Learned from the Piloting of the Training Materials

Lessons Learned from the Piloting of the Face to Face Training Workshops

Nearly all of the participants of the workshops, whatever their professional background, stated that their knowledge about victim oriented and restorative practice was enlarged and 'sharpened' while attending the face to face training workshop.

Participants highlighted some strong elements of the training such as the good information and background that was provided on both Dutch and European regulation and policy, the structure and set up of the workshop and the balance of theory and practice, the expertise and enthusiasm of the trainer and the highly interactive character of the training workshop.

The main suggestion for improvement that participants mentioned was the need for an in-depth follow up. A reasonable group of participants (8) stated that this workshop could serve very well as in introduction to victim oriented and restorative practice in the future. One suggestion was to incorporate it in the curriculum of organisations like victims support.

Lessons Learned from the Piloting of the Dutch E-training

Before designing the Dutch E-training interviews were held with a participant and two producers of RJ-trainings of IIRP. They advised us to take into account the following lessons that they learned over time. According to their vast experience key to a successful E-training is *active participation* and *interactivity*. That means amongst others that you should create possibilities for participants to chat with each other and make the virtual communication as *personal* as possible. Make sure that participants are asked to interact with each other, to comment on each other "homework" since they learn at least as much from each other than from the comments of the E-trainers and from reading written materials. And last but not least: the best mix is a combination of face to face events (training, seminars) and E-learning. In other words: a *mix of online and off line educational* activities. This advice was taken to heart while designing the Dutch E-training.

An important lesson we learned during the pilots is that it's important to create incentives for participants to finish the E-training. The E-training was offered for free and each E-training was fully booked within the week. However after enrolment quite some participants didn't actually start participating. Making participants pay a fee might have prevented this. Also certification is to be recommended to motivate participants to fully finish the training. Another aspect was that the timing of the first pilot was challenging (during the summer holiday), so official holidays should be taken into account when planning an E-training.

Most participants of the E-training, mainly professionals in the age group between 30 and 65 years, were unfamiliar with E-training in general and needed some time to get acquainted with the virtual learning environment. Despite this nearly everybody informed us that overall the technical threshold to participate was not very high.

Participants that finalized the E-training were positive about the training and were glad 'to be given this opportunity'. Due to the fact that the second pilot of the E-training was still running while writing this chapter we cannot provide an overall evaluation of the E-training.

Conclusions about the Educational Tools

The first pilot of the E-training proved that it's important to create intermediate deadlines and other incentives for participants to keep on track and finalize the E-training (certification etc.).

The content of the training was in general positively evaluated, both by the participants of the face to face workshops as the E-training. Some practical tips of participants about the used materials have been taken into account to further improve the reader and powerpoint presentations.

A combination of face to face educational activities and (interactive) E-learning seems a powerful and effective tool to train and empower professionals.

Attention needs to be paid to participants that have been (secondary) victimised themselves, since a training around topics such as victim oriented and restorative practices can stir up emotions and open old wounds. Therefore follow up support should be offered if needed.

Critical Thinking and Vision for the Future

The Implementation of the Victim's Directive in the Netherlands

The Netherlands are well on it's way with implementing the legal framework that is required by the European Victim's Directive. The necessary legislation and national victim policy is nearly ready and in 2015 the new policy on mediation in penal matters will be enacted.

Also when it comes to safe provisions for victims the Netherlands can be seen as a good practice: a sound national infrastructure of victim support and judicial victim care exists and adequate financial support is present. Victim in Focus provides nationwide victim offender talks that take place mainly outside of the criminal justice system and HALT can be seen as a form of diversion that's well embedded in the practice of the police and public prosecution.

The implementation of other judicial forms of restorative justice are however still in it's infancy. The current pilots in which a variety of restorative justice approaches are being tested are however encouraging. The hope is that these pilots result in new, clear referral procedures and good practices. A bottleneck that however still doesn't seem to have been solved is the financing of the different forms of restorative justice. Also a plan for additional education of 'gate keepers' and other stakeholders is urgently needed.

The Need for a Change of Culture

Victim oriented practices within judicial organisations are being stimulated for some time by the Ministry of Safety and Justice. For many judicial organisations and practitioners it's however relatively new to pay attention to victim's rights and needs in a systematic way. It's therefore not surprising that our research indicated that there is a need for cultural change within judicial organisations. Extra attention needs to be paid to the following aspects:

- *Changing professional patriarchal attitudes*
  Not only criminal justice professionals but also some victims support practitioners tend to think and decide for (vulnerable) victims. It's crucial that they learn to actively inquire about the exact needs of each individual victim. Extra vulnerable victims should not be protected too much, but be given the opportunity to empower themselves. This means that vulnerable victims should not be shielded from restorative justice procedures but that the restorative justice procedure should be tailored to the specific needs of these victims so participation is safe for them.
  The rule of thumb is here: don't do things TO or FOR victims but act WITH them.
- *Preventing the instrumentalization of victims*
  Judicial professionals are used to giving priority to the needs of the criminal justice system. The motivation of judicial professionals to refer to restorative justice providers can therefore be quite instrumental: it's quicker, cheaper, it reduces the workload of the criminal justice system etc. This can endanger the rights and interests of victims.
  Judicial professionals therefore have to learn how to adequately balance the rights and interests of offenders and the criminal justice system with the rights and interests of victims.
- *Creating access for all victims to restorative justice services*
  A consequence of the fact that the motivation of judicial professionals to refer to restorative justice

providers can be quite instrumental is that not all victims get equal access to restorative justice. Therefore critical attention has to be given to create referral procedures that put the needs of victims in the centre and not organisational needs.

To bring about these cultural organisational changes a combination of measures is necessary: the development and implementation of adequate policies and referral procedures, safeguards for (extra vulnerable) victims, projects to change the organisational culture and training for professionals.

Recommendations for the Future

Professional Development

A lot of professionals working within the penal system still lack an adequate attitude, the knowledge and skills to implement a victim oriented and restorative approach. Tailored education is therefore needed. A combination of off line training (face to face workshops etc.) and interactive online E-training that's well tailored to the needs of the target group seems most feasible and effective and is therefore recommended.

Cross-national Learning

The implementation of the European Victim's directive is stimulating a more victim oriented and restorative criminal justice system in the different European countries.

In this respect cross-national learning is of the highest importance to ensure that European countries can get inspired by good practices and support tools developed elsewhere.

The results of the RJE-project will contribute to this development. Moreover Restorative Justice Nederland developed two pan-European tools that can be used by judicial organisations all over Europe to bring victim oriented and restorative practices to the next level: an organisational maturity grid restorative practices for judicial organisations and a similar grid for victim oriented practices.

These tools can be used as self-assessment tool to find out in what development phase your organisation is and what is necessary to bring the organisation to the next level. These tools can be used by one organisation at a time, but the 'training & gaming workshop' in Belfast also learned that it's quite educational and inspirational to use this tool by different organisations from different countries in one workshop. Restorative Justice Nederland is offering these training & gaming workshops for interested organisations all over Europe.

Another pan-European tool Restorative Justice Nederland developed is the Five Step Implementation Plan that can be used by national policy makers all over Europe to help them implement and enforce the Victim's Directive in a systematic way.

From Ideology to Grounded Evidence Based Practice

Too long the Dutch debate has been on 'restorative justice being 'soft' and only favourable to the offender. The current attention for victim oriented practices creates a new opportunity for creating a more restorative criminal justice system. However the risk is that practices are steered by ideologies and not by realistic needs and wishes of victims and offenders.

Victim's are not only instrumentalized by some judicial practitioners but also by some politicians, decision makers and 'victims'groups. Specific political and ideological driven people think they know exactly what victims need: more legal rights, more emotional and practical support, more empowerment or more participation in alternative processes of conflict resolution. In practice it's up to the individual victim to decide and express what he or she really needs. That means it's core to actively ask the victim what is needed, listen well and act accordingly. To avoid ideological blindness it's important to establish a good system of evaluation of victim oriented and restorative practices, so practices can be grounded in empirical research and not in ideological paradigms.

A Victim-led Criminal Justice System?

Recently – and for the first time in Dutch history - restorative justice has become explicitly part of the Dutch national policy for victims, which implies that restorative justice is (also) seen as being in the interest of victims (under certain conditions). This is a shift from earlier days, when there was not a sound social and political base to implement judicial forms of restorative justice, since it was mainly seen as being in the interest of offenders.

This shift is due to the priority that the Ministry of Safety and Justice has given to victim oriented practices as part of the implementation of European Victim's Directive.

A lot of practitioners feel it's positive that victim oriented and (as a part of that) restorative practices are stimulated within the context of the criminal justice system. The question is however what the right balance should be between the rights and interests of victims and the rights and interests of suspects/offenders.

During the workshops and E-trainings of RJN a question often discussed was: "Is it desirable to create a victim led criminal justice system"? Practitioners that work for judicial organisations that mainly deal with offenders (probation, detention centres etc.) voiced that the balance shouldn't tilt too much to the side of victims.

It's crucial to also keep safeguarding the rights and interests of offenders and when the rights of both parties are contradictory, make a well-funded judgement. Other professionals agreed to that too, also because it's not clear in all cases who is the victim and who's the offender. Therefore the rights of both parties must be taken into account in a balanced way.

After an offender-led criminal justice system, that has been the dominating paradigm for far too long, RJN feels that the new ideal and practice should not be a victim-led criminal justice system, but a well-balanced system in which the interests and rights of both victims and offenders are safeguarded.

Notes

1 This led to the publication *"Waar zit de ruimte voor slachtoffers? De waarde van herstel in en rond het klassieke strafproces."* Drs. Gert Jan Slump en prof. mr. Marc Groenhuijsen. Published in "Hoe te reageren op misdaad? Op zoek naar de hedendaagse betekenis van preventie, vergelding en herstel". University of Tilburg, 2013. See: https://pure.uvt.nl/portal/files/1577125/Waar_zit_de_ruimte_voor_slachtoffers_1_.pdf

2 Four articles were written (two by Anneke van Hoek and two by Gert Jan Slump) in 2013 and 2014 in which specific aspects of the RJE project were highlighted. See: www.suggnome.be/pdf/nieuwsbrief_jg14nr1.pdf, www.suggnome.be/pdf/nieuwsbrief_jg 14nr2.pdf, www.suggnome.be/pdf/nieuwsbrief_jg14nr3.pdf and www.suggnome.be/pdf/nieuwsbrief_jg15nr1.pdf.

3 *Restorative Justice (in the) Netherlands: a valuable enterprise.* Anneke van Hoek, *Resolution,* Edition 48, Summer 2013, p. 8 – 9. Restorative Justice Council, London.
4 RJN has produced a substantial article that will be published in the last isssue of the Dutch-Flemish *Tijdschrift voor Herstelrecht* in 2014.
5 RJN has also written an article that will be published in the first issue of *Sancties* in 2015.
6 *Restorative Justice in Europe: slachtoffers, herstelrecht en herstelgerichte (jeugd)detentie. Bespreking van Nederlandse en Vlaamse literatuur.* Anneke van Hoek, Gert Jan Slump, RJN, March, 2013. See: http://www.restorativejustice.nl/uploads/file/Literatuuronderzoek_RJN_RJE_NL_def.pdf
7 The results per juvenile detention centre are not representative, but the *combined* results are pretty reliable. To give an example: in total 73% of the respondents says that it's "very important that the detention period is also aimed at restoration". This percentage lies for all four detention centres with a certainty of 95% between the 64% and 82%.
8 *Restorative Justice in Europe: Resultaten van het veldwerk (work stream 2). Deel I: De implementatie en bekrachtiging van de Europese Slachtoffer Richtlijn: state of the art, stappenplan en groeimodel. Deel II: Slachtoffer- en herstelgericht werken in de fase van de tenuitvoerlegging: casestudy Justitiële Jeugdinrichtingen.* Anneke van Hoek, Gert Jan Slump. Restorative Justice Nederland, November 2013. See: http://www.restorativejustice.nl/uploads/file/RJE_WS2_RJN_definitief_def.pdf
9 *Tijdschrift voor Herstelrecht,* 2014, nr. 4 and *Sancties,* 2015, nr. 1.
10 Victims can also come into contact with medical staff or staff from other organisations (insurance companies etc.), so it would also be good if these 'second circle' of organisations could inform victims about restorative justice through leaflets or other means of communication.
11 In the Netherlands the Minister of Justice stimulates all judicial organisations to increase victim awareness in their work. This has led to different activities to change the organisational culture and professional attitude of judicial professionals and to develop new working methodologies in which the victim comes in focus in a systematic way.
12 The IIRP (http://www.iirp.edu), an American based graduate school for restorative practitioners, has worldwide the most experience in developing E-trainings in this domain.
13 See www.learningstone.com

References

Blad, J.R. & J. Pauwelsen: *Rentray: de justitiële jeugdinrichting als rehabilitatiecentrum. Een onderzoek naar de mogelijkheden van herstelgerichte detentie.* Rotterdam, Erasmus University Rotterdam, 2003.

Council of Europe, European Commission for the Efficiency of Justice (CEPEJ) (2007): *Guidelines for a better implementation of the existing recommendation concerning mediation in penal matters',* CEPEJ, 2007.

Department of Safety and Justice: *Recht doen aan slachtoffers,* The Hague, 2013.

Dierx, Janny & Anneke van Hoek (ed.): *Mediation in strafzaken. De praktische toepassing van restorative justice en herstelrecht.* Nr. 10 mediation series, Sdu publishers, The Hague, 2012.

European Parliament and European Council: *Directive 2012/29/EU of the European Parliament and of the Council of 25 October 2012 establishing minimum standards on the rights, support and protection of victims of crime, and replacing Council Framework Decision 2001/220/JHA*

Ferwerda, Henk & Ilse van Leiden, *De schade hersteld? Een onderzoek naar herstelbemiddeling bij jeugdige delinquenten in Vlaanderen.* Bureau Beke, Arnhem, 2013.

Jansen-Van Driel, Jeanet: *Herstel en Detentie, een onderzoek naar de mogelijkheden van herstelgerichte detentie in relatie tot de geestelijke verzorgingspraktijk.* Doctoraalscriptie Universiteit voor Humanistiek, Renswoude, 2004.

Pemberton, A., Slachtofferbewegingen en herstelrecht: over het belang van de realiteit achter de stereotypen, *Tijdschrift voor Herstelrecht*, volume 11, issue 4, pp. 28-45, The Hague, 2012.

Ten Boom, A & K.F. Kuypers, M.H. Moene: *Behoeften van slachtoffers van delicten: een systematische literatuurstudie naar behoeften zoals door slachtoffers zelf geuit*, Research and Documentation Centre of the Department of Justice, The Hague, 2008.

Van Hoek, A. & G. J. Slump: Inventarisatie herstelrechtelijke projecten en activiteiten in Nederland van 1980 tot heden en buitenlandse voorbeelden, *Stichting Restorative Justice Nederland / Ministry of Safety & Justice*, Amsterdam/The Hague, 2011

Van Hoek, A. & G.J. Slump: De toepassing van herstelrecht in Nederland: bouwstenen voor een toekomstvisie. *Stichting Restorative Justice Nederland/ Ministry of Safety & Justice*, Amsterdam/The Hague, 2011

Van Hoek, A. & G. J, Slump, M. Leijten, A. Ochtman: De toepassing van herstelrecht in Nederland: toekomstvisie en advies. *Stichting Restorative Justice Nederland/ Ministry of Safety & Justice*, Amsterdam/The Hague, 2011

Wolthuis, A.: *Herstelrecht, een kinderrecht. Voorstellen voor integratie van herstel in het hart van het jeugdstrafrecht*. Boom Lemma publishers, The Hague, 2012

More Justice for Crime Victims in Bulgaria

*Dobrinka Chankova**

Abstract

This chapter examines "The Bulgarian Project" – a part of "Restorative Justice in Europe: Safeguarding Victims and Empowering Professionals" (RJE) project, whose main purpose is to explore victims-related theory, practices, services and policies in Bulgaria, including the state of play of restorative justice. It is meant to support the successful national implementation of Directive 2012/29/EU of the European Parliament and of the Council Establishing Minimum Standards on the Rights, Support and Protection of Victims of Crime, as well as Bulgaria's efforts to become a better and safer place for crime victims where restorative justice is widely applied. It provides a summary review of Bulgarian literature, findings from surveys conducted among crime victims, professionals from the criminal justice system, service providers working with victims, and practitioners applying restorative practices as well as the prospects for restorative justice in Bulgaria. Recommendations for implementation of the Victims' Directive and further application of restorative justice in Bulgaria as a relevant instrument for victims are submitted.

The Crime Victim's Status in Bulgarian Law and Practice

For a long time, crime victims were the "forgotten party" in the Bulgarian criminal justice system. They were totally neglected and marginalized, while the attention fell exclusively on the offender. Protection of the procedural rights of the perpetrators of crime was even enhanced by the Bulgarian legislator and judicial practice. However, the rights of crime victims were not equally protected.

Despite the fact that Bulgaria had already declared adherence to the 1985 United Nations Declaration of Basic Principles of Justice for Victims of Crime and Abuse of Power and to the other relevant UN and Council of Europe instruments, crime victims remained for decades in the periphery of the attention of the legislature, state institutions and even non-governmental organizations (NGOs). It was only some research centres and University professors that paid due attention to crime victims and regularly sent alarming messages about their legal status and actual situation (Miteva, 1977; Bochev, 1986; Stoinov, 1993).

Fortunately, recently the victims of crime in Bulgaria seem to be receiving increased attention from governmental institutions, NGOs, academia, etc. The victims have been rediscovered and recognized. From an "invisible" object of social reality and criminal proceedings, often isolated from their own case, they have become a more noticeable figure in law, political strategies and media. This attention was prompted by the negotiations and pre-accession process for Bulgaria's full membership in the European Union when numerous recommendations for applying the minimum standards for protection of victims of crime have been made to the government. The National Strategy for Support and Compensation of Crime Victims (2006), the Strategy for Continuing the Judicial Reform in the Context of full EU Membership (2010), the National Concept for Penal Policy of the Republic of Bulgaria for the

* Professor Dobrinka Chankova (Chair of the Institute of Conflict Resolution, Bulgaria) contact chankova@yahoo.com

period 2010-2014 and the Concept on the State's Policy on Juvenile Justice (2011) are among the most important documents demonstrating this new trend in the Bulgarian crime policy.

It will not be an overstatement to say that one of the greatest recent achievements was the Criminal Procedure Code 2005.[1] The Code regulated for the first time the procedural status of the injured party in a separate chapter. After the amendments from 2008,[2] the current standing of crime victims in criminal proceedings could be described as follows:

According to Article 74 of the Criminal Procedure Code, the person who has suffered pecuniary or non-pecuniary damage from the crime shall be an injured party. After the death of the injured party, this right shall pass on to his/her heirs. The injured party enjoys specific rights both in the pre-trial and court proceedings. Most of these rights can be exercised in full during the court proceedings when the injured party can be constituted as a private prosecutor, private complainant or civil claimant. However, according to Article 75 of the same Code, during the pre-trial proceedings the injured party has the following rights: to be notified of his/her rights in the criminal proceedings; to receive protection of his/her safety and that of his/her close persons; to be informed about the course of the criminal proceedings; to take part in the proceedings; to appeal the acts resulting in the suspension or termination of the criminal proceedings; to have a counsel. The injured party is entitled to these rights if s/he has explicitly requested to take part in the pre-trial proceedings and has stated a summoning address in the country. In summary, the injured party currently enjoys a relatively high status in the criminal proceedings; s/he is no longer merely a "witness".

As a candidate country for EU accession, the Republic of Bulgaria had to transpose Council Directive 2004/80/EC of 29 April 2004 relating to compensation to crime victims. This was done by adopting the Support and Financial Compensation for Crime Victims Act 2006.[3] The objective of this Act is to recognise and guarantee the rights and lawful interests of crime victims, according to the European and international standards. It provides for various types of support such as psychological, legal, medical, etc., as well as financial compensation from the state, although rather limited.

A separate chapter of the Support and Financial Compensation for Crime Victims Act deals specifically with informing crime victims of their rights. It is an obligation of the bodies of the Ministry of Interior and the victim support organizations.

The National Council for Support and Compensation of Crime Victims, which was established with the Ministry of Justice in 2007, is the body competent to consider victims' applications for financial compensation. In view of the need to raise public awareness and knowledge of the opportunities provided for by the Support and Financial Compensation for Crime Victims Act, the Ministry of Justice has developed a specialised Internet site.[4]

Lately Restorative justice (RJ), one of the most attractive modern policies in criminal justice worldwide and a recognized instrument for crime victims' protection, has finally received some attention in Bulgaria. The Mediation Act 2004[5] introduced mediation as an alternative method for resolution of family, civil, administrative and other disputes between natural and/or legal persons. A much praised achievement of this act is Article 3, paragraph 2, which provides for mediation in criminal matters, as envisaged in the Criminal Procedure Code. Bulgaria belongs to the continental system of law; hence for mediation in criminal matters to be implemented, a detailed legislative regulation is required. Despite the explicit requirement of the law to that end, the Criminal Procedure Code 2005 did not provide for any cases where mediation could be applied and left this issue to subsequent amendments. Although proposals *de lege ferenda* (for the future legislation) in this direction were submitted by academia and NGOs to the Ministry of Justice and Parliament in 2008, RJ is not a fact of law yet. Nevertheless, the current legislation leaves room for the application of restorative justice methods in relation to the so called complainant's crimes where the criminal proceedings are instituted upon the victim's initiative. Restorative practices are also applied in juvenile cases, in prisons, in community matters, although on a limited scale.

In the meantime, a number of NGOs have started to successfully implement trainings of mediators, judges, prosecutors and other professionals in the field. The National Association of Mediators, the Institute for Conflict Resolution (ICR), the Union of Bulgarian Jurists and others work intensively in this area.

The academic community, also made their own contribution. For instance, special courses in alternative dispute resolution, restorative justice and mediation in criminal matters have been introduced in the New Bulgarian University and South-West University, as well as in the Institute for Postgraduate Studies with the University for World and National Economy. According to sociological surveys, restorative justice enjoys wide support among criminal justice practitioners and the society at large (Chankova, 2006; Chankova, Georgieva and Bakalov, 2008).

Although many initiatives for crime victims have been recently undertaken in Bulgaria, the practice shows that they still need more attention, protection and justice. That is why the project "Restorative Justice in Europe: Safeguarding Victims and Empowering Professionals" (RJE) was considered timely and necessary.

Review of the Bulgarian Literature on Crime Victims

One of the first tasks according to RJE project work stream 1 was to make an overview of the existing relevant Bulgarian literature - a theoretical premise for developing protocols and guidelines for enhancing the safeguards for victims and for elaborating training materials and programmes for professionals with the aim of improving their skills and knowledge on how they treat and interact with victims in the RJ process.

The review emphasized that victimology, the study of victimization and crime victims, is a relatively new domain of knowledge in Bulgaria. It has been developed predominantly as a part of criminology during the last decades. However, a good amount of literature had already been published (Belova, 1998; Stankov, 1999 and 2001; Fikov, 2009).

The issue best explored in the specialized Bulgarian literature is the legal status of crime victims in criminal procedure ((Chinova and Ivanova, 2005; Doychinova, 2010; Chinova, 2013). Another topic well studied is the victimization as a process of transforming a given person, group of people or society into potential or real victims (Miteva, 1980; Panev, 2004).

In the meantime, restorative justice has been gaining more and more supporters in Bulgaria and a good volume of literature has been published (Chankova, 1996, 2002 and 2011; Trendafilova, 2001; Panev, 2008; Genova, 2012). The bibliography sets out all historical, legal and social arguments for introducing RJ and particularly victim-offender mediation (VOM) in the Bulgarian criminal justice system. The legal concept, principles, objectives and key values of restorative justice are analysed and the distinguishing features of this relatively new approach to crime are discussed. RJ advocacy in the Bulgarian literature acknowledges a radical reformulation of the State's role and responsibility with regard to crime, which is usually expressed in terms of the "principle of subsidiarity". Instead of the State or its institutions to assume direct and primary responsibility for dealing with crime and its aftermath, its chief function should be to act as facilitator, information giver, provider of resources and deliverer of services. The State should serve as the ultimate arbiter of fairness, and provide the court-based forum for delivering restorative outcomes only in cases which cannot be adequately resolved by the relevant communities or specialized structures.

Due attention is paid to the different restorative justice models. The literature describes the essence and peculiarities not only of the major, widespread practices such as VOM, family group conferences (FGC), or community group conferences, but also explores less widely used models such as restorative conferencing, restorative cautioning, sentencing (peace-making) circles, committees for truth and reconciliation, referral orders, restorative disposals etc. The conclusion made is that most of these practices are particularly applicable to juvenile crime but that they are also successfully used in relation to adult offenders. Applied predominantly to petty crimes in the past, today there is evidence that they are appropriate instruments in relation to serious crime, too.

A critical analysis of putting restorative justice into practice is developed in the Bulgarian RJ literature; concerns and sceptical counterarguments about the "bright" restorative horizons are also examined. The assertions of victim support organizations, claiming that they are in a better position to protect the interests of the victims and that restorative justice remains primarily offender-oriented, are discussed as well.

Special theoretical attention is paid to the latest developments in Bulgaria related to the problems of implementation due to the unknown benefits of restorative justice and the existing "vested interests" in delivering justice. Findings from sociological surveys that encourage the immediate implementation are cited. A critical and constructive analysis of the Mediation Act, the legal basis for some restorative practices, is also made. Proposals for using restorative justice in criminal law and criminal procedure, in juvenile delinquency, as a service in favour of victims, in prisons and probation services and by the police, are developed as well. Amendments to the relevant acts are developed and the ways ahead are indicated.

In particular, a theoretical model of victim-offender mediation, adjusted to the Bulgarian legal and social environment, has been elaborated. The necessary safeguards for victims' rights such as legal aid, confidentiality of the procedure, neutrality of the facilitator etc. are developed and ensured. Potential risks are also discussed and suggestions to reduce the possible negative impact are made. Proposals *de lege ferenda* are submitted to the attention of the Bulgarian legislator. Some practical guidelines are offered, too.

While achievements do exist on theoretical level, many deficits in practice remain. Bulgaria lags behind other countries and RJ practically is in an embryonic stage of development. Only basic manuals, flyers, brochures, sample protocols etc. have been developed, aiming to support victims participating in RJ schemes, still very limited in number. The safeguards are mainly worked out by victim support services. Some procedural documentation, respectively due safeguards related to victims' participation in the RJ process, are elaborated exclusively in the frameworks of pilot projects.

Findings from surveys conducted among crime victims, professionals from the criminal justice system, service providers working with victims, and practitioners applying restorative practices, regarding crime victims protection and perspectives of restorative justice in Bulgaria

According to the second work stream of the RJE project, the Institute of Conflict Resolution has done fieldwork to explore the current state of affairs and prospects for crime victims' protection and restorative justice, as well as the application of Victims' Directive.

Fieldwork: Summary of the Responses

In compliance with the project work plan, a total of 10 victims of different crimes were interviewed in-depth through a semi-structured questionnaire. It was not an easy task to find respondents due to the very limited scope of application of RJ in Bulgaria, and the rather small number of centres offering restorative practices. Only five of the victims who agreed to be interviewed had participated in restorative processes, mostly VOM. The rest have been duly informed about the essence, principles, objectives and models of RJ and the above mentioned Directive, so their answers could be considered relevant and have been counted. The participants in the interviews are adult men and women who have suffered damage from different complainants' crimes with regard to which the acting legislation allows VOM.

The following answers have been received to the questions posed:

1. *Are you familiar with the Bulgarian/international law concerning victim protection?*
   Summarized, the responses describe a rather alarming picture. Although the survey has only a qualitative character and is not representative on a national scale, it is indicative that half of the crime victims do not have almost any knowledge about the legal and other types of protection. The rest of the respondents have only limited knowledge. This is a sign that on a national level there is not enough information and education about crime victims' rights. Respectively, urgent measures are necessary to fill in the vacuum so that this vulnerable group can be adequately protected.

2. *Do you think that good policies for victims exist in Bulgaria?*
   Most of the respondents (six) answer in a negative way. The rest give rather ambivalent answers pointing out some good intentions declared and their poor implementation. The negative evaluation of the existing policy for crime victims is more than evident. The positive sign is that the majority of victims (except one) do not consider victim protection only within the criminal justice system (CJS) but acknowledge other mechanisms like RJ. Dissatisfaction is expressed with the fact that RJ is not legally instituted and that the State does not promote it enough. This appeal for modern policies towards victims has to be heard.

3. *Do you think that good practices towards victims exist in Bulgaria?*
   Again, there is a great dissatisfaction with the victims' protection practices. Six respondents claim that victims are totally or considerably neglected. Two find the existing practices not efficient. Contemporary approaches like VOM, FGC, and restorative conferencing are still rare and not everybody has access to them. Only one respondent is fully satisfied with the dissemination of VOM, while one respondent says he has no info.

4. *What do you want from restorative justice?*
   The answers to this question show that victims, being duly informed, rightly and fully understand RJ ideology, benefits and potential. Even those of them who have not undergone RJ process give adequate answers. From RJ the victims expect mainly:

   - active participation
   - pecuniary compensation (financial or in-kind, according to their needs)
   - apology

- moral satisfaction of being heard and understood
- short and time-saving procedures
- support and good opportunities for restoration of relationships and social bonds
- correction of the offender
- taking responsibility not to commit the act again
- restoration of their sense of security etc.

Remarkably, rarely victims express revenge and expect severe penal sanctions. This is indicative of the victims' evolution and of their new needs.

5. *What do you understand by "victim's satisfaction" with justice procedures?*
   The answers to this question are related to the previous ones. Victims expect from traditional justice more or less the same as they expect from RJ. Definitely, even the most severe punishment is not enough. Victims will be satisfied when they have been treated with respect, professionalism and without discrimination, when they have received a more central role in the process. They need to be protected through protection orders or other relevant measures in order to avoid secondary or repeated victimization. Pecuniary compensation is important but the moral dimension should not be underestimated. Most wish to receive a sincere apology, to see that the offender understands the harm he has caused and his repentance.

6. *What do you think are the best and safest ways to implement restorative justice?*
   The victims interviewed insist that RJ should be statutory. For this purpose the Criminal Procedure Code has to be amended. While RJ is still a novelty for the conservative continental law system, it should be introduced step by step, starting with petty crimes and first time offenders and juveniles; after relevant assessments, its application should be expanded. The presence of a lawyer/lawyers is still considered essential for protection of the parties' rights and supervision of the CJS authorities. Voluntariness, informed consent and confidentiality are seen as a conditio sine qua non. Opinions are expressed that the introduction of RJ should follow the established models in the European and other countries in order to avoid mistakes.

7. *What are the best ways for enforcing the Victims' Directive?*
   The new Directive is warmly received by almost all interviewed victims although some of them heard of it for the first time. They see a good stimulus for improving and expanding services for crime victims. The respondents are unanimous that it should be transposed in the national law as soon as possible. The Directive should be broadly popularized through information campaigns, mass-media etc., and has to be fully implemented.

8. *How can NGOs and the criminal justice system cooperate better?*
   The majority of the interviewed see in NGOs a good resource for cooperation with the CJS. The main roles NGOs can play are launching information campaigns, providing education, delivering services to victims, compensating the lack of State's involvement. NGOs could be particularly useful in the application of RJ practices. In this way the overload of the justice system could be reduced. However, more dialog, trust and respect from the formal system are needed, according to the respondents.

9. *What is necessary to raise the general victim awareness about RJ options?*
   Most victims see a potential in making CJS authorities and lawyers more pro-active in informing the parties concerned about RJ and its opportunities. Some think that professionals should be legally obliged to spread this knowledge. The second option are direct information campaigns dedicated to RJ and the Victim Directive. Next come books, articles, the Internet, different fora, education in universities, schools etc.

10. *What do you think about the RJ services in which you have participated /have they met your expectations and needs/?*
    As has already been mentioned, only five victims have undergone RJ procedures. They all are positive and satisfied although in a somewhat nuanced way.

11. *At which stage of the criminal justice system (police, prosecution, courts, post/pre-sentence, prison, probation, ALL) do you think restorative justice is most appropriate?*
    Although the answers are split – four respondents think it should be applied on the initial stage, and four – at every stage, the important thing is that the informed victims are positive that RJ should be applied. As to when – this is not of vital significance.

12. *How satisfied are you with your experience in RJ? /in %*
    In correlation with the previous answers, two respondents express 100% satisfaction, two – 90%, and one – 50%.

13. *Would you recommend RJ to other victims?*
    Regardless of their diverse personal experience, eight of interviewed victims will definitely recommend RJ to other victims. Two will act according to the peculiarities of the particular case, but they remain positive.

14. *Any other comments:*
    As an additional comment some victims express hope that RJ will be successfully implemented within the CJS soon.

Summary of the Responses by Professionals from the Criminal Justice System, Service Providers Working with Victims, and Practitioners Applying Restorative Justice

In compliance with the work plan of the project, five focus group discussions took place. The focus groups included the following sample groups:

- prosecutors
- investigating policemen
- practitioners, applying RJ
- representatives of specialized NGOs
- academics.

Each focus group consisted of four members who responded to an inquiry in writing. There was a preliminary selection of the participants according to their competence about RJ and victims' issue, and their personal experience. This appeared to be quite difficult bearing in mind the small-scale Bulgarian experience in victim-related work and RJ.

Initially it was planned to form a separate focus group of criminal judges but only two judges with competence in the field responded. That is why a new focus group of academics was formed but the answers of the judges are also included.

So, 22 persons in total were inquired. Focus groups' representatives came from the whole country – from three different prosecutor's offices, two police stations, four NGOs and mediation centres, free-lance RJ practitioners and three high education institutions and research centres.

The summary has the following structure. The responses to each question by all focus groups are systematically analysed and at the end the opinion of the judges is given. To avoid repetitions, the responses of the prosecutors are analysed in detail, and after that the dissenting or concurring opinions of the remaining four groups or the confirmation of the answers are given briefly. Of course, some deviations from this structure were inevitable.

1. *What do you Want/Expect from Restorative Justice?*

The prosecutors' focus group gives the most detailed answers. From RJ they expect:

- protection of victims' rights
- speedy proceedings
- reducing the CJS's overload
- victims' satisfaction (material and moral)
- positive influence on the offender with educative and corrective effect
- therapeutic effect on the victim and offender, etc.

The investigating policemen emphasise on rehabilitation and apology, restoration of a sense of security and cost effectiveness of the process. Practitioners expect RJ to "return the conflicts back to their proper owners" and to involve them in seeking an appropriate decision.

NGOs' representatives underline that RJ helps raising the quality of life, restoring the relationships between the parties involved and putting the focus on victims. The academics, reconfirming the answers already given, state that hey expect active public involvement for helping victims restore physically and mentally and reintegrate into society. All focus groups understand rightly the ideology of RJ and consider it as a part of global justice.

2. *What do you Understand by "Victim Satisfaction" with Justice Procedures?*

The sophisticated nature of satisfaction with justice is well explained in the responses of all focus groups. According to the prosecutors and policemen, the retributive consequence, that is the punishment, is hardly enough. Much more important are the moral satisfaction, financial compensation and restitution, the active participation in the process and the feeling that the victim has been recognized and heard.

The practitioners add that the victim should not only accept the restorative result but would like also to know that the offender "has changed the course". The other focus groups agree more or less with the opinions expressed.

3. *What do You Think Are the Best and Safest Ways to Implement Restorative Justice?*
According to the prosecutors, substantial and procedural laws should explicitly regulate RJ. Safeguards for equal treatment and access to services are required. RJ should be applied in due course and with maximum speed and should ensure fast restoration of the harm inflicted. Special attention has to be paid to juvenile delinquency. RJ should be applied only once, towards first time offenders and juveniles who have committed petty crimes.
The policemen insist on following the models applied abroad.The practitioners emphasize on training of all applying RJ practices to avoid misuse and dissatisfaction. The NGOs' representatives consider voluntariness and informed consent as particularly important. RJ should be applied in symbiosis with CJS – an opinion shared by judges as well. The academics insist on introducing RJ in schools and universities.

4. *What are the Best Ways for Enforcing the Victims' Directive?*
The prosecutors consider transposing the Directive and establishing mechanisms for its implementation including seminars for professionals a *conditio sine qua non*. They recommend that the national legislation provides for more rights for victims since the Directive establishes only the minimum standards. Brochures for victims would be of great help.
According to the police representatives, full harmonisation of domestic legislation with the Directive and other European legal acts is a prerequisite for observing the European standards. Widespread information campaigns are certainly necessary. According to the practitioners, soft-law acts are just as important as is high-ranking legislation. The NGOs put the accent on education. The academics require specific measures to be undertaken: free services for crime victims should be offered by the public sector (police) or in co-operation with NGOs, risk assessment needs to be done, etc. According to judges the state authorities should be more concerned and more pro-active towards victims.

5. *How can NGOs and Criminal Justice System Co-operate Better? Are There Any Challenges That You Are Facing When Trying to Work Together?*
Three prosecutors have no experience in this regard. The other one sees good opportunities for co-operation on the basis of dialogue, mutual trust and respect. The policemen share this opinion. The practitioners insist on better symbiosis and see opportunities for working together in the framework of different projects, trainings etc. Logically, the NGOs' representatives believe that there are many unused niches for co-operation – in elaborating State policies, programmes, bills, etc. So far the official justice system underestimates the role of NGOs, there is lack of trust. According to them, the State receives support from NGOs and thanks to that it can work better. The academics criticize the paid services of the NGOs for victims, and sometimes their numerous requirements, especially towards the police. Judges find that NGOs should be the active part since they are more flexible. It is positive that all focus groups see good opportunities for co-operation.

6. *How can Victims be Made Better Aware of their Restorative Justice Options?*
According to the prosecutors and policemen, the victims have no or have only a fragmented idea about RJ. That is why a broad-scale information campaign is needed urgently. They recommend the use of Internet resources, TV and radio broadcasting, specialised training. A normative obligation

for and education of law enforcement authorities to familiarize victims with RJ is necessary, also according to the practitioners, judges and NGOs. The academics consider popularizing "success stories" and introducing RJ in the universities' an schools' curricula to be a good instrument.

7. *How can Offenders be Best Equipped with the Social and Apology Skills for a Meeting?*
   All focus groups consider relevant enrolment in educational and correctional programmes and courses, and psychological consultancy services. The role of society is underlined. The accent is put on juveniles.

8. *What should a Facilitator do if a Victim is Re-victimised?*
   Again, all focus groups claim that new, stronger measures for victims' protection should be undertaken besides the peculiarities of the case and consultations with specialists.

9. *Are there any Best Case Studies from Bulgaria and the OtherCountries where Restorative Justice is Implemented Safely and with Adequate Satisfaction Rates for Victims?*
   Here the answers are rather diverse according to the personal competence and experience. The prosecutors and judges have no experience. The policemen point out to VOM. The practitioners, NGOs' representatives and academics show in-depth knowledge of a comparative aspect and see some positive results in Bulgaria.

10. *How relevant are Materials from Other Countries / How Applicable in a Different National Context?*
    According to the majority of the prosecutors, the national peculiarities are not so important, hence the foreign experience could be used. The policemen find them relatively significant, having in mind the historical, sociological, psychological and other specifics. This is the opinion of the rest focus groups, too. According to judges, the foreign practices should be adapted to avoid contradiction with imperative national legal regulation.

11. *Will Practitioners in Different Institutions be Interested in Workshops/Training on RJ?*
    All focus groups are strongly in favour as such training is missing in their education so far.

12. *Will Key Professionals find Training Materials, Protocols, Guidelines & Best Practice Guidance useful when Applying RJ in Different Contexts, Services & Agencies?*
    Again, the focus groups are unanimously positive. The policemen find such materials obligatory. The academics think that these manuals should be detailed and should not contain only general directions.

13. *What sort of Training or Guidance have You received to Help you Work with Victims, especially those of Vulnerable Groups?*
    The prosecutors, judges and policemen find that this training is traditionally neglected in the Bulgarian legal education and judicial practice. That is why they have to compensate the knowledge deficit with individual work. The practitioners and NGOs' representatives are logically the best prepared focus groups. Most of them have received specialized education and in-service training but they think that extra training would be welcome. The academics do not work with victims directly.

14. *Do you Feel Confident that you have the Knowledge and the Tools to work directly with Victims in a Safe Way and Especially within the Context of the Victims' Directive?*
The prosecutors' answers are rather ambivalent. Two feel confident to work with victims, at least to a certain degree, the rest are sceptical about their preparedness. The policemen definitely need training to work within the context of the Victims' Directive. RJ practitioners and representatives of the NGO sector are more or less convinced that they are prepared for the abovementioned purpose but will welcome further training. Nowadays judges do not possess the relevant tool-kit to work with victims. As has already been mentioned, the academics research this issue and do not have direct contacts with victims.

15. *What Knowledge and Skills do Professionals Working with Victims, Lack and/or Need?*
The answers could be summarized as follows. Professionals with different educational background work with victims, so they may feel knowledge deficit in certain fields. Most frequently, in-depth psychological, victimological and socio-anthropological knowledge is missing. Working with children as victims requires specific knowledge and skills. The communicative and other social skills are insufficient in general.

16. *What Tools do Professionals Working with Victims need to Create Better Safeguards for Victims?*
The prosecutors need detailed legislation, working schemes, education and financing. The policemen find good networking between different institutions and NGOs essential. For practitioners and NGOs, the team work is of ultimate importance. According to the academics and judges, the effective services and individualized approach to different victims are of great significance.

17. *Should the State Finance RJ?*
Three of the prosecutors are in favour, one believes that the State should co-operate with NGOs. The policemen assert that the State should fund RJ, mainly in order to protect victims' rights. According to the practitioners, it is not realistic to expect that the State will fully finance RJ. That is why special funds have to be established and other financial resources should be ensured. But the State should explicitly express its support (including a financial one) in order to raise RJ credibility. The NGOs' representatives naturally answer positively. The academics and judges find financial State support essential for vulnerable groups.

18. *What are the Advantages or Disadvantages of Legislating Restorative Justice?*
The well-known advantages of legislating RJ are stated in details by all focus groups. That is why the accent will be put on potential disadvantages. The prosecutors express fear that in some cases RJ could be considered as too soft a response to certain offenders. That is why it should be applied very carefully. According to the policemen, the lack of coercion (in general) and good faith in executing the agreement reached could create problems. RJ practitioners find the lack of sufficient information and safeguards for victims critical. They add that the organization of restorative processes is difficult, time and effort-consuming and sometimes expensive. The NGOs' representatives point to limitations in applying RJ in relation to recidivists and criminals with low education who demonstrate lack of bona fide. The scientists see potential risks in misuse of RJ values, and judges refrain from answering due to lack of practice.

19. *How much Victims Know about Restorative Justice?*
    All focus groups are unanimous that victims know too little and definitely not enough about RJ.

20. *What do Restorative Justice Practitioners need in order to Implement Restorative Justice Safely and according to the Victims' Directive?*
    In summary the answers point to:

    - adequate legislative framework
    - detailed information
    - specialized training, both in theory and practice
    - good cooperation between institutions
    - trust and social support
    - financing

21. *What are the Key Challenges for Criminal Justice Agencies in Implementing Restorative Justice?*
    The interviewees indicates as main challenges the following:

    - overcoming stereotypes and the conservatism inherent to the justice system
    - lack of stability (in some cases) of final acts
    - novelty of the RJ idea for the continental law system
    - lack of sufficient information about RJ providers
    - shift of focus from the offender to the victim, etc.

22. *What do Professionals think will be the Key Challenges in Implementing the Victims' Directive? Could National Legislation on RJ or a Specific RJ Directive Help Significantly?*
    Again, according to the respondents, adequate legislation and machinery for its implementation are of key importance. Many new services and facilities should be provided for victims, and this is not always easy. A specific Directive could be of great help and could accelerate the process of introducing RJ in Bulgaria.

23. *Any Other Comments:*
    The numerous questions in the inquiry do not leave much space for further comments. However, hope is expressed that better services for victims and RJ will be a fact in Bulgaria soon, and there is willingness to work to establish these.

Brief Overview of Piloting Training Materials in Bulgaria

According to RJE work stream 3, the coordinator, IARS, had to produce protocols and guidelines for providing RJ in the interest of the victim and the offender with the aim of improving victims' safeguards in RJ services, and the consistent implementation of minimum standards throughout Europe; training materials and programmes for professionals (e.g. prison and probation staff, police, prosecutors, victim support workers) with the aim of improving their skills and knowledge about how they treat and interact with victims, as well as best practice guidelines that would enhance multi-agency and cross-sector co-operation among RJ/victim services and national agencies with the aim of minimising the risks of secondary and repeated victimisation when interacting with victims. The deliverables were written in English and translated into Bulgarian (by the ICR), German, Dutch and Greek. They should be implemented in the five member-states that take part in the project and disseminated across the EU. It was envisaged that the piloting in Bulgaria – work stream 4 – would be done by the UK team but inevitably the ICR team was largely involved.

The piloting was organized through face-to-face training in June 2014 in Sofia and Blagoevgrad, with participants from other cities - more than 40 people in total. The training methods and materials were well received by a largely diverse audience - students, lawyers, practitioners from the criminal justice system, NGO activists, mediators etc. Ben Lyon's training style which was tailored to the specific audience was highly appreciated. However, the training package which was originally written in English had to be adapted to the Bulgarian context.

The Faculty of Law and History at the South-West University hosted the large-scale and most successful training on 19 June 2014, in the presence of the Dean. Trainings were also organized on 16 June 2014 at Sofia Bar Association and on 17 June 2014, with the active involvement of the ICR members. The participants were also happy to receive certificates of attendance that IARS managed to accredit through Continuing Professional Development (CPD) status.

During the piloting it became clear that there was some major work going on in Bulgaria, let that be mediation or restorative justice. There is an apparent need for victims and perpetrators in the country to resolve harms through dialogue and action. This is currently being catered for by a range of very experienced and knowledgeable practitioners. However, although practice is more or less developed, there is a clear need for legislation, such as the Victims' Directive, to support this work and the participants involved.

The training was very well received. The evaluation that was posted on the internet[6] as well as the one that was made available by the IARS through evaluation forms that were filled in by the participants bear clear evidence of the success of the training. In summary, from a total of 40 evaluation forms returned back, it can be concluded that the vast majority, more than 90% of the participants, agree or strongly agree that the course has helped them to understand clearly the Victims' Directive and its RJ-related articles. In addition, the learning programme is evaluated as easy to access and navigate, the course materials are coherent and well developed, the programme delivery methods effectively enable studying the Victims' Directive, the course is important for the participants' professional development and has challenged them intellectually. Almost all expect to apply the knowledge gained from the course, enabling them to perform their job better. Remarkably, 97% say that the information received will help to collaborate better with victim-related service providers, and 100% claim that they would recommend this course to others. Only between 2 and 5% express some degree of dissatisfaction with the course, the very tiny remaining part are neutral.

The most powerful aspect of the training sessions were the group exercises, in particular the process of recovery timeline where the audience was asked to share case studies of the victims' journey after a crime. This allowed participants to begin an open, reflective review of their work. By reflecting on these experiences, one can hope to promote better understanding between practitioners and participants. The interactive work with case stories was also successful, drawing upon the group training and experience to display their ability to work with the Directive.

Information campaign

The information campaign "Restorative justice in the interest of the victim and the offender" was served as a tool for dissemination, policy development and awareness raising (work stream 5) in "The Bulgarian project". It was launched at an early stage of RJE and is still on-going, with the aim to continue after the project ends. All activities throughout the duration of the project and theirs results were largely announced in public through the internet, the media, at conferences and face-to-face meetings. Moreover, the ICR members were extremely pro-active and creative and used every opportunity, creating even new ones to raise public awareness and knowledge about the Victims' Directive and RJ. These efforts resulted in many publications in scientific journals and newsletters, presentations during national and international events, updating websites, radio broadcasting, various celebrations and happenings, more than 40 meetings with professionals, policy makers and academics, distribution of brochures and leaflets, etc.[7] Dissemination activities were very well accepted, we felt some kind of "hunger" for information. This is a strong evidence that the project is more than timely and needed.

Reflecting on the Overall Finding of the Bulgarian RJE Project

Although currently there is a rather comprehensive legal framework for crime victims' protection in Bulgaria, many of its aspects could be criticized. The acting legislation is not perfect, and is not properly and fully applied. One of the deficits of the legal regulation is that the injured party is excluded from the procedure for settling the case by an agreement between the public prosecutor and the accused party's defence counsel (plea bargaining). There are not enough efficient procedural mechanisms for the full implementation of the stipulated rights. Because of the low rate of crime detection and sentenced persons, a significant number of the victims cannot avail themselves of their rights. The lengthy procedure often takes away the due restitution and reparation.

Moreover, the victims of violent crimes are not well protected by the Support and Financial Compensation for Crime Victims Act. According to the National Council for Compensation of Crime Victims Database, very few of them (less than 30 yearly) receive limited compensation. Next, the list of crimes envisaged by the law is rather narrow. Sometimes the compensation is paid too late. In general, crime victims do not know their rights due to lack of access to information.

There are problems with the existing infrastructure and co-ordination between different agencies working in the field. Indeed, a number of non-governmental organizations have been registered that work for the protection of victims of violence, human trafficking and other forms of organized and conventional crime. Usually these are established for the benefit of victims but within the framework of different projects. When their funding comes to an end, the organizations suspend their services. Presently, there are very few specialized governmental structures working in this area.

There seems to be a "gap" between the declared good objectives and the low level of their implementation. That is why public discontent is increasing and the risk of raising punitive populism is more than evident.

Lack of proper RJ provisions in the legislation is also a great problem. It is highly unacceptable that RJ is practiced in the "shadow of the law" and is a function of the initiatives of progressive practitioners. There are enough studies, elaborated bills, trained and motivated professionals. What is missing is a good will from the state institutions.

Although the Bulgarian government claims that it is trying to observe the European standards, paradoxically, crime victims are not the new "icon" of our penal policy yet. So, Bulgarian criminal justice system is definitely not victim-led. But it should be – it is possible and desired, according to the research and surveys results. Implementing the Directive, fostering vigorously victims' rights and RJE deliverables could accelerate this process.

However, the answers of the interviewed victims and professionals during the project should be carefully interpreted. They reflect the opinion of specially selected, informed respondents, and not of the whole groups. Nevertheless, these answers present a disturbing picture - highly insufficient information or even lack of information on a large scale about national and supra-national legal and other options for victim protection.

The dissatisfaction with Bulgarian policies and practices for crime victims support requires re-definition of the existing approaches. It is especially valid regarding RJ. Crime victims start to see in RJ a reliable instrument for protection. Unfortunately, as stated above, it remains non-regularized. This deprives many potential beneficiaries from the opportunity to use it.

The interviewed focus groups' answers show their familiarity, understanding and support for RJ. Although its application is very limited, all inquired acknowledge the advantages of RJ. They should be given a chance to apply RJ immediately.

Some improvement is observed in relation to the training provided in the framework of the project. In general, the time envisaged for training was insufficient for genuine interactive education. Not all translated materials were used, e.g. movies. Too much "homework" was left to the participants. The case studies should better correspond to the Bulgarian environment. However, all these could be corrected in future trainings, and this is the meaning of piloting.

Recommendations for the Implementation of the Victims' Directive Restorative Justice Provisions in Bulgaria

It is time that RJ practices and victim support schemes in Bulgaria progress faster and deeper. In this regard the significance of the Victims' Directive is obvious, although quite cautious in promoting RJ and paying attention predominantly to safeguards. There are already quite active NGOs launching information campaigns, implementing various projects, pilot schemes, lobbying, training, and networking. Academics are one of the main proponents of RJ and victims' interests. Training and university education in RJ principles and practices are rapidly developing. This is a great resource that could be used.

Bulgarian policy makers need to "wake up" and adopt a modern criminal policy, including RJ. So far RJ potential is not properly understood, that it is why it is not a priority for the government. This should also explain why it remains underdeveloped and marginalized in the country.

However, the decision makers should act now, as the Directive has to be transposed by 16 November 2015 and relevant legislative measures for proper victim protection and regulation of RJ should be undertaken. Crime victims do deserve more and better justice. RJ should not be confronted with the existing CJS, a symbiosis with this system would be more efficient and productive. A special focus should be put on vulnerable victims.

Meanwhile, during the piloting and implementation phase, particular attention should be paid to the distribution of knowledge among RJ and victim services' providers and professionals in order to achieve compliance of their practices with the European standards.

Relevant documentation such as protocols and guidelines, training materials and best practice guides should be adopted on a national level and disseminated without delay as they are much needed. The RJE project deliverables are a great source in this regard. Large-scale information campaigns about the Victims' Directive should start immediately.

Financial, administrative and organizational support from the State is also essential. Such a big reform cannot be implemented without the involvement of State institutions.

Regular university training and continuing education of the criminal justice professionals and victim support practitioners about the principles, values, benefits etc. of RJ is a must. However, to establish a more restorative and victim-friendly climate in the country, we have to start as early as in schools.

Co-operation on national and international level should be intensified through by establishing networks, study visits, organizing conferences, exchanging information, etc.

In summary, a lot remains to be done for the full implementation of the Victims' Directive RJ provisions and minimum standards for victim protection in Bulgaria.

Notes

1 *State Gazette* No 83 of 18 October 2005, in force as of 29 April 2006.
2 *State Gazette* No 109 of 23 December 2008.
3 *State Gazette* No 105 of 22 December 2006, in force as of 1 January 2007.
4 http://www.compensation.bg, last accessed 25 August 2014
5 *State Gazette* No 110 of 17 December 2004.
6 https://www.surveymonkey.net/results/SM-35RLGGJ8/, last accessed 25 August 2014
7 For the Information campaign see www.icr-bg.org/Projects.htm, last accessed 25 August 2014

References

Belova, N. (1998) "Victimology problems in Bulgarian criminological literature", *Research works of The National Institute of Criminology*, v. 2, Sofia: NIC

Bochev, S. (1986) "Crimes against adults and some measures for their limitation", *Research works of The National Institute of Criminology*, v. 13, Sofia: NIC

Chankova, D.(1996) "Mediation as an Innovation in the Criminal Procedure", in Kornezov, L., Margaritova, S. and Chankova, D. (eds.) *A Century of Criminal Code and Current Issues of Criminal Legislation 1896-1996*, Sofia: Ministry of Justice

Chankova, D.(2002) *Victim-Offender Mediation*, Sofia: Feneya

Chankova, D.(2006) "Applicability of Victim-Offender Mediation in Bulgaria According to the Law Enforcement Authorities", Scientific Proceedings of Law and History Faculty at South-West University "N. Rilski" - *Blagoevgrad*, Vol.2, No 1

Chankova, D. (2011) *Restorative Justice. A Comparative Analysis*, Sofia: Avangard Prima

Chankova, D., Georgieva, E. and Bakalov, G. (2008) "Findings of Surveys on Applicability of Victim-Offender Mediation in Bulgaria", *Legal Tribune*, No 1

Chinova, M. and Ivanova, M. (2005) "The Crime Victim at the Stage of Pre-Trial Proceedings", *Contemporary Law*, No 4

Chinova, M. (2013) *Pre-trial Procedure according to the Criminal Procedure Code. Theory and Practice*, Sofia: Ciela

Doychinova, V. (2010) "Right to protection of crime victims according to the Bulgarian Criminal Procedure Code and the minimum international standards", *Legal Thought*, No 1

Fikov, S. (2009) "The victims do not know their rights", *Society and Law*, No 3

Genova, V. (2012) *Police and social conflicts*, Sofia: NIC

Miteva, J. (1977) *Basic victimology problems*, Sofia: NIC

Miteva, J. (1980) "Victimology studies and crime problems", in *Crime prevention* (compendium), Sofia: NIC

Panev, B. (2004) "Global sources for criminalization and victimization of society", *Legal World*, No 2

Panev, B.(2008)"About Applicability of Mediation in Criminal Proceedings", *Legal Tribune*, No 1 Stankov, B. (1999) *Crime in Bulgaria and its victims*, Sofia: Paralax

Stankov, B. (2001) *Victimology*, Varna: VFU

Stoinov, A. (1993) *Crime victim*, Sofia: University Press

Trendafilova, E. (2001) *The changes in the Criminal Procedure Code from 1999*, Sofia: Ciela

RJE Closing Seminar, hosted by the Restorative Justice Nederland - October 2014, The Netherlands. © IARS

Repositioning the Victim: Comparing and Learning

*Theo Gavrielides**

Abstract

In Europe, we are at a critical point as we prepare for criminal justice reforms that will arguably see the victim been moved from the margins to the centre of State attention. While a 'victim-led criminal justice system' is questioned, a discussion about such a system may help address a paradox that we have experienced since the Middle Ages. It is after all with big words that researchers have historically managed to grab politicians' attention and spark a debate within mainstream media. While we provoke by talking about a 'victim-led criminal justice system' and investigate the potential of restorative justice, this conclusive chapter attempts a comparative overview of the RJE research findings, the guest papers and the extant literature in the hope that next steps can be identified in the long road of repositioning the victims in criminal justice. Lessons can be drawn for the international community as it grabbles to manage expectations, reforms and institutional restructures in the midst of a global financial crisis.

A Reminder

We tend to forget that the criminal justice system is a modern construct. In other periods and cultures, the response to, what we call today, 'delinquency' did not fall within the legal positivistic understanding of 'crime' adopted by our modern Western societies. In fact, what we understand today as 'crime' was seen by the early communities as a conflict between individuals. Consequently, the terms "offender" and "victims" were coined as a result of this legal positivistic framework.

Even more importantly, we also seem to forget that in the pursuit of justice, those who had been hurt, and we now call victims, used to have a central role in the decision making process. In fact, there is a general agreement in the literature that in Europe, victims' roles in criminal proceedings started to deteriorate only during the Middle Ages , and that the major change occurred in the 9th century (Fry, 1951). In Europe, this process was complete by the end of the 12th century (Rossner, 1989), when the 'State' had taken control of conflicts (Christie, 1977). Michalowski (1985) claimed that formal law emerged as a means of controlling property and relations, and that the concept of individual property and the history of law were from then and on inseparable.

In consequence, as the rights of the 'State' gradually overshadowed those of the victim and the individual, the criminal justice system was no longer victim-focused. What also emerged from this

* Dr. Theo Gavrielides (Founder and Director of Independent Academic Research Studies, Co-Director of the Restorative Justice for All Institute, Visiting Professor at Buckinghamshire New University and Adjunct Professor at Simon Fraser University, School of Criminology), Unit 14, Dock Offices, Surrey Quays Road, Canada Water, London SE16 2XU, UK, T.Gavrielides@iars.org.uk +44(0)20 70644380.

development was the division of law between 'public' and 'private'. According to this new paradigm, 'crime' was mostly dealt with as an act against the State and the public interest, while offences against individuals' rights were pursued separately as 'torts'. The terms "offender" and "victims" started to be used and the criminal justice system became state-focused and state-led. A paradox was thus created whereby the criminal justice system was structured around the State without victim involvement.

Political philosophers Jeremy Bentham (1748-1832) and John Austin (1790-1859) argued that the law is a phenomenon of large societies with a 'sovereign'. This can be a determinate person or group who have supreme and absolute de facto power (Austin, 1832 [first published 1873]; Bentham, 1838; 1843). The laws in these societies, including our Western countries, are a subset of the sovereign's 'commands'. These are general orders that apply to classes of actions and people, and are backed up by threat of force or sanction. This imperatival positivist theory identifies the existence of legal systems with patterns of command and obedience that can be ascertained without considering whether the sovereign has a moral right to rule or whether his commands are meritorious.

It took humanity two World Wars and a number of other civil conflicts to come to the table and agree minimum standards of behaviour for States. These were intended to control this State-led attitude including that impacting on criminal justice. We called them "human rights' and recorded them in international documents such as the Universal Declaration on Human Rights (UDHR). According to the same convention "human rights refer to the basic rights and freedoms to which all humans are entitled", or as Article 1 states: "All human beings are born free and equal in dignity and rights. They are endowed with reason and conscience and should act towards one another in a spirit of brotherhood". Human rights are minimum standards that are available to everyone simply because of their humanity. Therefore, concepts such as citizenship and democracy are not prerequisites for someone's right to be human or the enjoyment of those standards that protect this qualification.

Inspired by the UDHR, Europe signed its own agreement known as the European Convention on Human Rights (ECHR) of which the European Union (EU) is a member. Therein, it introduced minimum standards for everyone in the European region. Article 6 is particularly relevant to the criminal justice process as it enshrines the right to a fair trail for all. It acts, or should have acted, as a reminder that offenders, victims and their families are first and foremost human beings whose involvement in the criminal justice process should be treated with respect. The Article also acts as a reminder of the human value, which is higher than the manifestation of state power and control of the criminal justice process.

Undoubtedly, the criminal process and the administration of criminal justice by State agents is the field of battle in which human rights are tested. Therefore, questions were raised by communities, the victims' movement and other civil society organisations about states' behaviour and compliance. Through the use of the ECHR, they began to put pressure on states and Europe's regional bodies, the Council of Europe and the EU. Academics and researchers also played their part. For example, victimologists such as Hans von Hentig (1887-1974), Benjamin Mendelsohn (1900-1998), Margery Fry (1874 – 1958) and Stephen Schafer claimed that victims were being ignored by the criminal justice system, and proposed a formal use of restitution . In 1970, Stephen Schafer said "if one looks at the legal systems of different countries, one seeks in vain a country where a victim of crime enjoys a certain expectation of fully restitution for his injury" Schafer (1970: 117).

Europe and its Union had no other choice but to respond to these pressures. I have already described the legislative and policy steps that the EU has taken to bring balance to our modern criminal justice system (Chapter 5). The latest step, the Victims' Directive explicitly regulates restorative justice while it introduces basic standards that must be respected when involving victims. Why after all should we assume that an alternative justice process such as restorative justice is a safer bet for victims?

The Victims' Directive assumes that policy, legislative and institutional reforms will take place in Member States. I have concerns about this expectation for two principal reasons. First, the cultural, societal and historical traits of our criminal justice systems are factors that may hinder this intention. Second, Europe and the international community are faced with a global financial crisis. Asking States to make reforms during a climate of financial austerity might put additional pressure. Of course, this is not to suggest that reforms may help cut down the spiralling costs of criminal justice. But this is not a narrative that has been developed by the EU, which will need to convince local politicians and civil society. Legislation alone will not suffice. A wider and inclusive debate is needed. This is also a debate for the wider international community and not just Europe. The Victims' Directive is only one attempt to move victims out of the shawdows.

This chapter attempts to critically present the key themes emerging from the RJE research (Part II and III), the book's international guest chapters (Part I) as well as recent data from the extant literature. The purpose is two fold. Firstly, I aim to present a critical and comparative narrative in order to assist an international debate about a victim and rights focused criminal justice system. By conceptualising the issues as these emerge from the most recent literature and research, I hope that a more informed and inclusive dialogue is encouraged. The role of users and especially victims is highlighted within this conceptual framework. Secondly, I attempt to posit recommendations in the hope of assisting the implementation of the Victims' Directive. This was also one of my key ambitions when I applied to the EC for financial support for the RJE project. It is through evidence and a critical reflection of reality that policy development and reforms should take place. The base on which I found these recommendations is the conceptual framework that we built through the RJE research and the other evidence recorded in this volume. I take this bold step knowingly that not all my readers will agree with my conclusions. This is partly intentional as no debate start with absolute consensus.

A New Conceptual Framework for Victim Policy

Lets Talk about Victims when we Talk about Victims

One of the most consistent findings of this volume is how differently the concept of a victim is perceived across Europe and internationally, and how much each national political and societal circumstances influence the way victim support services are understood and prioritised by individual governments. This cannot be taken lightly in the implementation of an EU-wide Victims' Directive or indeed of any international attempt for more rights for victims. For instance, if the concept 'victim' is used by a Member State too narrowly, this might be an obstacle for the enactment of the rules of the Directive. As we build our conceptual framework, we need to make sure that when we talk about victim we indeed talk about victims!

Looking at how the term victim is understood and is catered for by all Member States and not just the RJE participating countries, it is possible to distinguish two broad classifications (see Table 1 overleaf). These two classifications are not mutually exclusive. Classification 1 refers to how broadly or narrowly a Member State interprets the term victim. Classification 2 refers to how a Member State provides victim support services.

Table 1: Conceptualising the term 'victim'

Conceptual Classification 1: Base: How broadly or narrowly the term victim is interpreted	**Model 1**: Member States that have developed legal and policy structures that provide support services to the victim, the latter interpreted both in a general (any victim of crime) and specific contexts, e.g. victim of terrorism (Austria, Belgium, Germany, Ireland, the Netherlands and the United Kingdom). **Model 2**: Member States that have laws and provisions only for specific types of victims (e.g. children, women, victims of terrorism) and do not cater more generally for any person who has been harmed due to crime (Bulgaria, Croatia, Cyprus, Hungary, Italy, Latvia, Lithuania, Poland and Spain).
Conceptual Classification 2: Base: Types of services provided to victims	**Model 1**: Member States that provide services to victims only as part of their role in the criminal justice process (e.g. legal aid, prosecution) or as consumers of health and social care services (Croatia, Greece, Spain and Poland). **Model 2**: Member States that go beyond the customary provision of victims' services through their legal, health and social care arm by providing bespoke and specialist support either through their own institutions or by funding civil society organisations (Bulgaria, Cyprus, Czech Republic, Hungary, Italy, Poland and Slovakia).

Starting with Classification 1, we identify two Models. Model 1, within Classification 1, refers to countries that have developed legal structures, services and policy frameworks that service the victim both in the general understanding of its notion as well as its specialist context (Austria, Belgium, Germany, Ireland, the Netherlands and the United Kingdom). In effect, this means that their legislative frameworks provide not only for services to victims of specific groups such as children and women, but also for any person who has suffered harm as a result of a criminal offence (physical, mental or emotional harm or economic loss). Model 2, within Classification 1, refers to countries which acknowledge victims only in a specific context, namely as abused women, abused children and victims of trafficking/terrorism (Bulgaria, Croatia, Cyprus, Hungary, Italy, Latvia, Lithuania, Poland, and Spain). These Member States have not yet developed victim support services that are provided in a generic context, i.e. for any person who has been harmed.

Moving on to Classification 2 we can once again distinguish two separate models, this time focusing on how generic or specialist victim support services are provided. Model 1, within Classification 2, includes countries that provide services to victims only as part of their routine criminal justice service provision (e.g. through the police, prosecution, legal aid) or as consumers of routine health and social services (Croatia, Greece, Poland, and Spain). Model 2 within Classification 2 includes countries that go beyond the customary provision of legal, health and social services to victims by providing specialist services either through the government arm (e.g. central and local government bodies, public sector providers, the formal criminal justice system) or by funding civil society organisations (e.g. Bulgaria, Czech Republic, Cyprus, Hungary, Italy, Poland and Slovakia).

Although standardisation in the implementation of victim support services does not seem to be feasible, it is important when considering the implementation of the Victims' Directive to achieve and attain a baseline in relation to minimum standards for protection, availability and quality control. For instance, Article 9 of the Directive states that victim support services shall provide as a minimum: information, advice and support which is relevant to the rights of victims' emotional and psychological support; as well as advice relating to financial and practical issues . These standards shall be guaranteed in all Member States but not necessarily implemented in the same way. A shared understanding of the term victim must have a baseline across Europe and according to our findings this is still not the case.

Collapsing Assumptions: Listening to Victims

Due to the historical reasons explained above, the current criminal justice system is based on the assumption that victims are better off when not directly involved in the pursuit of justice for what happened to them. The same assumption is also made by many policy makers and criminal justice agents. This is not a phenomenon exclusive to one EU member state. Our new conceptual framework for victim policy must collapse these assumptions.

Looking at the RJE findings and the arguments emerging from the international guest chapters, our conclusion is that victims do want to talk, or at least to be given the opportunity to talk, about what matters to them and how they think their best interests can be pursued and protected in the criminal justice system. The same applies to their views on restorative justice whether they have had the chance to experience it directly or have only just been introduced to it. In going forward with our new narrative for victim policy, this must be taken into account.

Chapters 1 and 3 of this volume, written by victims of crime, are indicative of the power and contribution that victims' views can have in constructing evidence-based policy that is driven not by trivial and political interests, but by the needs of those it aims to serve. Turning our attention to the research carried out by the RJE, just in the UK, within a period of two months of fieldwork, 64 victims answered our online survey. Furthermore, out of the 39 victims who were approached for the in-depth interviews, 24 agreed to take part (success rate of 62%). In fact, the UK research with victims showed that the more complex the crime, the more chances there were for victims to want to speak up and take part. 24% of those who took part in our research identified themselves to be victims of hate crime, 17% of street crime, 14% victims of rape (female), and 15% of serious violent crime. 7% said they were victims of gang crime while the highest percentage (29%) said that they were burgled. 3% said they had a family member murdered. 68% of the victims were female, while the majority were between 46-55 years old. One victim said: "The government should open a debate about what is the most important reform for victims. There are many ways to shift what might appear as what victims want". Another victim said: "The government has responsibility to open up a debate about what victims want". In the Greek research, the demographics of the victims who took part also support the above conclusion. The complexities of the case (e.g. domestic violence, sexual violence) often make them feel the need to speak up and indeed help shape a better system.

Our conclusion creates an even bigger responsibility for civil society, the state and the European Commission. As victims want to meaningfully take part in policy making and the improvement of their criminal justice experience, structures must be put in place to ensure that their engagement is done according to the Victims' Directive and its intentions of safeguarding their rights as equal participants.

Generic, Specialised and Mixed Victim Support Services

According to the Victims' Directive, member states should not only assure support services for specific groups of victims and vulnerable groups (such as women and children), but also attend the necessities of anyone who has been harmed due to crime. In this regard, we identify within our conceptual framework a generic, a specialised, and a mixed model of victim support services.

The generic model means that the service is available to all victims of crimes without restrictions of any kind. A specialised model means that services are provided only for certain groups of victims affected by particular categories of crime. A mixed model means that services have been structured in order to cater both for specialist groups of victims as well as anyone who has been harmed by crime. This organisation is an indication of how much progress has been made in the Member States in understanding, and thus catering for, the complex needs of victims.

For instance, victims of domestic violence require specialist support. A generic service will not capture the sensitivities surrounding their psychological and other such needs. Looking at Hungary as an example, it has established a generic model, providing victim support services to any individual who has been harmed due to crime. No specialist provision has been developed for specific types of victims. On the contrary, other Member States (e.g. Austria, Croatia, Denmark and Finland) combine generic and specialist support systems, which cooperate together through different types of referral mechanisms. In Denmark, victim support services operate under a mixed model that provides victim support services through the various police districts, but also several specialist organisations supporting specific groups. Some examples include the National Organisation of Woman's Shelters and the Joan-Sisters organisation, which protect woman's rights in the context of violent crimes. Indeed, Denmark could be mentioned as an example of a country where public and private agencies work together, providing a mixed model of victim support services .

Bulgaria, Cyprus, Greece, Italy, Latvia, Lithuania, Romania and Slovenia have not developed services that support all individuals who have been harmed due to crime. They only have a specialised structure of services focusing on selected groups such as women and children. One reason for this might be related to an international legislative trend that places an emphasis on the protection and support of specific groups such as victims of domestic violence, women, children, and victims of terrorism. It is important to say that the functioning of the victim support services does not necessarily reflect the list of provisions and rights contained in their legislation. For instance, the codes of criminal procedure normally protect victims' procedural rights without restrictions relating to the type of crime committed against them. In this regard, the right to be informed, the right to legal assistance, the right to participate in judicial procedures and the right to receive psychological support are apparently contemplated by most European legislation. Italy and Greece are examples of countries that have developed a legislative framework to protect and support specific groups of victims, such as victims of trafficking and sexual exploitation, victims of forced labour and victims of sexual violence. In both countries, the institutional support for victims is also focused on services for specific groups.

State-based vs Community-led Victim Support and Restorative Justice Services

A number of authors in this volume as well as the recent literature are becoming increasingly concerned about national and EU wide developments in policy and law that are taking restorative justice further away from its community nature. The tendency to regulate, legislate and administer its delivery through centralised and formalised structures and controls are rooting out the very heart of a notion that was original introduced by aboriginal, indigenous and other localised communities as a response to state based interventions (Braithwaite 2002; Gavrielides; 2011). Our conceptual framework for a new victim policy must be one that embraces both State-based and community-led victim support and restorative justice services, and supports them where and when appropriately.

Looking more closely at the Classification relating to who provides victim support services, Model 1 refers to countries that have put victim support services almost entirely in the hands of the state (Belgium, Croatia, Hungary and Poland). In contrast, other countries (Germany, Finland, and the United Kingdom) have adopted Model 2 whereby support services depend principally on civil society. As an example of Model 1, legislation in Belgium, specifically the Code of Criminal Procedure, the law on police services and the Act concerning the organisation of an integrated police, have assigned to criminal justice agents the responsibility to provide the service immediately after a crime has occurred. Furthermore, the Protocol on the establishment of an integrated victim policy (7 April 1998) and The National Forum for Victim Support Policy have improved the coordination and cooperation between bodies dealing with victims. Moreover, the Flemish legislation establishes a 'quality criteria' and equal accessibility for every kind of victim to these services.

In Croatia, victim support services are also run almost entirely by the state. Following the EU Framework Decision 2001, the country has strived to enhance their legal and institutional framework in relation to victims' rights. The procedural legislation of Croatia enforces fundamental rights for victims such as the right to be informed, the right to legal assistance, the right to emotional and psychological support, the right to privacy and protection from secondary victimisation among others. Also, like many other EU Member States, Croatia has legislated to guarantee the right to financial compensation for damages caused by a criminal offence. In relation to victim support policy, the Croatian Ministry of Justice operates together with the National Committee for Monitoring and Improving the Victim and Witness Support System. The latter body is responsible for the development of strategies to improve and standardise the treatment of victims at a national level. The committee provides advice on how to enhance legislation and improve national policy on this matter. Additionally, this body has evaluation and monitoring functions over all the institutions working and involved with victims .

In Hungary, another example of Model 1, the most important piece of victim related legislation is the Victim Support Act. According to the Act, the victim support service must be provided not only for those directly harmed by the crime but also for their family members, friends and any other individual who may also be affected when a crime is committed. However, there is no consistency between the Victim Support Act's definition and the narrow concept of victim contemplated in the Code of Criminal Procedure. Hungary is also one of the EU countries where a generic support service exists to help victims independently of the type of crime that has affected them. Moreover, this country does not have a specialised service to deal with victims of particular type of crimes.

In Poland, there is a specialised victim support service for children, older and disabled persons, supervised and coordinated by the Victim Support Network. The police play a major role in providing the service in many localities, especially with regard to victims of domestic violence. The Polish Charter of Rights of a Victim assures several fundamental rights for victims such as the right to assistance, freedom from victimisation, access to justice and the right to mediation (among other rights). The passing of non-statutory Charters is a practice observed in other Member States such as the UK, the

Netherlands and Ireland. Although there is not yet any evidence of their effectiveness, they may constitute a promising practice in the assistance of the Victims' Directive implementation and the better provision of victim support services. In addition, the Polish criminal procedure permits the participation of the victim as an auxiliary prosecutor giving a voice to victims. In fact victims in Poland are allowed to act as an auxiliary prosecutor, 'alongside the public prosecutor (as the accessory auxiliary prosecutor) or in place of the public prosecutor' . However, compared to the provision of victim support services in other Member States (e.g. the Netherlands) these developments seem currently to be far behind the minimum EU requirements. For example, victim support services in the Netherlands are provided to any person who has simply been harmed and may not have been officially included in the criminal justice process. This may include restorative justice services, psychological and advice services to individuals who perceive themselves as victims due to a criminal activity although that particular activity may have never been prosecuted.

The United Kingdom is an example of Model 2 as the state, in addition to its own public service provision of victims' services, also provides financial support to voluntary and community sector victim support organisations without being formally responsible for the direct provision of the service. Nonetheless, the United Kingdom Government is responsible for developing and implementing policy on victims through the Ministry of Justice (2011). In order to provide the service, 'Victim Support' - the leading charity supporting victims - is funded through a grant received from the Ministry of Justice. At the same time, Victim Support receives charitable income through grants and donations. In a similar way, the functioning of non-governmental victim support services in Ireland relies on the state's financial support. Since the 1980s, civil society has a strong presence promoting victims' rights and supporting them in their needs. Nevertheless, public bodies such as the 'Support of Victims of Crime' and the Victims of Crime Office exist to monitor the quality of victim support services delivered by other state agencies and non-governmental organisations.

However, even in countries where the provision of victim support services is mainly in the hands of civil society (e.g. Finland and Germany), the state also contributes by providing support for specific groups of victims. In Finland for example, the state has a double role to play, delivering services to victims of human trafficking and victims of discrimination, while also funding civil society for the provision of generic victim support services.

In the Netherlands, 20 victim organisations were merged into one called *Victim Support Netherlands*. This offers legal, practical and emotional support to victims of various kinds. This organisation serves as a platform to coordinate and facilitate the service across the country working directly with the state and its agents. On the other hand, Germany can be seen as an example of decentralisation of the service. In this country, the functions developed by the public sector to support victims are different depending on each state. For instance, the German Ministry of Justice is only responsible for the coordination of victim support in the state of Mecklenburg-Vorpommern. The remaining states in Germany are not subjected to a national coordinator . In Denmark, there is also a national coordinator, which facilitates a generic victim support service provided through different police districts.

In contrast, other countries in the EU have adopted a unified or national victim support model. This is not a common trend across the EU and it mainly refers to the Netherlands, Denmark and the United Kingdom. In some countries (United Kingdom, Germany, Netherlands, Ireland) the state is responsible for both funding and providing victim services directly through their ministries and public bodies. The Ministry of Justice seems to be the central government department in most Member States that is tasked with coordinating responsibilities for victim support services. Other ministries such as the Ministry of Labour, Ministry of Health and Ministry of Interior also have a prominent role to play. In several EU countries, victim support services rely exclusively on the civil society and practically no financial support is given by the state (e.g. Bulgaria, Cyprus, Hungary, and Poland).

There is a long way to go before victim policy supports equally State-based and community-based interventions. As indicated, victim support services across the EU are generally provided through the cooperation of public bodies and private organisations. Fears are also expressed that restorative justice provision is gradually becoming a state monopoly.

For instance, one of the themes that dominated the discussions at the UK RJE focus group with experts related to the current development of restorative justice. The participants claimed that restorative justice is currently being promoted by government and certain government funded organisations "through top down structures that control its agenda and forms of manifestations" (quote from a practitioner). This was not thought to be in the interest of the victim, while concerns were expressed about the need to first change the criminal justice culture before the Victims' Directive can be genuinely implemented.

A senior probation manager said during this focus group that restorative justice is being promoted within their Probation Trust as "a quantifiable commodity that must be compared against existing practice. This takes restorative justice away from its key principles". Similarly, another probation officer said, "In our restorative justice unit, restorative justice is as top down as you get. The research on restorative justice is pointing in one direction i.e. it needs to be bottom-up. But all our funding comes from NOMS [government] and therefore it is hard to change the existing culture. This ultimately does not serve victims". The research with professionals from Greece where restorative justice is provided primarily through the law, as well as from Germany support the above finding.

This concern was also validated through the fieldwork with victims. For example, one victim who in fact progressed to becoming restorative justice practitioner said: "I stopped implementing restorative justice as the government is now seeing it as a way to get youth to say sorry for their actions". Another victim said: "My overall concern about restorative justice is its further implementation without consideration of victims' human rights and the power relations, including economics, that exist in society. For me, as a White, middle class professional with two degrees, getting a poor, Black kid to say sorry, seems an insult to justice and the injury that was caused".

Indeed it is questionable whether yet another piece of legislation such as a Directive can encourage implementation back to its original path and direction. In fact, it is troubling that in its very articles the Directive encourages strict regulation and standardisation of restorative justice as if it is part of the same system that the state owns and controls. The intention to protect victims overlooks the nature of restorative justice as a non-state based intervention that falls outside of the traditional way of delivering justice. This, of course, does not mean that restorative justice cannot be provided in parallel to the criminal justice system. It also means that protection can indeed be initiated but not through the same legal structures that the state provides for its own justice methods (see Gavrielides and Artinopoulou, 2013).

Practitioners in the RJE research seem to agree that restorative justice should be provided both within and outside of the criminal justice system and that this should include partnerships with community and civil society organisations, which seem to have taken the principal burden in the implementation and innovation of restorative justice in most EU member states.

RJE participants in the UK, the Netherlands and Germany also expressed the view that there are already plenty and adequate legislative and institutional arrangements for the protection of victims in the criminal justice and restorative justice process. Nevertheless, there is a considerable gap in the implementation of these intentions. This should serve as a lesson for the Directive and its implementation. They also pointed out that the real challenge is not the passing of these regulations at the national level, but their enforcement. This is also a message shared in this book's first and third chapter written by victims of crime.

Relating also to the issue of enforcement, there was consensus across the RJE participating countries that there is almost no information on the Directive's implications while most relevant agencies are even unaware of its existence. Practitioners and other professionals who took part in our programmes also seemed to agree that it is questionable whether legislation alone can help with the implementation of restorative justice. In fact, attempts and resources directed into legislative initiatives may destruct from the actual issue, which according to most revolves around community engagement and community leadership.

It was concluded that there are strong power structures within the victims and restorative justice movements as well as the criminal justice system that make victims and offenders suspicious of restorative justice processes. Gatekeepers often treat victims in a patronising or tokenistic manner despite the existence of guidance and regulations. In fact, there are fears that this deterioration will continue as funding is being rolled out to mainstream restorative justice too quickly and without consideration of its complex, local and fluid nature.

Victims' Confidence and Engagement made Possible

The new conceptual framework for victim policy must be built on the assumption that increased victim confidence and engagement with the criminal justice system is pursued and achieved. We know that criminal justice agents, particularly those working within prosecution and the police, have historically struggled to engage victims as witnesses. Reasons that have been recorded by the extant literature and our research indicate a lack of confidence and trust in the system, fear of re-victimisation, lack of information and a sense that they are merely being used as part of a system that does not treat them as its central focus.

The chapters in this book suggest that meaningful victim engagement is possible provided that we encourage a victim-focused criminal justice system that allows certain procedures to be victim-led or victim driven. Here, we must stress that none of the chapters advocated in favour of an entire victim-led criminal justice system. The evidence, however, have argued in favour of certain criminal justice procedures for being victim-led. This relates not only to the traditional criminal justice system, but also to restorative justice processes.

Another model that is rather visible in the way support services are provided to victims across EU Member States is in relation to countries that do so via offender focused services, such as probation, and those that have distinct victim focused providers. For example in Sweden, victim support services are managed only by organisations specialised in the treatment of victims. Conversely, in Germany the police and the Social Services of the Judiciary are public institutions that deal with both victims and offenders. There are also countries that will allow a combination of the two. So for instance, while in the United Kingdom the probation service will also cater for some types of victims, such as those of domestic violence, sexual abuse and hate crime, the state will also fund generic and specialist victim focused organisations to provide support both in the context of the criminal procedure but also in terms of psychological and medical assistance.

Looking exclusive at the UK and restorative justice, when asked what they understood by it, victims pointed out that a restorative justice that is not victim-led or victim focused is not a restorative justice at all. Some indicative answers include:

> *"To give victims the chance to tell offenders the impact of their crime, to have questions answered e.g. Why me? It should hold offenders to account for what they have done, helps them understand the real impact of what they've done, to take responsibility and make amends".*

> *"It has a focus on victims' needs as well as calling offender to account for their actions and see the impact of the crimes".*

> *"Redressing the balance - giving back dignity to the victim - being able to say I am not a victim anymore".*

> *"A recovering process for the victim and a reflective process for the offender on his actions and bringing together the offender and the victim to allow an apology to take place".*

> *"Justice that is not just a punishment system for the people who have broken the law. A system that tries to restore an offender to the person they were before they started committing crime. To reconnect them to the emotions of life and living amongst people that they should not harm as they themselves should not wish to be harmed in their life time".*

Similarly, in Greece, Germany, the Netherlands and Bulgaria, victims pointed out that confidence in the criminal and restorative justice processes is possible provided that certain standards are met. Overall, there was consensus that preparation is key to participating, and that the level of it should depend on the crime that was committed and the personality and needs of the people involved.

The majority of victims who took part in the RJE research stressed that when the process is initiated by them, the chances of success are higher in their mind. Victims were also asked what type of information they were given in order to decide whether to opt for restorative justice. Again, the answers varied from "Nothing", to "Full information about the process and timescales". Some said that they just received an email or a quick phone call. One victim who had undergone restorative justice said: "The process was absolutely the opposite to a victim centred practice. I was not treated with any respect or consideration. If I wanted information, I had to chase for it. My victim experience was not a good one".

Some victims in Greece and the UK mentioned the importance of the meeting location both for the actual process, but also for agreeing to take part. All of them highlighted that a neutral space was key with the majority opting for a public place. There was agreement that restorative justice must remain voluntary both at its initiation as well as during its implementation. "At any point, the victim or the offender can change their mind. Neither side can feel under pressure to participate or to decide on outcomes. This is something that I experienced because the agency wanted resolution", one victim said.

A Balanced Approach to all Key Stakeholders made Possible

In the pursuit for a more balanced criminal and restorative justice system it is easy to forget that offenders, the state and the community are also key stakeholders. While moving victims from the shadows of the criminal justice system, our new conceptual framework for victim policy must not to do injustice to the other justice players.

For instance, practitioners who took part in our research pointed out that victims are not always the most vulnerable in the criminal and restorative justice processes. Examples were given of extremely vulnerable juveniles undergoing restorative justice while in prison settings. Issues around posttraumatic disorder, suicidal tendencies and the ability to process pain were mentioned. One practitioner said: "Even when we explain the restorative process to offenders, they still do not realise that they will be emotionally charged over it. They are always surprised when victims are insulting them. They understand at a superficial level that they will go into a meeting with a victim, but they do not really expect to be emotionally affected. Maybe we should prepare them better by showing them documentaries, videos or training material". Another practitioner said: "The victim might have a confrontational attitude against the offender. We don't want a frustrated offender. That would be a negative outcome attributed to a restorative justice meeting. So, safeguards need to protect both sides". The Directive does point out that in the pursuit of victims' rights, offenders should not be harmed. However, this requirement is very much under hidden.

The RJE research also pointed out that "victims sometimes feel vulnerable, sometimes they don't. It is necessary, however, that victims have trust in the facilitator. Necessary skills are being able to listen and have empathy". Another practitioner said: "Most victims are concerned about safety and mainly emotional safety. They are concerned about not being re-traumatised or being wound up by other participants. If their hearts are in the right place then their attitude towards the meeting and the offender will be right". These fears must be addressed before proceeding with restorative justice", the practitioner said. "The Directive must be implemented in a manner that safeguards victims from these fears so that they do not become realities. The consequence will be detrimental for all parties involved". One practitioner said: "What helps make victims feel safe in restorative justice is bringing with them people they trust. It can be a friend or a spouse. The friends will be there to advocate for them when they are overcoming a conference. It is very frightening for people to feel that they are coming in alone. Can the Victims' Directive secure this"?

A number of practitioners pointed out that "restorative justice has its own timescales" and that it can often be time consuming in criminal justice terms. "We have to accept resistance at the beginning. We have to explain the process really well and hear victims' stories. It is only then when people will start to become more open to the possibility of restorative justice" one practitioner said. One practitioner said: "Unlike what happens in a criminal court when the jury gives the verdict, in restorative justice there is no magical climax! The process should be over only when the parties have come to terms with or recovered from the harm caused. Never lead parties into a single-event conference. Restorative justice is a long term process of change".

There was also consensus that there is no evidence to believe that restorative justice would not be appropriate with certain crimes. In relation to offenders with mental health problems, one practitioner said: "We take special measure in the pre-work for these people. Especially, we prepare them for what might happen in terms of the behaviour of the person with the mental health problems and in most situations they know the person well". Someone else said: "Everyone should be allowed to restorative justice if the circumstances are right. Now, you have to be careful especially in situations of sexual assault. However, this doesn't mean that they can do restorative justice". Another practitioner said: "It is not the nature of the offence that dictates where restorative justice can happen but more the circumstances around it". A practitioner with expertise in complex cases such as domestic violence said: "There are no restrictions as to where restorative justice can be used. However, careful assessment and consultation with the victim (and the offender) will exclude some. Every contact with either party should be reparatory and restorative in itself".

Learning to Follow Victims' Journey

Our conceptual framework for a more inclusive victim policy must be grounded on the real needs of victims prior, during and after the criminal justice and restorative justice process Here, I attempt to group them into two broad categories:

I. General Needs, encompasing:

Emotional Needs

Recognition of the victim and of what happened, restoration of relations, apologies, direct emotional support, aftercare, specific care, certain characteristics of the emotional support.

The Need for Information

Information about the CJS, about the role of the victim in the CJS, about the offender (background, motives, crimes), about prevention and about the process of healing.

The Need for Practical Support

Help with paperwork, procedures, medical support, crisis management, transport, etc.

The Need for Financial Compensation

Financial compensation by the offender, support with financial procedures, etc.

The Need for Safety and Security

Creation of immediate safety (sometimes by providing a shelter/new home), prevention of re-victimisation, etc.

II. Specific Needs in relation to the Criminal Justice and Restorative Justice Processes

Specific needs include: the need to be treated respectfully and with care by CJ-officials and restorative justice practitioners, swift reaction by the police and other criminal justice professionals that they come in contact with, the need to have legal assistance, to have a strong legal position and the possibility to be heard and give input into the criminal justice procedure (procedural justice), the satisfaction that the output of the CJ process gives (the sentence/sanction), the need that the offender becomes aware of the consequences of his own behaviour and will refrain from crime, the need to get into contact with the offender and sometimes their families. For example, a number of victims and professionals pointed out that the implementation of a psychological service delivered by mental health professionals should be available to support victims in their needs before, during and after the trial. In this regard, beyond the domestic context of European jurisdictions, the International Criminal Court has created special units managed by professionals salaried and employed by the Court itself in order to help victims in dealing with the psychological aftermath of a crime. In the context of the EU, Article 9 of the Victims' Directive states that support services shall as minimum provide "(c) emotional and, where available, psychological support".

Steps to Implementing our New Conceptual Framework: Recommendations

What is Possible: Resources and Funding

When implementing our conceptual framework for victim policy we must remain realistic placing our action and reforms within the given financial, political and cultural circumstances. Taking the Victims' Directive and the RJE project as an example, a question that was repeatedly raised by a number of practitioners and stakeholders who took part in our research revolved around resources. Providing a holistic service to victims is important while following their entire journey prior, during and after the criminal justice and restorative justice process. But how possible is this given the budgetary cuts in many EU justice systems?

The general practice is that in most Member States either the total (e.g. Hungary, Romania) or primary responsibility for funding victim support services lies with the state. A distinction can be made between services provided to victims as part of the criminal procedure and those provided to them above and beyond their role in legal proceedings. This includes reforms in the legal aid legislation including that of France, Greece, Italy, Spain, and the United Kingdom. Under this group of services, Member States' obligation to ensure that victims are compensated for their loss due to the crimes are also included. Provisions for compensation in some countries (e.g. Italy), were not introduced until the EU Framework Decision was passed in 2001. This is a good indicator of the role that EU-wide initiatives and instruments can have on individual Member States and the harmonisation of minimum standards for victim service provision.

In some countries (e.g. Luxembourg, Netherlands, and the United Kingdom), funding of services that do not relate to the role of victims in the criminal process also comes from private income, donations and project-funded activities. This is possible when victim support services are not provided exclusively by the state arm, but through NGOs. For instance, in the United Kingdom where the charity sector is much stronger than in many other EU countries, the key body providing services to victims, Victim Support, is increasingly relying on private and charitable income. This is also true for the smaller victim support providers in the country. With some exceptions (e.g. Austria, Germany) "due to their non-governmental background, victim support organisations are in principle mostly financed privately, i.e. sponsors, donations, membership fees, volunteers etc." . Similarly, in Germany "Independent volunteer support services ... receive no public funding and are financed predominantly by membership fees, donations and allocations of fines by the courts" .

The bulk of victim support services, independently of whether these relate to their legal, psychological and emotional needs are provided by volunteers. It can safely be said that the area of victim support is for Member States and the EU one of the areas where civic society is mostly energised, and thus where the biggest savings are made in terms of public service delivery. It is also an area where democracy and civil participation in action takes place. Where the state realises and respects this, there is also investment in the form of training and funding. As a consequence, better and more victim support services are developed and state accountability is strengthened.

Denmark is one example where, although the National Commission of the Danish Police takes responsibility for channelling funds to the local service through the umbrella organisation Victim Support Denmark, there is still an acknowledgement that individual volunteers must also be supported and rewarded.

Most Member States consider their obligations to fund victim support services addressed (whether of a legal nature or not) simply because they are responsible for the running of key criminal justice organisations (such as the police, probation, prosecution) or health and social care providers. Some countries consider their funding obligations complete simply because they run social care services. For instance, in Bulgaria "no specific requirements were identified for the special victim support services. The general requirements for all service providers under the Regulations for Implementation of the Social Assistance Act are that the service provider is obliged to provide to the client written information about social services it provides."

When it comes to specialist victim support services that are outsourced to non-governmental providers, the models vary as some countries do not chose this option while others open up this opportunity to competition. Some Member States tend to repeat funding for the same organisations. For instance, the Cyprus government over the years has outsourced victim support service only to one organisation while, in the United Kingdom, Victim Support has traditionally been the biggest and most stable receiver of multi-million pound grants. The same applies to the Netherlands for Victim Support Netherlands as well as Finland (Victim Support Finland receives 70% of its budget from the state). This approach hinders innovation and diversity as well as the ability to drill down into the needs of local and marginalised communities.

Another aspect in relation to funding is how this is allocated by the state. Again, where the service is beyond the role of the victim in the criminal procedure, the models that can be identified are threefold. Some countries fund organisations directly by commissioning services through their central government departments (e.g. Romania). Other countries have set up specialist Committees that are cross governmental or on some occasions may even have representation from the voluntary sector as well as experts (e.g. Belgium: Commission for Financial Aid and the Commission and Fund for Financial Aid to Victims of Deliberate Acts of Violence and to Occasional Rescuers). In France, the National Council for Victims, chaired by the Minister of Justice, is responsible for funding and coordination of victim support services. In Ireland, the Commission for the Support of Victims of Crime is responsible for funding and coordination as well as policymaking and strategy. In Sweden, the Crime Victim Compensation and Support Authority administers the Fund for Victims of Crime, which receives most of its income from convicted perpetrators.

EU Member States also receive funding for victim support from the EU and the UN. The levels of this support are not uniform while only some countries (Croatia, Cyprus, Hungary and Spain) acknowledge the significance that this contribution has. Independent victim support organisations may receive funding directly from the EU which they would often combine with their own independent income generation which may include donations and carrying out projects for private organisations and businesses (e.g. Cyprus, the United Kingdom). Some countries, such as Croatia, have introduced programmes that are funded directly by other countries whether these are from Europe or elsewhere. For instance, 1.3 million euros have been invested in a 4 year victim support system programme in Croatia with investment from the United Nations development fund as well as funding from the Netherlands, Spain but also the US and OSCE. The use of assets and money acquired by the state from criminals is an innovative method of funding victims support services and a good way of compensating those directly affected by the activities that generated this surplus in the first place (e.g. Germany).

Where the Church has a strong role and presence in a Member State, some victim support services may receive direct funding from its faith institutions (e.g. Estonia). However, these tend to prioritise victims of the same faith or of specific crimes and ages. Another innovative way to raise independent funds is the support by the state of special initiatives such as fundraising through the selling of a Victim Support Magazine (e.g. see Finland). Another community that has funded victim support services directly is that of academics and professional practitioners. For instance, in Lithuania, the Association of the Support of Crime Victims, which is one of the lead independent organisations providing victim services, is an entirely personal initiative of victim support practitioners and researchers. They fund it through their own projects and through membership fees that they charge individuals and organisations for receiving certain benefits from their activities.

In the UK RJE research faith institutions practising restorative justice were explicitly mentioned and so was central government. One practitioner said: "There can be pressure from faith institutions to forgive the offender in a hasty way ... forgive the offender and move on, and there can be a sense that if you don't forgive that you are not a good Christian ... that you are not living up to the expectations of your faith". Someone else said: "The victim has to be honoured in the restorative justice journey. The role of the facilitator is very important in ensuring that the practice pursues what the victim wants. Forgiveness should be the last thing on their minds". A practitioner with expertise in complex cases including sexual violence said: "The danger in the UK is that victims are being encouraged, persuaded, educated, even coerced into attending single-event conferences which they never wanted to do and may not serve any purpose other than to satisfy the needs of the facilitator and the agency".

One model that seems to be working for generating independent income for victim support services can be found in Lithuania where "resources for the Fund of Crime Victims are payments imposed by courts in criminal cases, recovered sums, resources from the state budget (assignations) and other lawfully obtained sources" . Another good practice model that was identified was the direct engagement of victims in the identification of the types of services they need, and the providers they prefer to use. For instance, the Irish government has made a priority the direct empowerment and engagement of victims in the provision of services. In 2005, the Ministry of Justice and Equality established the Commission for Support for Victims of Crime, which, among other responsibilities, holds an annual Consultative Forum, which is attended by representatives of all funded voluntary organisations providing services to victims. The purpose is to hold them to account and also to listen to what victims really need.

The Option of Restorative Justice made Possible

It is clear that the Directive has no intention to promote restorative justice. It only aims to regulate restorative justice where it is already provided by a member state. Therefore, the purpose of Article 12 is merely to safeguard victims' rights within existing practices. It does not intend to create new ones.

However, it has become apparent from our research and the extant literature that an option that is not communicated to victims is not an option at all. Put another way, how can victims decide what to opt for and how to protect themselves if they are not aware of restorative justice? A recent survey that was conducted by the Restorative Justice for All International Institute asking "Do victims know about restorative justice" showed that out of the 77 responses 34% said "They know nothing at all", 62% said "They know very little" and only 4% said "They know enough" . It is wrong to assume that restorative justice is offered by the state in the same way as any other criminal justice process, and that victims have access to it. It is hardly known amongst criminal justice professionals. Thus Article 12 remains weak and almost without context.

True, some member states where restorative justice is already implemented have adequate structures for complying with the Directive. However, crucial setbacks were identified in certain cases such as the UK and Ireland while the RJE research and the extant literature seem to suggest that we have a long way to go before re-victimisation and secondary victimisation can safely be avoided. It is also apparent that in Greece and other countries such as France and Switzerland the impact on victims of the criminal process is disproportionate compared to what the justice process aims to give to them while in other countries assessment of the effectiveness of the system is impossible.

Here, we have to ask whether the EC has a responsibility to provide victims with the alternative restorative justice option. We know for example that Cyprus, Italy and Estonia do not have restorative justice at all, while in many countries, including Bulgaria, it is offered only on an informal basis and in the shadows.

What we do know is that in all RJE participating countries, more information about restorative justice was requested from victims, offenders and professionals. This was not necessarily in the form of printed material. Case studies and real live examples were thought to be the best way to increase awareness while online information, email and the use of videos and audio were all recommended. The majority of our victims-participants felt that all victims should be offered the chance to choose restorative justice over the traditional criminal justice process. However, there were conditions attached to this and most of them were covered by the expectations included in the Victims' Directive.

Some victims who took part in the RJE said that it shouldn't be up to the court to decide whether a restorative justice intervention should take place or not. "If the courts decide then there is a risk of undermining the voluntary nature of the processes while we add yet more gatekeepers for a justice process that should be community led". Someone else said: "There is a risk to base the decision on another agenda different than the interests of the parties if it is all in the hands of professionals and judges".

Standards and Standardisation: Achieving a Balance

The Victims' Directive is strong on standards. It is hoped that by being clear and strict, the Directive can create a baseline across Europe for the safe delivery of victim support, criminal justice and restorative justice services. The burden is principally placed on state services to respect these standards. To understand the role of the state, a distinction must be made between two large groups of victim support services.

According to my first model, providers of the aforementioned services are part of the criminal justice procedure. These are screened and regulated as part of the justice mechanism. This will relate to their qualifications as civil servants, lawyers, judges, prosecutors, social workers police officers, psychologists etc. Each Member State has its own legal framework for the recruitment, attainment and development of criminal justice, civil service and public sector staff. It has to be stressed here that these are general civil servants or criminal justice agents and not exclusive victim support service providers. The RJE research suggests that the majority of services to victims particularly those provided within the criminal justice context (legal aid, compensation, witness etc.) are provided through criminal justice agents. Put another way, where victim support services are exclusively provided by agents of the criminal justice system, such as probation staff, prosecutors and the police, their training and the standards they need to respect are very much defined by their professional bodies and the agencies that employ them. In general terms, the state feels that it has an obligation to oversee only when (a) services are provided directly by its public arm, and (b) funding is provided directly by its government departments.

According to my second model, providers of the aforementioned services are independent (especially in relation to support that falls outside the criminal justice process). These are very much unregulated and unmonitored by state bodies. Some organisations may develop their own quality, accreditation and training standards and frameworks. They then self-regulate and self-monitor to ensure compliance (e.g. see Weisser Ring in Germany, Victim Support in the United Kingdom, Victim Support Netherlands, Victim Support Finland (RIKU), INAVEM in France). Where there is a funding relationship, the sponsoring government body may require certain standards that in most cases reflect human rights and other criminal law legislation. However, this is not uniform across Member States.

In Cyprus, the only system in place that can be considered as a quality management procedure is the Internal Audit Unit, which operates under the Social and Welfare Services. This provides general audit that is not focused on victim services. The unit is staffed with two people, which is an indicator of the level and scope of the scrutiny that takes place. Some countries have clearly stated their concern in relation to victim support service staffing. For instance in Hungary, most of the victim support staff have been replaced by young and inexperienced officers. The state does not have control over this recruitment, which seems to have been influenced by the lack of financial resources.

The registration of organisations as specialist victim support organisations is also not a matter of government control. Most countries deal with this under general guidelines and legislation for NGOs. For example, if a victim support service is registered in a country as a charity, NGO or a non-profit, then the general rules will apply. If the service falls within a specialist profession such as legal or medical, then the general rule is that the relevant regulator (e.g. the Law Society in the United Kingdom for legal professionals) would expect registration in order for services to be legitimate and accredited. Regulators are independent of government but controlled under national legislation and national standards. There are no regulators of victim support services in any Member State. As indicated by the UK RJE research, an attempt to impose registration of victim related restorative justice practices in the United Kingdom has backfired and a lot of criticism has been received both in terms of the interference of government and the lack of independence of the registering body (Gavrielides, 2013).

The lack of transparency and the many issues that are at stake for the registering body, as well as those expecting to be registered, has raised concerns in terms of how genuine this process is and what criteria are being used. It is also a costly process that excludes and indeed disregards the voluntary nature of these services, which are not carried out for profit but largely as part of civic society breaching a gap in public service provision .

In Belgium for instance, "Services for Victims of Crime must carry out tasks and respect principles enacted by the law ... [and] have to apply for official recognition with an official notice from the Ministry of Welfare, Health and Family of the relevant community" . Similarly, in Estonia, the Victim Support Act provides some guidance on the requirements for a victim support service provider, but again the requirements are rather broad. In France, the approving of associations that deliver victim support services is provided for by law but the procedure for obtaining a service agreement from the state is merely regulated via a circular and is not of a legislative nature. Arguably the most stringent regime in terms of registration is in the Netherlands, where the Justice Subsidies Act lays down the tasks in the field of victim support. Victim Support Netherlands then receives funds from the state to implement and to formulate quality standards.

In the case of vulnerable victims and especially children those providing both legal and non-legal services to them are more closely regulated, monitored and accredited. This is a consistent finding in almost all Member States. Some countries have Codes of Ethics relating to the handling of sensitive cases, especially those relating to the sexual abuse of women and children (e.g. Greece). Although not justiciable, these Codes provide a baseline of behaviour that is deemed acceptable but it is questionable whether a service provider can be held into account for breaching articles of such Codes. This is particularly true when the breach relates to a body that is not part of the state machinery.

An important caveat that cannot be stressed enough here is that in all Member States victim support service providers are heavily reliant on volunteers. The example of the Netherlands and the United Kingdom are striking, as over 80% of the workforce of victim support service is voluntary. However, the notion of 'volunteer' must not be confused with that of 'amateur'. Volunteers can be more qualified to provide victim services than paid staff. However, the need to continue attracting a voluntary workforce is always counterbalanced against the somewhat limited expectations that the state can have on individuals who give their time freely to support others. One good example of providing tailored support to volunteers is found in Denmark, where supervision is provided locally via regular meetings.

Practitioners' Training: Where to Invest

The training of practitioners in the implementation of a new conceptual framework for victim policy, including the Directive is a matter that raises several questions. I draw from our learning from the RJE project to posit recommendations. It is worth noting that during its 24-month life, the RJE project delivered 27 face-to-face training pilots in the five participating countries reaching 1,131 individuals and 383 organisations. Table 4 provides a summary of the pilots that were conducted face to face in the participating countries as well as a description of the organisations that were reached.

Before drawing these conclusions, I attempt to make two broad categorisations as to who provides victim support services in Europe whether these are within the criminal justice or restorative justice context. This is an important categorisation for the training and capacity building of victim support and restorative justice service providers.

Table 2: Delivery of victim support services in Europe

Categorisation 1: Victim Support Services provided by the public sector	**Group 1**: Delivery by professionals
	Group 2: Delivery by volunteers
Categorisation 2: Victim Support Services provided by the civil society organisations	**Group 1**: Delivery by professionals
	Group 2: Delivery by volunteers

The first categorisation includes those who deliver services as part of the public arm. Within this categorisation we can distinguish two groups. Group 1 includes professionals of public services providers (e.g. probation and police officers, healthcare professionals, lawyers, prosecutors). Group 2 within this categorisation includes volunteers recruited by public sector organisations. The second categorisation includes those who deliver services in the community and as part of civil society. Similarly to the first categorisation, Group 1 includes professionals and paid staff of civil society organisations whereas Group 2 here includes volunteers. The training that goes into these different groups varies significantly. What is also diverse is the combination of the different types of categorisations and Groups that EU Member States adopt.

The basic level of victim support service provision takes place under Categorisation 1, Group 1 as provision happens as part of the routine running of public services. The training that takes place here is offered as part of a public servant's expected qualifications and depends on the given role e.g. lawyers for legal aid provision, probation officers, healthcare professionals, etc.

All EU member states also seem to provide victim support services under Categorisation 1, Group 2. However, the requirements around training and the provision of specific skills and knowledge are not consistent here. In Austria, Bulgaria, Cyprus, Greece, Italy, Latvia, Malta, Poland, Portugal, Romania, Slovenia, Slovakia and Spain, there is either no information at all on expectations of volunteers' training or a simple acknowledgement that this matter is not regulated and thus each provider adopts ad hoc practice.

Belgium, Croatia, the Czech Republic, Denmark, Estonia, Lithuania, Luxembourg, the Netherlands, Sweden, and the UK provide victim support services under Categorisation 2. Member States that indeed allow provision at this level are split into two groups. Group 1 creates expectations around the training of both professionals and volunteers through the sub-contracting process (e.g. Czech Republic, Lithuania) or through the law (see Belgium , Estonia , Croatia , Luxembourg). This is particularly relevant for the training of professionals working for civil society organisations. However, the situation for volunteers working in civil society organisations, where applicable, is not as regulated. In fact, only a few Member States seem to provide training to volunteers as a self-regulated process by civil society service providers (i.e. Victim Support Denmark; the Weisser Ring in Germany, Finland, France, Hungary, Ireland, Victim Support Netherlands, Sweden; and, Victim Support England).

Investing in the training of professionals is a key strategic step for the implementation of our conceptual framework and indeed the Victim Directive. This must be done considering the budgetary cuts in member states and the available resources through the EU. For example, the RJE has produced both online and face to face training material that were piloted and are now available widely. Maximising these resources is an obligation of the EU and member states.

Our research seems to suggest that governments tend to opt for centralised training providers who promise "quick and dirty" training that will tick the boxes for the given provider (particularly those functioning with Categorisation 1. In particular, concerns were expressed about existing "ready-made training packages" that are being rolled out, accrediting professionals as restorative justice practitioners in a quick and cost effective manner. This was particularly true for the UK but also in Greece and other EU member states. Some practitioners said that the values and complexities of restorative justice are not captured during these short training sessions, which are designed to provide quick access to restorative justice processes so that diversion becomes possible within the given agency. It was agreed that such practice is in contradiction with both the letter and the spirit of the Victims' Directive. Reading the Directive carefully, one will notice that the training of practitioners and other professionals must be done in a genuine manner and by integrating it within existing curricula in an organic manner. The Directive also assumes a shift in culture in the given agencies.

Building and Maintaining Multi-agency, Cross-sector Partnerships

Undoubtedly one of the weakest areas in relation to victim support service provision whether within the criminal justice or restorative justice context is the cooperation is organisations' cooperation at national and European levels. In going forward with a new framework for victim policy including the implementation of the Victims' Directive, multi-agency and cross-sector partnerships must be genuinely fostered.

At national level, where there is a history of NGO victim support and more than one organisation provides services to victims, these tend to cooperate where there are structures and expectations to do so through their funding agreements with government. Where services are provided exclusively by the state then cooperation may take place between its various agencies (e.g. police, prosecution, courts), but there is no legislative requirement to do so. In general terms, there does not seem to be an obligation on the state to encourage cooperation between its own agencies or between its public arm and NGOs.

At European level, again there is no obligation or indeed any visible interest on behalf of the state to encourage cooperation with other state or NGO based services. What is consistent throughout Member States is that the lead victim support organisation in a Member State would subscribe as a member of Victim Support Europe. Strangely enough, Victim Support Europe restricts this membership to only national victim support organisations when it could have acted as a catalyst for cross-sector collaboration and strategic thinking.

Occasionally, there are exceptions to the above rule with some countries breaking the mould of working in silos. For example in Romania, the Probation Service collaborated with Victim Support in the United Kingdom to carry out a project on enforcing their services. Also, in Sweden an information campaign offering victim support services information to non-residents in Sweden was carried out as part of an EU funded Grotius II programme. In the United Kingdom, the RJE project could be considered a beacon for further collaboration as it brought together 5 Member States to develop victim led material that will help with the implementation of the Victims' Directive across Europe (Victim Support UK was also an associate partner).

Empowering Victims

Our conceptual framework was constructed by collapsing the assumption that victims do not want to be heard in the formation of victim policy. Therefore, in my recommendation for its implementation, including the Victims' Directive, I must include their direct empowerment and engagement. The RJE project identified and indeed piloted a number of methods through which this can be achieved.

For instance, an online free training course was created using the evidence from the victims' fieldwork. This was piloted over 50 times and has been made available to any victim for free. Furthermore, material that are included in this book (Part IV) and also online offer tools that can directly empower victims to claim and safeguard their rights whether prosecution has taken place or not. The role of civil society and the materialisation of a true democracy in Europe cannot be achieved without the true empowerment of individuals.

Concluding Thoughts

Despite its limited harmonising effect, the EU Framework Decision 2001 seems to have had a positive impact on all Member States. This took some time to materialise as the historical, cultural and societal context of Member States are stronger than the will and the arm of the European Commission. For example, where the role of the state was already advanced due to historical, cultural, economic and social reasons, the Decision had little impact in moving individuals and victims to a more central position in the criminal justice process. In countries, such as Bulgaria, Croatia, Cyprus, Hungary, Italy, Poland, and Spain, it acted as an important lever for: (1) creating a basic understanding of the term 'victim' (2) introducing legal and policy frameworks to cater for victim support services. In this chapter, I asked how ready is Europe and EU Member States for the Victims' Directive. Is the new EU law new wine in old wineskins?

As outlined in this book, Member States have traditionally prioritised the provision of victim services to groups that were seen as important by the international community (e.g. children, women, domestic violence victims and victims of human trafficking). However, the Framework Decision (and now its successor the Victims' Directive) introduced a new way of understanding the term 'victim' by stretching it beyond the specialist provision of services to selected groups of victims. The Victims' Directive expects Member States to cater for any individual who has been harmed due to crime. Although this was also encouraged by the Framework Decision, Member States such as Bulgaria, Croatia, Cyprus, Hungary, Poland and Spain did not take the extra step of providing these generic services whether they were provided within the criminal justice or restorative justice context. Some may argue that this is not only due to the historical and cultural background of these Member States but also due to the non-obligatory nature of the Decision.

This inconsistency continues until today. As noted by this book the most visible cluster here is between Member States that provide specialist victim support services (i.e. to abused women, children, victims of trafficking and terrorism) on top of the generic victim support services that they provide either through public sector organisations or NGOs, and, those that provide only minimum focused services to selected groups of victims. This inconsistency relates not only to the provision and availability of these services, but also in terms of their funding and accreditation. It also applies to the role of the state in terms of oversight, training and support for organisations that provide services at national levels. In relation to cross border service provision, there is almost no good practice or a significant development that is worth noting at this stage.

In going forward, the Victims' Directive has a key role to play in creating a baseline both in terms of how the term 'victim' is understood by Member States (in general and in specific contexts) as well as how services are structured and delivered to both categories of victims (general and specific). The already existing policy, strategic and legislative frameworks regulating the provision of services to women victims (OJ C 296 E, 2.10.2012), victims of terrorism (Council Framework Decision 2002/475/JHA) and children (Directive 2011/93/EU) as well as the UN initiatives (Convention on the Rights of the Child 1989, UN CEDAW 1979) must be aligned with the intentions of the Victims' Directive and national policy and legislative minimum standards. Issues of awareness, financing, culture and implementation must be addressed to this end.

While the role of the state varies across Member States in the provision, regulation and control of victim support services, this should be seen neither as a surprise nor as a disadvantage. Any Directive must respect the context within which it is implemented. However, some general rules seem to apply in the responsibility and role of the state in the provision of victim support services:

- Culturally and in relation to their attitude, understanding and treatment of the term 'victim', Member States form part of the EU community and as a result must subscribe to and consequently promote a unified baseline. This also relates to their agents whether they are to be found in criminal justice agencies (e.g. the police, prosecution, probation, courts) or healthcare service providers.
- A mixed model of service provision through the state arm and NGOs seems to be the way forward both in terms of increasing diversity and allowing completion but also in avoiding a monopoly and a one size fits all approach.
- Top down structures that provide services to victims in an exclusive manner are not recommended, and this includes controlling funds and the registration of victim support services. The RJE findings indicate the significant role that civil society plays in the provision of victim support services. Austria, Denmark, Germany, Italy, Latvia, Malta, the Netherlands, Poland, Portugal, Slovakia, Slovenia, Spain, Sweden, and the United Kingdom see a number of key victim support services being provided through non-governmental organisations and through partnerships with civil society. In fact, some Member States such as Malta do not provide victim support services through any Ministry or central government department. The EU has recognised the significance of strengthening civil society and this is manifested in a number of new programmes including Horizon 2020. Victim support services are no exception and this report bears evidence to this claim.
- Acknowledging that victim support is one of the key areas in which European citizens are active and where civic engagement becomes live is key in setting up structures both within public institutions and in communities that support, train and reward volunteers who provide services to victims either through organised or ad hoc ways. Involving volunteer providers (individuals) directly in the setting up of victim support policies is also recommended as a good practice.
- The obligation of states to provide services to victims as part of the criminal justice and restorative justice process (e.g. legal aid, compensation, representation) is as important as the need to ensure that psychological, emotional and other needs are met before, during and after the justice process. There is no uniformity in this. This must be addressed as part of basic human rights including that of access to justice, life, security and protection.
- Although minimum standards and the debate on quality control is desirable and useful in setting up minimum frameworks for the delivery of victim support services, the close control of these providers, their registration and the repeat funding of the same organisations will kill innovation and take out the very heart and soul that keeps them staffed and running with minimal support from the state. This is particularly true for restorative justice victim related services due to their strong community led nature as well the ability of practitioners to drill down into the needs and specificities of small and local communities and groups. Justice is rarely delivered at national and abstract levels. It is a concept that takes meaning and gains significance only when it has addressed the needs and the imbalance that have been distorted at the individual level.

Focusing on restorative justice, the victims who responded to our research and had participated in restorative justice had an overall positive experience and they would recommend it to others. The victims who were not offered restorative justice or chose not to participate in restorative justice did so principally because: (1) they did not believe that restorative justice can offer a better alternative (2) they had doubts about the offender's sincerity (3) they were suspicious of the agencies that offer the process. However, the majority of victims who took part in our research but had not gone through restorative justice said that they would opt for restorative justice had they known about it. It also seems that the three key barriers that prevent victims from opting for restorative justice are: (1) availability in the criminal justice system (2) low awareness (3) gatekeepers and power structures within the restorative justice and criminal justice professions.

In the eyes of victims, a successful justice process is one that takes into account their: (1) emotional needs (2) need for information (3) need for practical support (e.g. medical support, transport, childcare) (4) need for financial compensation (5) need for safety and security (6) need to be treated with dignity and respect (human rights standards). Victims want from restorative justice to be: (1) voluntary (2) safe (3) accessible (4) able to hold the offender accountable (5) timely ('justice delays – justice denies') (6) neutral and (7) independent. Among victims, awareness of the rights and protection standards included in the Victims' Directive is absent. This is also the case for professionals servicing victims as well as policy makers.

Restorative justice is not a process that can be standardised so that it can be initiated through automated structures and concluded with a guaranteed result. It may involve considerable timescales and shifting goalposts. A victim-focused restorative process is the only restorative justice that victims want, while its complexity and deep emotional impact means that offenders must also be protected. This is particularly true when applied in prison settings or with vulnerable individuals such as young offenders, those with mental health problems and those with psychological and emotional needs.

There seem to be strong interests and entrenched top down management of restorative practice particularly as more funds become available for its delivery. The Directive provides a framework for minimum safeguards, but our research did not give us clarity as to how the power structures within the various movements can be managed so that the Directive is successfully implemented. While the research alerts us to this conclusion, hopes are raised that the legislative nature of the Victims' Directive may indeed force agencies to think differently including empowering victims directly to seek justice and their protected rights. However, the Directive must not become a top down mechanism that will turn against itself and root out the community heart of restorative justice. How we empower volunteers and paid professionals to deliver restorative justice in line with the Directive will be a key question in the years to come.

In a shifting policy and legislative environment where the EC is determined to bring a change in how victims are served both within and outside of the criminal justice system, victims' voices must be heard. Whether the Victims' Directive brings the much-anticipated consistency that the EC wishes to see across its member states in how victims are treated, remains to be seen. We know that for the first time, restorative justice is regulated at the EU legal level as a process that is offered within as well as outside of the criminal justice system. Whether one belongs to the sceptic, adversary or advocate camp of restorative justice, we must accept that the Directive acknowledges all competing views while shifting its focus elsewhere. The Directive simply provides that if restorative justice is indeed going to be offered that it is offered respecting its standards. In

November 2015, these standards will have higher position over national legislation. They are not luxury entitlements. They stem from human rights conventions and namely the European Convention on Human Rights. They are minimum guarantees for those who have already been victimised by criminal actions.

However, I fear that despite good intentions, the EU has not convinced yet that cultural and attitudinal change must take place in order to reposition victims in the criminal process. This is not surprising given that victims remained in the margins of the criminal justice system since the Middle Ages. This paradox that is supported by power structures and top down arrangements of justice continue to be strong and the testimonies from victims, offenders and practitioners who took part in our research seem to support this conclusion. Restorative justice is not immune to these structures and power interests. Attempting to interpret the findings of our research, we conclude that victims and offenders feel that the existing "gatekeepers", entrenched practices and mind-sets are the true barriers in the implementation of the Directive's intentions. The practitioners and other experts who took part in our research confirm this conclusion. In fact, it seems that the more interest the government and funders are showing in restorative justice, the more defensive gatekeepers and entrenched practices become. This must be read as a warning for those wishing the Victims' Directive to succeed. As many victims said, "legislation alone will not do".

Furthermore, contrary to what criminal justice professionals believe, victims do want to talk and be included in the formation of practices and policies that impact on them. However, as the research reveals, the recent institutional and legislative changes that are taking place in Europe do not genuinely include victims. Consequently, current practice that is being developed may not serve victims' needs but the agendas of the gatekeepers and those who are in a position to dictate when, how and for which crimes restorative justice is offered. This is in contradiction with what victims want. It also goes against the hopes of many restorativists who in the early days of restorative justice saw it as a paradigm (Gavrielides, 2007), which can return "conflict as property" (Christie, 1977) to the parties, and an alternative process that helps us "change lenses" in how we view and deal with criminal and every day conflict (Zehr, 1990). A true democracy is one that not only offers its citizens the opportunity to participate but also supports them in doing so. As we become more honest about our intentions and available resources for criminal justice reforms, we must become more accountable for our choices not to include victims directly in policy making. This book advocated in favour of a victim-led, victim policy. It also presented evidence that such policy is possible and that victims want to talk. Therefore, an obligation is created for national and European governments to respond to this call.

Closing this chapter and book we must stress that none of its chapters advocated in favour of a victim-led criminal justice or restorative justice system. However, strong evidence was presented that suggested that certain elements of these systems must be victim-led or victim-focused. I have also argued that by using strong language, such as victim-led, the research community may finally gather some momentum and attract the attention of politicians and the media. Through this attention a debate may be sparked that will ensure implementation of the intentions and the letter of the Victims' Directive.

References

Austin, J. (1873) *Lectures on Jurisprudence, The Philosophy of Positive Law,* London: John Murray.

Austin, J. (1832) [first published] *The Province of Jurisprudence Determined,* Cambridge: Cambridge University Press.

Bentham, J. 1838-1843 'The Principles of Penal Law', in J. Bowring (ed) *The works of Jeremy Bentham,* Edinburgh: W. Tait.

Braithwaite, J. (2002) *Restorative Justice & Responsive Regulation,* Oxford: Oxford University Press.

Christie, N. (1977) 'Conflicts as Property', *British Journal of Criminology* 17(1), 1-15.

Fry, M. (1951) *Arms of the Law,* London: Victor Gollancz.

Gavrielides, T (2013). "Where is restorative justice heading?". *Probation Junior* Vol 5:1, 79-95.

Gavrielides, T. (2011). "Restorative Practices: From the Early Societies to the 1970s". *Internet Journal of Criminology* ISSN 2045-6743 (Online).

Gavrielides, T. (2007) *Restorative Justice Theory and Practice: Addressing the Discrepancy,* Helsinki: HEUNI.

Gavrielides, T. and V. Artinopoulou (2013). *Reconstructing the Restorative Justice Philosophy,* Ashgate Publishing: Furnham, UK. ISBN 978-1-4094-7071-7.

Michalowski, R. (1985) *Order, Law and Crime,* New York: Random House.

Random House (1968) *Random House Dictionary of the English Language,* New York: Random House.

Rossner, D. (1989) 'Wiedergutmachen statt Ubelvergelten', in E. Marks and D. Rossner (eds) *Tater-Opfer-Ausgleich: Vom zwischenmenschlichen Weg zur Wiederstellung des Rechtsfriedens*, Bonn: Unverdnderte Auflage.

Schafer, S. (1970) 'Victim Compensation and Responsibility', *Southern California Law Review* (43), pp. 55-109.

Zehr, H. (1990) Changing Lenses: *A New Focus for Crime and Justice*, Scottdale, Pennsylvania Waterloo, Ontario: Herald Press.

PART III:
CASE STUDIES & BEST PRACTICES

Intimate Partner Violence | United Kingdom| Case submitted by Ben Lyon, a founder member of the Register of Restorative Practitioners and an Associate of IARS, UK

This is a case history that many would not have allowed to be told, or taken place, or even considered. It was a case involving violence in an obsessive relationship. The identities of all concerned must be disguised. The exact location and circumstances are therefore restricted to those who facilitated and supervised the case. It took place in recent years and was initiated by the victim of the case, via a concerned professional.

The Offence

Amy lived alone now in her second story flat on the outskirts of town. She had initiated the contact with the facilitator because her assailant (Ralph) was approaching the end of his sentence and was becoming liable for parole. A violent and controlling relationship had led to a serious assault after which the offender had been imprisoned for some years. He was now nearing the end of his sentence and his inevitable release.

The Initial Consultation

Once a rapport was reached ,Amy expressed the long frustration of her relationship with the offender and the periods of sheer terror that followed his outbursts. She needed to ensure her long-term safety and to make her own assessment of his future intentions. His sentence was coming to an end, but hers would continue unless she could reassure herself. Her desired outcomes were stark and powerful:

She wanted to be able to sleep at nights. To move back into the bedroom that Ralph had previously broken into via a balcony. Furthermore she did not want to feel the need to keep an axe under the bed. Amy did not want to meet with Ralph because she knew she might show weakness and did not want to reinforce his obsession or to encourage him in any way. Therefore an indirect process was suggested and the male/female team drew up an agreed assessment and plan.

The Offender

Ralph was a confident man. He made no denial of the offence as charged, but sought to minimize any responsibility for his long-term behaviour. However he did want to break from his previous relationship and move on. If this could be managed then it would be good for both parties.

His offender manager welcomed this restorative initiative, as it gave him a further assessment of any residual risk of reoffending and enabled Ralph's rehabilitation into the community.

The Process

An indirect mediation was co-worked by a mixed gender team, following government guidelines on sensitive and complex cases. In particular all assessments and agreements were recorded and signed off with the consent of the participants.

All parties expressed their satisfaction that their outcomes had been achieved.

Amy eventually got rid of the hatchet. She moved back into the bedroom with the balcony and when last visited she reported that she sleeps peacefully at night now.

This mediation was entirely Amy's choice. She exercised her right to communicate and was empowered by the process.

It was facilitated safely and the risk to her and to others was greatly reduced. If anyone knows why are such cases should be suppressed perhaps they should explain to Amy.

Assault, 2014 | Victim with Learning Difficulties | United Kingdom | Case submitted by Stephen Cheetham, Reparation Worker | Cheshire West, Halton & Warrington Youth Offending Service, UK

Recently another restorative justice conference took place at Ditton Community Centre in Widnes. The offence was an assault on a 17-year-old male, Dan who has learning difficulties. There were 3 others responsible for the assault, one of which was a girl, Lauren 16, not directly involved in the offence but had lured the victim to a local park also attended the conference. This was a Divert case Ali Newton was dealing with in which she identified that a conference would be suitable. Both sets of parents were distraught for their children and this was apparent when both Ali and I began the preparations for the conference. The harmed person had become withdrawn and isolated himself for fear of going outside and meeting his attackers again. The female responsible displayed an appropriate level of remorse for her involvement and wanted the chance to let the victim know this would never happen again.

The conference was held in May 2014 at a local community centre. During the meeting I was able to support and encourage Dan in sharing what had happened and how the offence had affected him. His mum became extremely upset as her son's learning difficulties had made Dan a target for bullies all of his life and didn't seem fair that even now as adult he should still have to put up with it. Lauren's mum also became emotional while she heard about how her daughter had assisted in causing so much upset, furthermore because her own daughter had now become the bully.

During the meeting both young people were asked how they have been affected and what do they think needs to happen next. Dan asked for reassurance that this would never happen again and Josie sincerely apologised for her part in the offence and reassured Dan that nothing like this would happen again. Lauren's mum shared that her behaviour had come about as a result of hanging around with the 'wrong crowd'. It became clear she understood her actions were the result of peer pressure and hanging round with the wrong people.

As always, lots of emotions are displayed during such a meeting which is always encouraged by us during the preparation. Both parents were especially grateful at the end for creating an alternative opportunity to put what had happened right again and in so doing 'repairing the harm caused'.

Theft, 2013 | Minnesota, United States | Case submitted by Lindsey Burkhardt, Restorative Justice Coordinator, Clay County Attorney's Office, Minnesota, United States

On November 24th 2013, a woman left her purse in her unlocked vehicle as she quickly ran into her home to pick up her children. A group of young girls were walking down the street, noticed the purse, and took it out of the vehicle. Each of the girls played a role in the theft. Three of the girls were referred to a restorative justice programme by the Moorhead Police Department on February 10, 2014. The focus here is a conference held, though all girls participated in conferences with the victim.

The facilitator set up a pre-meeting to meet individually with the victim, and with the youth offender.

The youth offender, who is 13 years old, met with a trained facilitator and talked about the incident. She said she felt bad, and shouldn't have done it but sometimes when she's with her friends she feels like she needs to do what they are doing to 'fit in'. "I'm going to have to meet with that lady!" was her response when the facilitator shared information about the programme.

The victim came and met with the facilitator. She talked about the items in her purse that were missing, and never returned. She said that when her dad was dying, he gave her $2 bills, and told her that it can be a way to always remember him as they had been his. She talked about her feelings. She said she felt scared to be at home as they might know where she lived now. She had to have all the locks changed, call and cancel all of her cards, lost money for Christmas gifts, and most significantly to her, had lost the last thing her dad had given her. She said that her children really struggled for a long time, her son would always remind her to take her purse with her. And during Christmas said, "Maybe Santa will come next year mom!" She said that out of the entire ordeal, her two youngest were impacted the most due to this incident.

After working around all individuals involved schedules- a conference was set for March 5, 2014 in the afternoon.

The youth walked into the meeting room, and looked at the victim and said hello. The room felt very tense as the conference began. The meeting began by sharing names and going over guidelines. Then the youth was asked to share what happened. She began to tell the story of what happened that day, from the very beginning up until she spoke with the Moorhead Police Department. She said that they were all badgering each other to take the purse from the vehicle, and pressuring one another until the two youngest girls opened the van door to grab it, and an older girl grabbed it out. She explained her role in the matter, and took responsibility for her actions. She said she bought Cheetos with a $2 bill, and also that she had taken a coin.

When she finished, the victim said, "First, I want to thank you for your honesty, and to tell you that you are a beautiful young girl". The victim talked about the impact of that day on her, and her family. She asked about the envelopes in her purse, the youth said that one of the girls said, "Who carries mail in their purse?" And that they flushed them down the toilet. The victim told her it contained $500, and its purpose to buy Christmas presents for her children. The youth sat in awe, and said they all thought it was all mail. The victim asked about the $2 bills, the youth talked about buying the Cheetos with one. Tears began running down the victims face as she talked about losing her dad, and that being the one thing she had to hold on to in remembrance of him. As she cried, the youth began crying as her head dropped. The youth's mother began to cry as the victim continued to talk about changing her locks on her doors, not sleeping at night, and the fears her children had been having about the "bad guys" who stole their mom's purse.

The youth looked at the victim and said how sorry she was, and that she would do anything to take it back. She also said she would do anything to make it up to her. The victim told her there isn't anything that can bring back those $2 bills, and that's the hardest part. The youth told the victim that she gave the police officer the coin she had. The victim thanked her for that, and said it was the only thing recovered. They didn't find or get anything else back.

The two began to talk about a way to repair the harm that was caused. It was decided between both parties that Mae would do volunteer work/spring cleaning work around the victims yard when it started to warm up. She would complete twenty hours of service doing yard work and cleaning out a shed. Also, the youth offender would write two letters of apology, one to the two young children involved in the matter, and one to her mom.

The conference lasted over two hours. At the end of the meeting, the victim got up to leave the conference, and the youth got up- and asked her if she could hug her. They seemed to hold on to each other for a period of time, and you could sense that forgiveness was given. Not only did the youth complete the apology letter to the two young children, but she also brought gifts for the two children to make up for her wrongdoing.

Inter-personal Conflict, 2011 | Italy | Case submitted by Dr. Giuseppe Maglione, University of Florence, Department of Legal Sciences, Florence, Italy

The case described has been managed by the Victim-Offender Mediation centre in Florence, Italy, in 2011. It took approximately 4 weeks to conclude the mediation process. The centre's activity is placed within the framework of the criminal competence of the Justice of the Peace jurisdiction as regulated by the Legislative Decree 274/2000, par. 29.4. This is a pre-sentencing procedure (diversion), for adults, which implies the suspension of the trial for a given period (1 month), within which mediation has to be concluded. The procedure is confidential, on a voluntary basis and totally free of any financial charge (the mediators are volunteers from the non-profit organization *L'altro diritto*).

The case involved a former couple, in phase of divorcing at the moment the mediation took place. The charge was filed by the ex-husband against the ex-wife: the wife was not complying with the divorce judge prescription of allowing the husband's visits to their child aged 4, according to a tight schedule. The husband, after a while, decided to file a criminal complaint against the wife each time his right was denied by the oppositional wife's behaviour. After one year, the number of criminal complaints amounted at 40. The prosecutor decided to charge the wife and the Judge of the Peace in Florence was competent to decide. At the first hearing, the Judge decided to activate the VOM process, considering fulfilled the referral's conditions, beforehand established along with the mediators (existence of interpersonal conflict; need continuing relationship between the conflicting parties; proximity/interdependent parties; need clarification; potential relationship's degeneration, or at least stand-off with judgment).

The VOM center's case manager took contact with both parties' lawyers (defense counsel), and afterwards with parties. Both accepted the preliminary interviews.

The first interview took place one week after the referral, with the defendant (ex-wife), no lawyers present. The interview, with the mediation team (1 case manager and two mediators) lasted approx. 90 minutes. After the explanation of mediation's meanings and procedural aspects, the party was invited to the storytelling/conflict reconstruction. She described the wider context within which the charges took place. Crucial points were the husband's cheating behaviour (with a family friend), the aggressive husband's behaviour, the presence of a new and invasive partner, as well as the ongoing divorce trial which was really psychologically impacting both parties.

The other preliminary interview took place the day after. The mediators decided to invite also the new partner, due to her 'backstage role' in the conflict. The version was opposite to the other party's one except for three elements: the crucial role of the new partner, the psychological impact of the divorce, the centrality of the 'child happiness'. The new partner was open to mediation, coming up with ideas and suggestions.

The parties accepted to meet each other to discuss of the situation 'only for the child's advantage'. Before the agreed face-to-face meeting, the team met for the feasibility study. They assessed the feasibility of the mediation by examining some of the parties' features (minimum of mutual trust, trauma, expectations, demands, second-victimization, emotional self-control, logistical issues); any 'resonances' or emotional 'hooks' (the eventual mediator's emotional involvement in relation to that conflict); the parties' capacity to participate in an informed way both intellectually and emotionally to the mediation; the strategy to be used to conduct the mediation.

The final meeting occurred three weeks after the referral (two week after the interviews) at the presence of both parties. After the welcome and the introduction (mediation's rules and meanings and re-establishment of the parties' consent to access to the final meeting), the case manager invited the parties to describe in turn, the reasons of their presence in mediation. Mediators then encouraged parties to exchange their points of view, to describe the background of behaviours, but also their feelings, emotions, and hopes. Mediators had to buffer two different moments of emotional outburst, when parties touched on their life before the crisis and also on the child's need of having a peaceful and conducive family environment, heavily blaming each other.

The mediator managed the process breaking down complex problem arisen (their family history). The crucial move was to highlight a 'higher' but hidden (for the trial) interest: the child's one. Both parties accepted this, and on this basis agreed on: the visit at ex-wife's home without new partners; rule of behavior; re-scheduling of visits. They agreed also on a specific reparative measure: the wife accepted to allow the husband visits one time extra for each criminal complaint issued, i.e. 40 days in addition to those one decided by the divorce Judge. To be remarked that this idea came in the preliminary interview from the new husband's new partner. The session was concluded with remarks of the case manager and the writing and seal of the mediation agreement.

Due to the simultaneous presence of material and symbolical indicators and also a good atmosphere of the meeting, the mediation's outcome was considered as positive. A summary communication of the outcome was sent to the referring Judge who in the following hearing saw parties renouncing to the legal action. The charges were dropped and the trial closed. A follow-up assessment of the parties' conducts to the mediations' agreement was done three months after the mediation session. The agreement was described as 'functioning' and no additional criminal complaints were filled meanwhile.

This case shows some actual and potential strengths of VOM as restorative practice at procedural and substantial level. The procedure requires short time, is flexible and decided with parties, it is free, confidential and ethically regulated. Moreover, the VOM aims at overcoming the tight criminal-legal roles, for instance involving in the decision-making subjects external to the trial (the husband's new partner), it narratively offers new positions within which to see themselves and the conflict, identifying interests and needs beyond the façade of criminal charges, empowering parties at dealing with conflict, spreading effects beyond the disputants (the child, new partners, families, new families), reducing the judicial workload (40 charges).

Sexual Offending, 2002 | United Kingdom | Case submitted by Gabrielle Browne (victim of crime), UK

The Offender was 16 years's old and was a Sierra Leoneon National denied citizenship in 2002 due to his offending history. A prolific offender whose early offending included theft, robbery and arson before sexually abusing 11 women.

In the summer of 2002, he committed six sexual assaults in the Burgess Park for which he received a 2 year community sentence. He was released from custody just 7 days prior to this serious sexual assault – early release from a custodial term imposed for a separate robbery offence but had signed his agreement to the community sentence on Monday, 3rd March 2003.

The victim was a female, aged 37, married and living in Camberwell with her young family and had been running in preparation for the London Marathon in April of that year.

Just after 11 am on Thursday, 6th March 2003, the offender was hiding behind a wall near the canal path's entrance to Burgess Park. From here, he could see the victim approaching but she could not see him. He jumped out and blocked her path on the pretext of asking her the time. He spun 360o on his heels and pressed his left shoulder against her right and grinned. In the next second, his right arm whipped violently around her neck. She lost consciousness but he dragged her some 300m and began sexually violating her. When she came round again, she eventually fought back and he ran off. She called the police. The offender was arrested that morning. He was remanded but released on bail a few weeks' later, when the victim failed to pick him out of an identity parade. He committed further serious offences whilst on bail.

Subsequently, the victim suffered a double abuse by the criminal justice system, each agency failed in its responsibilities. Examples of this failure include:.

- The case was discontinued by the Crown Prosecution Service and the Police attempted to persuade the victim not to pursue charges. This was before full forensic analysis was returned. The strength of the forensic evidence led the offender to plead guilty on the first day of trial.
- The probation service failed to supervise the offender in the community on each and every release from prison. He continued to commit serious further offences.
- On several occasions, the Home Office failed to either consider the merits of his deportation or failed in their attempt to deport him. At one stage, a judge allowed him to remain in the country when the offender provided false information that he had no living relatives back in Sierra Leone. The offender was subsequently deported in 2012 and was met at the airport by his uncle.

No restorative intervention took place. The victim was not offered restorative justice either. It is doubtful whether the case was indeed appropriate for restorative justice for the victim. The offender pleaded guilty on the first day of trial, owing to the damning nature of the forensic evidence against him. However, he would not face up to the seriousness of his offending and the gravity of the harm he caused his victim.

Racial Abuse, 2014 | United Kingdom | Case submitted by Matthew Kemp, Business Development Officer, Midland Heart, Birmingham, UK

Case brief

On 26th May 2014 Police Officers were called to a report of racial abuse in a suburb which traditionally had a diverse ethnic population. There have been a number of large-scale disorders between different ethnic communities, with incidents known to escalate into criminal matters.

On this occasion, children who had been playing in the street had fallen out, this in turn led to an argument between their parents who until now had spoken but only in passing. Abusive words and threats were exchanged between the adults. The incident became more heated, racist remarks were directed towards the children. The incident was seen and heard by others including other children. Local cohesion within this multicultural area was at risk.

Instead of pursing prosecution against the parties involved the police passed the case to the Joint Restorative Justice team to assess.

Following a number of visits to engage both parties, a conference was agreed by a joint team from West Midlands Police and Midland Heart at an independent community venue on 26 June 2014, one month following the initial incident. The Restorative Justice Officers explained the practice of Fair Process. The conversation was at times intense as emotions were high and anger was felt by both. The flow of conversation brought about sincere apologies.

A particularly emotive point for one of those involved was the realisation that her racist abuse had led her neighbour's eldest daughter to worry that the entire street held racist views about her family. As a result of the conference;

- Each undertstood why they had acted in they way they did
- Agreements were reached where the families apologised for their behavior
- The families committed to working together to improve wider relations in the street

Conclusion

The conference proved to do more than simply restore- it improved the long term relationships between the families. In this case it not only gave closure to a situation, but an opportunity for a more prosperous future for the community.

Furthermore, the responsiveness of the Restorative Justice team to engage both parties at an early stage lessened the risk of future involvement of Health, Police and other services should the situation have escalated.

Neighbourhood Conflict, 2014 | United Kingdom | Case submitted by Matthew Kemp, Business Development Officer, Midland Heart, Birmingham, UK

In response to rising levels of antisocial behaviour (ASB) and increasing costs of managing cases, West Midlands Police and Midland Heart, a leading housing and care provider are working together on a innovative partnership. Both the Police and Midland Heart have funded Restorative Justice Co-ordinator posts to explore the benefits of resolving ASB, criminal behaviour and other community issues. Restorative Justice is being employed in areas of Birmingham where high volumes of ASB cases (36.1 ASB cases per 1000 population - Source: Recorded crime offences – www.police.uk (2014) are requiring a substantial amount of Police and third sector intervention.

Case brief

A conflict began following a report of noise nuisance on the 1st of April 2014 between two families living in the same apartment complex. The report initially stated that musical instruments were being played regularly and late at night from the property directly above one of the families. The noise was reportedly coming from an upstairs property affecting the neighbour living directly below.

There were multiple visits and letters sent by the Housing Officer to resolve the issue however, the situation persisted and relations worsened. The case was referred to the Restorative Justice team. The Restorative Justice partnership team contacted both parties and a visit was planned to fully explain the process to get an agreement to proceed to conference. On the 5th June the harmed party (victim) was visited two months after the first report, she was very responsive and agreed to take part. The victim's full participation was key, it gave them the opportunity to tell the harmers (offenders) how she felt and how the noise impacted her and her child.

In June, the offender was visited and was provided with a full explanation of the process. The offenders were surprised by the proposal, having previously been declined the opportunity to speak to their neighbour. A restorative justice conference was completed a few days later. It came to light that the noise disturbance was in fact the tapping of a foot whilst the resident played his instrument. Understanding the underlying causes meant that a resolution could be agreed whereby all parties compromised that the son would play his instrument at reasonable hours and away from areas with hard flooring. By bringing both parties together the source of the noise was identified and a comprise was made that satisfied both parties.

Conclusion

The restorative justice process highlighted how traditional methods of investigation and resolution had failed in identifying the real issue and only led to a heightened frustration. Restorative Justice assisted in the clarification of the facts in relation to the conflict and prevented the need for continued interventions from services and unnecessary tension between the families. In this case the process changed both parties thinking by promoting consideration for each other and thus achieved greater social cohesion an increased ability on the part of the individuals to resolve the issues they face.

PART IV:
EMPOWERING VICTIMS AND PROFESSIONALS: THE TOOLS

The materials below have been developed as part of the Restorative Justice in Europe project and seek to support victims in accessing their rights as detailed in Directive 2012/29/EU of the European Parliament and of the Council of 25 October 2012.

A toolkit for practitioners is also included. This aims to assist them in providing these rights to victims of crime and their families. Accompanying guidance notes are provided.

A Victim's Guide to Restorative Justice

Your own Assessment

This is a victim's guide to taking part in restorative justice, based upon the European Directive on the rights, support and protection of victims. You can use this to build up a profile of your own needs, wishes and any risks, or you can use it as a measure and guide to any restorative justice process offered by another person or agency.

The first point is that different people are affected differently by different crimes. You may feel that you simply want no part in this, or that you feel vulnerable or unready to consider the matter again. If that is the case then this is not a problem as participation in restorative justice is voluntary. You are under no obligation, legally or through civic duty to take part. On the other hand there may be benefits, such as making your views on the crime known, stating the effects that it has had for you, asking for an explanation, an apology and some form of reparation from the offender. At its best it can help deal with the harm caused by crime and for some it can be part of a healing process.

There are many definitions of restorative justice. Most definitions will be listed at the end of this document. However we will use the following definition from the Directive:

> *"Restorative justice means any process whereby the victim and the offender are enabled, if they freely consent, to participate actively in the resolution of matters arising from the criminal offence through the help of an impartial third party"*

As a victim of crime you will be entitled to an individual assessment of risk and this is part of the restorative justice process too. Someone may carry out this assessment for you, or you may do so yourself. We believe that restorative justice enables people to deal with the effects of the crime themselves. That this is something that you do yourself, or is done with you – rather than imposed on or done to you. You may want to follow this personal guide and self-assessment. None of the questions are prescriptive, they are only suggestions for your guidance and we have left some space for you to make notes if you wish:

First Thoughts & Your Own Assessment

Take some time to think about the crime or the incident that has caused you harm. What actually happened? What harm has been caused to you and how do you feel about this? What is the nature of the injury to you, or the loss, or the damage? If you feel to vulnerable or unready to do this then leave it for now.

Children and Young People

Another essential question is, how old are you? If you are under 18 then the Directive requires that you be given special consideration as a child, or young person. Different countries should have their own laws and special measures, including the fact that the parents must be involved and give consent.

The Crime

- What was the nature of the crime and the circumstances?
- What has the offender been charged with?
- Was it of a very serious nature, or a crime of terrorism, organised crime, human trafficking, gender-based violence, violence in a close relationship, sexual violence, exploitation, or hate crime?
- Do I have any official references to this?

Effects

These are just a few questions that might help you, but they are not definitive and it is best that you think this through for yourself:

- Have you suffered any emotional or psychological effects from this crime?
- Are there any physical effects as a result of the crime and are these continuing?
- Have you had any medical treatment relating to the incident?
- Has your attendance or competence at work suffered in any way?
- What about your financial position, your means of transport, or your housing?
- Are there any secondary victims? Has this impacted upon family members, children or partner and if so how?

Risk

- Do you have any fears or concerns about the offender, either now or in the future?
- Are you vulnerable in any way? This could be your emotional state or some other condition in your life.
- Do you feel that the justice system, or restorative process itself may force you to go over the incident too many times, or to be challenged in an unacceptable way?
- Are you angry about this incident (it is perfectly normal) and do you think that you can handle this?
- Is there any risk to the wider community, such as threats to neighbours or witnesses?

Serious Risk and Vulnerability

Do you think that you are at risk of secondary and repeat victimisation, or of intimidation and retaliation by the offender?

If so then the authorities should take notice of this and discuss with you any special measures that may be necessary for your protection. This will also be a matter to take into consideration when deciding whether to go ahead with any restorative justice process, and if so then how this should be done.

There are ways of facilitating restorative cases of a sensitive or complex nature, such as avoiding direct face-to-face contact, but you should not be put at any further risk, whether it is physical or emotional. If you consider that this is a concern for you then say so, tell the official or the facilitator concerned and make sure that it is recorded.

Relationships

- Did you know the offender at the time of the crime and if so, how?

You may have known the offender in a casual or circumstantial way, or in a more personal way. Victims who have a close relationship to, or a dependence on the offender can be particularly vulnerable and this should be taken into consideration.

Responsibility

- Has the offender admitted, or at least accepted responsibility for the crime and the harm done to you?

This may be a formal plea of guilty before a court, but it would be difficult to proceed without some statement of responsibility.

Information

- What information has been given to me about the RJ process?
- What is offered for me?
- Is this in writing and I have a copy?
- Do I want to meet the offender?
- Can I take part without meeting them directly?

The Restorative Justice Process

Within Europe there is a wide range of restorative justice services, such as victim-offender mediation, conferencing and sentencing circles. Some offender work in the community is considered to be restorative too. You can consider what may be offered in your case and whether you have any choice as to what would be best for you;

- What is being offered and what will happen?
- What is my part?
- Who is offering this and are they independent or from a criminal justice agency?
- What is the motivation, the reason that this process has been offered?
- Is my involvement necessary to meet any targets set for the facilitator or their agency?
- Will this process make any difference for the offender?
- What are the proposed benefits for me?

Informed Choice

- Have I been offered an "informed choice" as to what I want to do?
- Have I been asked to agree to this, and is this in writing?
- Do I have a copy of this?

My Wishes and Needs

This is your conclusion about what you want to achieve;

- What do I want from this process?
- How can it repair the harm for me?
- Is there anything I want to know or to ask of the offender?
- Do I have questions of the offender services, such as police, prison or probation?
- Do I want to express my thoughts and feelings to them?
- What could be done to make things better; for me and more generally?
- If we could come to some agreement, then what could I reasonably request or require?

A restorative process can result in an outcome agreement, where all those concerned agree to a course of action by the offender. You can consider what you would want this to include, and what is proportionate, from your perspective.

Confidentiality

Any discussions during restorative justice meetings should be kept absolutely confidential. However you should consider what is recorded, how the information is stored and with whom it will be shared. This assessment contains some very personal information that you may not want to be shared with the offender or their representatives, or maybe anybody at all. It is best to specify exactly what information you want to be passed on – and that which is absolutely confidential.

- What information about me is going to be recorded?
- Who will keep this and where?
- Will information about me be shared and if so with whom?
- What information may be shared with the courts?
- Will the offender, or any person associated with them get information about me?

Consent and Agreement

At the end of this assessment process you will want to check over what you have recorded. It is even more important that you check over what has been recorded if someone else has done this. You should agree any assessment or decision carried out on your behalf and this agreement, together with any consent to go ahead should be recorded. It is best that it is in writing and signed. Remember that restorative process is voluntary and all parties can withdraw at any stage.

- Do I have a copy of any meeting or assessment?
- Have I been asked formally whether I agree to take part in a restorative process?
- How has this been recorded?

A strong and confident victim will benefit from a restorative process, as well as contributing massively towards its success. We trust that this guide will help build that confidence and we hope that the harm done to you will be repaired.

Victim and Offender Profiles and Assessment Toolkits

Notes for use:

These documents are intended as toolkits for the use of restorative practitioners, working separately with victims and offenders. They should not be used unless the practitioner is trained and understands their use. They were designed as an aid and a record of the assessment process. They should guide a practitioner to good practice, as well as helping them and their supervisor/s to ensure that the necessary information and measures have been undertaken.

Information about parties to restorative processes should be treated with discretion and confidentiality is essential, particularly in relation to victims. Therefore these two documents should not be used and stored together. Data should be stored and safeguarded separately. Only information that has been agreed with each party should be passed on or shared. These toolkits give space for these items of information to be separated.

It is good practice that assessments are carried out together with the party concerned. It is part of the restorative justice ethos that the process is done "with" the client, not "to" the client. Nevertheless there may be some information regarding offenders that will need to be kept discreet to professionals.

The front page contains the basic information to create a file, plus the most fundamental points; the agreed aims of the process and the agreed information that can be shared.

The second page is an *aide memoire*, although this is not intended to be proscriptive, or complete. An individual practitioner could adapt this to their own, or agencies' needs. There is space to right notes alongside each point and the page can be printed off to use as a contemporaneous note. However some practitioners believe it better practice to conduct interviews face to face without constant note taking.

The third and fourth pages have individual boxes for the relevant topics. These topic boxes will expand as information is entered. The whole document can be updated and amended, but is designed to be a complete assessment for the case.

However it is more than a mere assessment of either party. Apart from obvious risks these toolkits build a fuller background to the parties concerned and there needs and views. They are intended to produce a profile of the forthcoming restorative case and should be used as such.

Victim Profile & Assessment

"In a respectful, tailored, professional and non-discriminatory manner"

Name:

Address:

Contact Details:

Date of Birth:	Age:

Offence(s):

Referral:	Agency and Contact No:

Date of Report:

Aims of Restorative Process:
(As agreed)

Information agreed to be passed on:

Non disclosure; any confidentiality agreement?

Practitioners Checklist Guide

Practitioners Notes

INTRODUCTION

- ○ Explain service (as RJ, not as formal witness) & listen

OPEN LISTENING & COMMUNICATION NEEDS

- ○ What do they want to say?
- ○ Not as a witness but freely
- ○ What do they want? Be open to self-expression
- ○ What do they want from the RJ process?
- ○ What do they want to hear/need from the offender?

EFFECTS

- ○ Emotional
- ○ Psychological
- ○ Physical
- ○ Any medical treatment or condition
- ○ Financial - insurance, transport, housing
- ○ Work, attendance, competence
- ○ Secondary victims, effects on others

RELATIONSHIPS

- ○ Attitude to offender
- ○ Relationship to offender – known? Close? Partner?
- ○ Relationship with other agencies?

RISK

- ○ Fears, concerns
- ○ Vulnerability
- ○ Re-victimisation – direct, or third parties
- ○ Will participation in RJ do harm?
- ○ Anger levels
- ○ Intimidation? Community safety?

PRACTICE ISSUES

- ○ Circumstances of case
- ○ Relationship with CJS – differentiate
- ○ Anniversaries
- ○ Timescale, discuss confidentiality
- ○ Other agencies – Victim support etc., others specify

REVIEW

- ○ What can be achieved? – Reasonable & Proportionate
- ○ What restorative processes are relevant?
- ○ What is the potential?
- ○ Offender's right to withdraw
- ○ Has this helped so far?

CONCLUSION

- ○ Formal notepad for agreed points to disclose
- ○ Agreed aims for process (to be measured at end of process)
- ○ Disclosure / confidentiality agreement?

AIMS

- ○ To be measured against outcomes (front page)

INFORMATION

- ○ Info that can be disclosed in mediation process
- ○ Evaluation permission – data / contact?

THE STORY & COMMUNICATION NEEDS

EFFECTS

RELATIONSHIPS

RISK

Physical and emotional

Specific protection needs (as per Articles 22 & 12)?
Special measures necessary?

PRACTICE ISSUES – THESE QUESTIONS NEED TO BE A MATTER OF RECORD

Full unbiased information re process given? Record and copy kept?

Has offender acknowledged responsibility?

Free and informed choice offered and made? By whom and how as it recorded?

Confidentiality and disclosure matters discussed? Recorded?

Special measures required? Is it of a complex nature that requires a senior practitioner?

PROPOSAL

Agreed with victim, led by victim

Agreed and countersigned by victim .... Date ....

Offender Profile & Assessment

"In a respectful, tailored, professional and non-discriminatory manner"

Name:

Address:

Contact Details:

Date of Birth:	Age:

Offence(s):

Referral:	Agency and Contact No:

Date of Report:

Aims of Restorative Process: *(As agreed)*

Information agreed to be passed on:
Non disclosure; any confidentiality agreement?

Practitioners Checklist Guide

Practitioners Notes

INTRODUCTION

- ○ Explain service (restorative perspective) briefly and listen

OPEN LISTENING & COMMUNICATION NEEDS

- ○ What do they want to say?
- ○ Not as defendant but freely
- ○ What do they want? Be open to self-expression
- ○ Why do they want from the RJ process?
- ○ What do they want to hear from victim?
- ○ What do they offer to victim?

EFFECTS

- ○ Emotional
- ○ Psychological
- ○ Physical
- ○ Any medical treatment
- ○ Financial, employment, housing
- ○ Secondary effects on others, family etc.
- ○ Any reports available to facilitator

RELATIONSHIPS

- ○ Attitude to victim
- ○ Relationship to victim, repeat victimisation?
- ○ Manipulation, control, abuse concerns?
- ○ Attitude to agency staff

RISK

- ○ Fears, concerns
- ○ Vulnerability
- ○ Risk of reoffending – Any relevant sentencing history.
- ○ Risk to community
- ○ Process risk – will RJ do harm?
- ○ Anger / emotional control
- ○ Intimidation or retaliation?
- ○ **Check other sources & discuss**

PRACTICE ISSUES

- ○ Circumstances of case
- ○ Relationship with CJS – differentiate
- ○ Anniversaries
- ○ Timescale, discuss confidentiality
- ○ Other agencies – prisoner support agencies, others specify
- ○ Contacts, e.g. lawyer, probation, prison officer

REVIEW

- ○ What can be achieved? – Realistic & Proportionate
- ○ What can they offer?
- ○ What restorative processes are relevant?
- ○ What is the potential?
- ○ Victim's right to withdraw
- ○ Has this helped so far?

CONCLUSION

- ○ Formal notepad for agreed points to disclose
- ○ Agreed aims for process (to be measured at end of process)
- ○ Disclosure / confidentiality agreement?

AIMS

- ○ To be measured against outcomes (front page)

INFORMATION

- ○ Info that can be disclosed in mediation process
- ○ Evaluation permission – data / contact?

THE STORY & COMMUNICATION NEEDS

EFFECTS

RELATIONSHIPS

RISK

Physical / emotional / vulnerability - N.B. to offender and to victim

Is there input or formal assessment from officials?

Specific protection needs (as per Articles 22 & 12)?
Special measures necessary?

PRACTICE ISSUES

Full unbiased information re process given? Record and copy kept?

Has offender acknowledged responsibility? Plea of guilty? Post sentence?

Free and informed choice offered and made? Is this part of system or sentence?

Does offender benefit from participation?

Confidentiality and disclosure matters discussed? Recorded?

Special measures required? Is it of a complex nature that requires a senior practitioner?

PROPOSAL

Agreed with offender. (If this is imposed as condition of sentence this should be noted)

Agreed and countersigned by offender .... Date ....

IARS Publications

IARS Publications is a branch of IARS, which acts as an independent, small publisher specialising in social science books and research studies. All our publications are peer reviewed by our international Editorial Board.

Authors who want to publish with IARS should submit an initial inquiry to the Editor-in-Chief Dr. Theo Gavrielides T.Gavrielides@iars.org.uk IARS Publications adhere to the Code of Conduct for Journal Editors.

To order please email **contact@iars.org.uk** or visit our online Book Store:

http://iars.org.uk/content/IARSpublications

IARS member are entitled to a 10% discount on all publications. To find out how to become a member please see the information on page 257 or go to the IARS website:

http://www.iars.org.uk/content/join-us-member

By buying our publications you support the charity as every pound we receive is re-invested into our programmes. We are a registered charity and all our services are NOT for profit making. Postage is based on Royal Mail prices

IARS strives for and guarantees 100% customer satisfaction. We take great care to describe accurately the bibliographic details, condition and authenticity of what we sell. In the unlikely event that there has been an error in any of these areas, we will be happy to provide a full refund of the cost of purchase on return of the item. Please see below for further details of sales policies, including our return policy.

All prices are net. As a charity, we are not registered for VAT and all our services are not for profit. Prepayment is required except for bona fide buyers.

IARS Restorative Justice Training Programmes

IARS has a history of delivering high quality face to face and online training packages to individuals and organisations. We have supported several organisations including public services, third sector organisations and policy bodies in our three areas of expertise: Justice - Equalities - Young People. We have also helped them introduce a user-led element into their way of thinking, research and policy work. IARS is a CPD training provider and all our courses and events are accredited with CPD points.

IARS is offering bespoke training packages that suit to organisations; if you would like to request more information please contact us at **contact@iars.org.uk**. Our members receive a special discount of 10% to all our training packages. If you are not member and you want to join see the information on page 265.

Victims' Rights and Restorative Justice

Having being piloted 21 times in five different countries with over 1,131 individuals and 383 organisations, the Victims' Rights and Restorative Justice Training Programme has been developed to equip restorative justice professionals with the tools and knowledge that they need to conform with the new Victims' Directive focusing on its restorative justice requirements. It will also increase their knowledge on how to treat and interact with victims. The training programme is certified (*20 CPD points*), and it is the output of the two year EU funded project "Restorative Justice in Europe: Safeguarding Victims And Empowering Professionals"(RJE), that aims to facilitate the implementation of the EU Victims' Directive 2012/29/EU establishing minimum standards on the rights, support and protection of victims of crime.

The training programme is also available as an e- course and can be accessed at

http://www.rj4all.info/ content/RJE-etraining

Free e- course for Victims' of crime: Asserting your rights

The course aims to empower victims by increasing their knowledge of their rights in the criminal justice and restorative justice process as these are protected EC Victims' Directive due to come into force in November 2015. According to the EU the goal of the new Directive "is to improve the real, day-to-day situation of millions of victims of crime across Europe to the greatest extent possible". IARS is responding to this Call through the release of this e-training course. This includes information on victims' rights, support and protection. The training programme can be undertaken by victims of any crime, based in the UK, Europe and internationally. The course is the output of the two year EU funded project **Restorative Justice in Europe: Safeguarding Victims and Empowering Professionals**.

To access the training course please visit **http://www.rj4all.info/content/victimscourse**